Diabolo

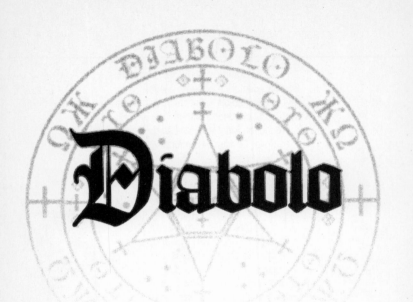

Diabolo Vol. 2
created by Kei Kusunoki & Kaoru Ohashi

Translation - Beni Axia Hirayama
English Adaptation - Jackie Medel
Copy Editor - Suzanne Waldman, Aaron Sparrow
Retouch and Lettering - Anthony Daulo
Production Artist - Louis Csontos
Cover Design - Raymond Makowski

Editor - Bryce P. Coleman
Digital Imaging Manager - Chris Buford
Pre-Press Manager - Antonio DePietro
Production Managers - Jennifer Miller and Mutsumi Miyazaki
Art Director - Matt Alford
Managing Editor - Jill Freshney
VP of Production - Ron Klamert
Editor-in-Chief - Mike Kiley
President and C.O.O. - John Parker
Publisher and C.E.O. - Stuart Levy

A 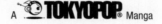 Manga

TOKYOPOP Inc.
5900 Wilshire Blvd. Suite 2000
Los Angeles, CA 90036

E-mail: info@TOKYOPOP.com
Come visit us online at www.TOKYOPOP.com

ISBN: 1-59532-233-7

First TOKYOPOP printing: December 2004
10 9 8 7 6 5 4 3 2 1
Printed in the USA

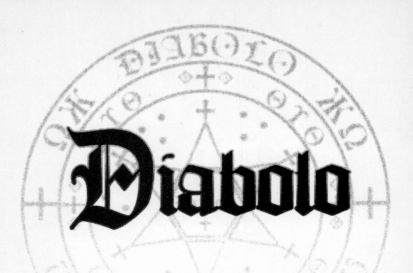

Diabolo

Vol. 2

Created By
Kei Kusunoki & Kauro Ohashi

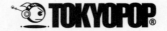

HAMBURG // LONDON // LOS ANGELES // TOKYO

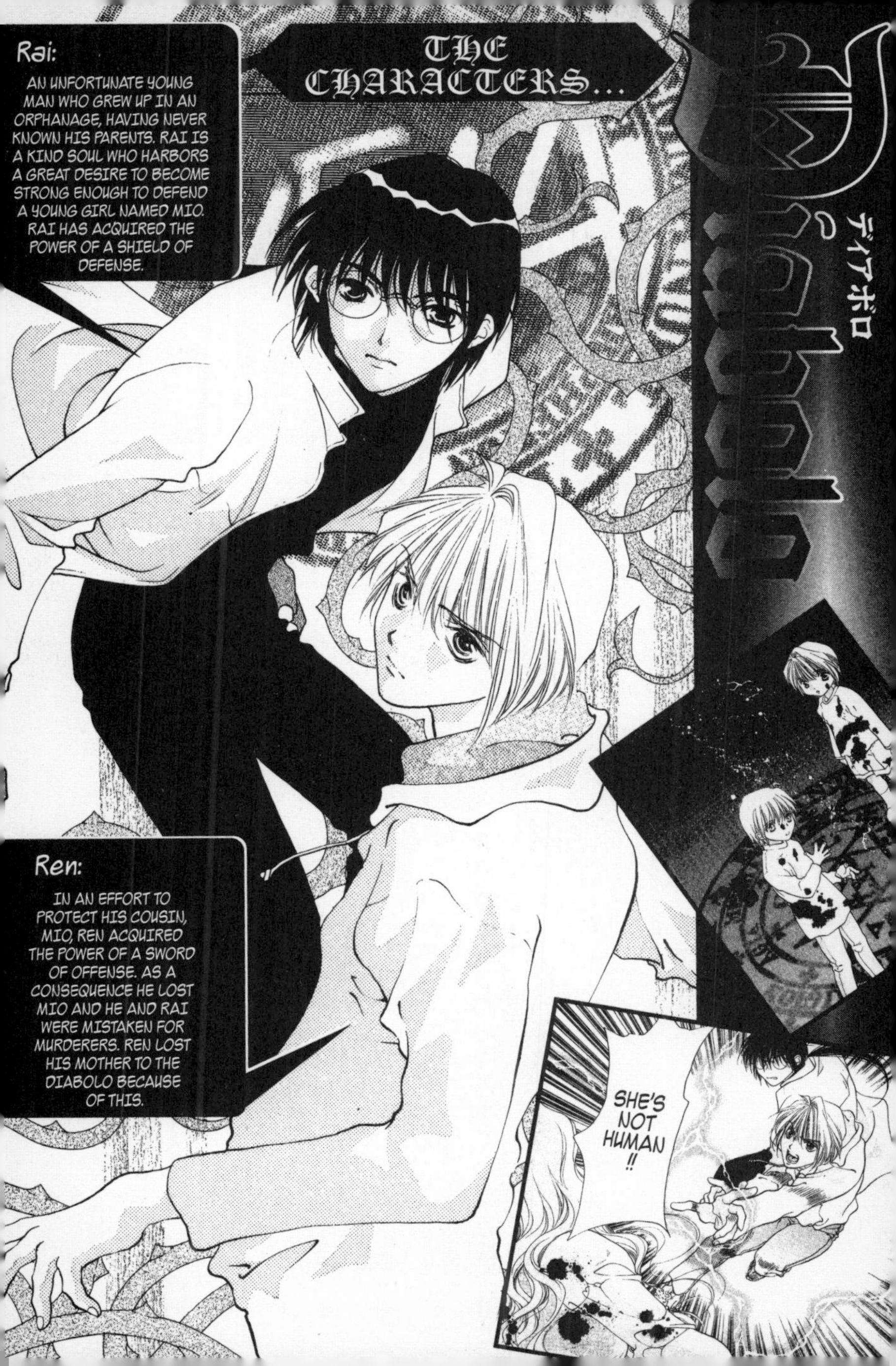
Diabolo
ディアボロ
THE CHARACTERS...
Rai:
AN UNFORTUNATE YOUNG MAN WHO GREW UP IN AN ORPHANAGE, HAVING NEVER KNOWN HIS PARENTS. RAI IS A KIND SOUL WHO HARBORS A GREAT DESIRE TO BECOME STRONG ENOUGH TO DEFEND A YOUNG GIRL NAMED MIO. RAI HAS ACQUIRED THE POWER OF A SHIELD OF DEFENSE.
Ren:
IN AN EFFORT TO PROTECT HIS COUSIN, MIO, REN ACQUIRED THE POWER OF A SWORD OF OFFENSE. AS A CONSEQUENCE HE LOST MIO AND HE AND RAI WERE MISTAKEN FOR MURDERERS. REN LOST HIS MOTHER TO THE DIABOLO BECAUSE OF THIS.
SHE'S NOT HUMAN !!

Nema

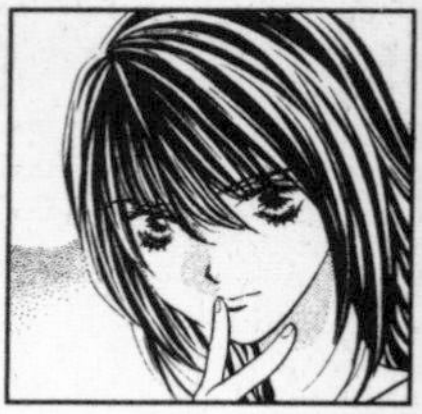

THE MYSTERIOUS AND BEAUTIFUL YOUNG GIRL WHO REPEATEDLY APPEARS BEFORE REN AND RAI. SHE IS THOUGHT TO BE THE DIABOLO WHO GUIDED REN AND RAI TO THE RITUAL, BUT THERE ARE OTHER THEORIES.

Mio

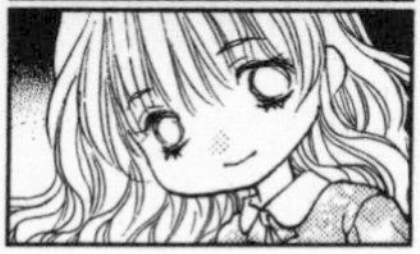

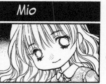

REN'S COUSIN WHO WAS FREED FROM THE VIOLENCE OF HER PARENTS. SHE DISAPPEARED BECAUSE OF REN AND RAI'S RITUAL JUST BEFORE SHE WAS TO ENTER AN ORPHANAGE.

Hiromi

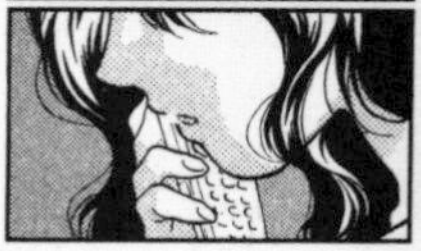

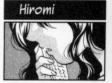

A YOUNG LADY WHO HAD FALLEN TO THE DEVIL'S SNARE WHILE SEEKING BEAUTY. SHE NOW HELPS GATHER INFORMATION FOR REN AND RAI AFTER THEY SAVED HER.

The Story Thus Far...

THEY SAY THAT THOSE WHO FALL PREY TO THE "DEVIL'S SNARE" ARE GRANTED THE POWER OF THE DIABOLO. AT AGE 17 THEY LOSE THEIR SOULS AS THE POWER PEAKS, AND AT 18 (THE TOTAL OF THE NUMBERS 6-6-6) THEY GO INSANE.

10 YEARS AGO, TWO YOUNG BOYS, REN AND RAI, TOOK PART IN A STRANGE RITUAL IN AN EFFORT TO SAVE REN'S BELOVED COUSIN, MIO. AS A RESULT, MIO WAS LOST, AND THE BOY'S WERE CAUGHT IN THE DEVIL'S SNARE. NOW, ALTHOUGH THEY STILL RETAIN THEIR OWN SOULS, REN AND RAI ALSO POSSESS POWERFUL OCCULT ABILITIES. USING THESE POWERS, THE TWO CURSED BOYS CONTINUE THEIR QUEST TO FIND AND SAVE MIO, ALL THE WHILE AIDING THOSE WHO HAVE FALLEN INTO THE EVIL CLUTCHES OF THE DIABOLO EVEN IF THIS MEANS KILLING THEM. IN ADDITION, REN AND RAI HAVE PLEDGED TO KILL EACH OTHER ON THEIR 18TH BIRTHDAY.

A YOUNG GIRL NAMED HIROMI, WHO HAVING BEEN RESCUED BY REN AND RAI, HAS NOW VOWED TO ASSIST THEM IN THEIR WAR AGAINST DIABOLO. BUT MIO IS STILL MISSING, AND THE DIABOLO'S INFLUENCE IS QUICKLY SPREADING AMONG THE WORLD'S YOUTH AS THE MASTER DIABOLO IS MAKING KNOWN THE PRESENCE OF SIX GREAT SPIRITS...

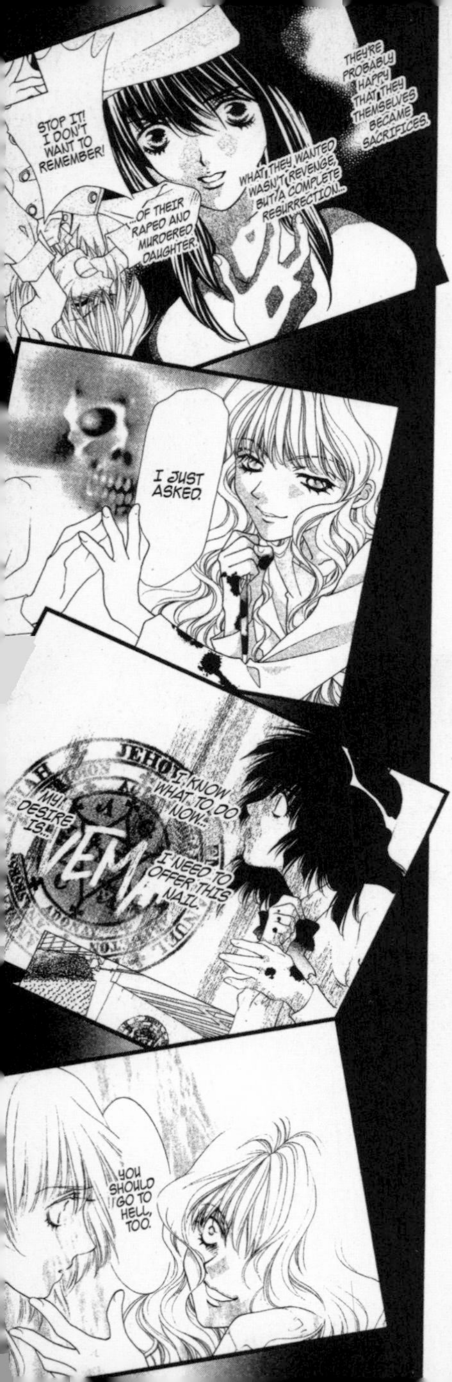
THEY'RE PROBABLY HAPPY THAT THEY THEMSELVES BECAME SACRIFICES.
WHAT THEY WANTED WASN'T REVENGE, BUT A COMPLETE RESURRECTION...
STOP IT! I DON'T WANT TO REMEMBER!
...OF THEIR RAPED AND MURDERED DAUGHTER.
I JUST ASKED.
I KNOW WHAT TO DO NOW...
I NEED TO OFFER THIS NAIL.
MY DESIRE IS...
YOU SHOULD GO TO HELL, TOO.

Diabolo 2

CONTENTS

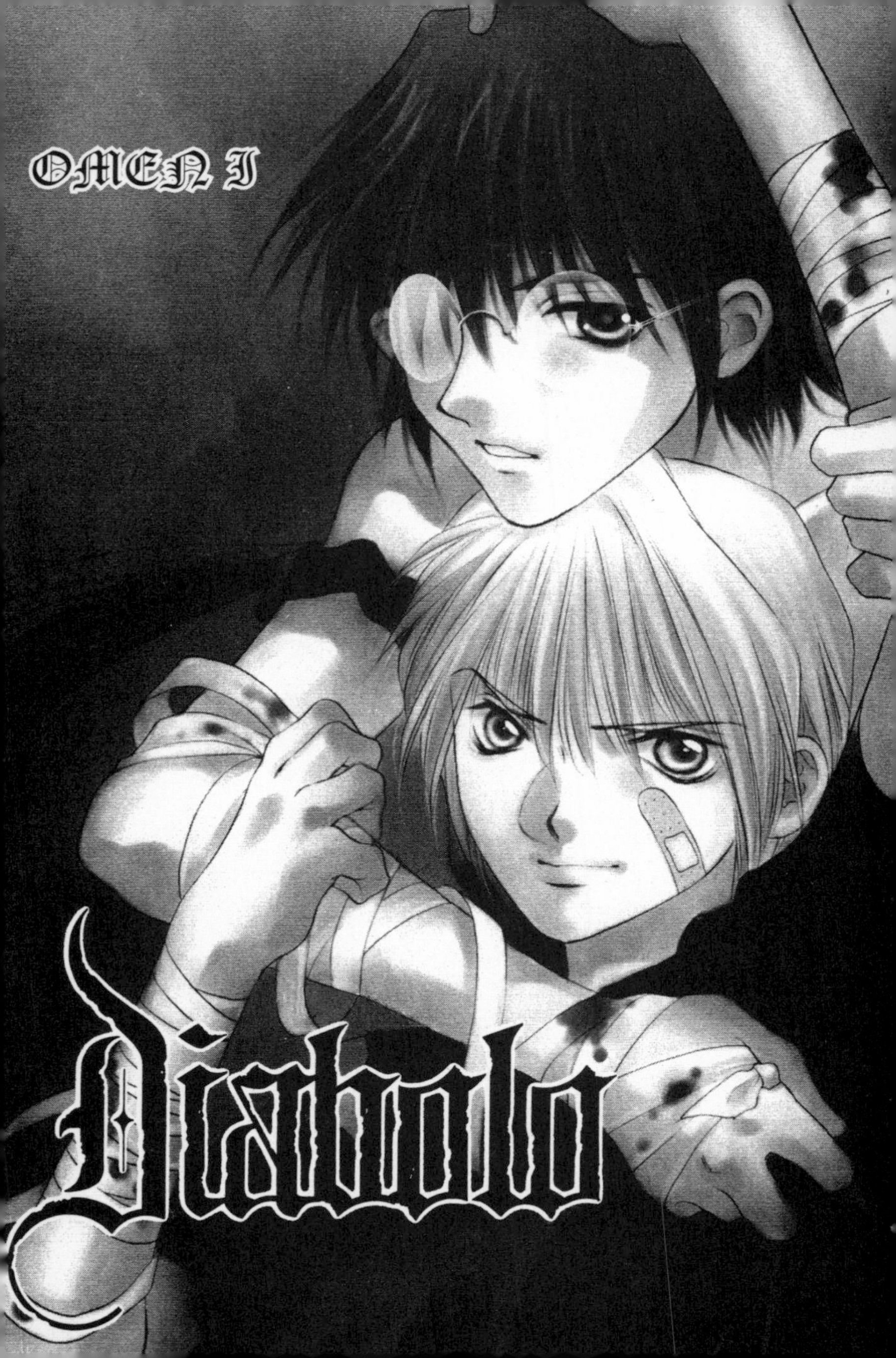
OMEN I
Diabolo

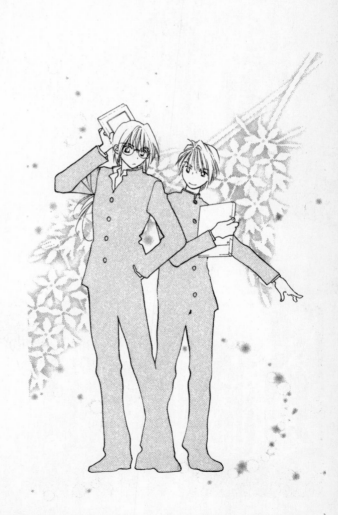

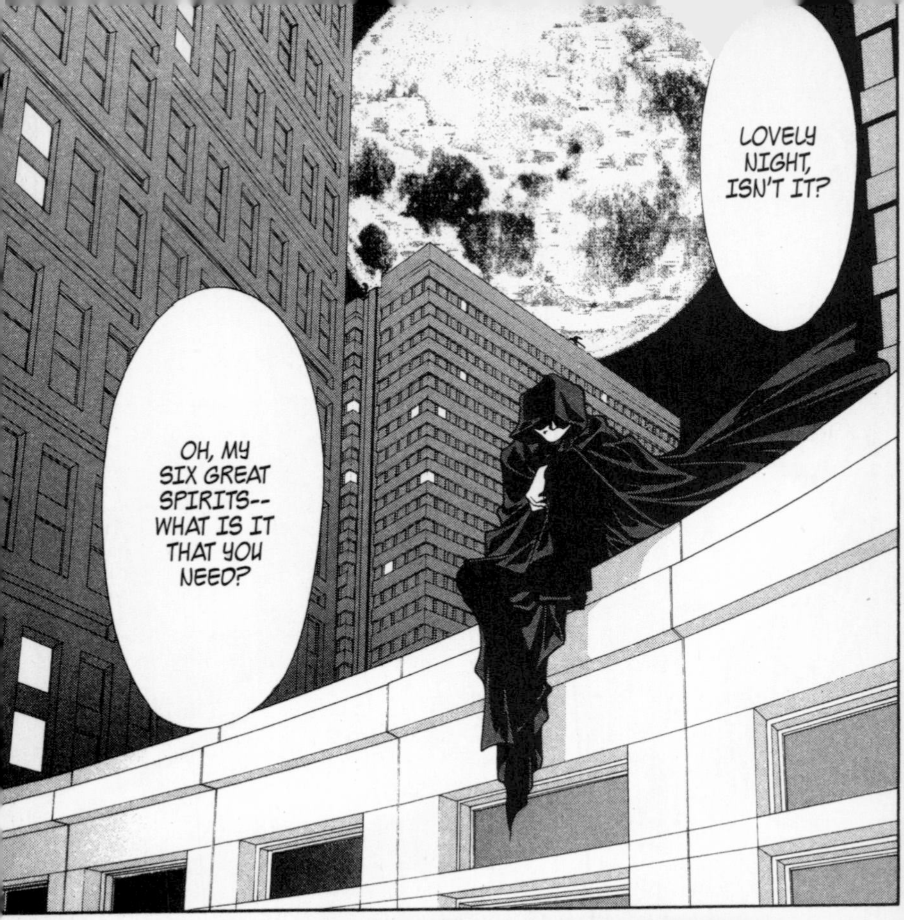
LOVELY NIGHT, ISN'T IT?
OH, MY SIX GREAT SPIRITS-- WHAT IS IT THAT YOU NEED?
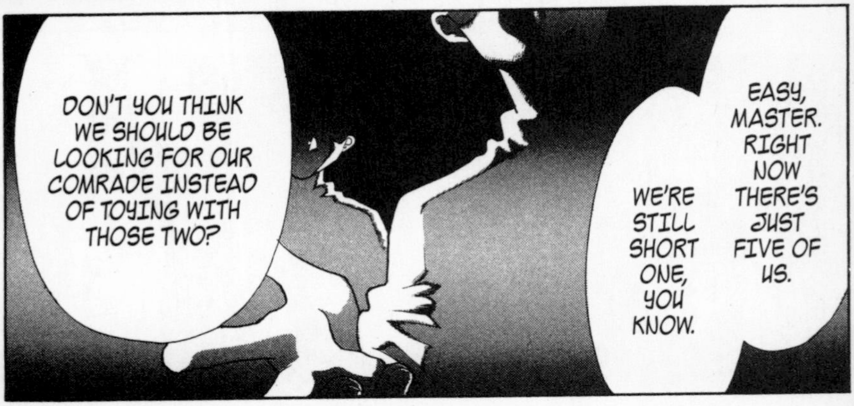
EASY, MASTER. RIGHT NOW THERE'S JUST FIVE OF US.
WE'RE STILL SHORT ONE, YOU KNOW.
DON'T YOU THINK WE SHOULD BE LOOKING FOR OUR COMRADE INSTEAD OF TOYING WITH THOSE TWO?

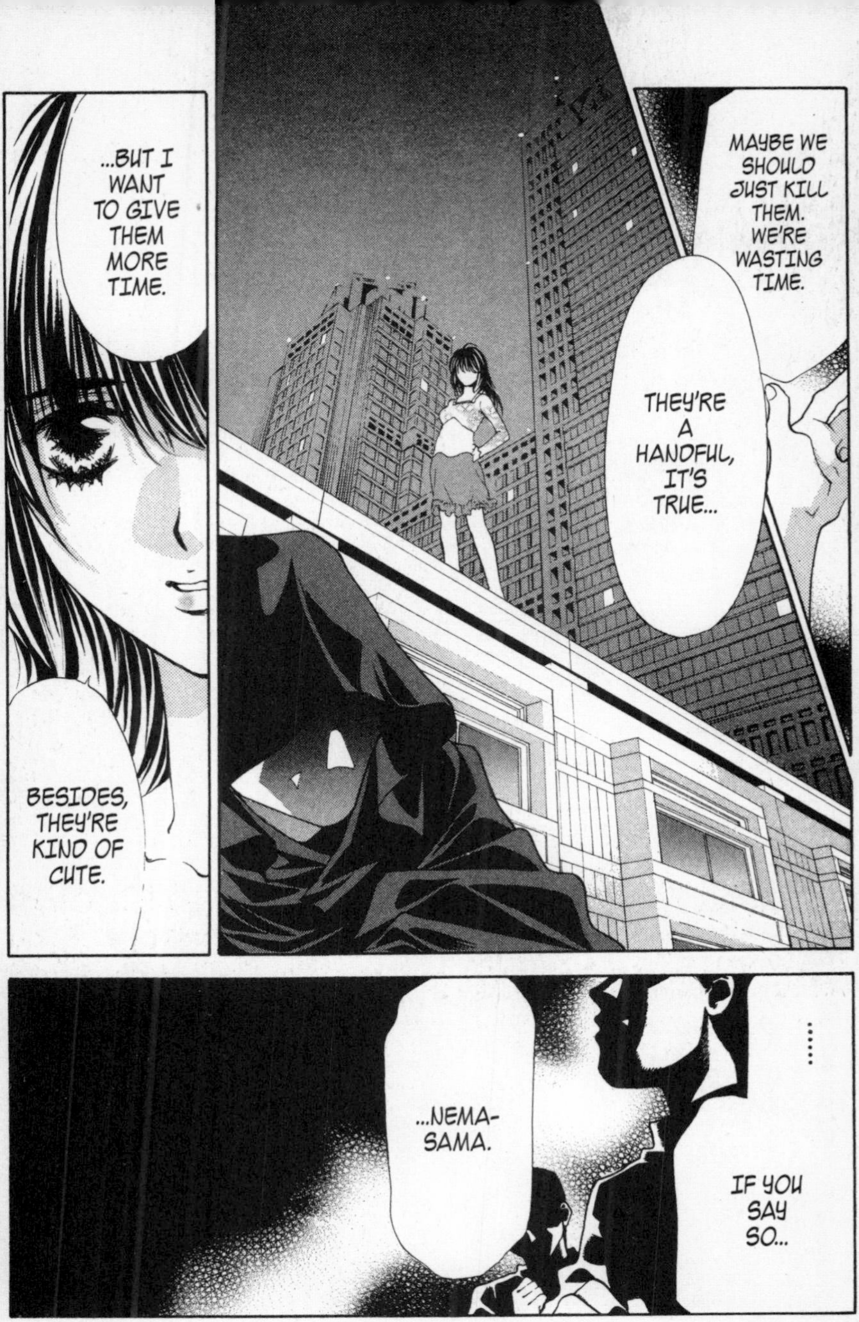
MAYBE WE SHOULD JUST KILL THEM. WE'RE WASTING TIME.
THEY'RE A HANDFUL, IT'S TRUE...
...BUT I WANT TO GIVE THEM MORE TIME.
BESIDES, THEY'RE KIND OF CUTE.
......
IF YOU SAY SO...
...NEMA-SAMA.

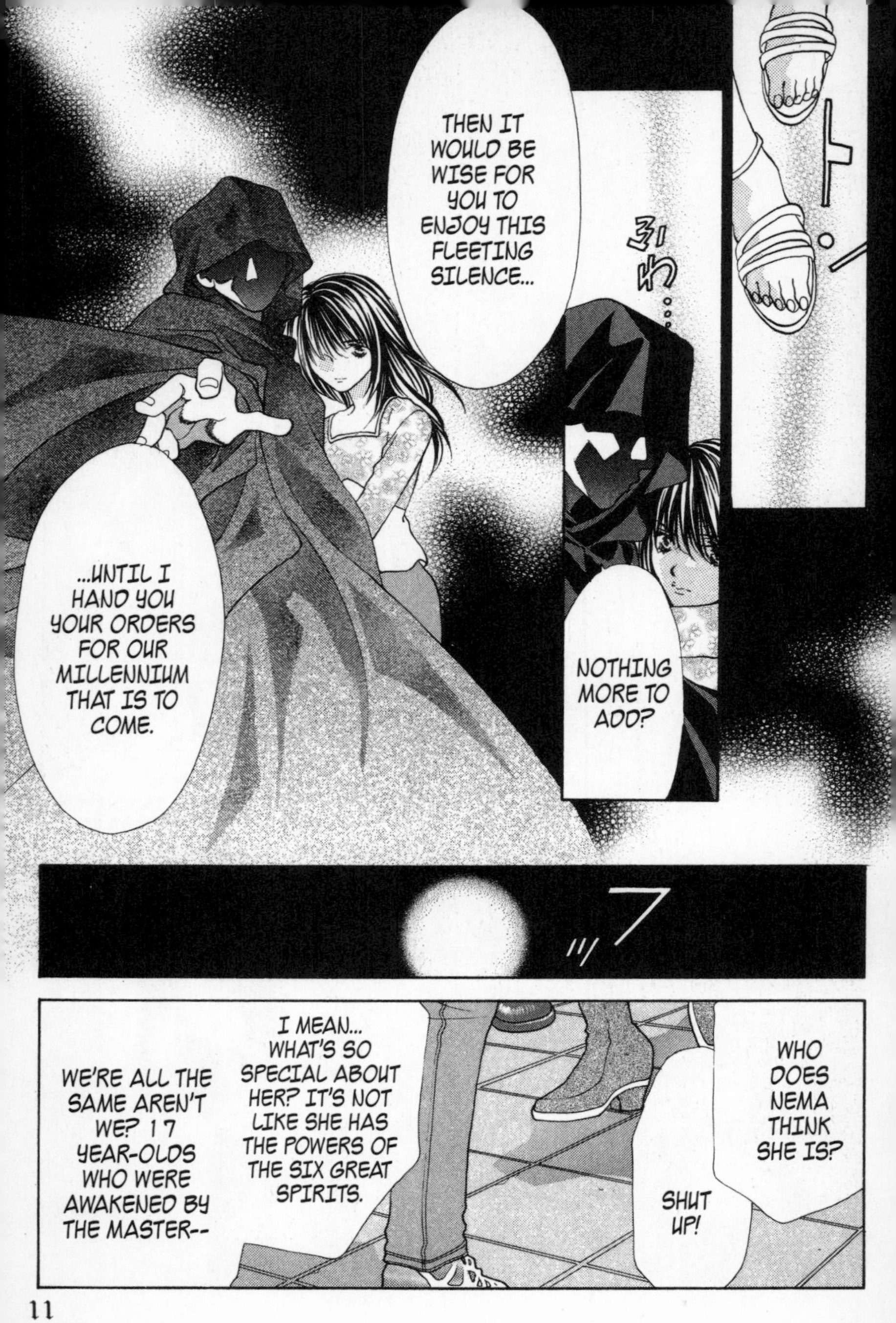
ふわ…
NOTHING MORE TO ADD?
THEN IT WOULD BE WISE FOR YOU TO ENJOY THIS FLEETING SILENCE...
...UNTIL I HAND YOU YOUR ORDERS FOR OUR MILLENNIUM THAT IS TO COME.
WHO DOES NEMA THINK SHE IS?
SHUT UP!
I MEAN... WHAT'S SO SPECIAL ABOUT HER? IT'S NOT LIKE SHE HAS THE POWERS OF THE SIX GREAT SPIRITS.
WE'RE ALL THE SAME AREN'T WE? 17 YEAR-OLDS WHO WERE AWAKENED BY THE MASTER--

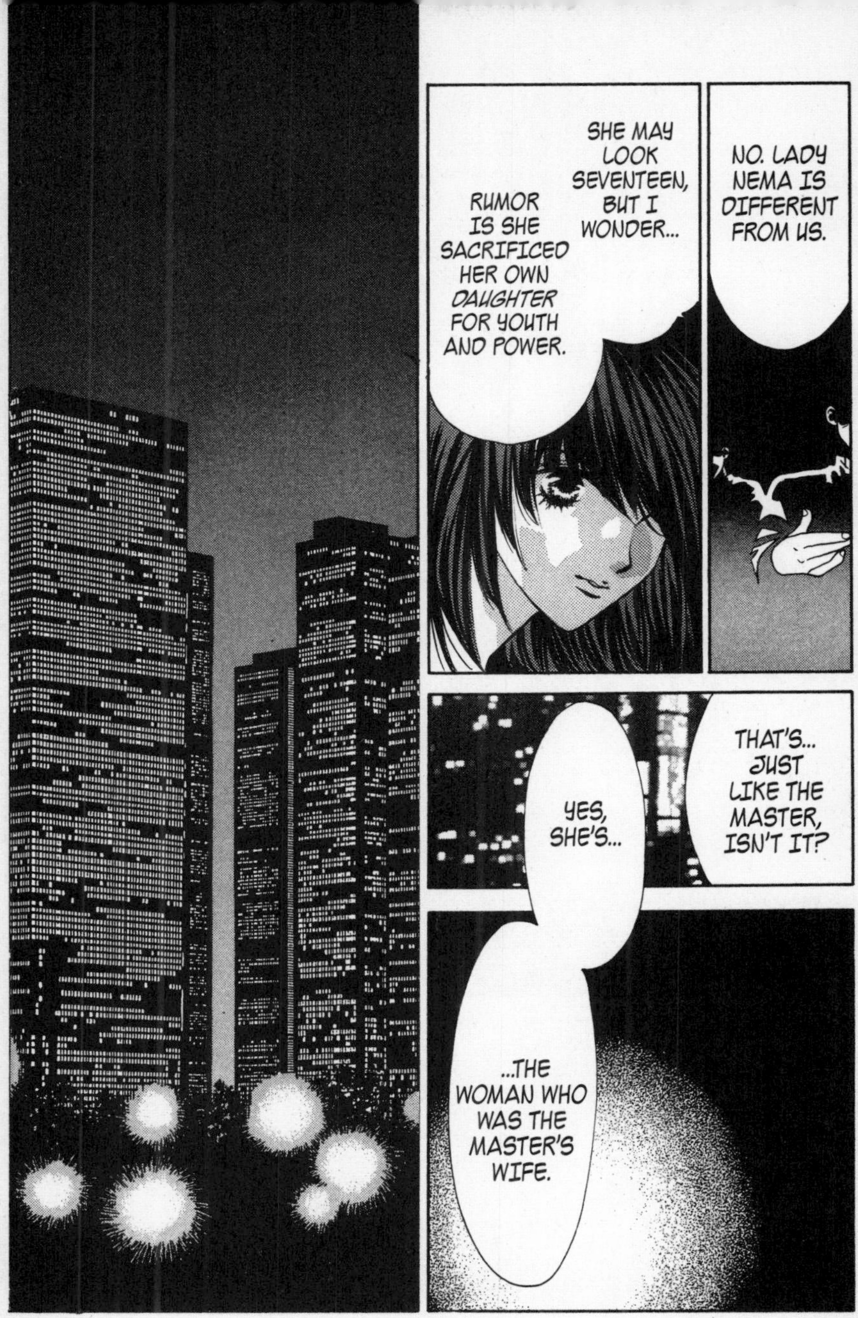
NO. LADY NEMA IS DIFFERENT FROM US.
SHE MAY LOOK SEVENTEEN, BUT I WONDER...
RUMOR IS SHE SACRIFICED HER OWN *DAUGHTER* FOR YOUTH AND POWER.
THAT'S... JUST LIKE THE MASTER, ISN'T IT?
YES, SHE'S...
...THE WOMAN WHO WAS THE MASTER'S WIFE.

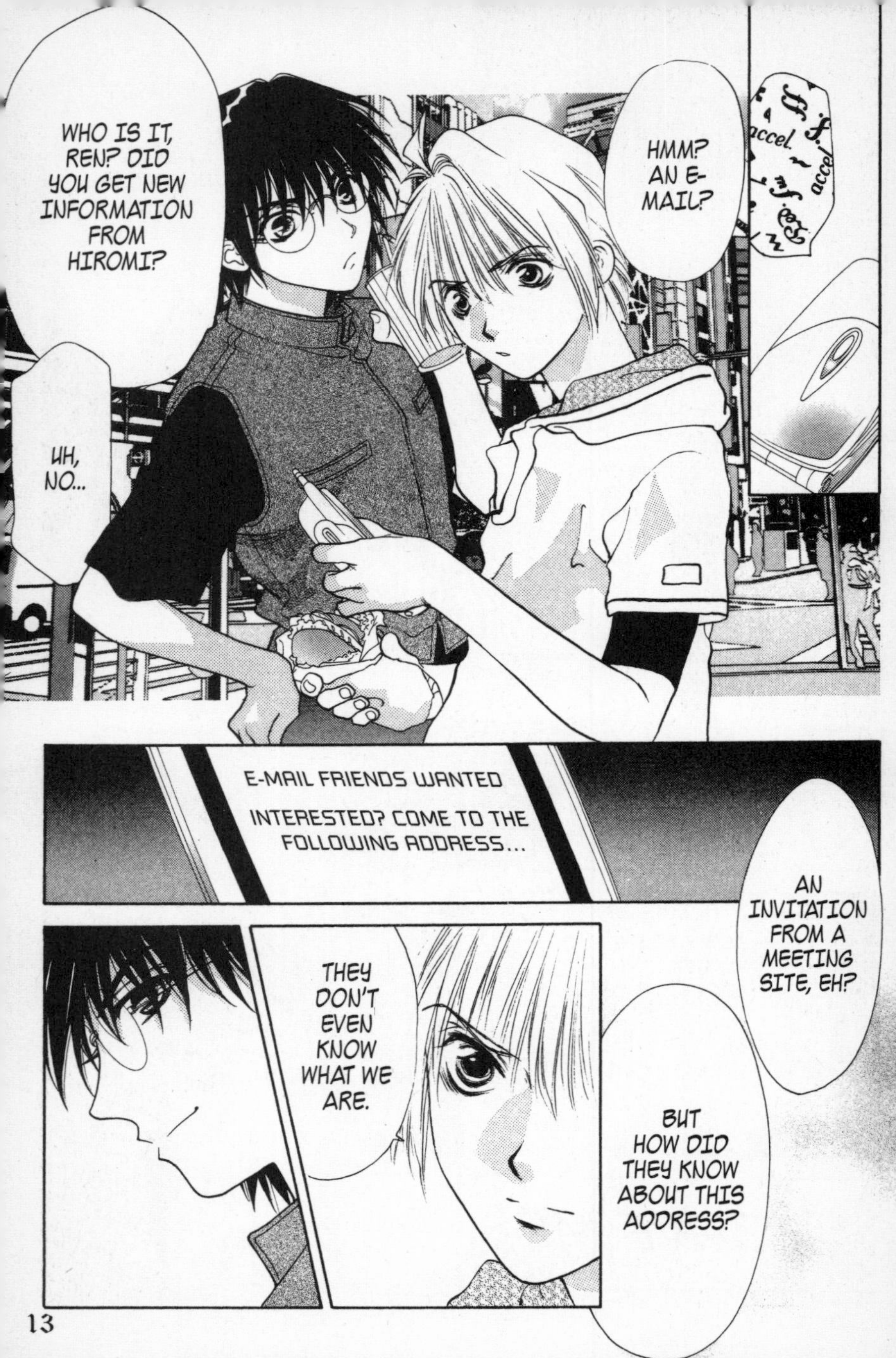
HMM? AN E-MAIL?
WHO IS IT, REN? DID YOU GET NEW INFORMATION FROM HIROMI?
UH, NO...
E-MAIL FRIENDS WANTED
INTERESTED? COME TO THE FOLLOWING ADDRESS...
AN INVITATION FROM A MEETING SITE, EH?
BUT HOW DID THEY KNOW ABOUT THIS ADDRESS?
THEY DON'T EVEN KNOW WHAT WE ARE.

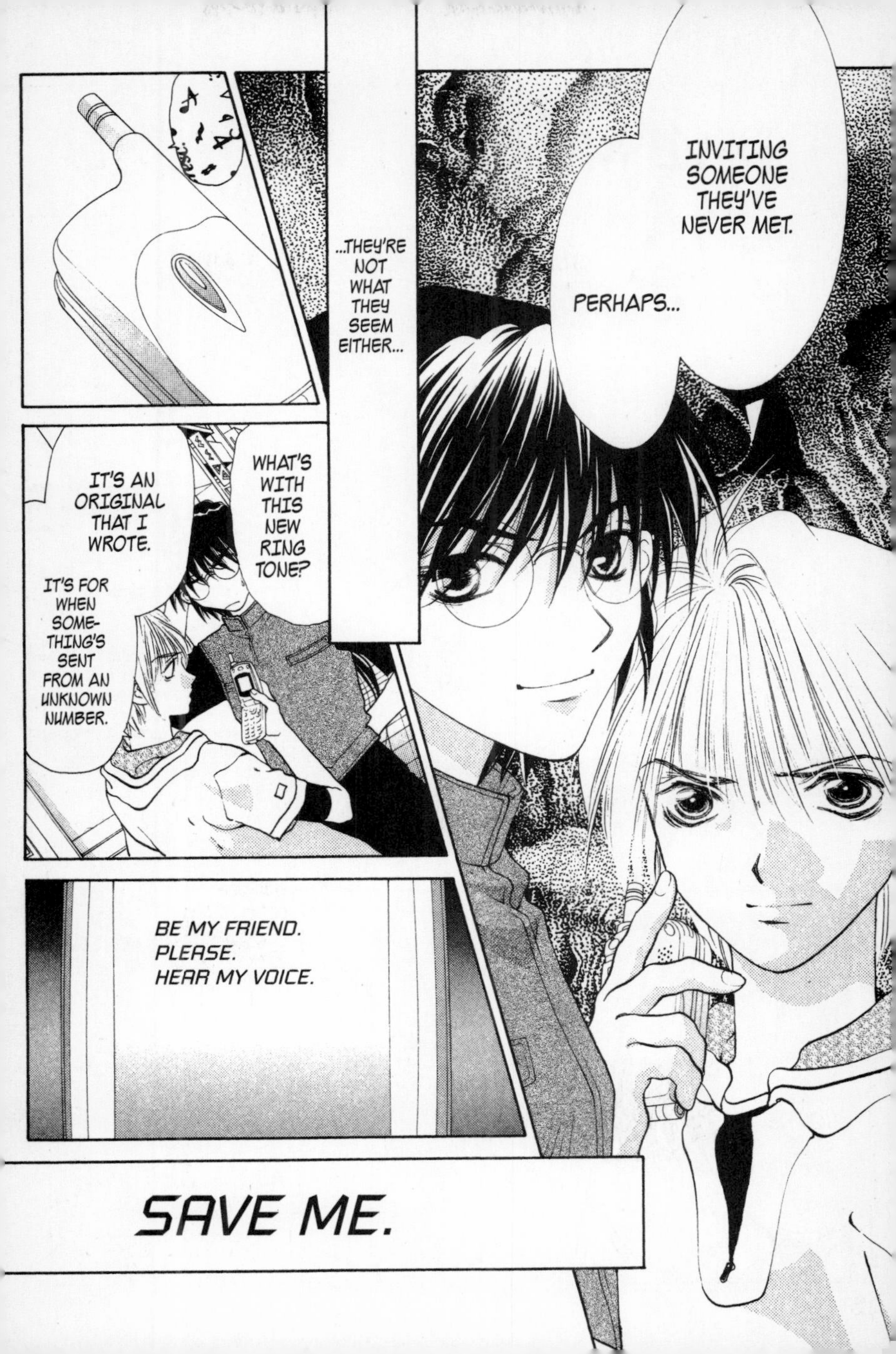
INVITING SOMEONE THEY'VE NEVER MET.
PERHAPS...
...THEY'RE NOT WHAT THEY SEEM EITHER...
WHAT'S WITH THIS NEW RING TONE?
IT'S AN ORIGINAL THAT I WROTE.
IT'S FOR WHEN SOME-THING'S SENT FROM AN UNKNOWN NUMBER.
BE MY FRIEND.
PLEASE.
HEAR MY VOICE.
SAVE ME.

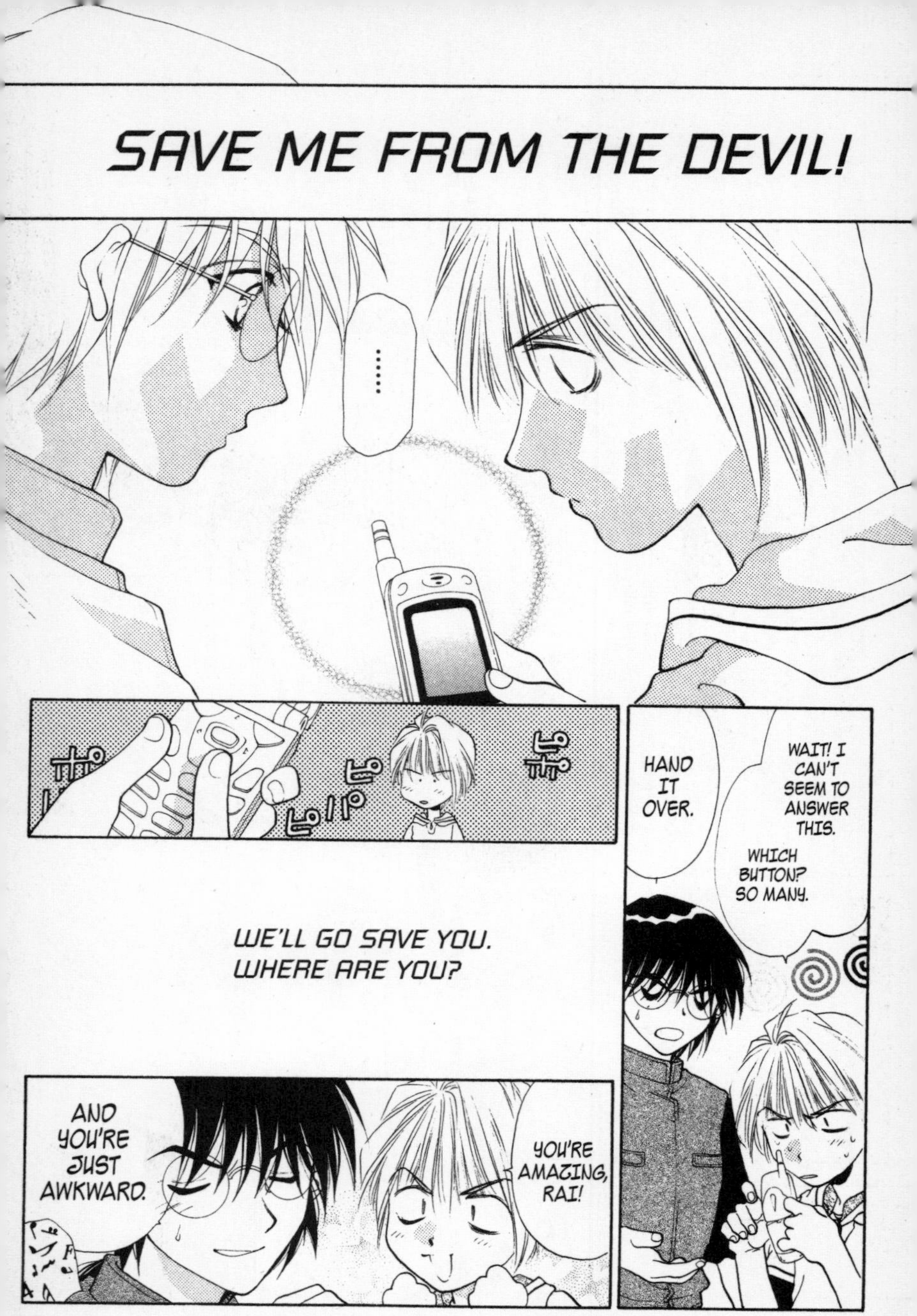
SAVE ME FROM THE DEVIL!
......
HAND IT OVER.
WAIT! I CAN'T SEEM TO ANSWER THIS.
WHICH BUTTON? SO MANY.
WE'LL GO SAVE YOU. WHERE ARE YOU?
YOU'RE AMAZING, RAI!
AND YOU'RE JUST AWKWARD.

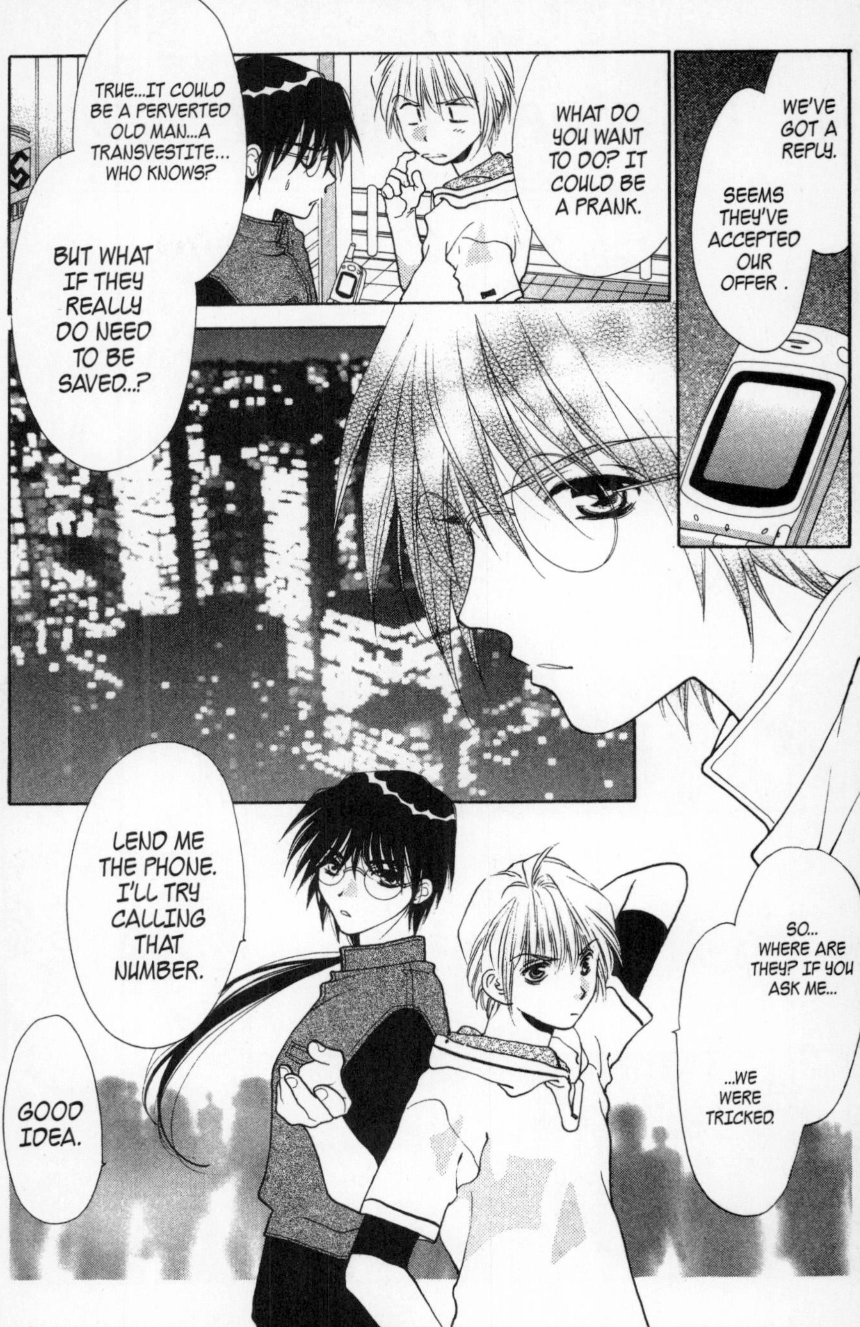
WE'VE GOT A REPLY.
SEEMS THEY'VE ACCEPTED OUR OFFER .
WHAT DO YOU WANT TO DO? IT COULD BE A PRANK.
TRUE...IT COULD BE A PERVERTED OLD MAN...A TRANSVESTITE... WHO KNOWS?
BUT WHAT IF THEY REALLY DO NEED TO BE SAVED..?
SO... WHERE ARE THEY? IF YOU ASK ME...
...WE WERE TRICKED.
LEND ME THE PHONE. I'LL TRY CALLING THAT NUMBER.
GOOD IDEA.

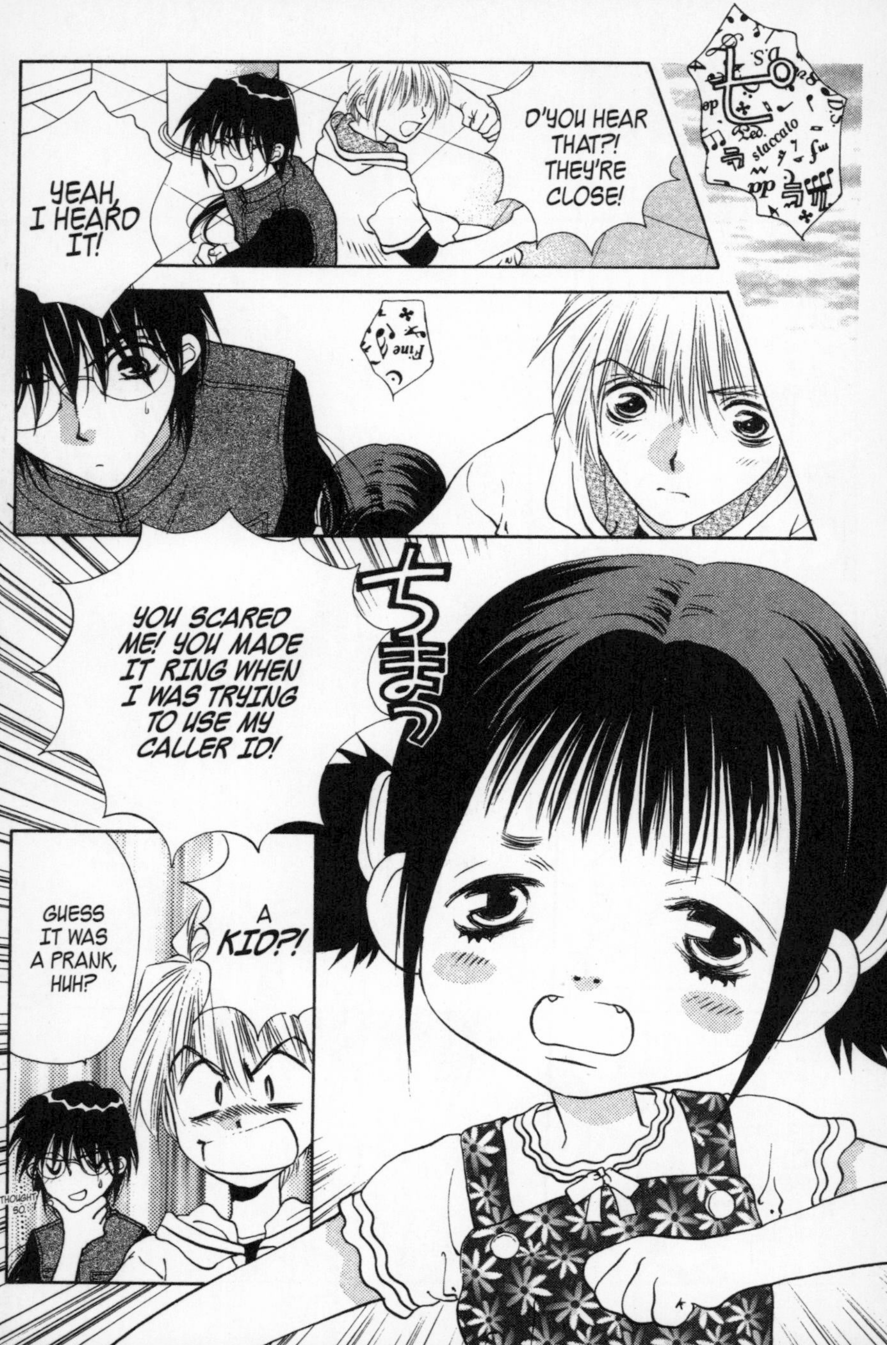
D'YOU HEAR THAT?! THEY'RE CLOSE!
YEAH, I HEARD IT!
ちまっ
YOU SCARED ME! YOU MADE IT RING WHEN I WAS TRYING TO USE MY CALLER ID!
A KID?!
GUESS IT WAS A PRANK, HUH?
THOUGHT SO.

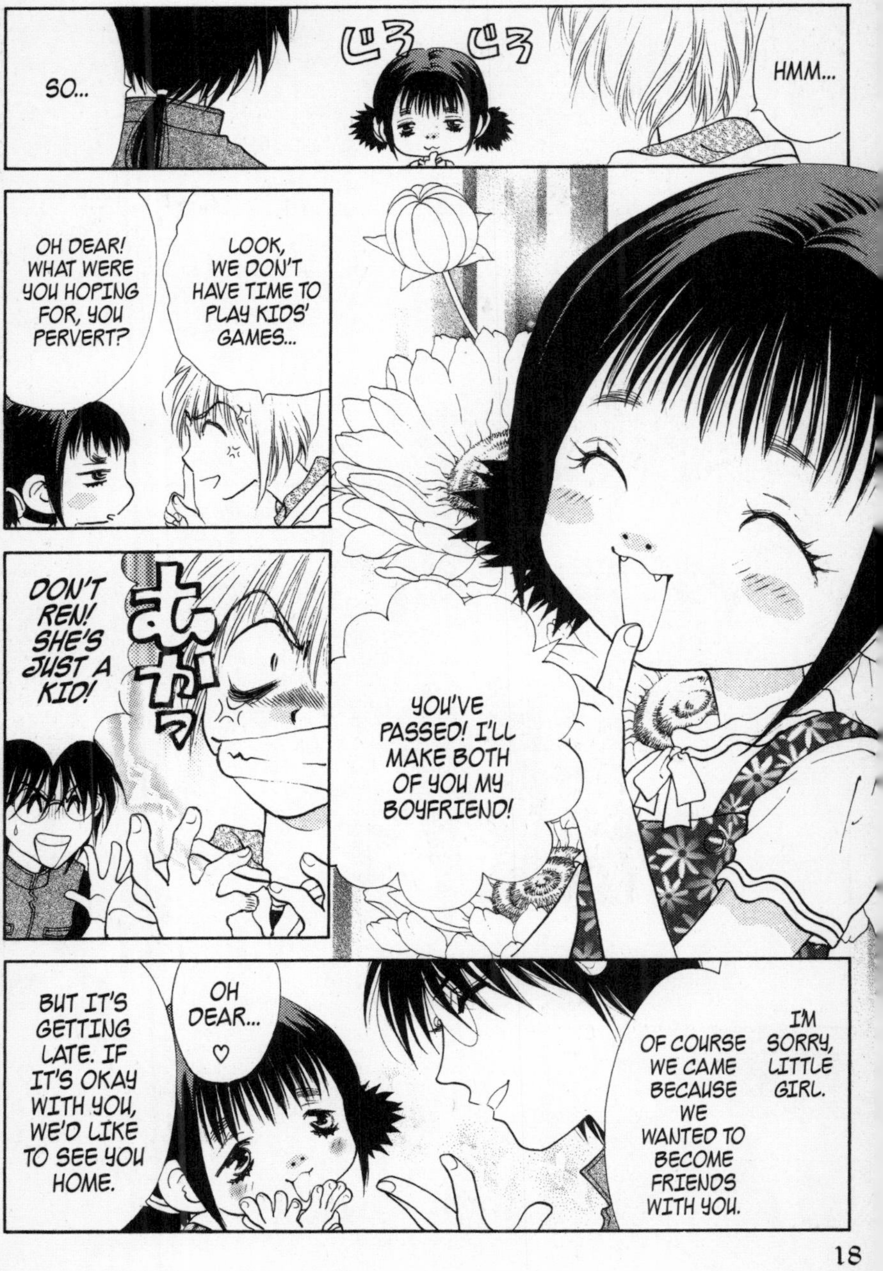
HMM...
じろ じろ
SO...
YOU'VE PASSED! I'LL MAKE BOTH OF YOU MY BOYFRIEND!
LOOK, WE DON'T HAVE TIME TO PLAY KIDS' GAMES...
OH DEAR! WHAT WERE YOU HOPING FOR, YOU PERVERT?
むかっ
DON'T REN! SHE'S JUST A KID!
I'M SORRY, LITTLE GIRL.
OF COURSE WE CAME BECAUSE WE WANTED TO BECOME FRIENDS WITH YOU.
OH DEAR... ♡
BUT IT'S GETTING LATE. IF IT'S OKAY WITH YOU, WE'D LIKE TO SEE YOU HOME.

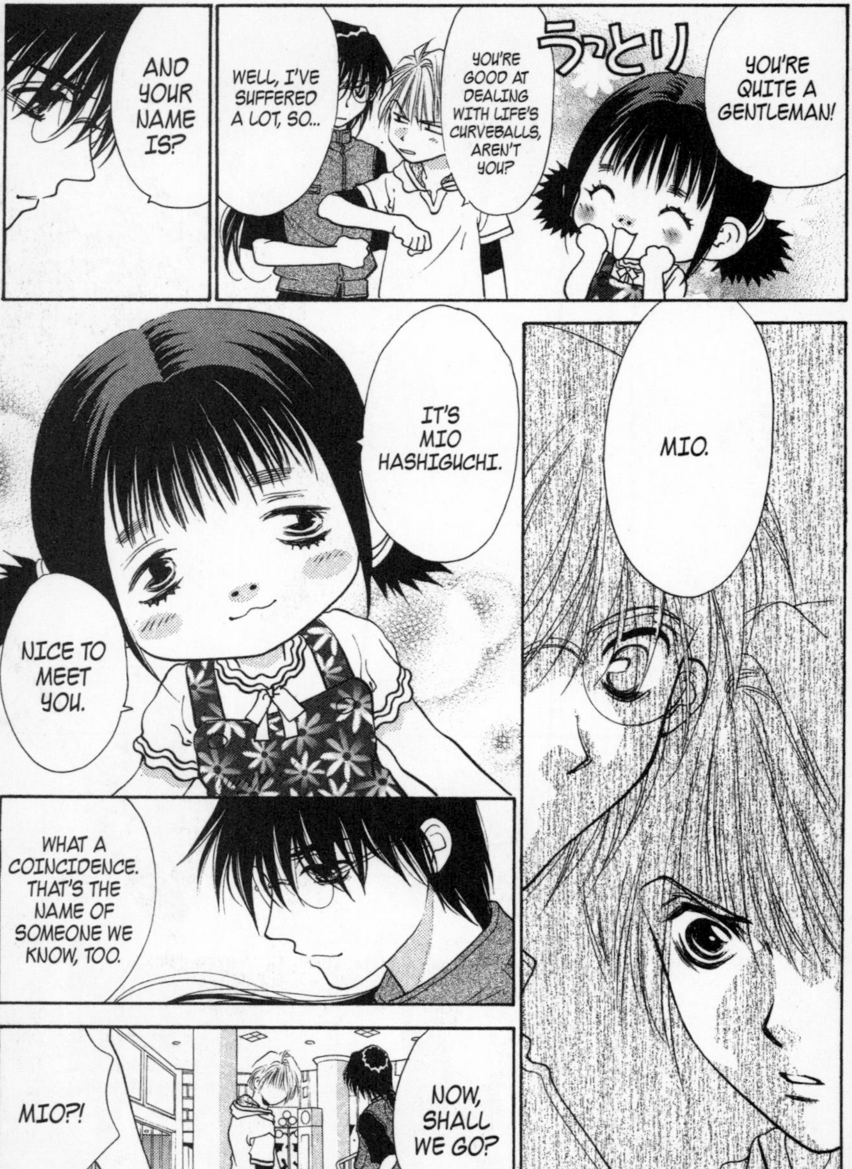
うっとり
YOU'RE QUITE A GENTLEMAN!
YOU'RE GOOD AT DEALING WITH LIFE'S CURVEBALLS, AREN'T YOU?
WELL, I'VE SUFFERED A LOT, SO...
AND YOUR NAME IS?
MIO.
IT'S MIO HASHIGUCHI.
NICE TO MEET YOU.
WHAT A COINCIDENCE. THAT'S THE NAME OF SOMEONE WE KNOW, TOO.
NOW, SHALL WE GO?
MIO?!

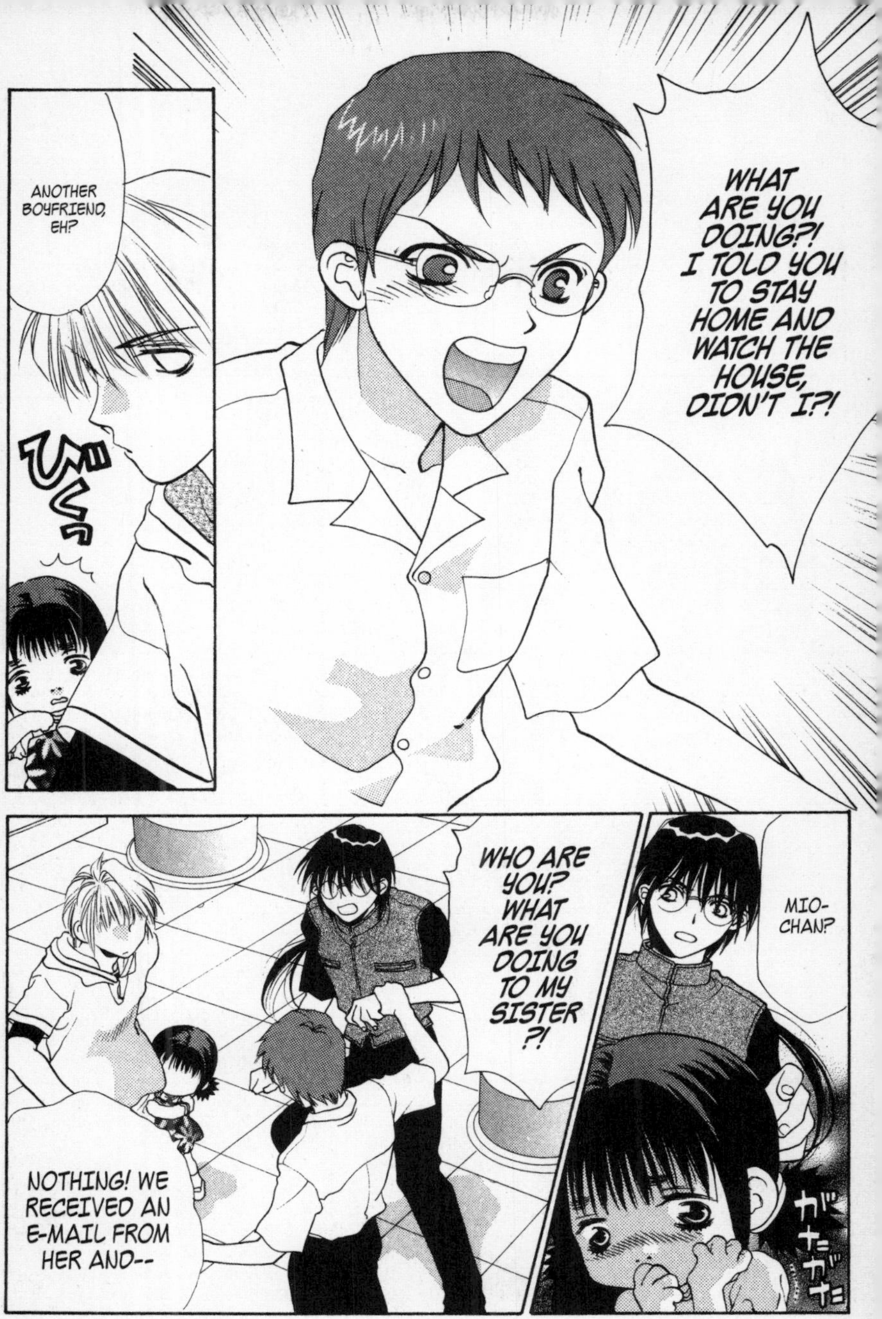
WHAT ARE YOU DOING?! I TOLD YOU TO STAY HOME AND WATCH THE HOUSE, DIDN'T I?!
ANOTHER BOYFRIEND, EH?
びくっ
MIO-CHAN?
ガタガタ
WHO ARE YOU? WHAT ARE YOU DOING TO MY SISTER ?!
NOTHING! WE RECEIVED AN E-MAIL FROM HER AND--

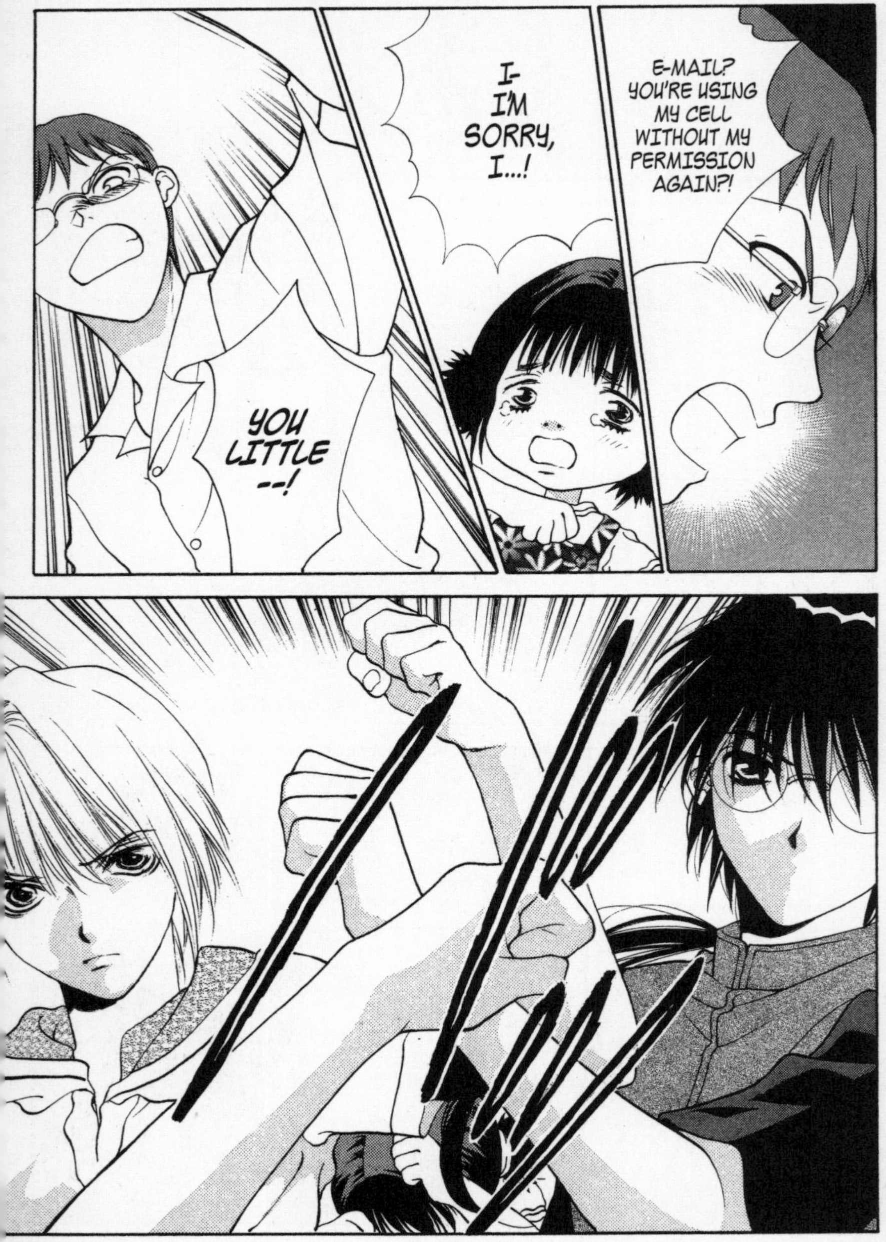
E-MAIL? YOU'RE USING MY CELL WITHOUT MY PERMISSION AGAIN?!
I- I'M SORRY, I...!
YOU LITTLE --!

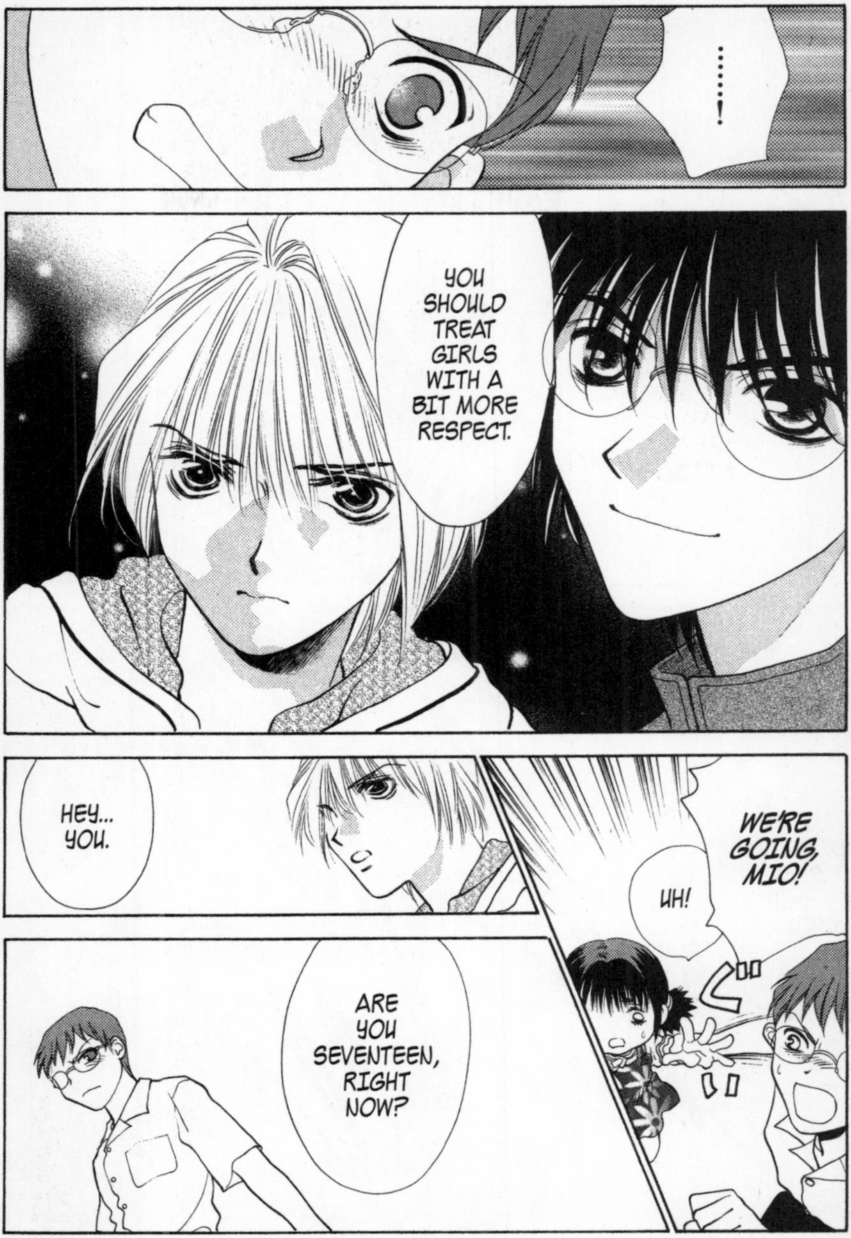
……!
YOU SHOULD TREAT GIRLS WITH A BIT MORE RESPECT.
WE'RE GOING, MIO!
UH!
HEY... YOU.
ARE YOU SEVENTEEN, RIGHT NOW?

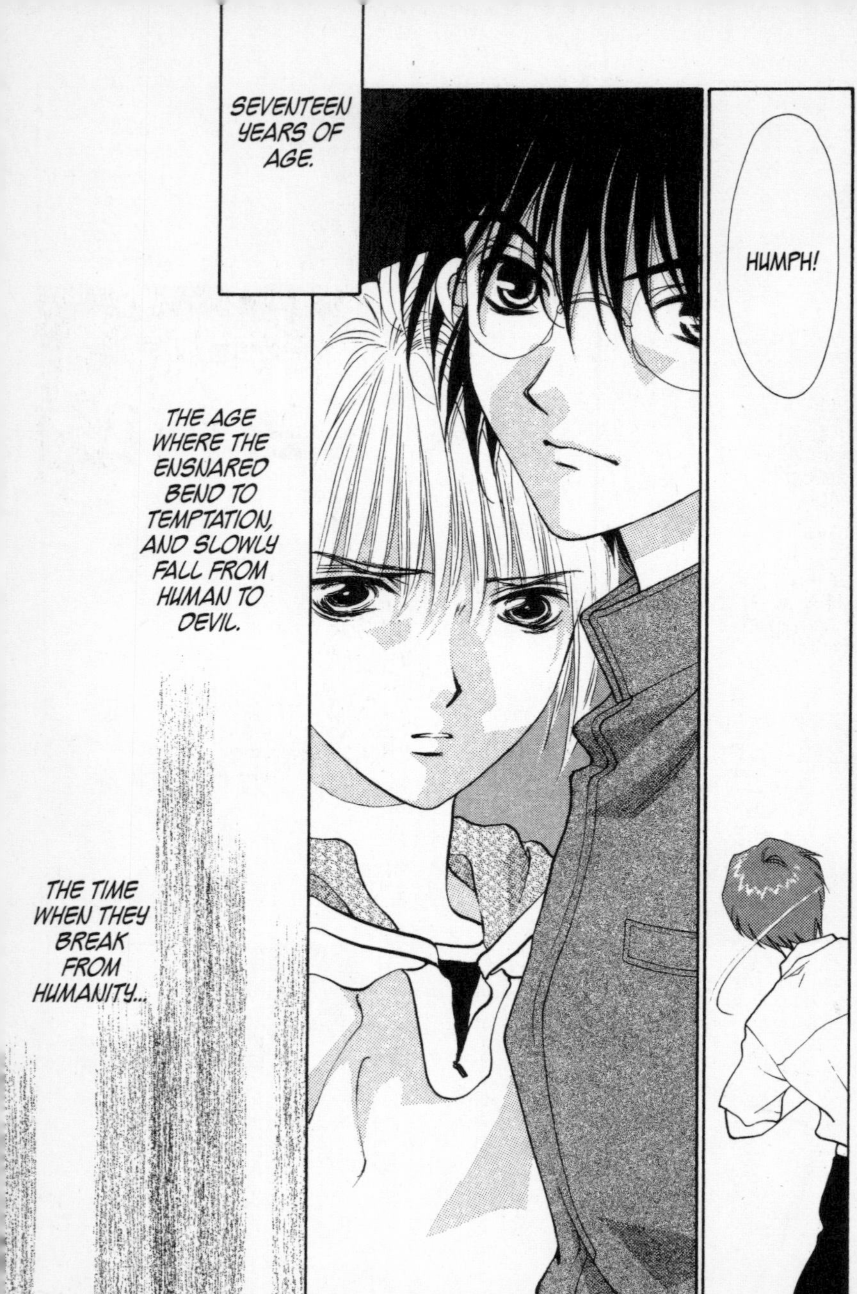
HUMPH!
SEVENTEEN YEARS OF AGE.
THE AGE WHERE THE ENSNARED BEND TO TEMPTATION, AND SLOWLY FALL FROM HUMAN TO DEVIL.
THE TIME WHEN THEY BREAK FROM HUMANITY...

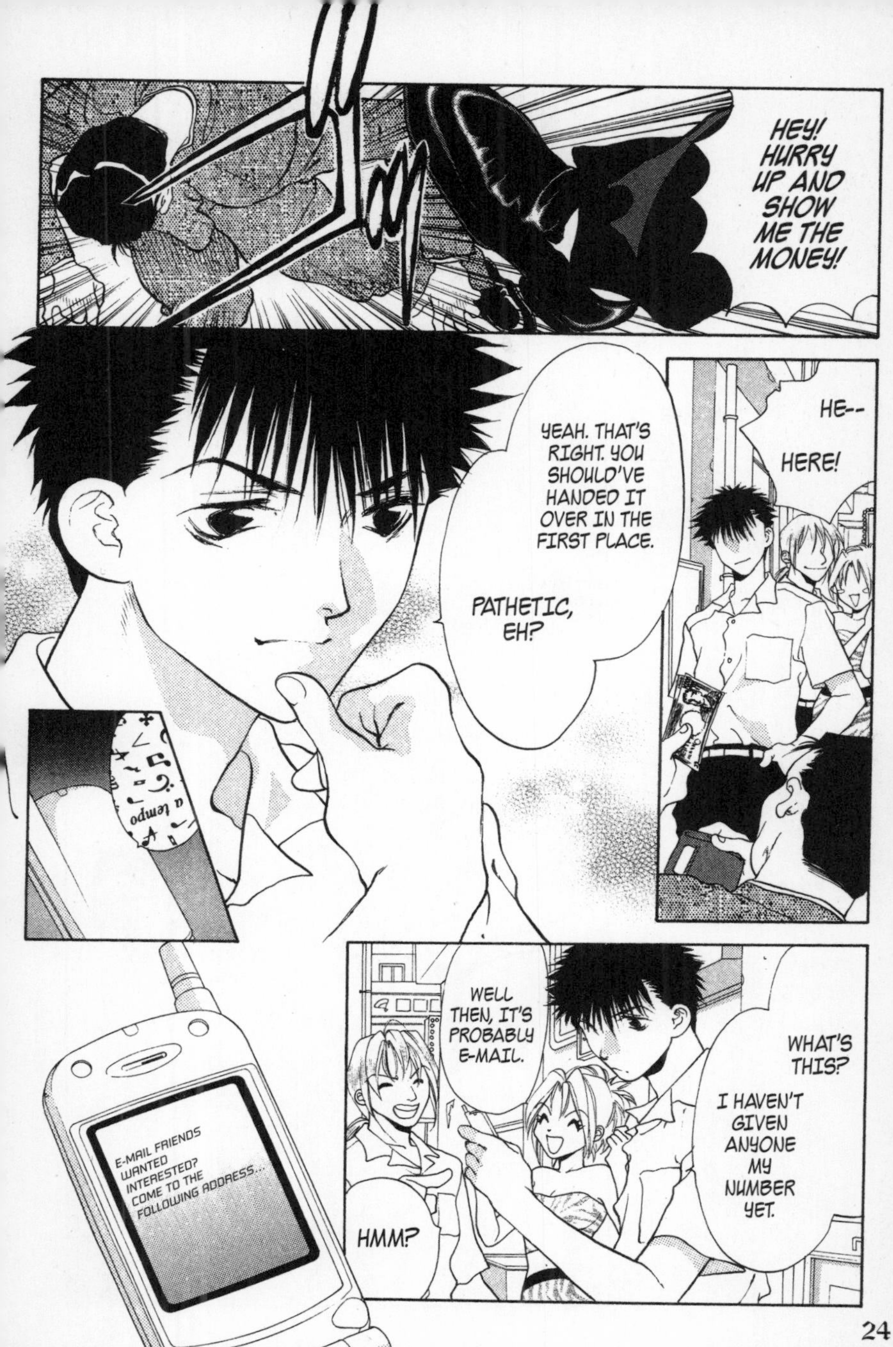
HEY! HURRY UP AND SHOW ME THE MONEY!
HE--
HERE!
YEAH. THAT'S RIGHT. YOU SHOULD'VE HANDED IT OVER IN THE FIRST PLACE.
PATHETIC, EH?
a tempo
WHAT'S THIS?
I HAVEN'T GIVEN ANYONE MY NUMBER YET.
WELL THEN, IT'S PROBABLY E-MAIL.
HMM?
E-MAIL FRIENDS WANTED
INTERESTED? COME TO THE FOLLOWING ADDRESS...

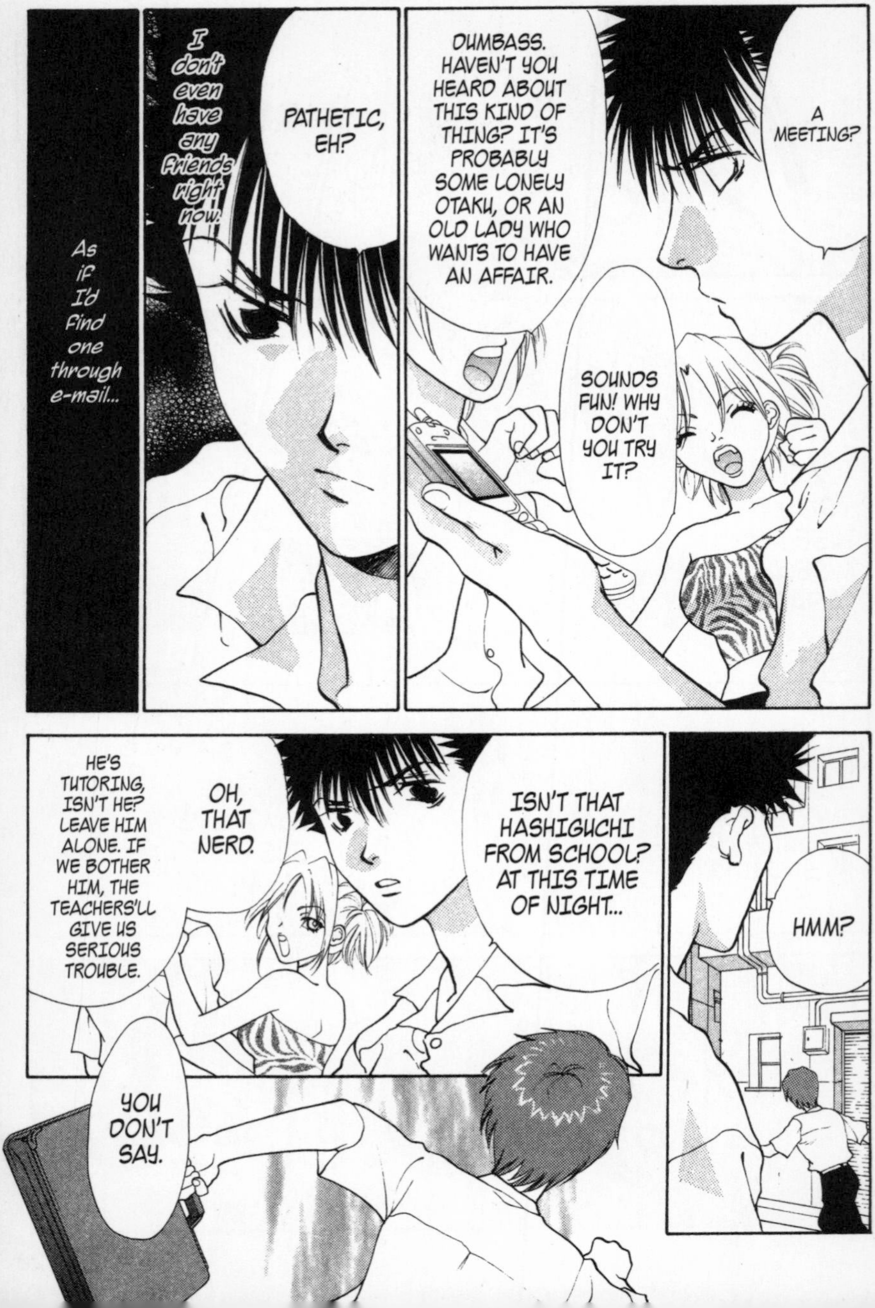
A MEETING?
DUMBASS. HAVEN'T YOU HEARD ABOUT THIS KIND OF THING? IT'S PROBABLY SOME LONELY OTAKU, OR AN OLD LADY WHO WANTS TO HAVE AN AFFAIR.
SOUNDS FUN! WHY DON'T YOU TRY IT?
PATHETIC, EH?
I don't even have any friends right now.
As if I'd find one through e-mail...
HMM?
ISN'T THAT HASHIGUCHI FROM SCHOOL? AT THIS TIME OF NIGHT...
OH, THAT NERD.
HE'S TUTORING, ISN'T HE? LEAVE HIM ALONE. IF WE BOTHER HIM, THE TEACHERS'LL GIVE US SERIOUS TROUBLE.
YOU DON'T SAY.

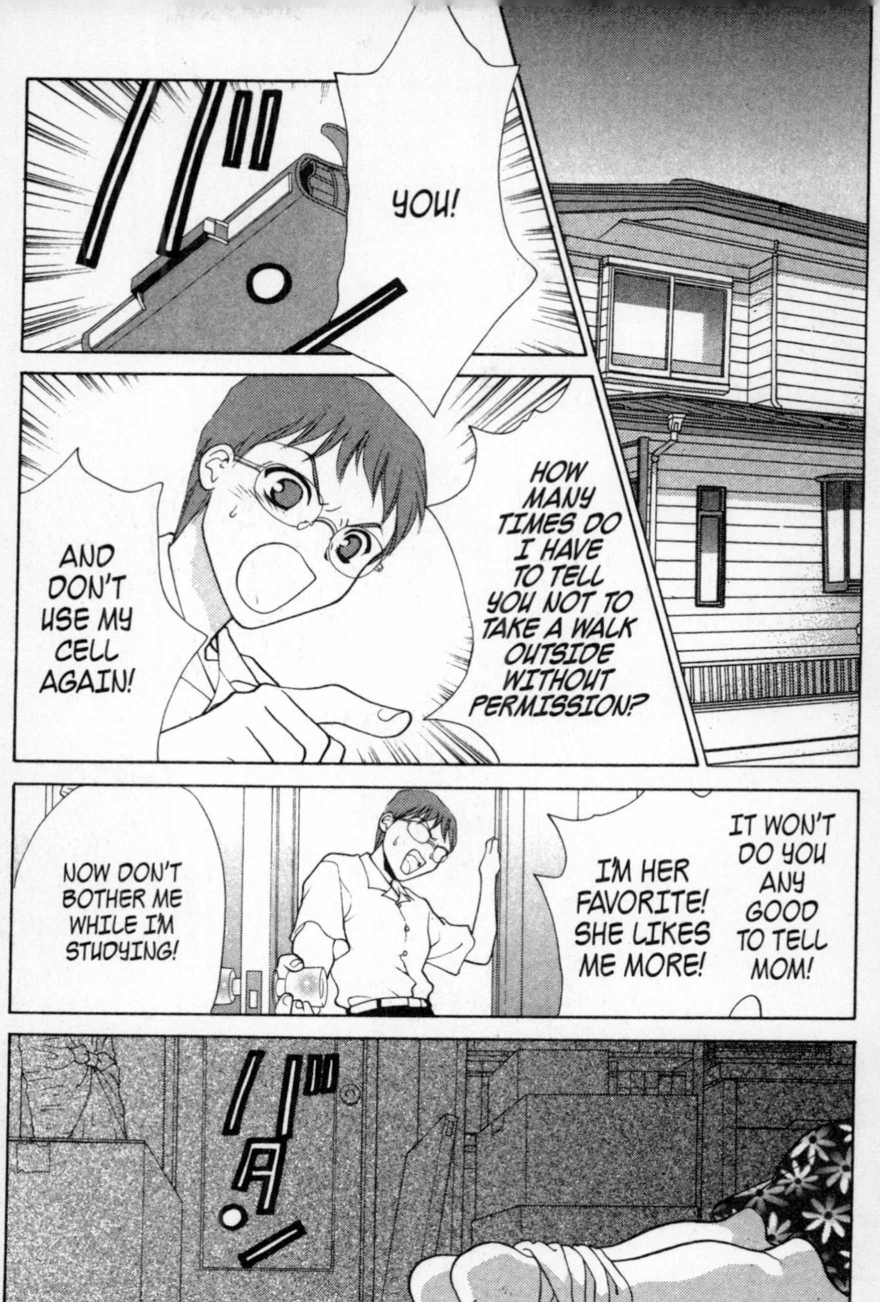
YOU!
HOW MANY TIMES DO I HAVE TO TELL YOU NOT TO TAKE A WALK OUTSIDE WITHOUT PERMISSION?
AND DON'T USE MY CELL AGAIN!
IT WON'T DO YOU ANY GOOD TO TELL MOM!
I'M HER FAVORITE! SHE LIKES ME MORE!
NOW DON'T BOTHER ME WHILE I'M STUDYING!

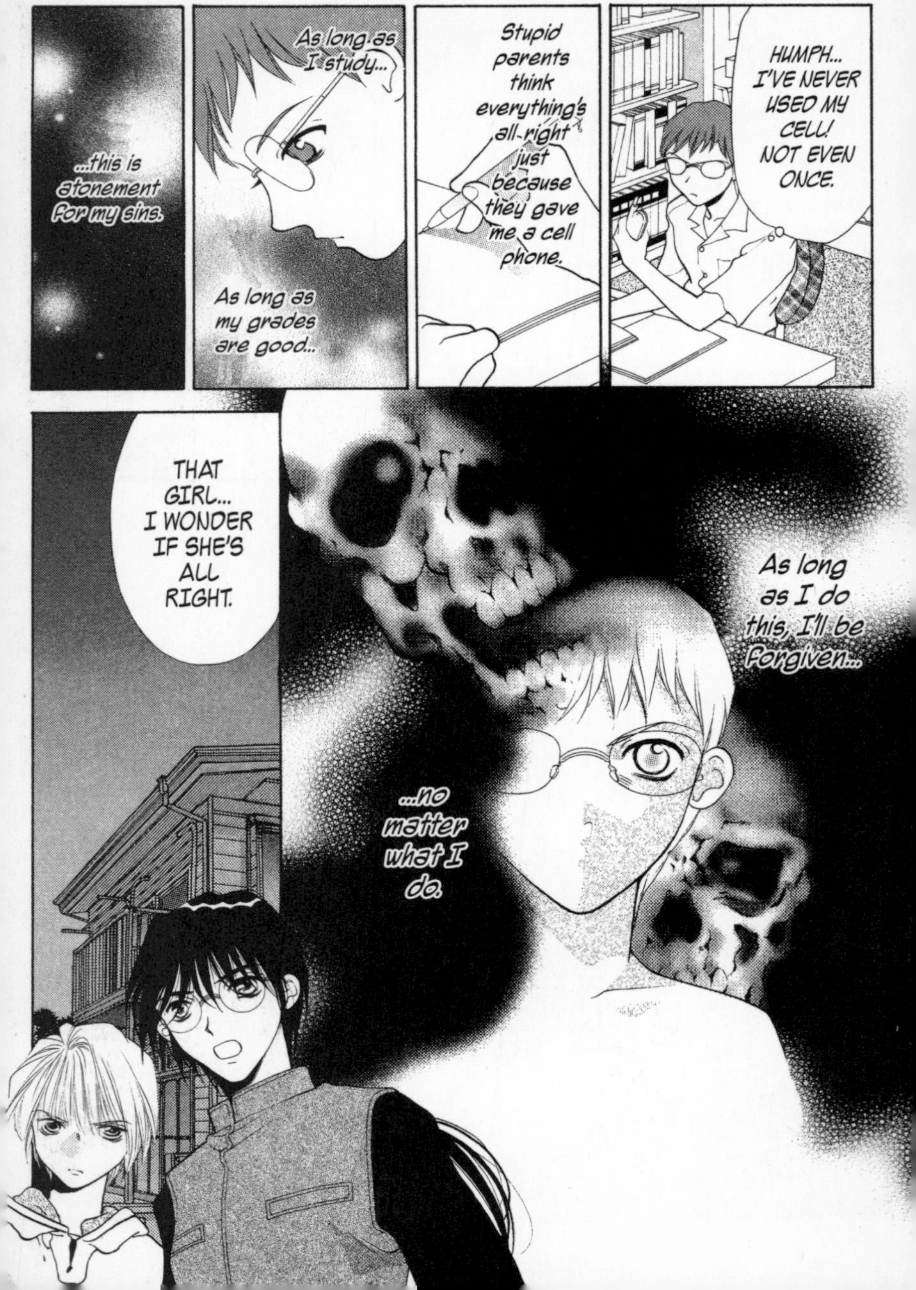
HUMPH... I'VE NEVER USED MY CELL! NOT EVEN ONCE.
Stupid parents think everything's all-right just because they gave me a cell phone.
As long as I study...
As long as my grades are good..
...this is atonement for my sins.
As long as I do this, I'll be forgiven...
...no matter what I do.
THAT GIRL... I WONDER IF SHE'S ALL RIGHT.

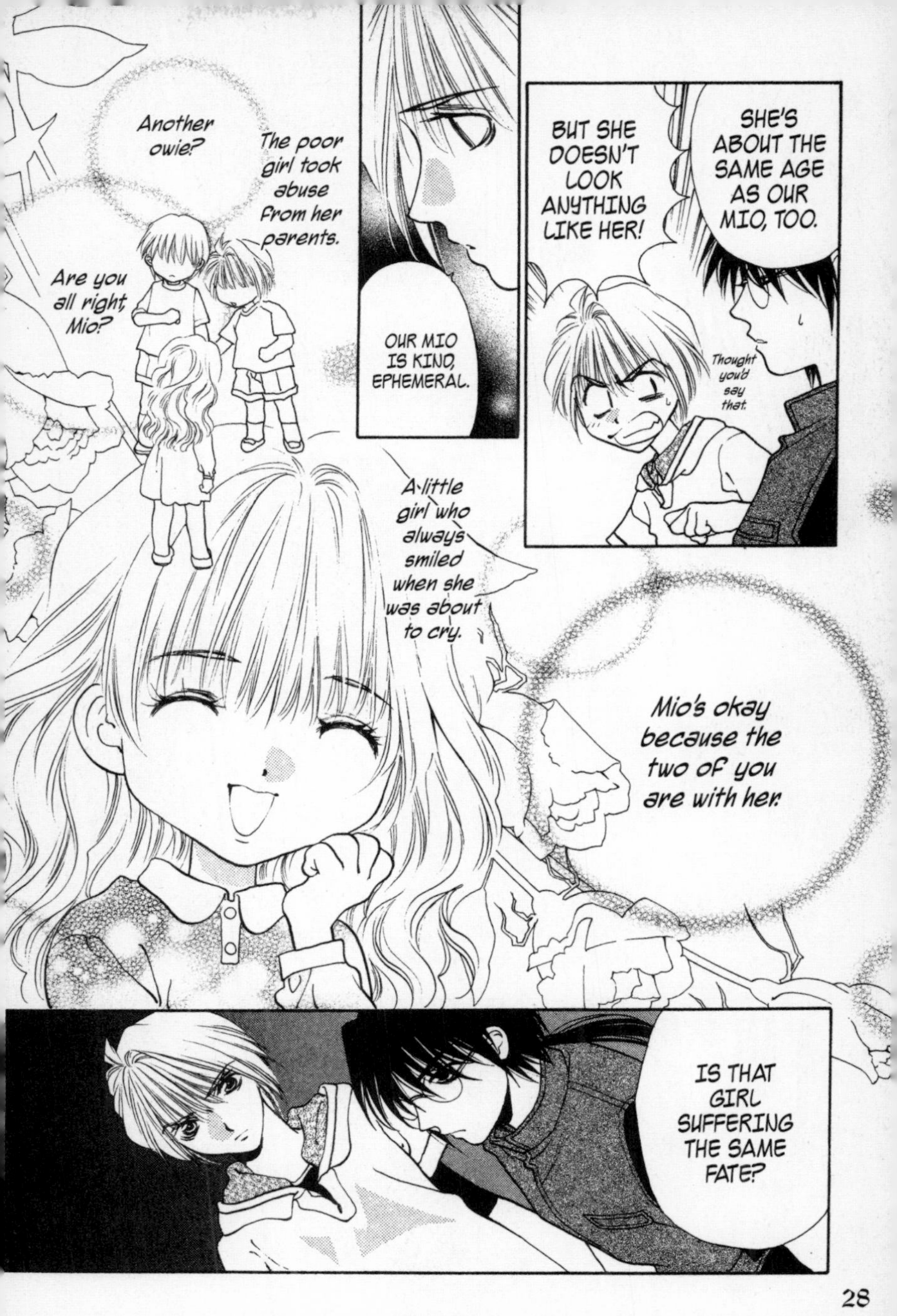
SHE'S ABOUT THE SAME AGE AS OUR MIO, TOO.
BUT SHE DOESN'T LOOK ANYTHING LIKE HER!
Thought you'd say that.
OUR MIO IS KIND, EPHEMERAL.
The poor girl took abuse from her parents.
Another owie?
Are you all right, Mio?
A little girl who always smiled when she was about to cry.
Mio's okay because the two of you are with her.
IS THAT GIRL SUFFERING THE SAME FATE?

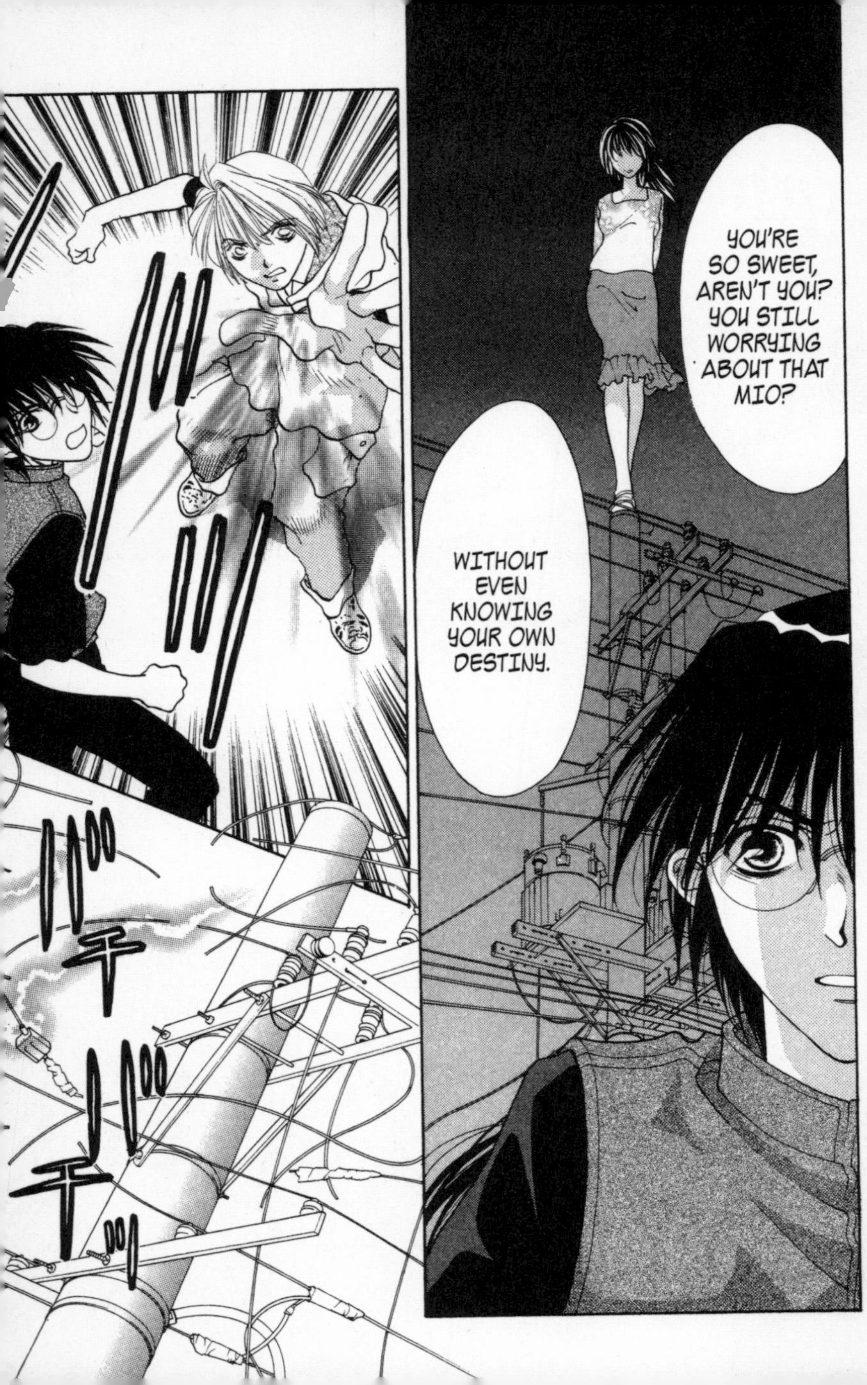
YOU'RE SO SWEET, AREN'T YOU? YOU STILL WORRYING ABOUT THAT MIO?
WITHOUT EVEN KNOWING YOUR OWN DESTINY.

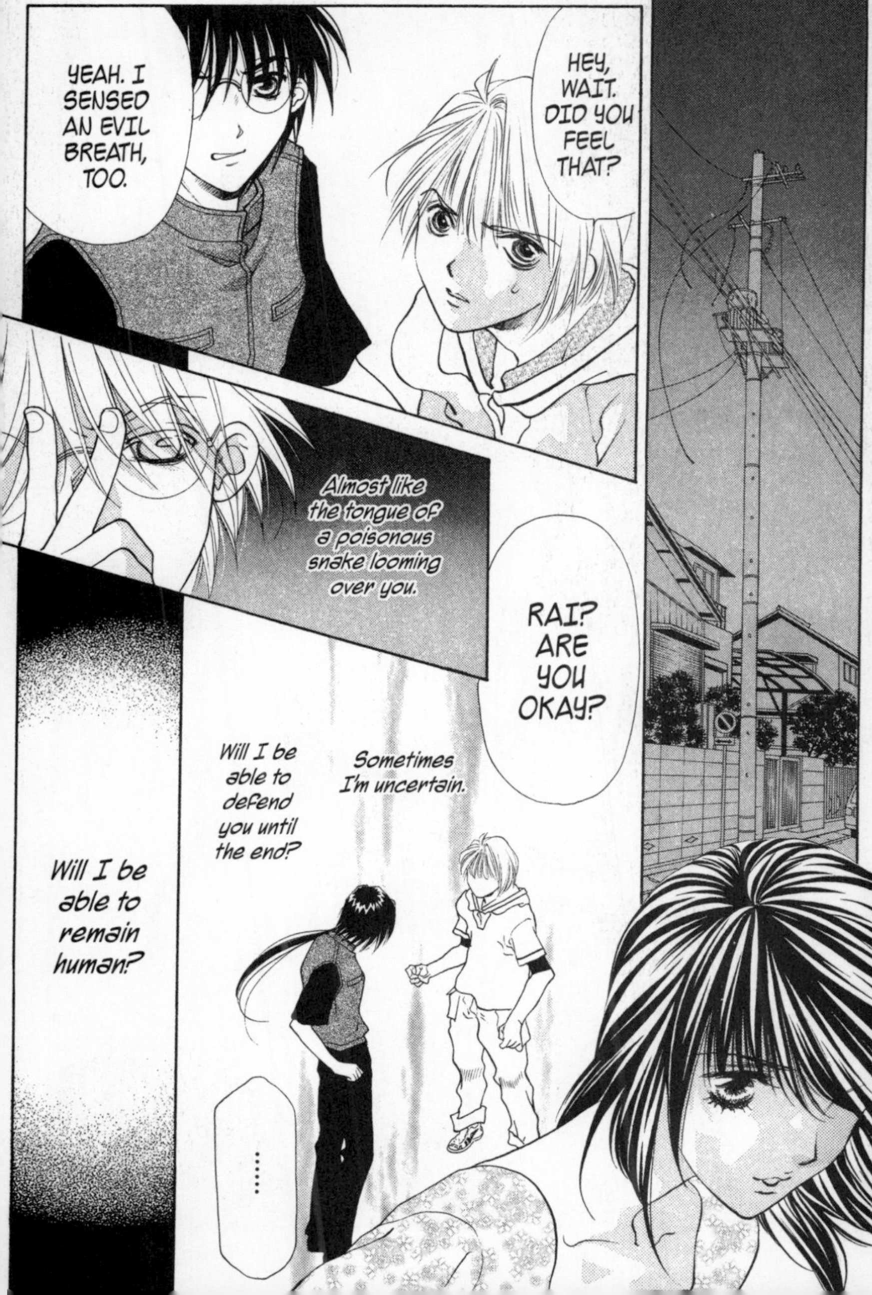
HEY, WAIT. DID YOU FEEL THAT?
YEAH. I SENSED AN EVIL BREATH, TOO.
Almost like the tongue of a poisonous snake looming over you.
RAI? ARE YOU OKAY?
Sometimes I'm uncertain.
Will I be able to defend you until the end?
......
Will I be able to remain human?

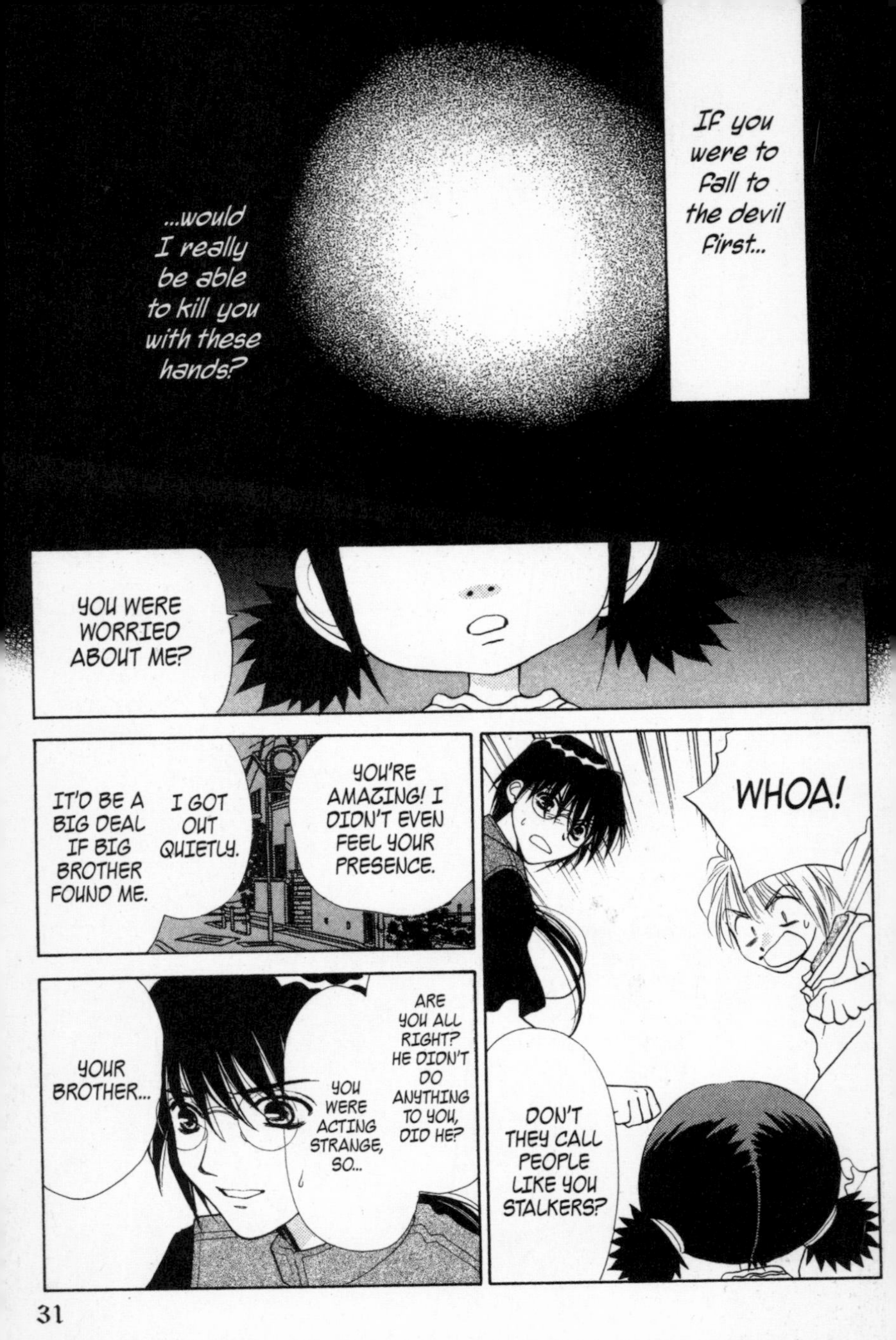
If you were to fall to the devil first...
...would I really be able to kill you with these hands?
YOU WERE WORRIED ABOUT ME?
WHOA!
DON'T THEY CALL PEOPLE LIKE YOU STALKERS?
YOU'RE AMAZING! I DIDN'T EVEN FEEL YOUR PRESENCE.
I GOT OUT QUIETLY.
IT'D BE A BIG DEAL IF BIG BROTHER FOUND ME.
ARE YOU ALL RIGHT? HE DIDN'T DO ANYTHING TO YOU, DID HE?
YOU WERE ACTING STRANGE, SO...
YOUR BROTHER...

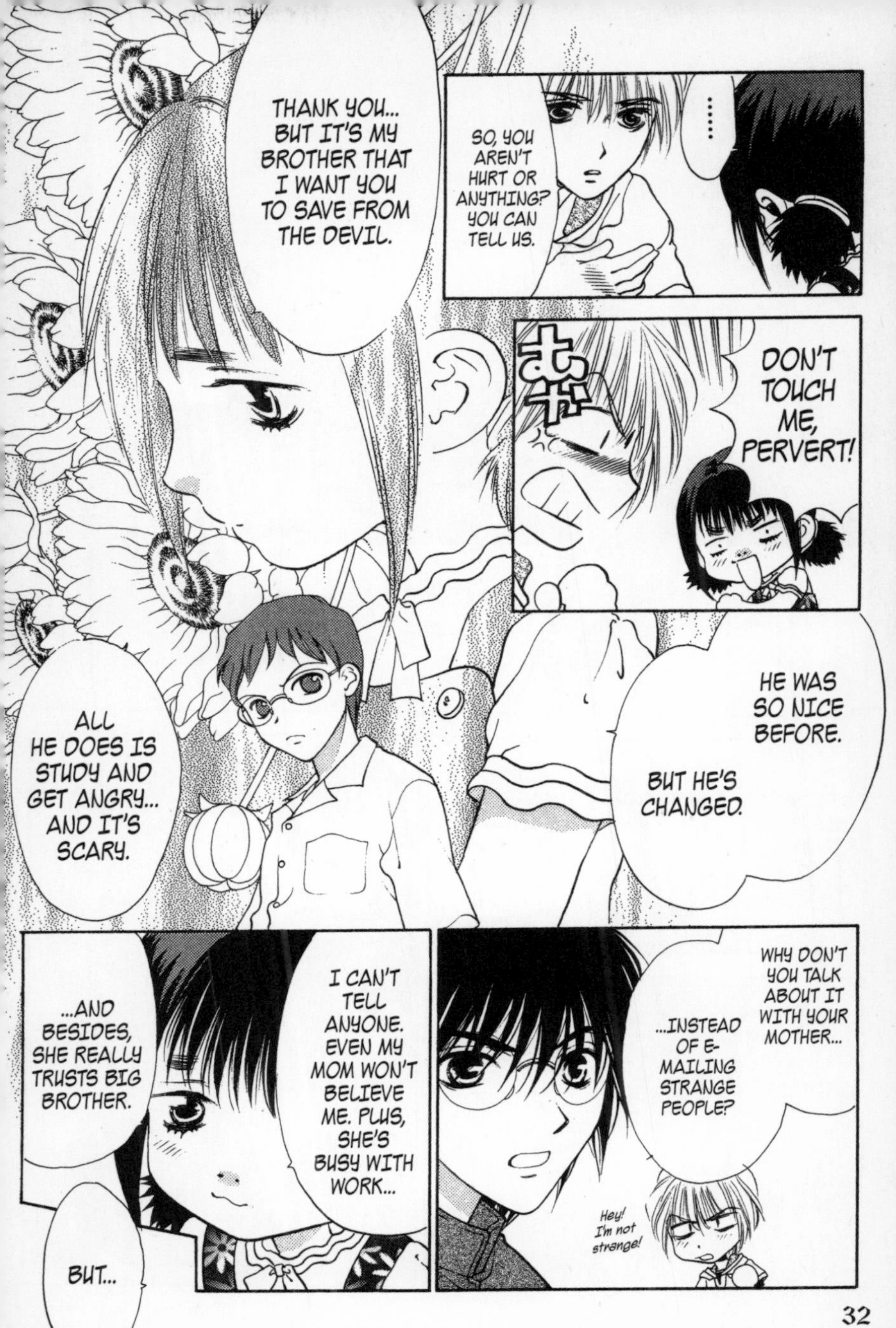
SO, YOU AREN'T HURT OR ANYTHING? YOU CAN TELL US.
……
DON'T TOUCH ME, PERVERT!
THANK YOU... BUT IT'S MY BROTHER THAT I WANT YOU TO SAVE FROM THE DEVIL.
HE WAS SO NICE BEFORE.
BUT HE'S CHANGED.
ALL HE DOES IS STUDY AND GET ANGRY... AND IT'S SCARY.
WHY DON'T YOU TALK ABOUT IT WITH YOUR MOTHER...
...INSTEAD OF E-MAILING STRANGE PEOPLE?
Hey! I'm not strange!
I CAN'T TELL ANYONE. EVEN MY MOM WON'T BELIEVE ME. PLUS, SHE'S BUSY WITH WORK...
...AND BESIDES, SHE REALLY TRUSTS BIG BROTHER.
BUT...

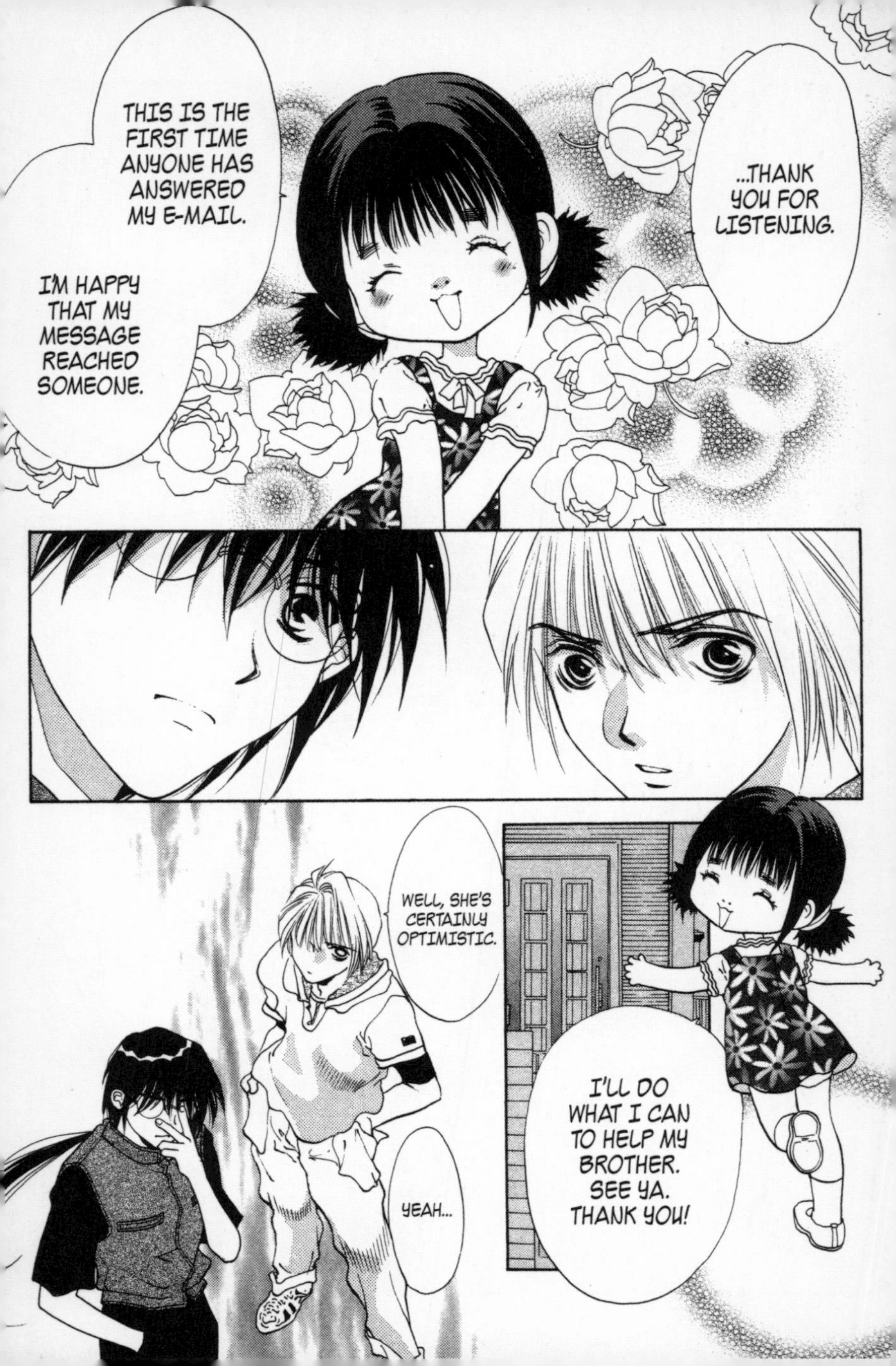
...THANK YOU FOR LISTENING.
THIS IS THE FIRST TIME ANYONE HAS ANSWERED MY E-MAIL.
I'M HAPPY THAT MY MESSAGE REACHED SOMEONE.
I'LL DO WHAT I CAN TO HELP MY BROTHER. SEE YA. THANK YOU!
WELL, SHE'S CERTAINLY OPTIMISTIC.
YEAH...

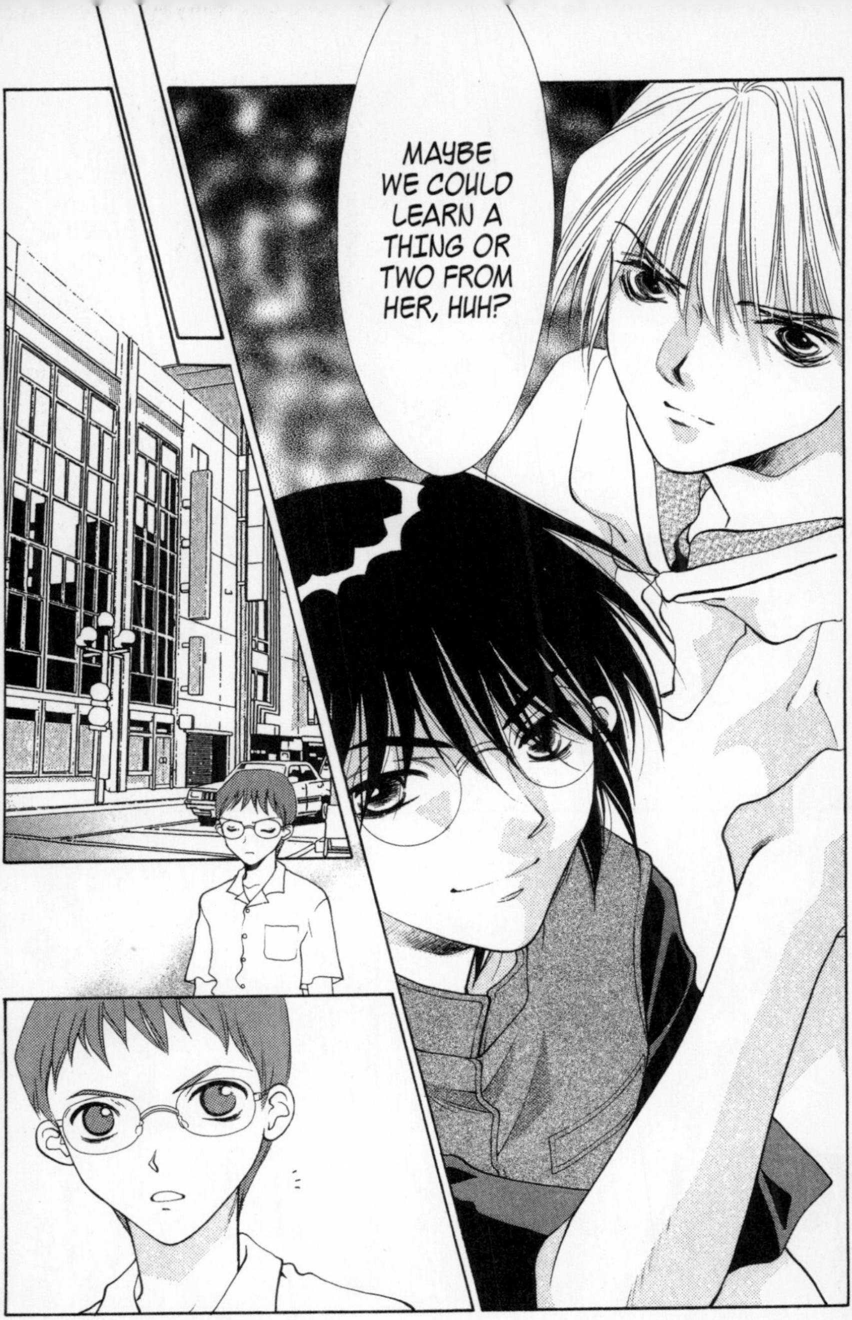
MAYBE WE COULD LEARN A THING OR TWO FROM HER, HUH?

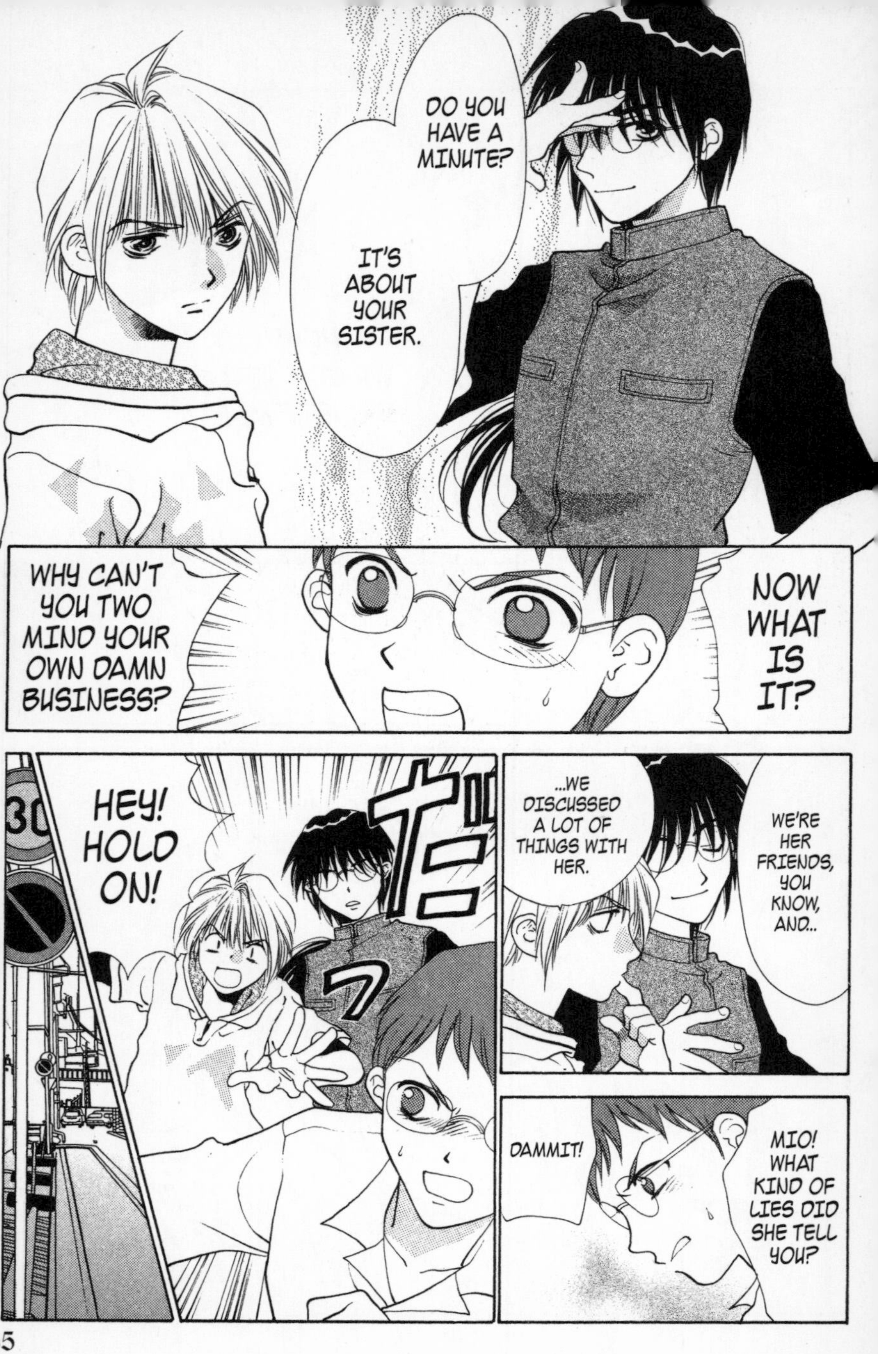
DO YOU HAVE A MINUTE?
IT'S ABOUT YOUR SISTER.
NOW WHAT IS IT?
WHY CAN'T YOU TWO MIND YOUR OWN DAMN BUSINESS?
WE'RE HER FRIENDS, YOU KNOW, AND...
...WE DISCUSSED A LOT OF THINGS WITH HER.
MIO! WHAT KIND OF LIES DID SHE TELL YOU?
DAMMIT!
HEY! HOLD ON!
30

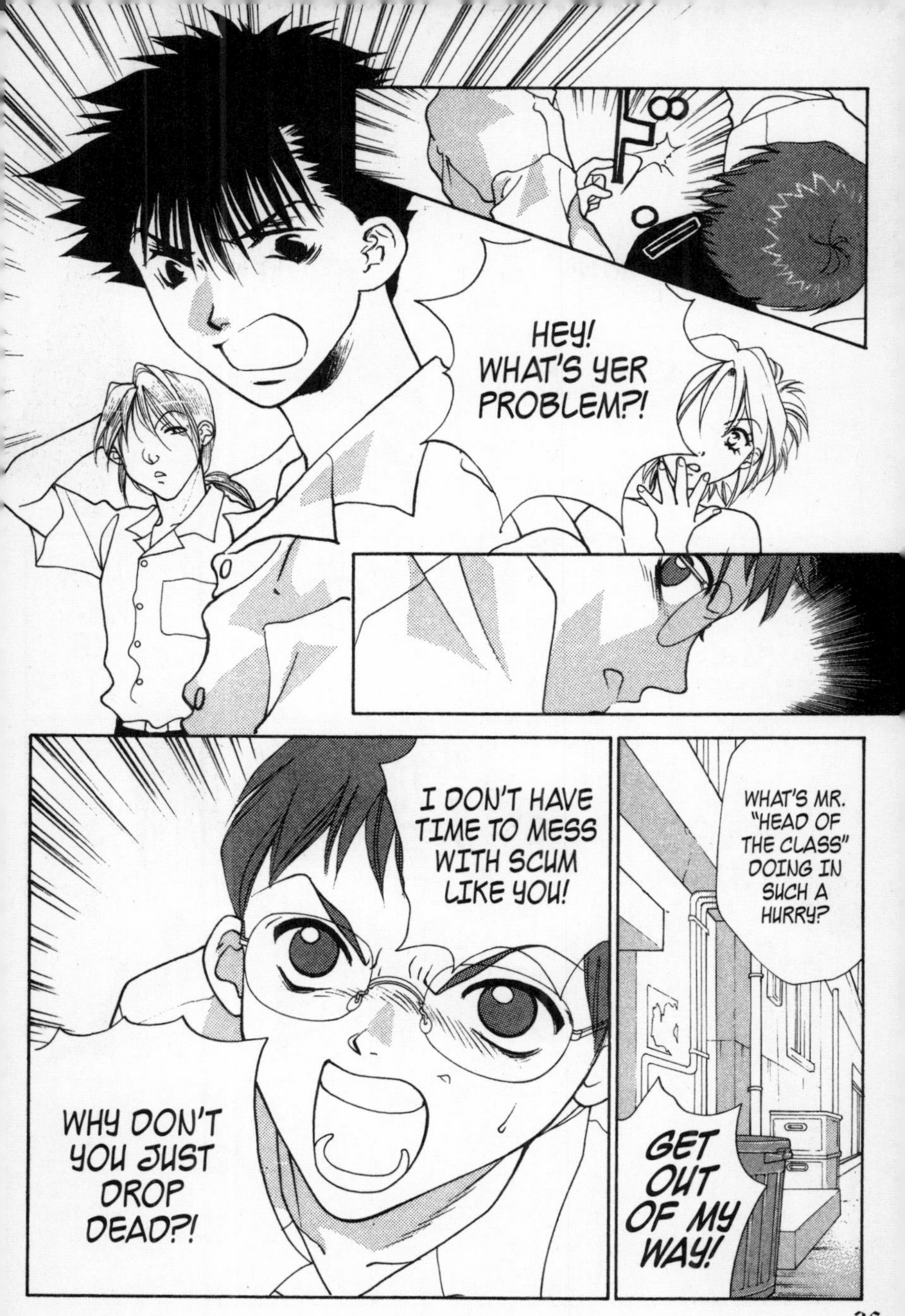
HEY! WHAT'S YER PROBLEM?!
WHAT'S MR. "HEAD OF THE CLASS" DOING IN SUCH A HURRY?
GET OUT OF MY WAY!
I DON'T HAVE TIME TO MESS WITH SCUM LIKE YOU!
WHY DON'T YOU JUST DROP DEAD?!

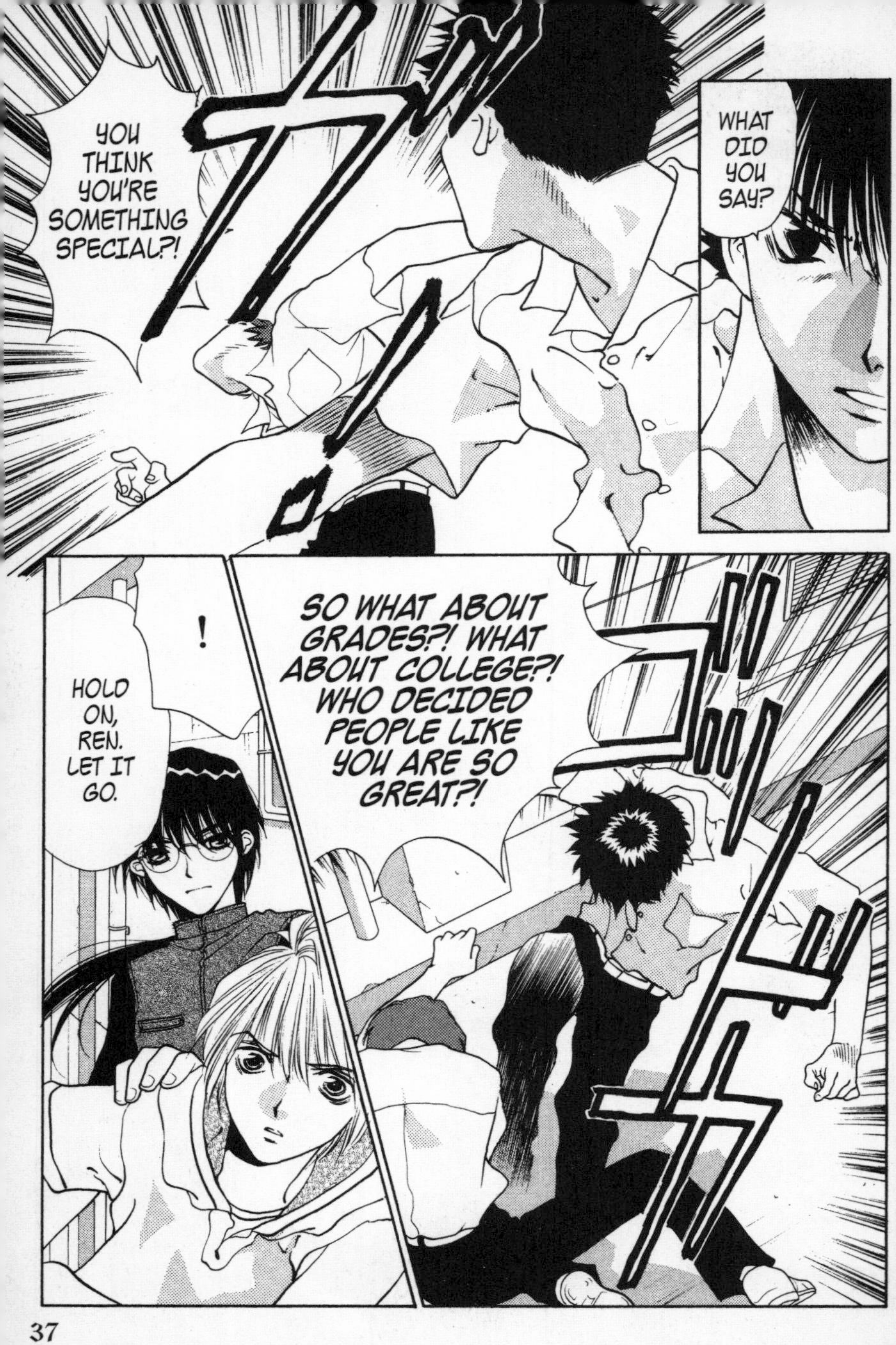
WHAT DID YOU SAY?
YOU THINK YOU'RE SOMETHING SPECIAL?!
SO WHAT ABOUT GRADES?! WHAT ABOUT COLLEGE?! WHO DECIDED PEOPLE LIKE YOU ARE SO GREAT?!
!
HOLD ON, REN. LET IT GO.

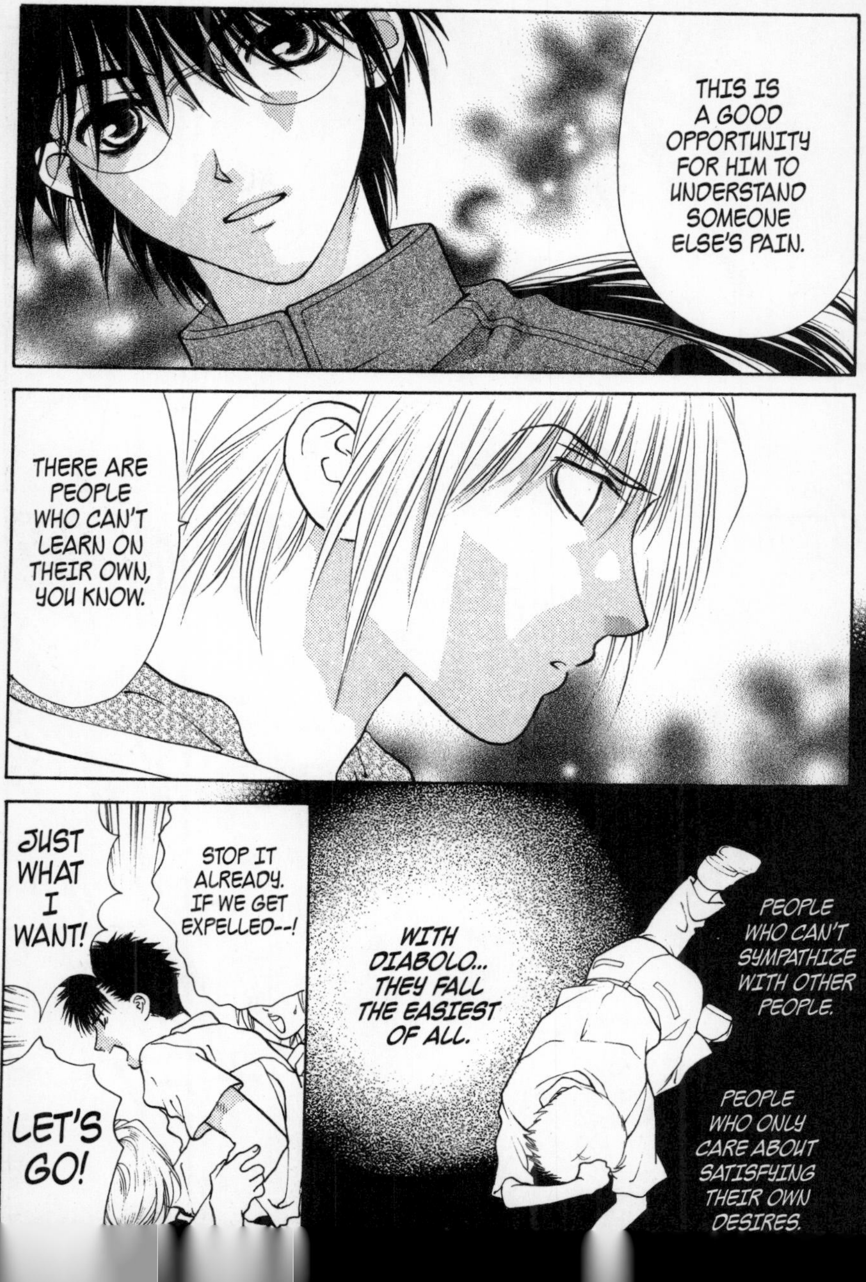
THIS IS A GOOD OPPORTUNITY FOR HIM TO UNDERSTAND SOMEONE ELSE'S PAIN.
THERE ARE PEOPLE WHO CAN'T LEARN ON THEIR OWN, YOU KNOW.
PEOPLE WHO CAN'T SYMPATHIZE WITH OTHER PEOPLE.
PEOPLE WHO ONLY CARE ABOUT SATISFYING THEIR OWN DESIRES.
WITH DIABOLO... THEY FALL THE EASIEST OF ALL.
STOP IT ALREADY. IF WE GET EXPELLED--!
JUST WHAT I WANT!
LET'S GO!

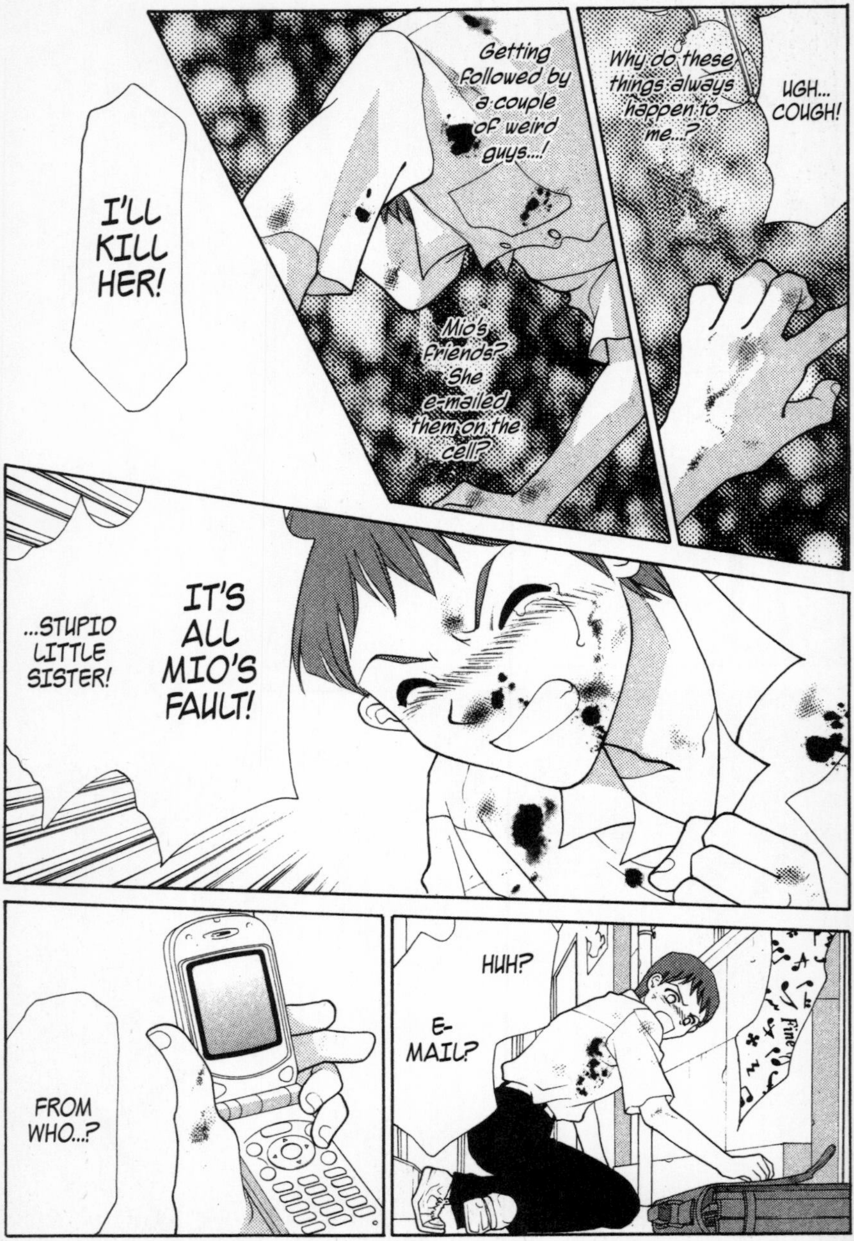
UGH... COUGH!
Why do these things always happen to me...?
Getting followed by a couple of weird guys...!
Mio's friends? She e-mailed them on the cell?
I'LL KILL HER!
IT'S ALL MIO'S FAULT!
...STUPID LITTLE SISTER!
Fine
HUH?
E-MAIL?
FROM WHO...?

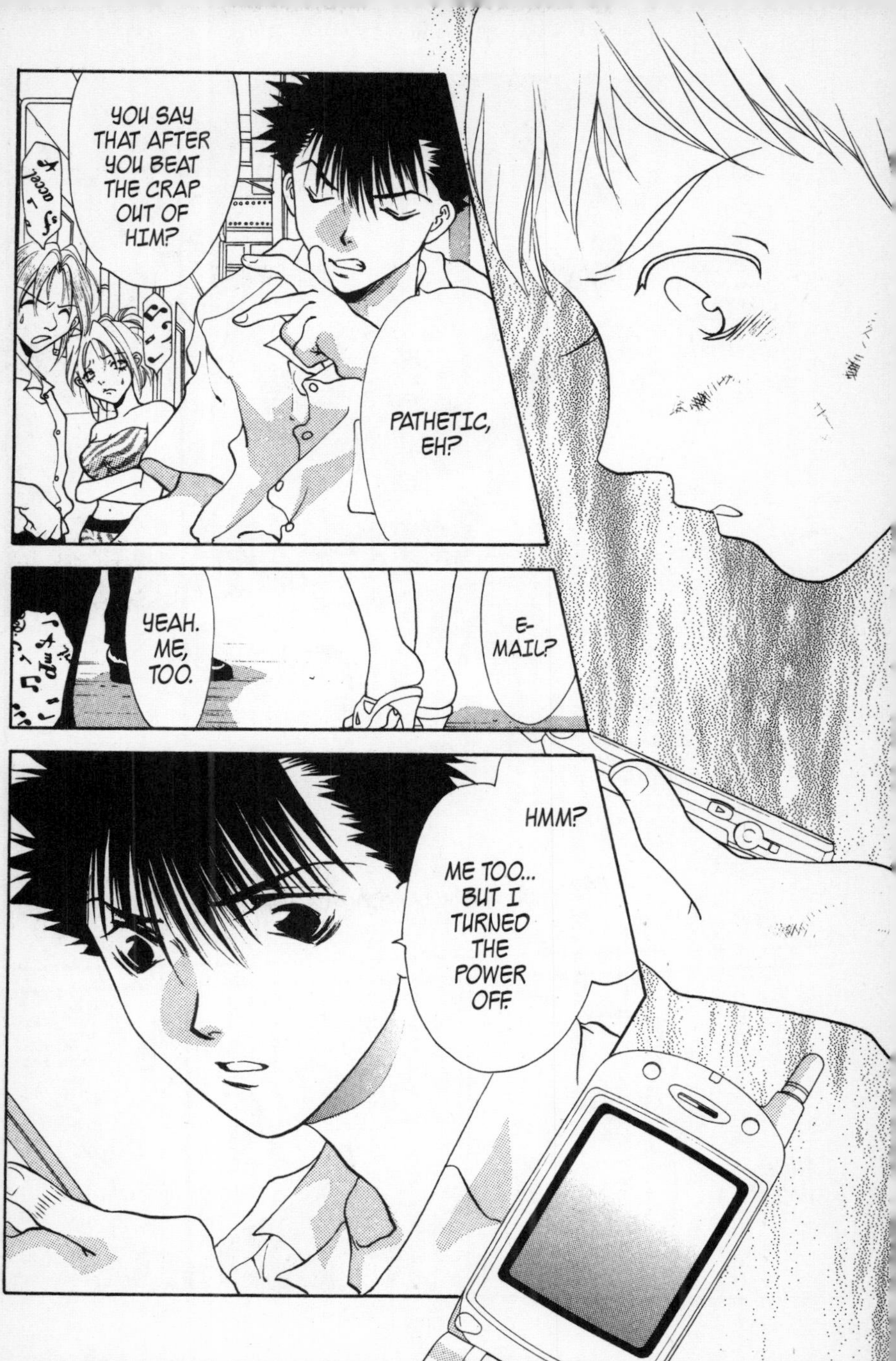
PATHETIC, EH?
YOU SAY THAT AFTER YOU BEAT THE CRAP OUT OF HIM?
E-MAIL?
YEAH. ME, TOO.
HMM?
ME TOO... BUT I TURNED THE POWER OFF.

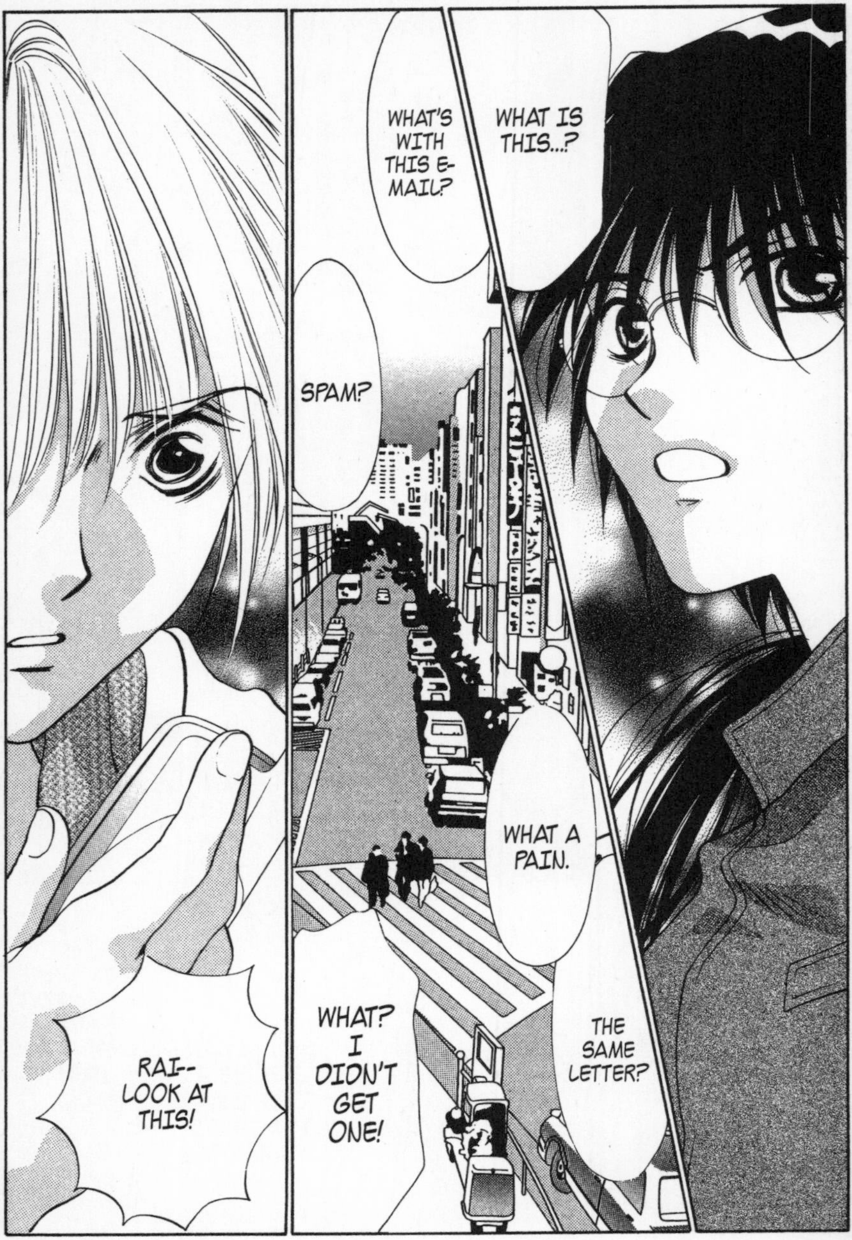
WHAT IS THIS...?
WHAT'S WITH THIS E-MAIL?
SPAM?
WHAT A PAIN.
THE SAME LETTER?
WHAT? I DIDN'T GET ONE!
RAI-- LOOK AT THIS!

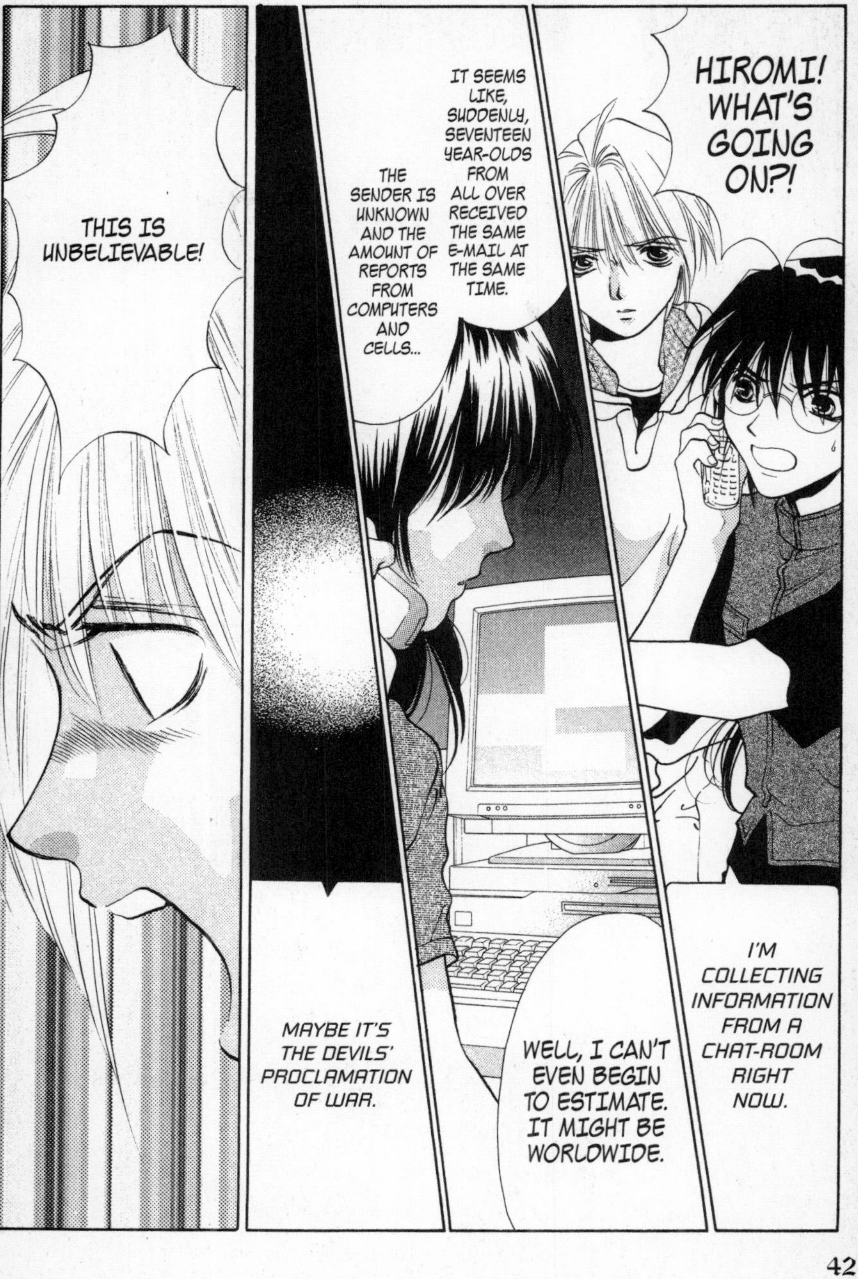
HIROMI! WHAT'S GOING ON?!
I'M COLLECTING INFORMATION FROM A CHAT-ROOM RIGHT NOW.
IT SEEMS LIKE, SUDDENLY, SEVENTEEN YEAR-OLDS FROM ALL OVER RECEIVED THE SAME E-MAIL AT THE SAME TIME.
THE SENDER IS UNKNOWN AND THE AMOUNT OF REPORTS FROM COMPUTERS AND CELLS...
WELL, I CAN'T EVEN BEGIN TO ESTIMATE. IT MIGHT BE WORLDWIDE.
MAYBE IT'S THE DEVILS' PROCLAMATION OF WAR.
THIS IS UNBELIEVABLE!

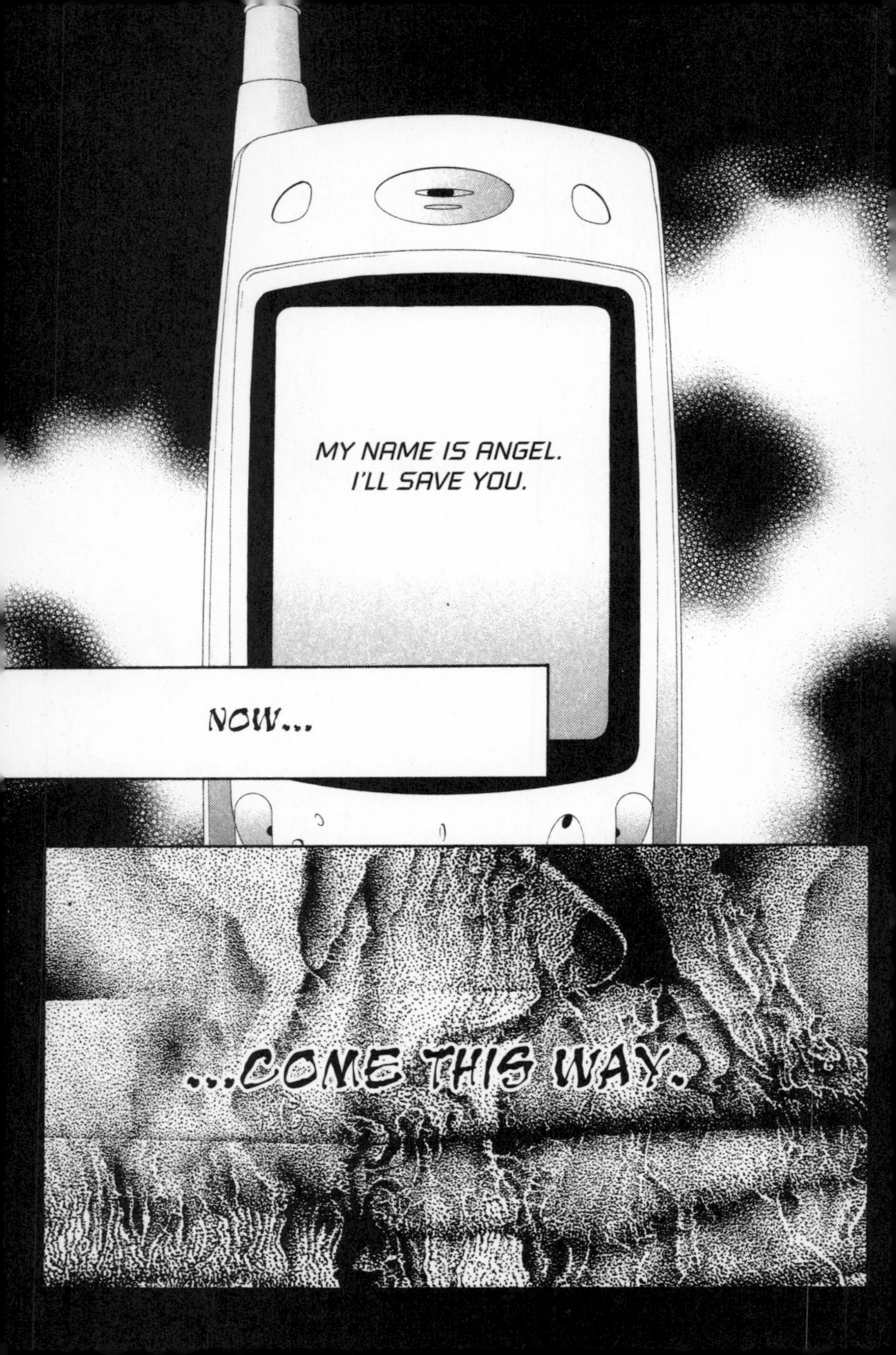
MY NAME IS ANGEL.
I'LL SAVE YOU.
NOW...
...COME THIS WAY.

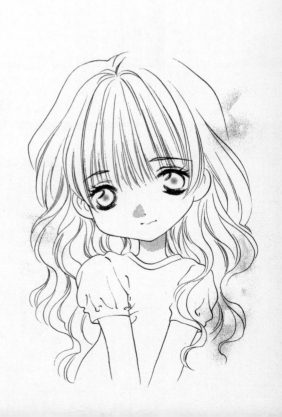

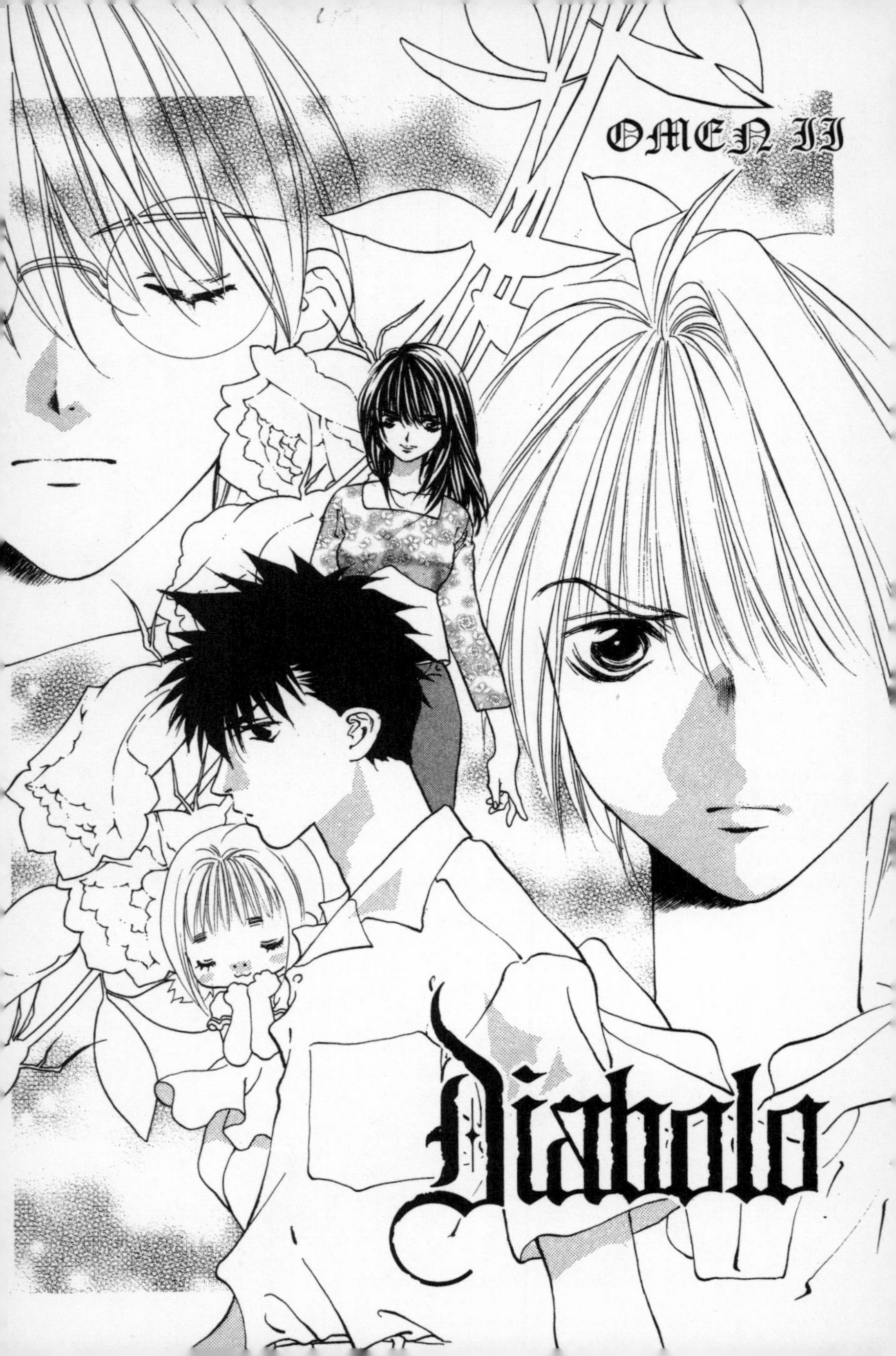
OMEN II
Diabolo

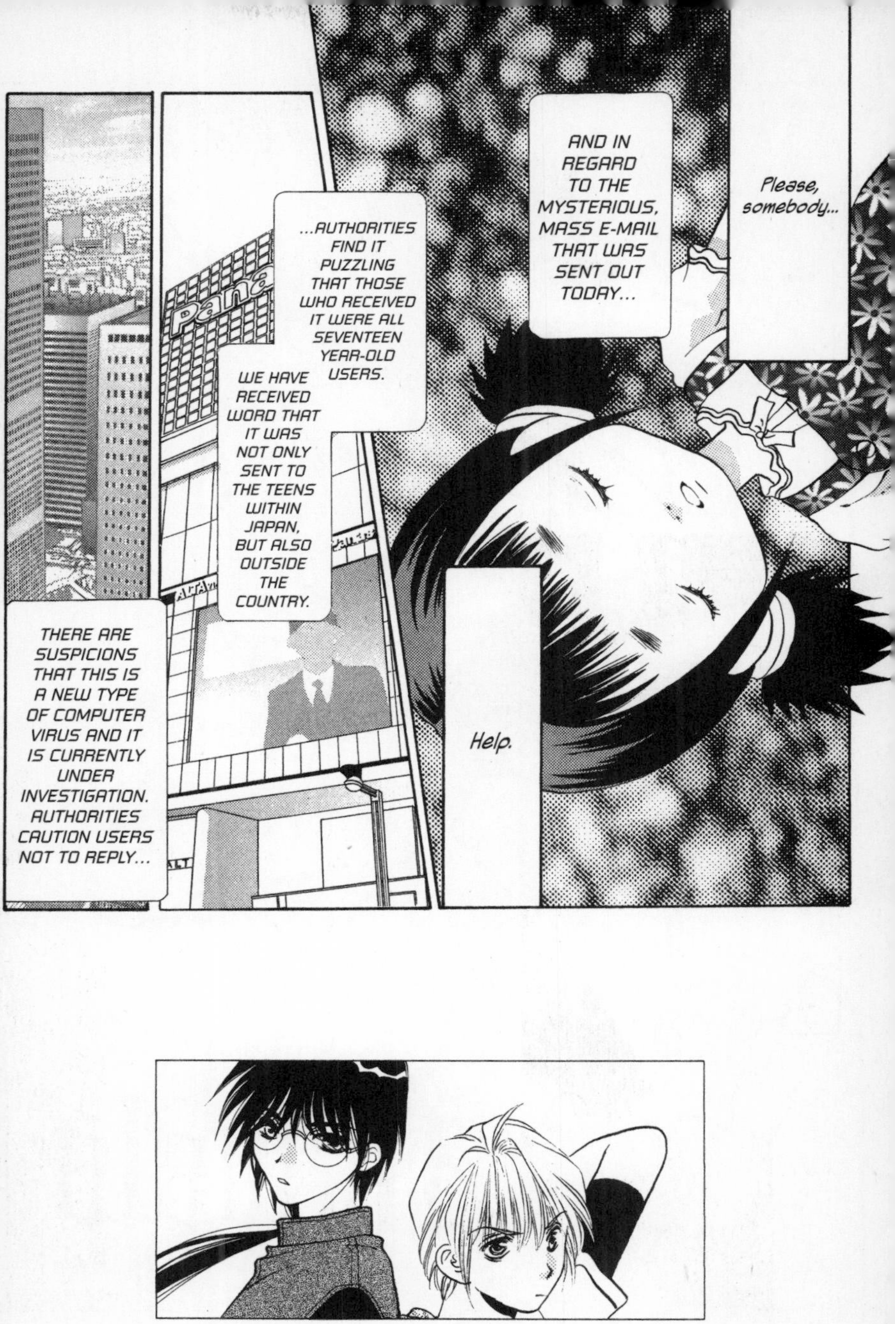
Please, somebody...
AND IN REGARD TO THE MYSTERIOUS, MASS E-MAIL THAT WAS SENT OUT TODAY...
Help.
...AUTHORITIES FIND IT PUZZLING THAT THOSE WHO RECEIVED IT WERE ALL SEVENTEEN YEAR-OLD USERS.
WE HAVE RECEIVED WORD THAT IT WAS NOT ONLY SENT TO THE TEENS WITHIN JAPAN, BUT ALSO OUTSIDE THE COUNTRY.
THERE ARE SUSPICIONS THAT THIS IS A NEW TYPE OF COMPUTER VIRUS AND IT IS CURRENTLY UNDER INVESTIGATION. AUTHORITIES CAUTION USERS NOT TO REPLY...

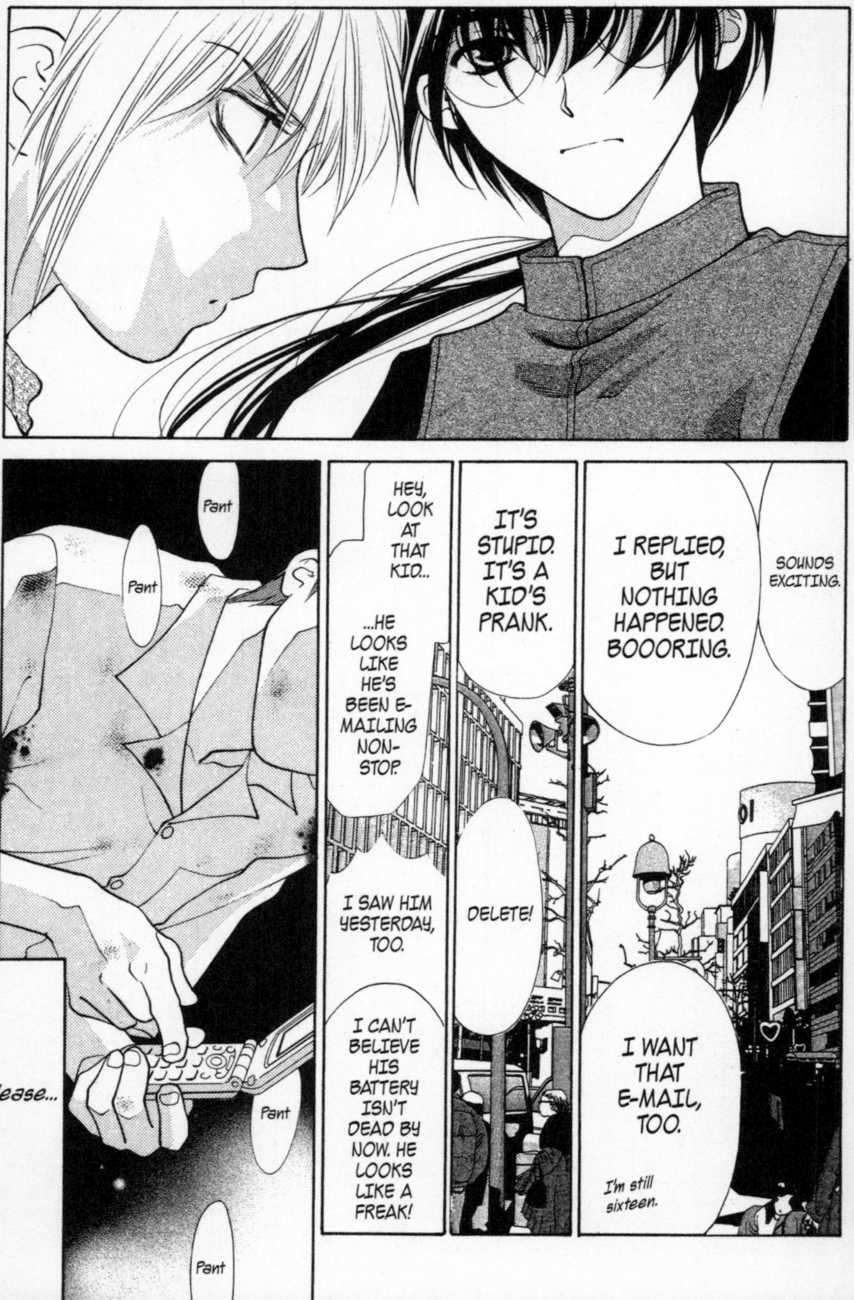
SOUNDS EXCITING.
I REPLIED, BUT NOTHING HAPPENED. BOOORING.
I WANT THAT E-MAIL, TOO.
I'm still sixteen.
IT'S STUPID. IT'S A KID'S PRANK.
DELETE!
HEY, LOOK AT THAT KID...
...HE LOOKS LIKE HE'S BEEN E-MAILING NON-STOP.
I SAW HIM YESTERDAY, TOO.
I CAN'T BELIEVE HIS BATTERY ISN'T DEAD BY NOW. HE LOOKS LIKE A FREAK!
Pant
Pant
Please...
Pant
Pant

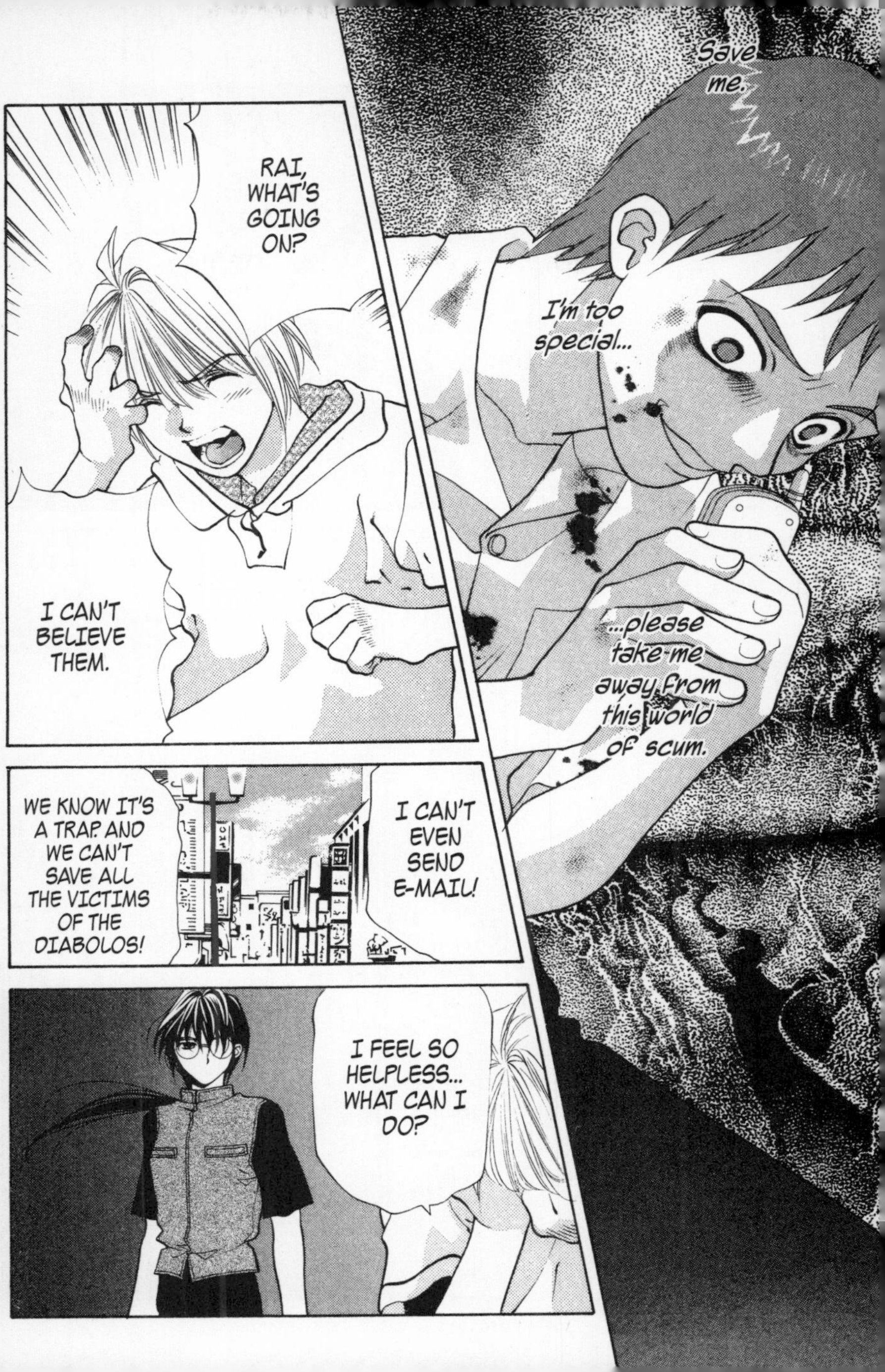
Save me.
I'm too special...
...please take me away from this world of scum.
RAI, WHAT'S GOING ON?
I CAN'T BELIEVE THEM.
I CAN'T EVEN SEND E-MAIL!
WE KNOW IT'S A TRAP. AND WE CAN'T SAVE ALL THE VICTIMS OF THE DIABOLOS!
I FEEL SO HELPLESS... WHAT CAN I DO?

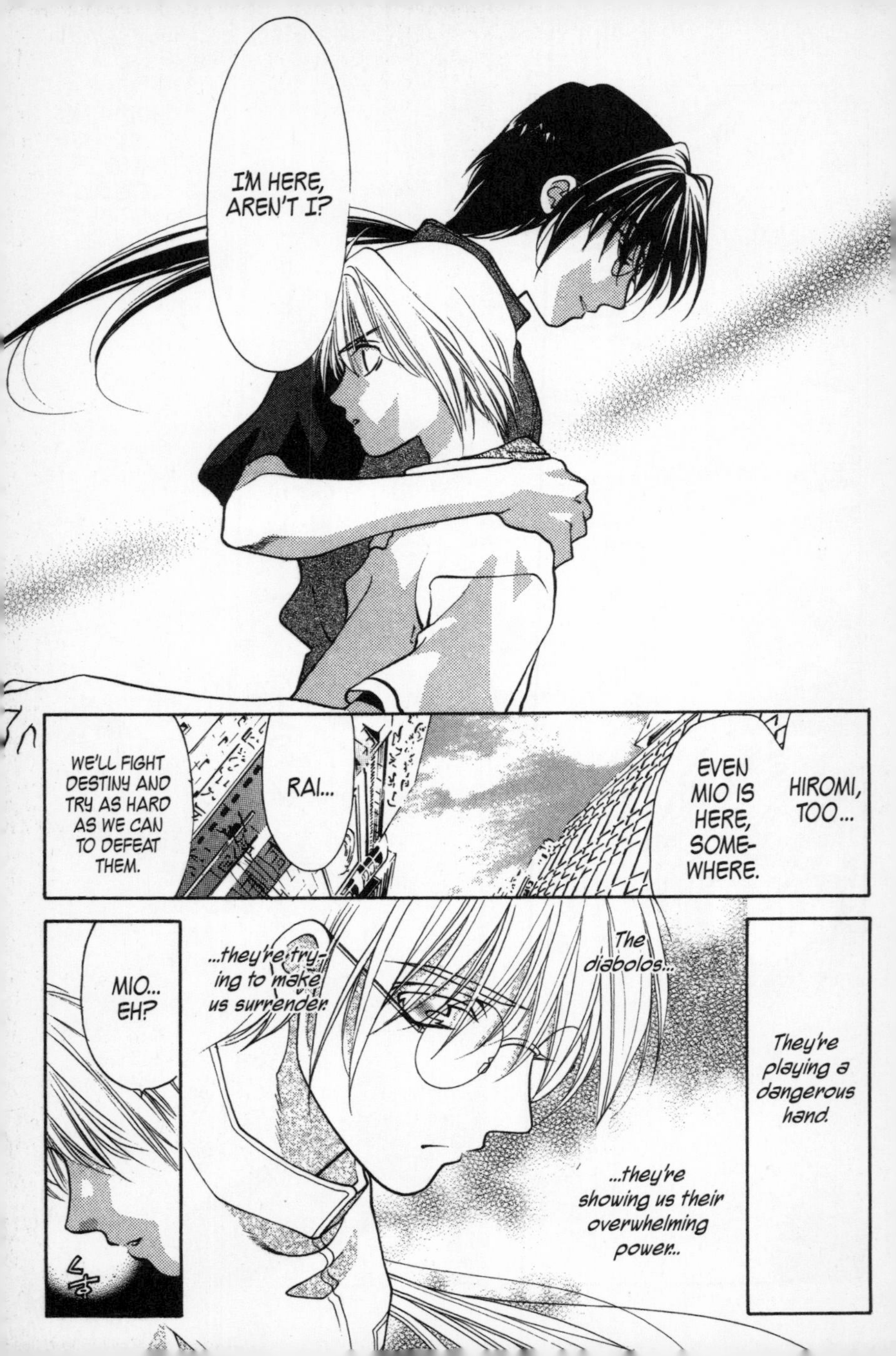
I'M HERE, AREN'T I?
HIROMI, TOO...
EVEN MIO IS HERE, SOME-WHERE.
RAI...
WE'LL FIGHT DESTINY AND TRY AS HARD AS WE CAN TO DEFEAT THEM.
They're playing a dangerous hand.
The diabolos...
...they're try-ing to make us surrender.
...they're showing us their overwhelming power...
MIO... EH?

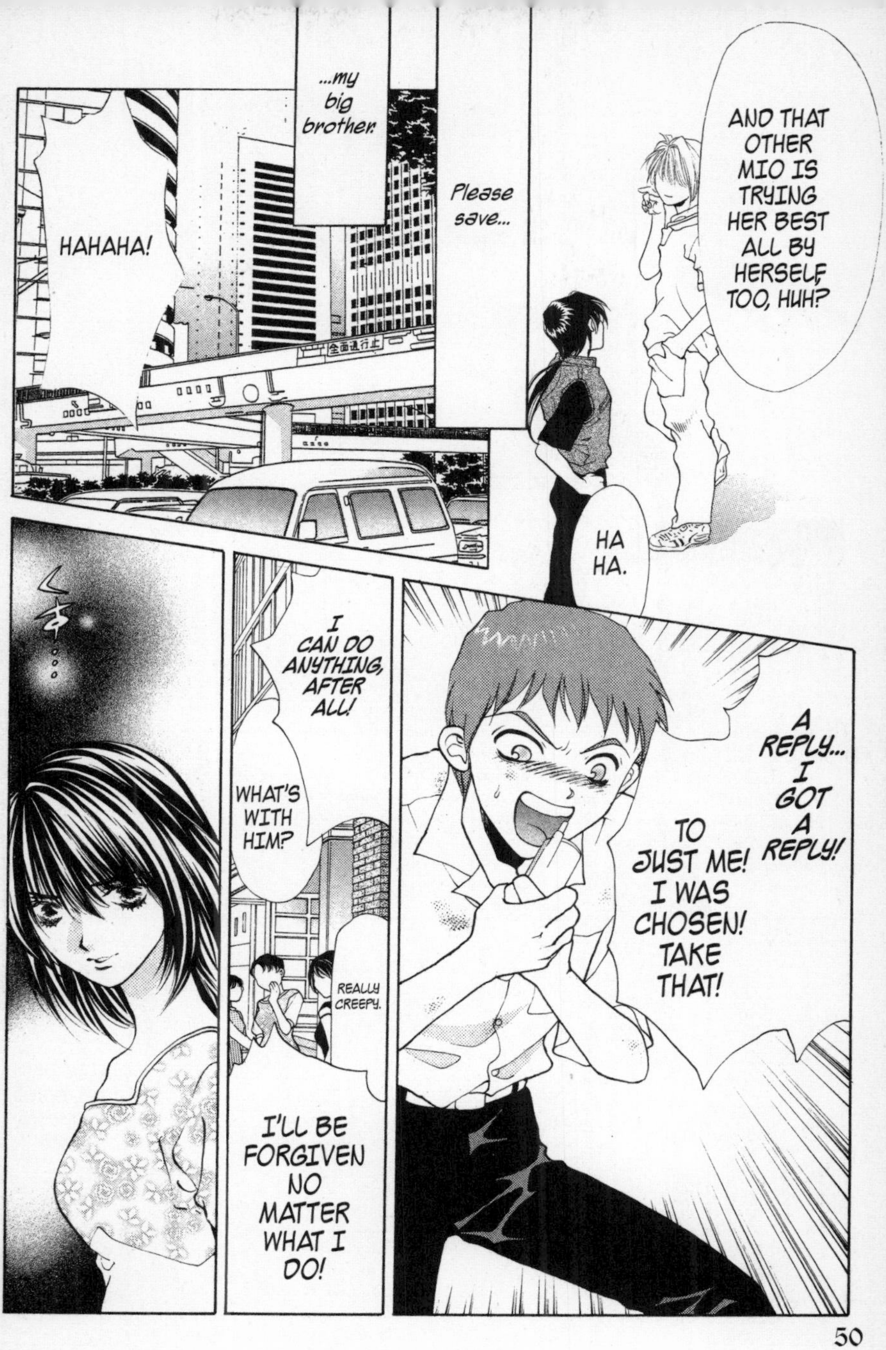

AND THAT OTHER MIO IS TRYING HER BEST ALL BY HERSELF, TOO, HUH?
HA HA.
Please save...
...my big brother.
HAHAHA!
A REPLY... I GOT A REPLY!
TO JUST ME! I WAS CHOSEN! TAKE THAT!
I CAN DO ANYTHING, AFTER ALL!
WHAT'S WITH HIM?
REALLY CREEPY.
I'LL BE FORGIVEN NO MATTER WHAT I DO!
くす…

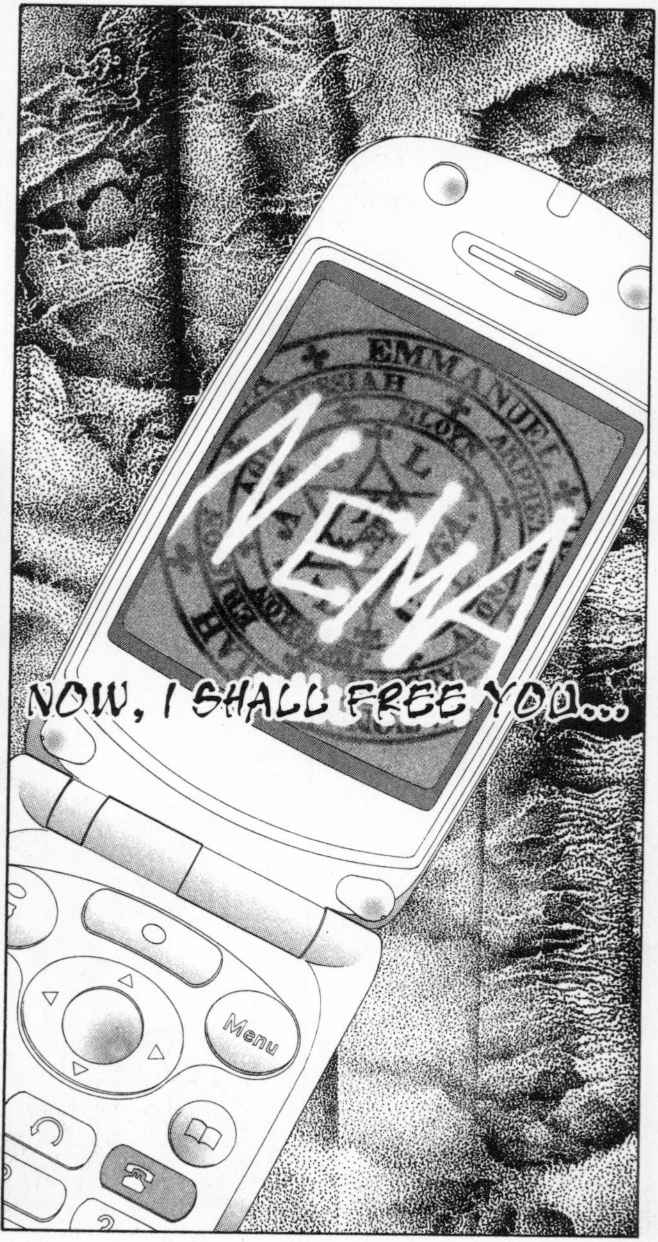
EMMANUEL
NOW, I SHALL FREE YOU...
Menu
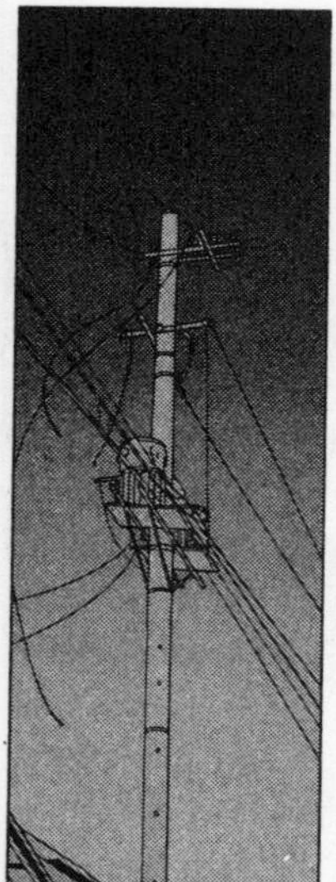

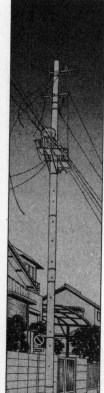

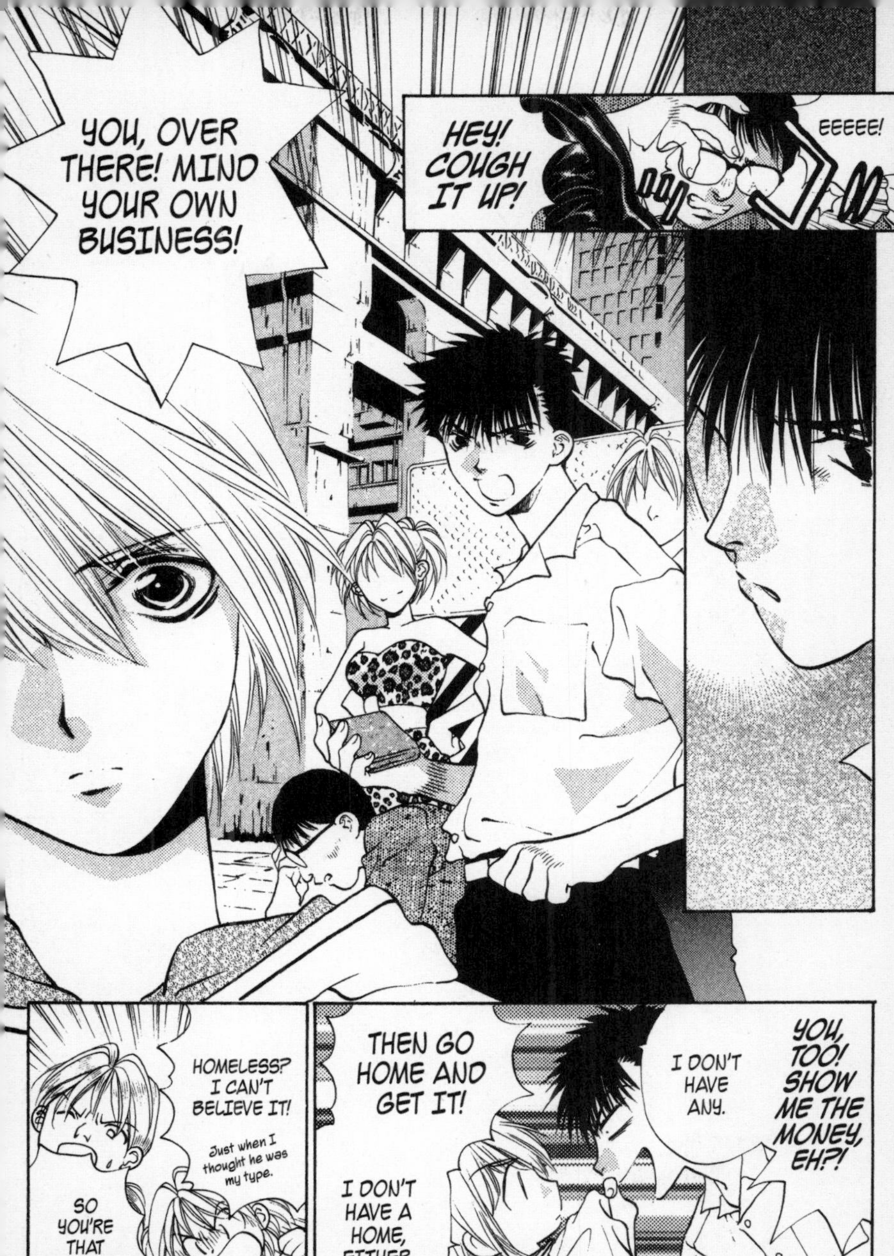
EEEEE!
HEY! COUGH IT UP!
YOU, OVER THERE! MIND YOUR OWN BUSINESS!
YOU, TOO! SHOW ME THE MONEY, EH?!
I DON'T HAVE ANY.
THEN GO HOME AND GET IT!
I DON'T HAVE A HOME, EITHER.
HOMELESS? I CAN'T BELIEVE IT!
Just when I thought he was my type.
SO YOU'RE THAT DESPERATE, HUH?

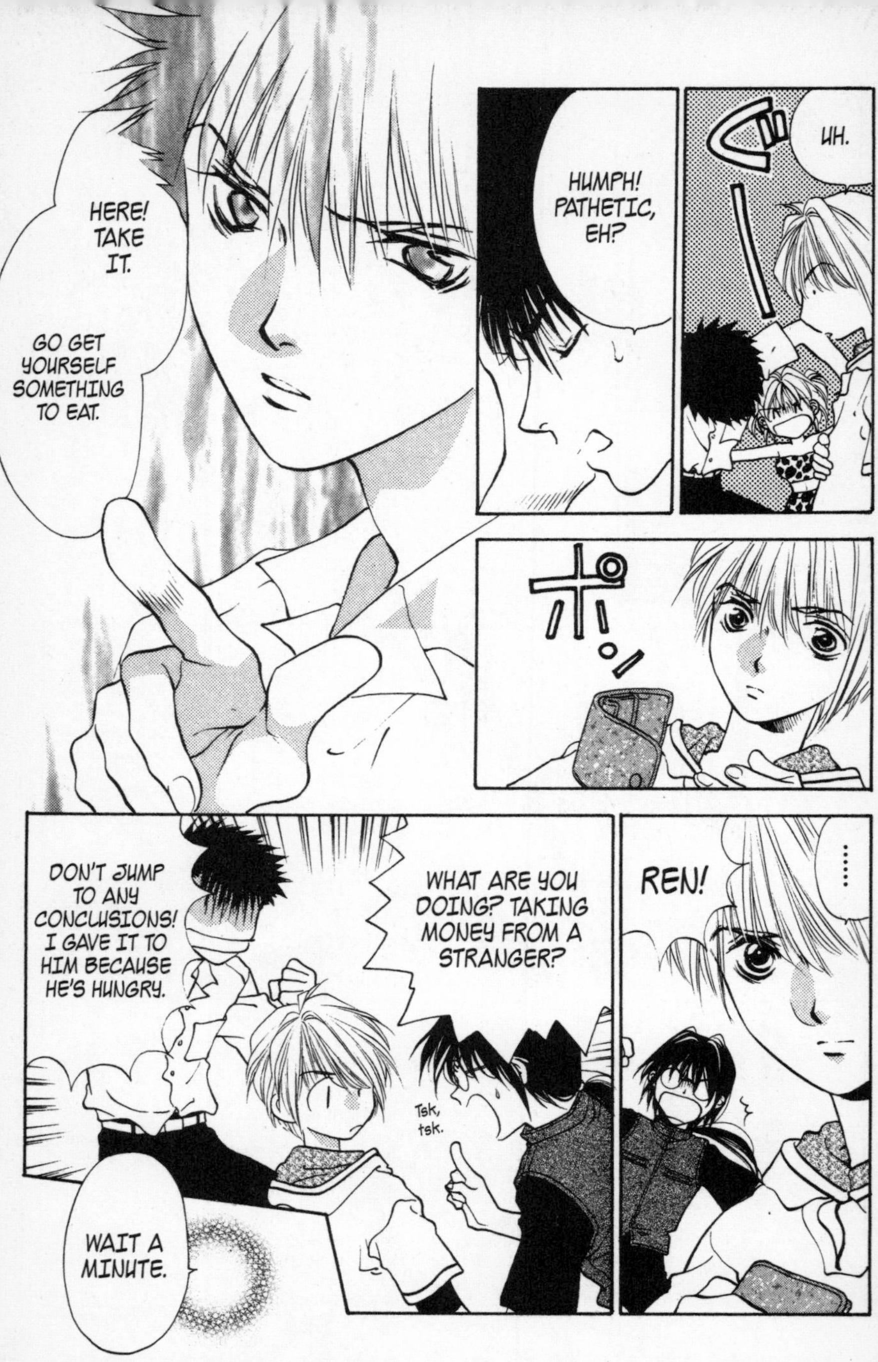
UH.
HUMPH! PATHETIC, EH?
ポイ
HERE! TAKE IT.
GO GET YOURSELF SOMETHING TO EAT.
......
REN!
WHAT ARE YOU DOING? TAKING MONEY FROM A STRANGER?
DON'T JUMP TO ANY CONCLUSIONS! I GAVE IT TO HIM BECAUSE HE'S HUNGRY.
Tsk, tsk.
WAIT A MINUTE.

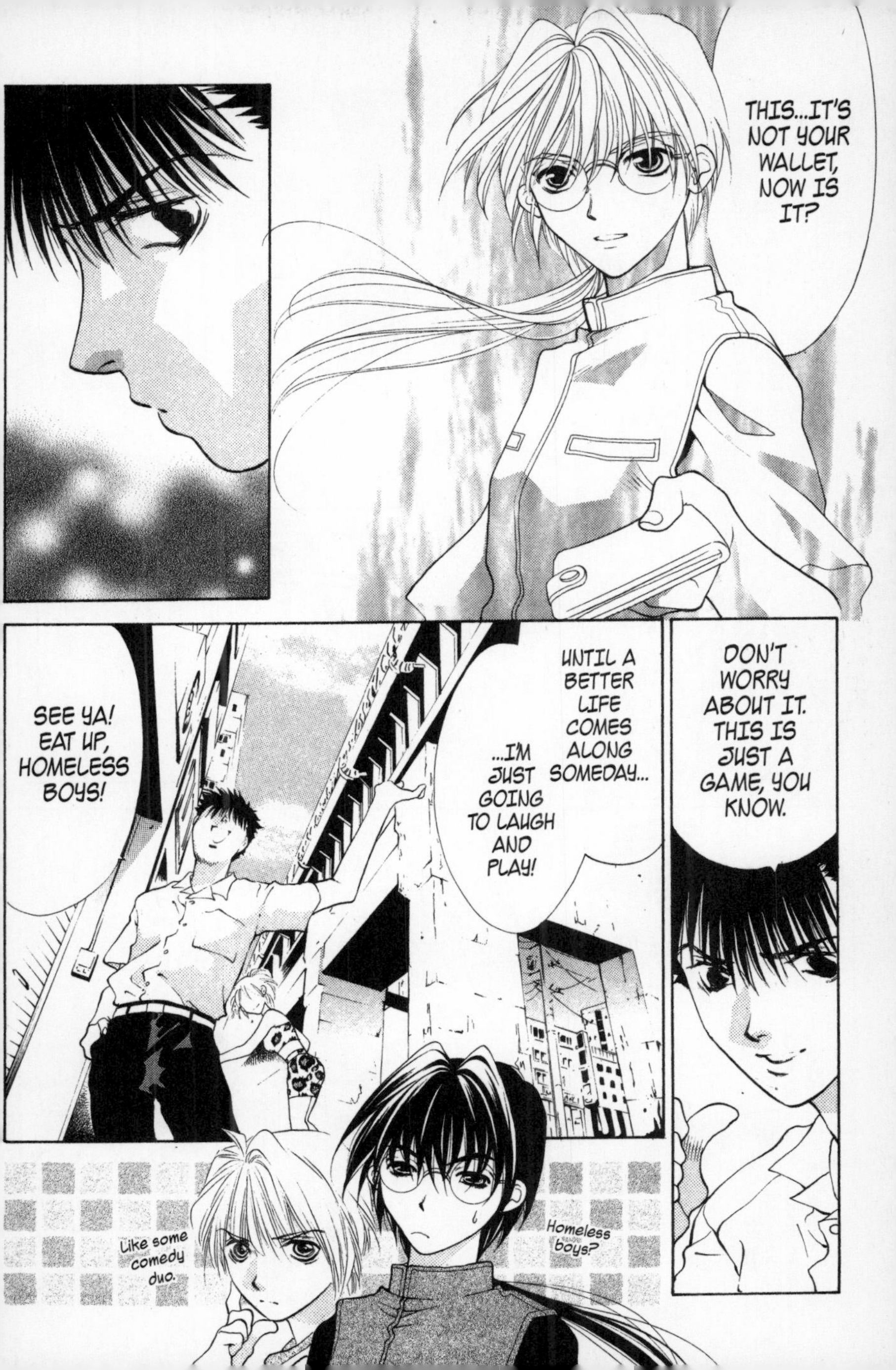
THIS...IT'S NOT YOUR WALLET, NOW IS IT?
DON'T WORRY ABOUT IT. THIS IS JUST A GAME, YOU KNOW.
UNTIL A BETTER LIFE COMES ALONG SOMEDAY...
...I'M JUST GOING TO LAUGH AND PLAY!
SEE YA! EAT UP, HOMELESS BOYS!
Homeless boys?
Like some comedy duo.

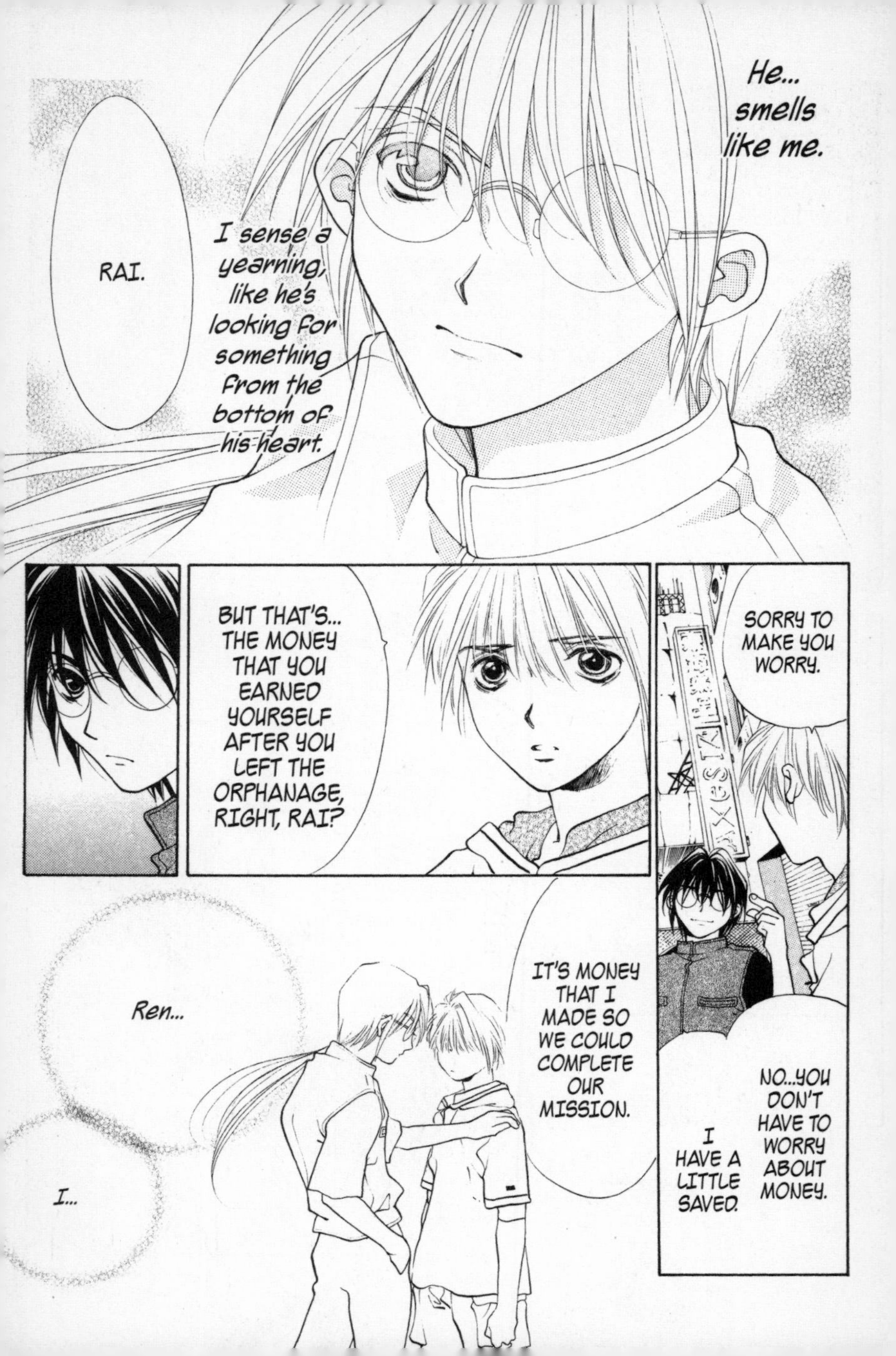

He... smells like me.
I sense a yearning, like he's looking for something from the bottom of his heart.
RAI.
SORRY TO MAKE YOU WORRY.
NO...YOU DON'T HAVE TO WORRY ABOUT MONEY.
I HAVE A LITTLE SAVED.
BUT THAT'S... THE MONEY THAT YOU EARNED YOURSELF AFTER YOU LEFT THE ORPHANAGE, RIGHT, RAI?
IT'S MONEY THAT I MADE SO WE COULD COMPLETE OUR MISSION.
Ren...
I...

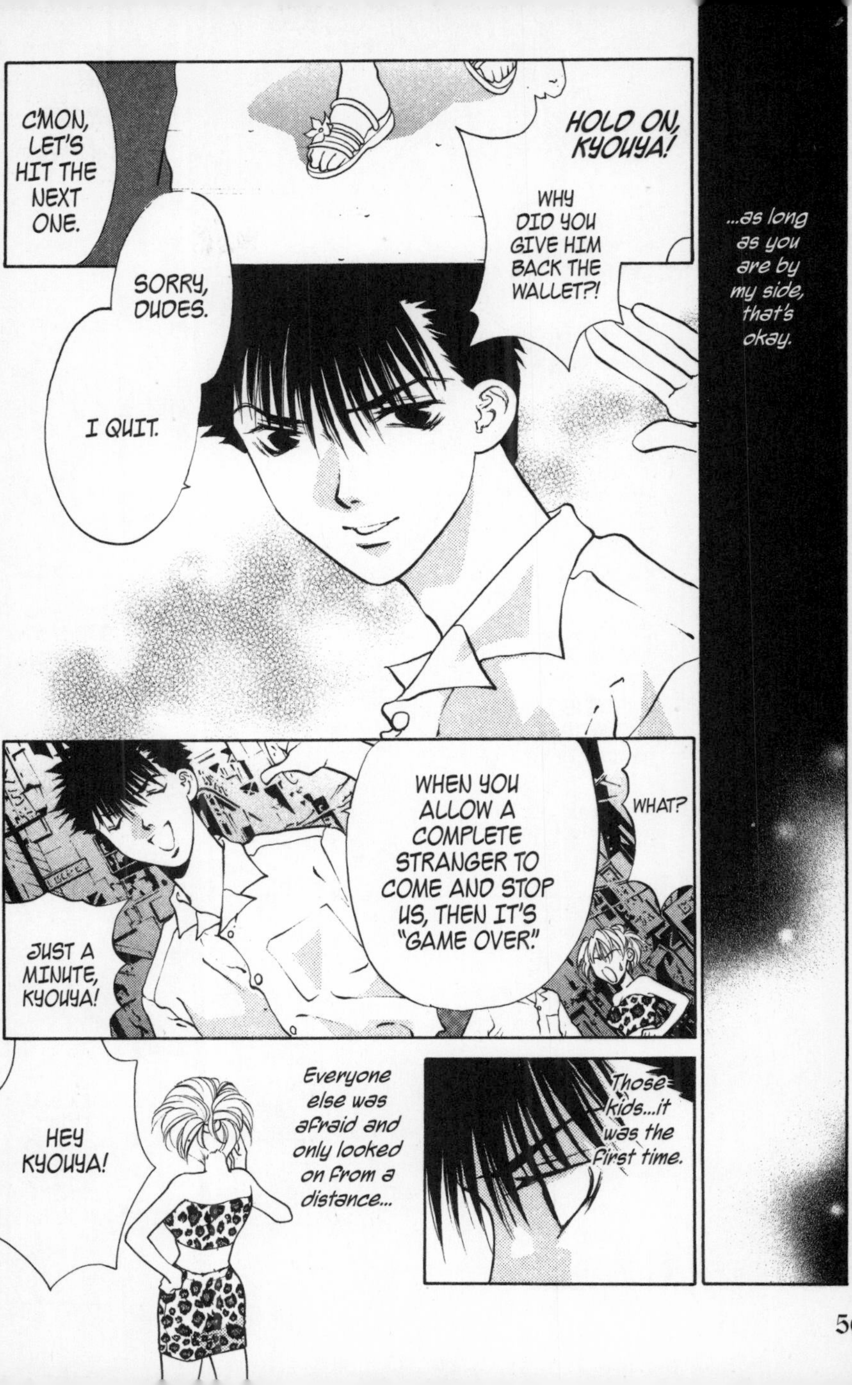
...as long as you are by my side, that's okay.
HOLD ON, KYOUYA!
C'MON, LET'S HIT THE NEXT ONE.
WHY DID YOU GIVE HIM BACK THE WALLET?!
SORRY, DUDES.
I QUIT.
WHAT?
WHEN YOU ALLOW A COMPLETE STRANGER TO COME AND STOP US, THEN IT'S "GAME OVER."
JUST A MINUTE, KYOUYA!
Those kids...it was the first time.
Everyone else was afraid and only looked on from a distance...
HEY KYOUYA!

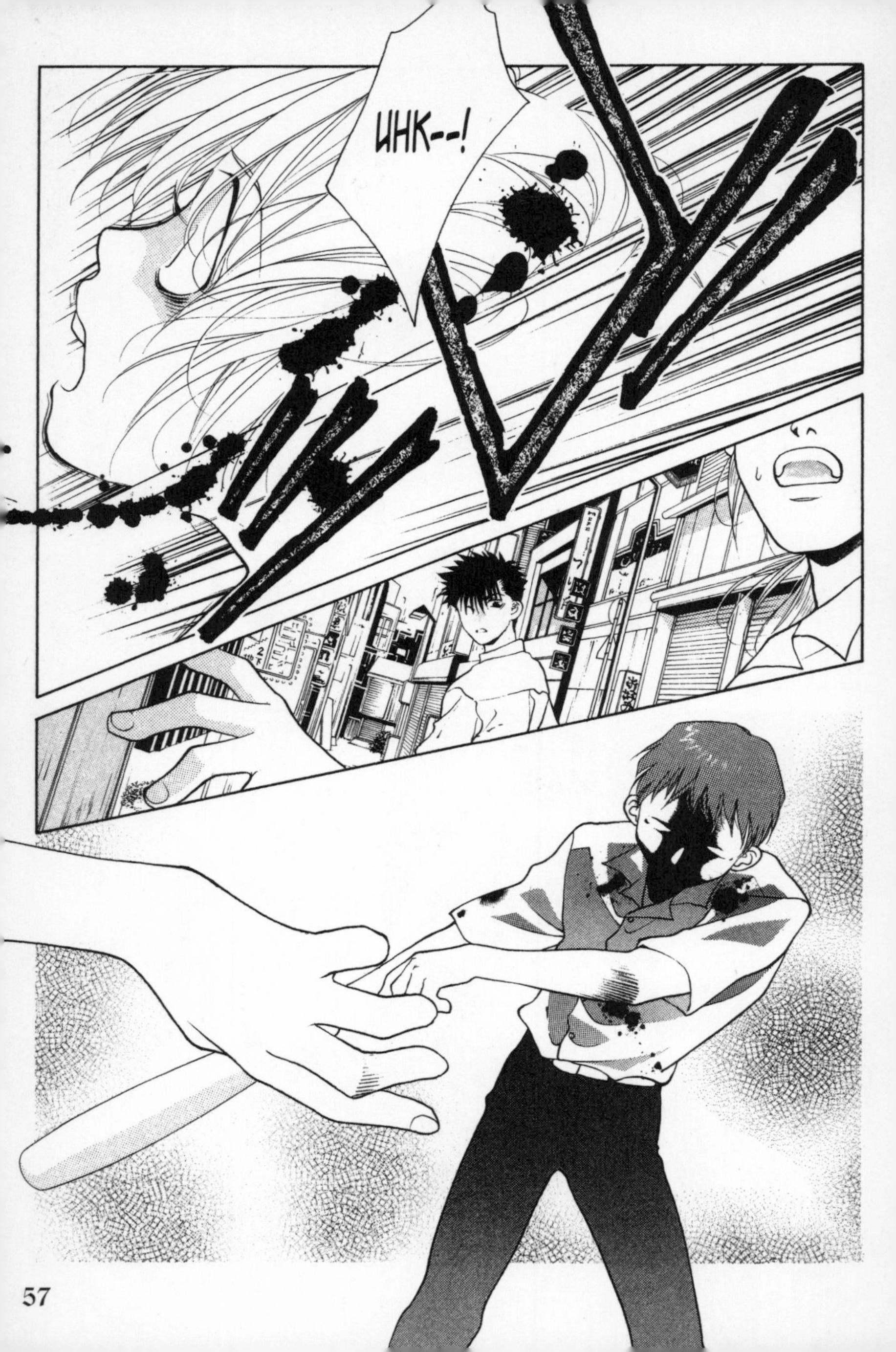
UHK--!

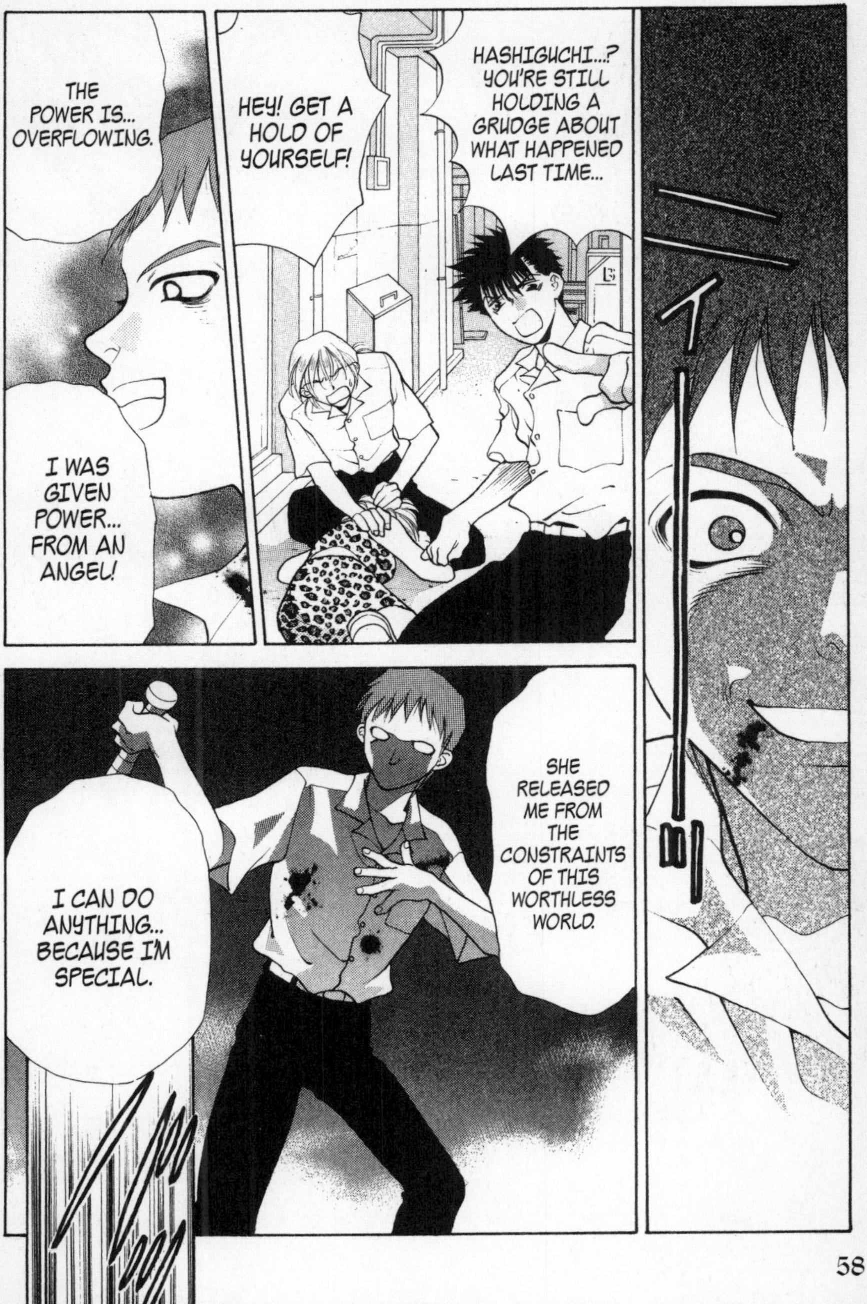

HASHIGUCHI...? YOU'RE STILL HOLDING A GRUDGE ABOUT WHAT HAPPENED LAST TIME...
HEY! GET A HOLD OF YOURSELF!
THE POWER IS... OVERFLOWING.
I WAS GIVEN POWER... FROM AN ANGEL!
SHE RELEASED ME FROM THE CONSTRAINTS OF THIS WORTHLESS WORLD.
I CAN DO ANYTHING... BECAUSE I'M SPECIAL.

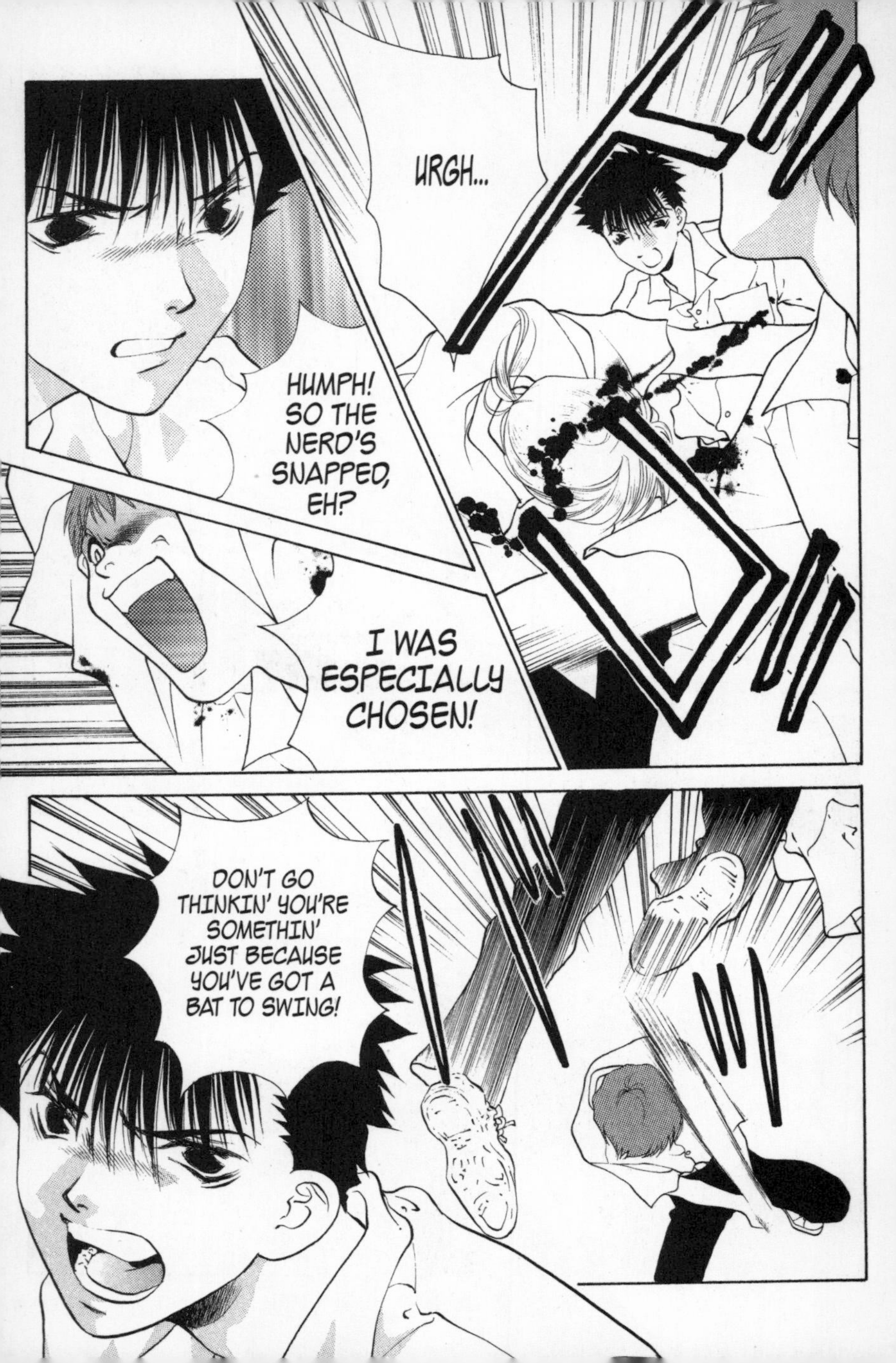
URGH...
HUMPH! SO THE NERD'S SNAPPED, EH?
I WAS ESPECIALLY CHOSEN!
DON'T GO THINKIN' YOU'RE SOMETHIN' JUST BECAUSE YOU'VE GOT A BAT TO SWING!

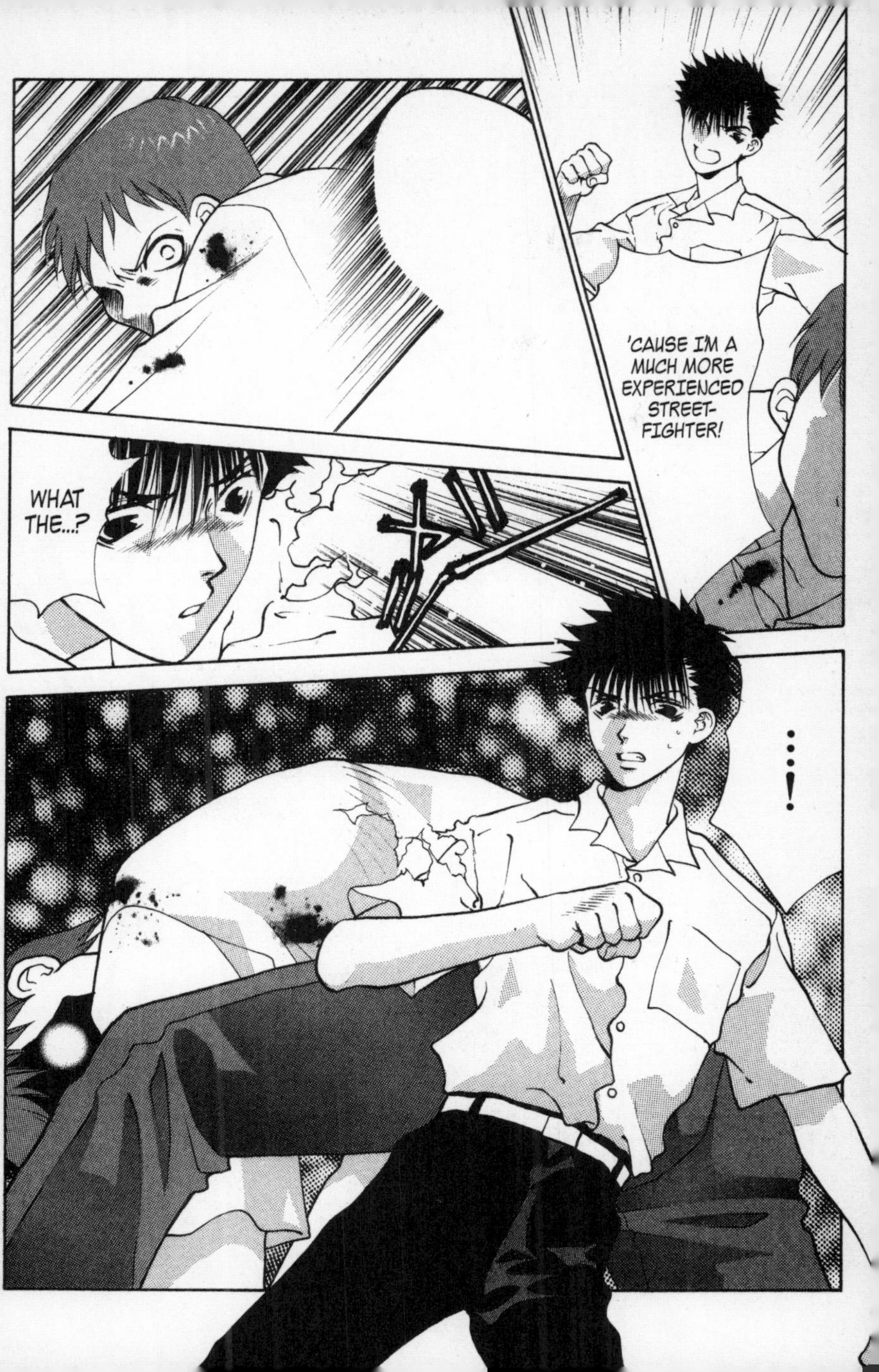
'CAUSE I'M A MUCH MORE EXPERIENCED STREET-FIGHTER!
WHAT THE...?
...!

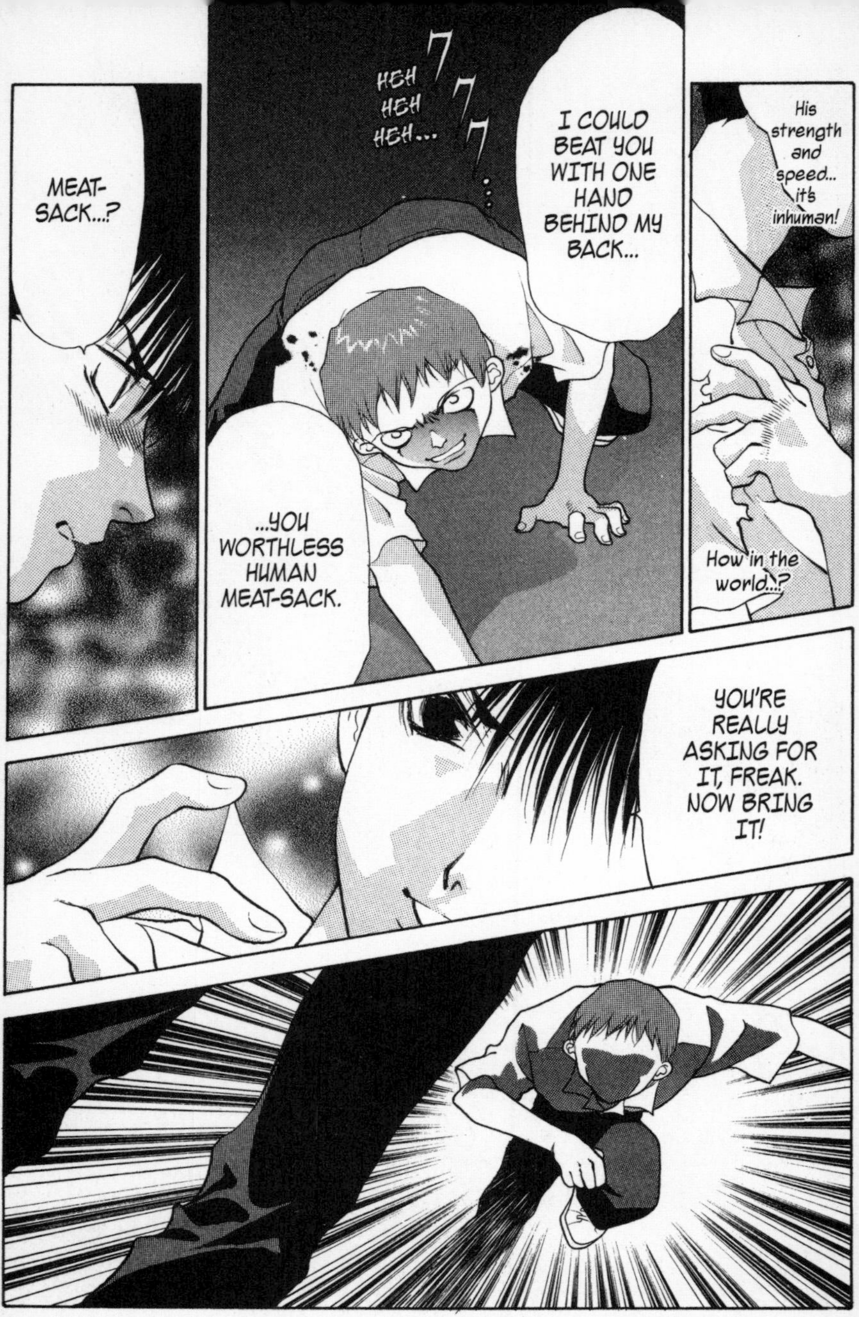

His strength and speed... it's inhuman!
How in the world...?
I COULD BEAT YOU WITH ONE HAND BEHIND MY BACK...
HEH HEH HEH...
...YOU WORTHLESS HUMAN MEAT-SACK.
MEAT-SACK...?
YOU'RE REALLY ASKING FOR IT, FREAK. NOW BRING IT!

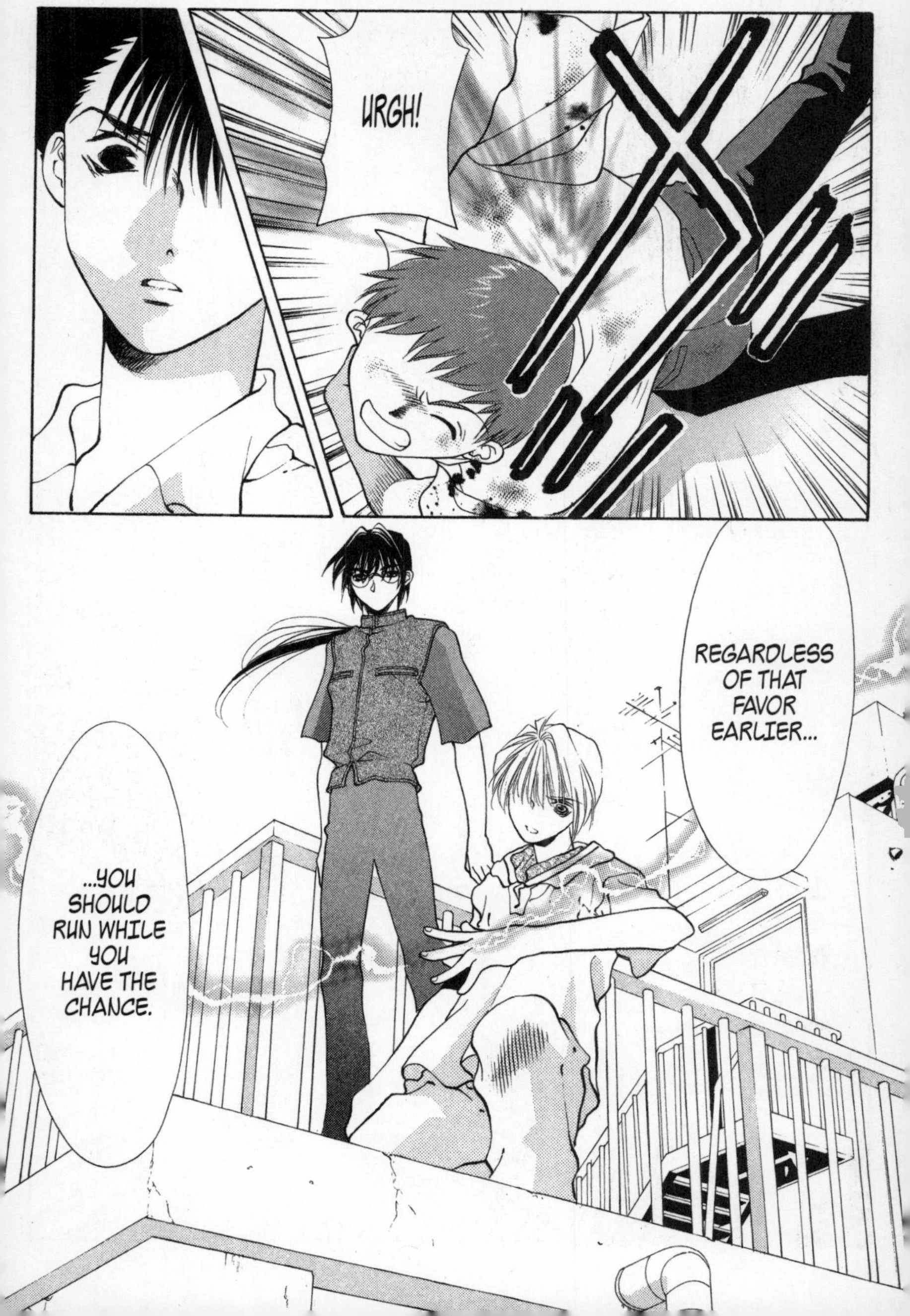
URGH!
REGARDLESS OF THAT FAVOR EARLIER...
...YOU SHOULD RUN WHILE YOU HAVE THE CHANCE.

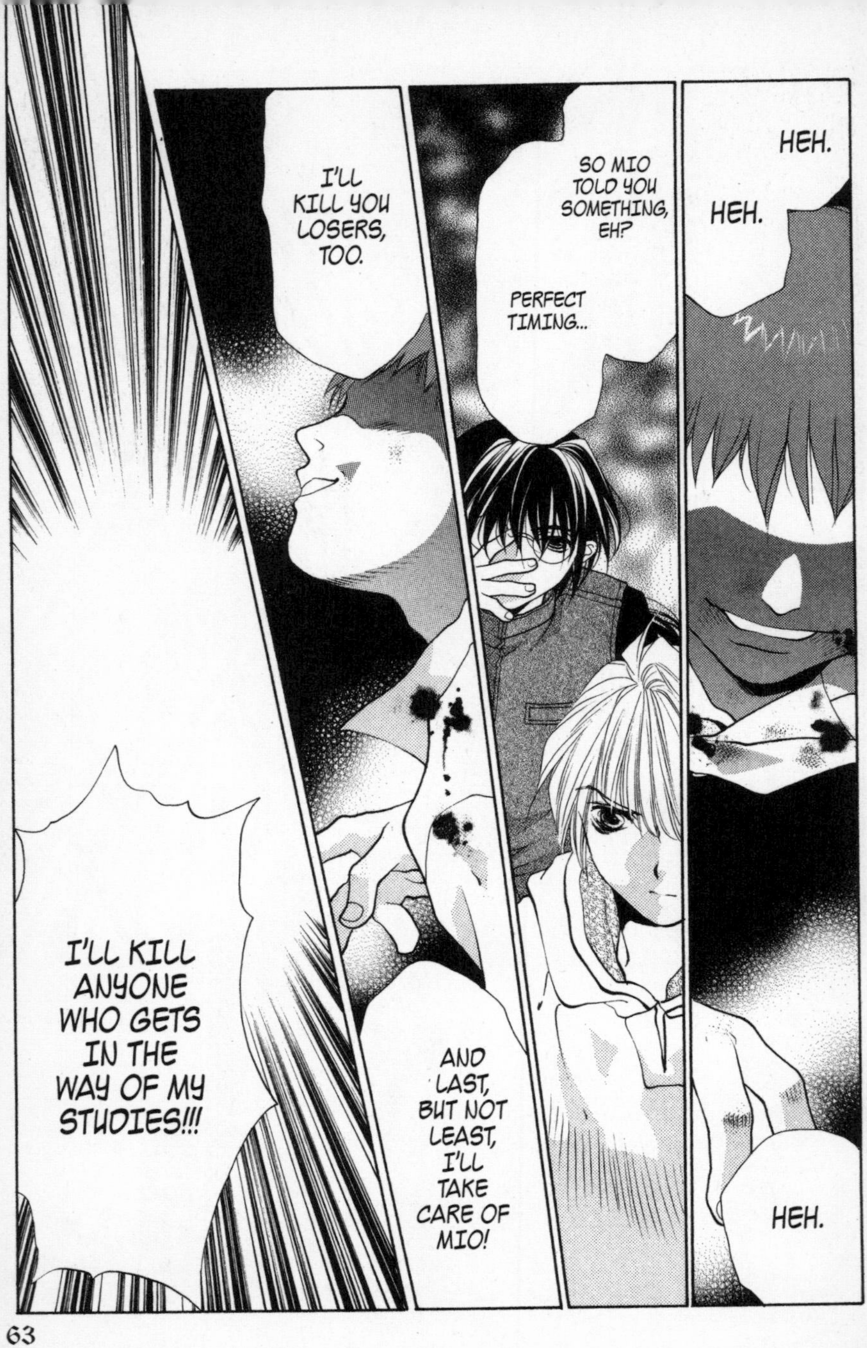
HEH.
HEH.
HEH.
SO MIO TOLD YOU SOMETHING, EH?
PERFECT TIMING...
I'LL KILL YOU LOSERS, TOO.
AND LAST, BUT NOT LEAST, I'LL TAKE CARE OF MIO!
I'LL KILL ANYONE WHO GETS IN THE WAY OF MY STUDIES!!!

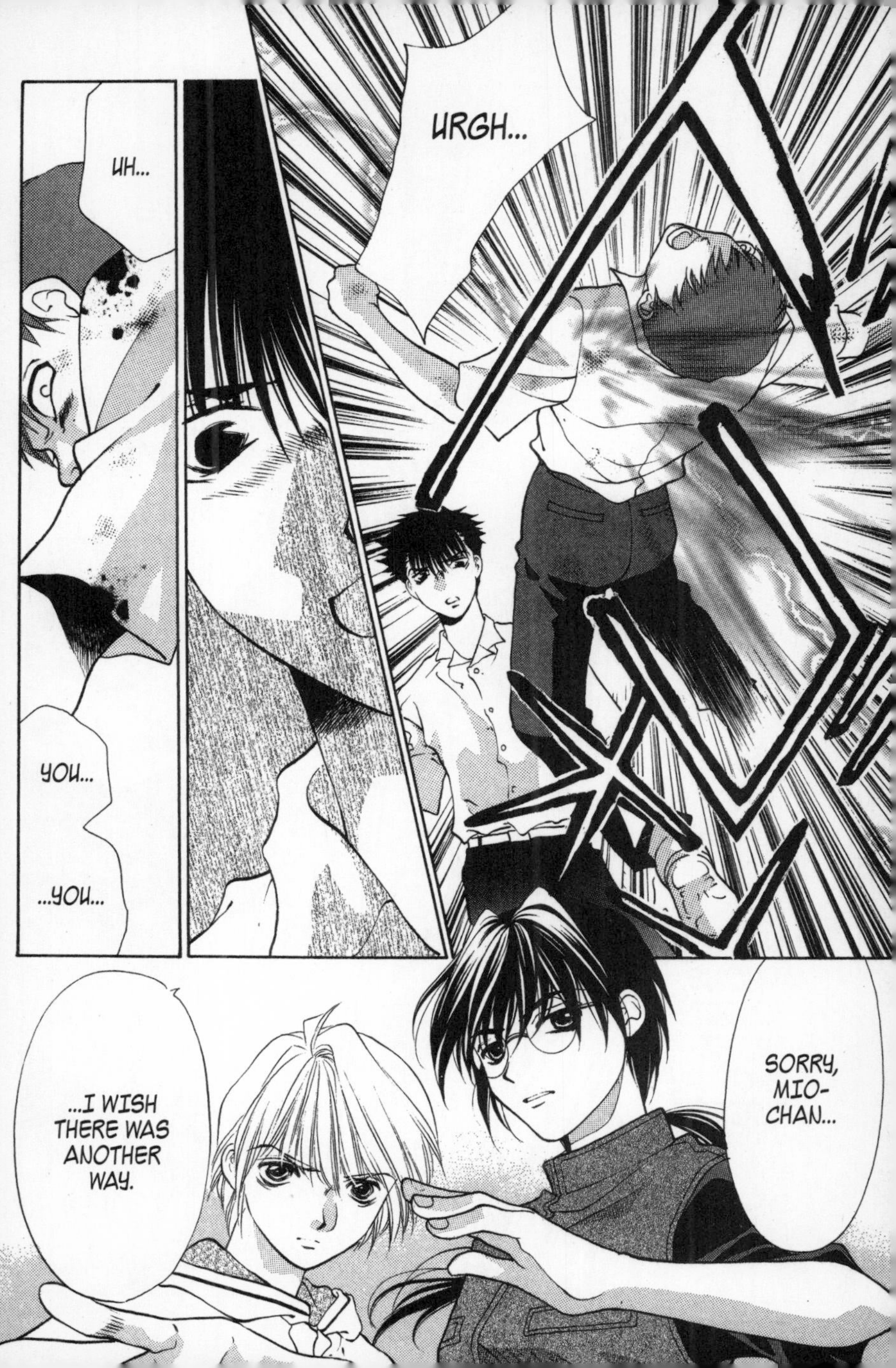
URGH...
UH...
YOU...
...YOU...
SORRY, MIO-CHAN...
...I WISH THERE WAS ANOTHER WAY.

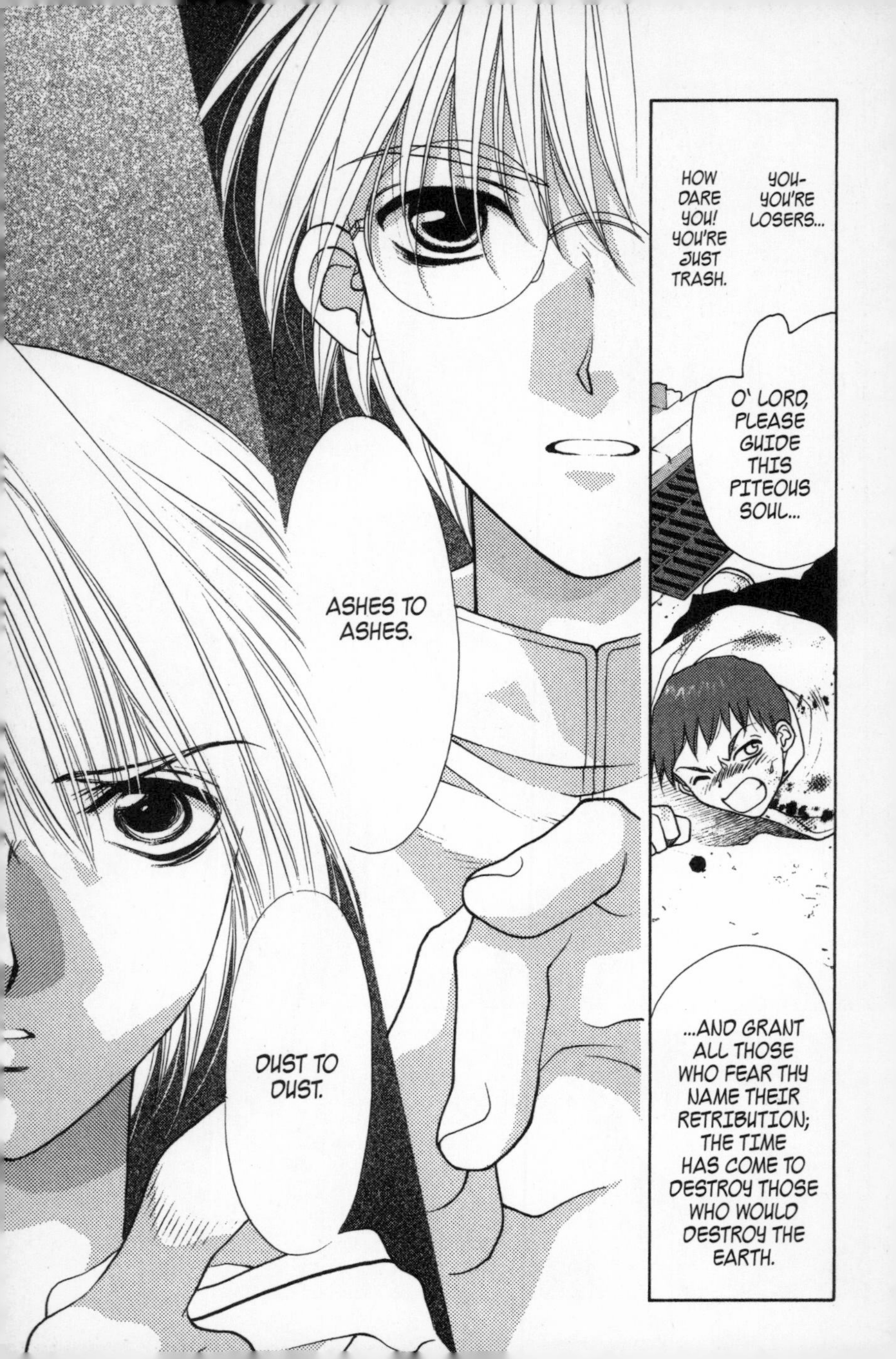
YOU- YOU'RE LOSERS...
HOW DARE YOU! YOU'RE JUST TRASH.
O' LORD, PLEASE GUIDE THIS PITEOUS SOUL...
...AND GRANT ALL THOSE WHO FEAR THY NAME THEIR RETRIBUTION; THE TIME HAS COME TO DESTROY THOSE WHO WOULD DESTROY THE EARTH.
ASHES TO ASHES.
DUST TO DUST.

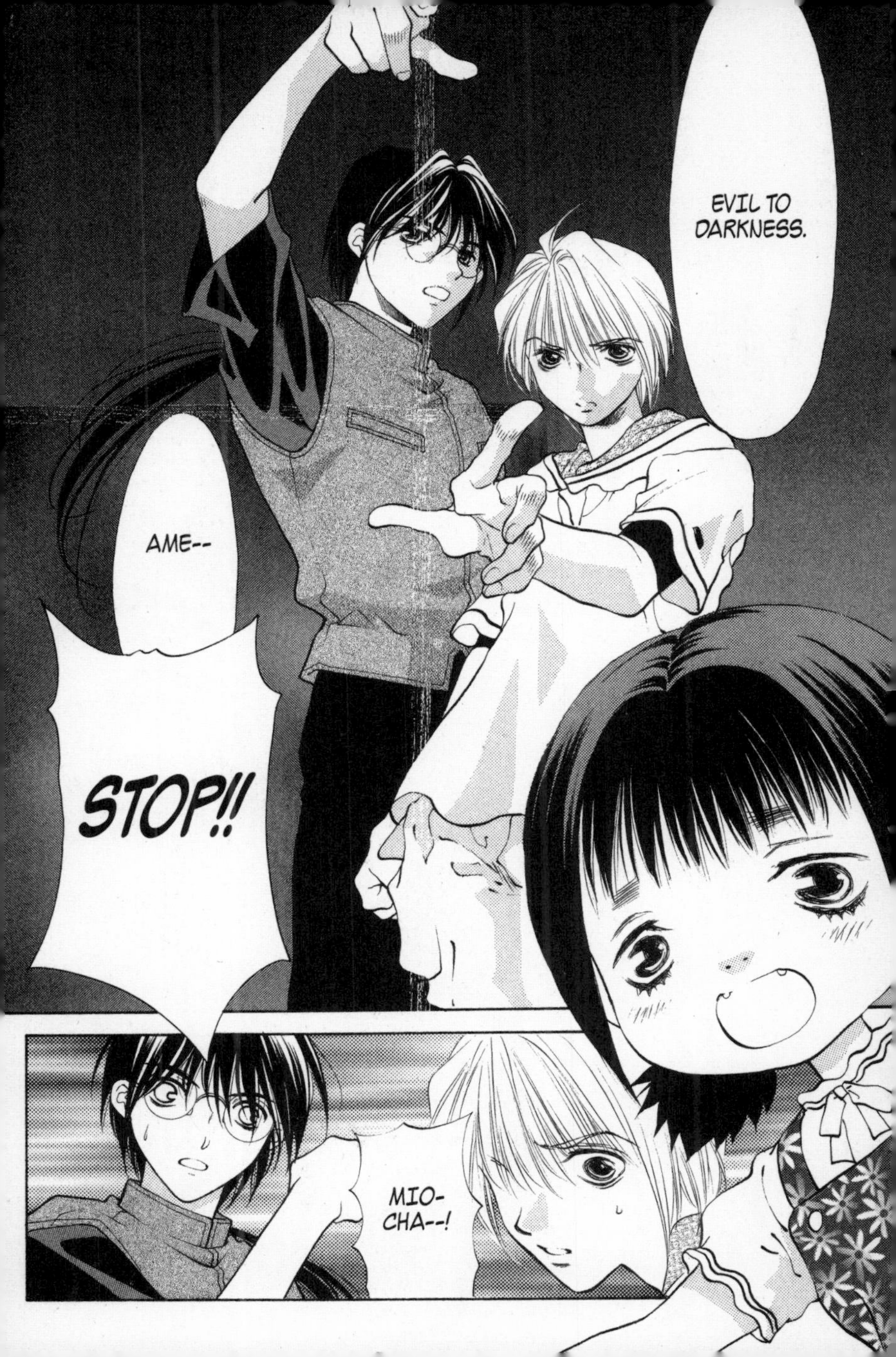

EVIL TO DARKNESS.
AME--
STOP!!
MIO-CHA--!

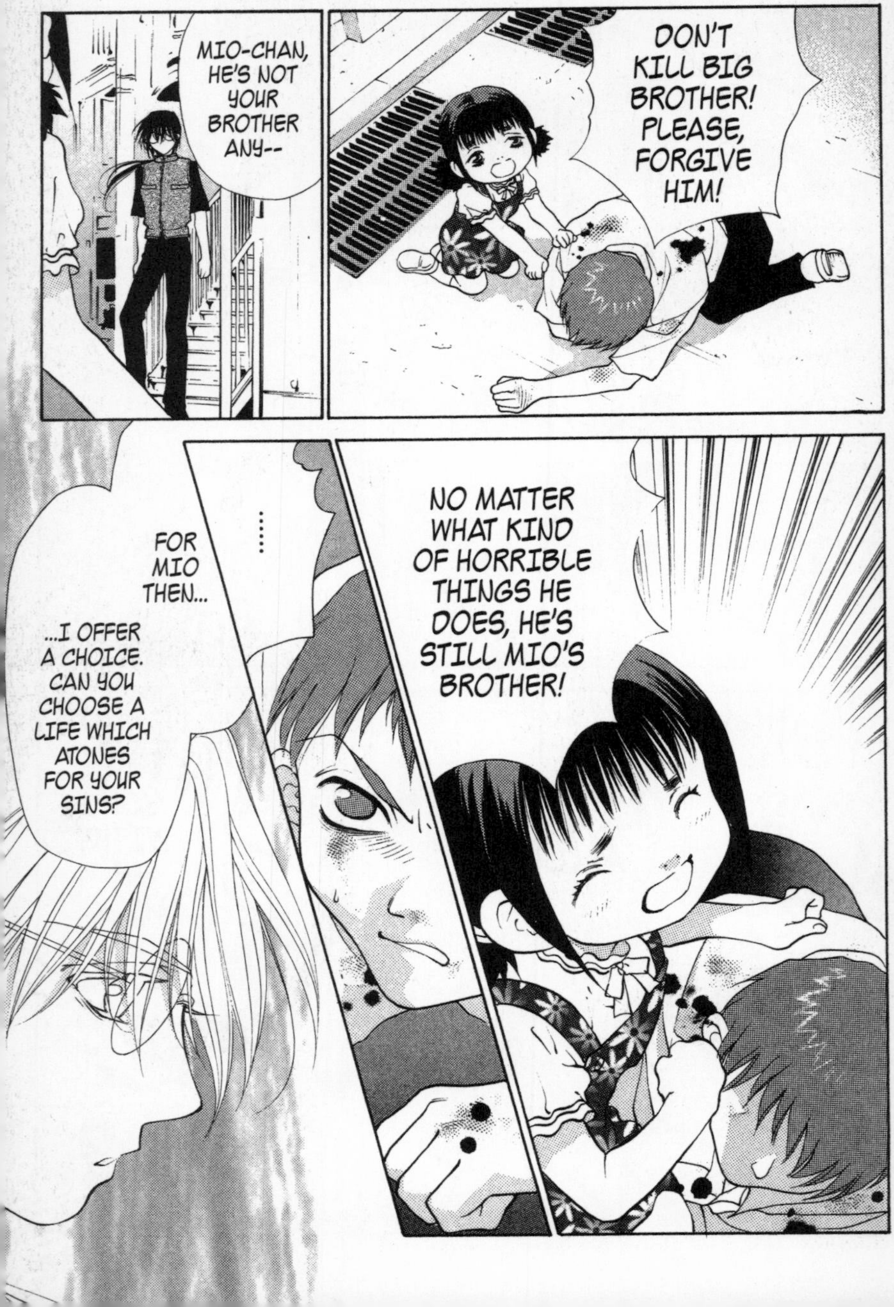
DON'T KILL BIG BROTHER! PLEASE, FORGIVE HIM!
MIO-CHAN, HE'S NOT YOUR BROTHER ANY--
NO MATTER WHAT KIND OF HORRIBLE THINGS HE DOES, HE'S STILL MIO'S BROTHER!
......
FOR MIO THEN...
...I OFFER A CHOICE. CAN YOU CHOOSE A LIFE WHICH ATONES FOR YOUR SINS?

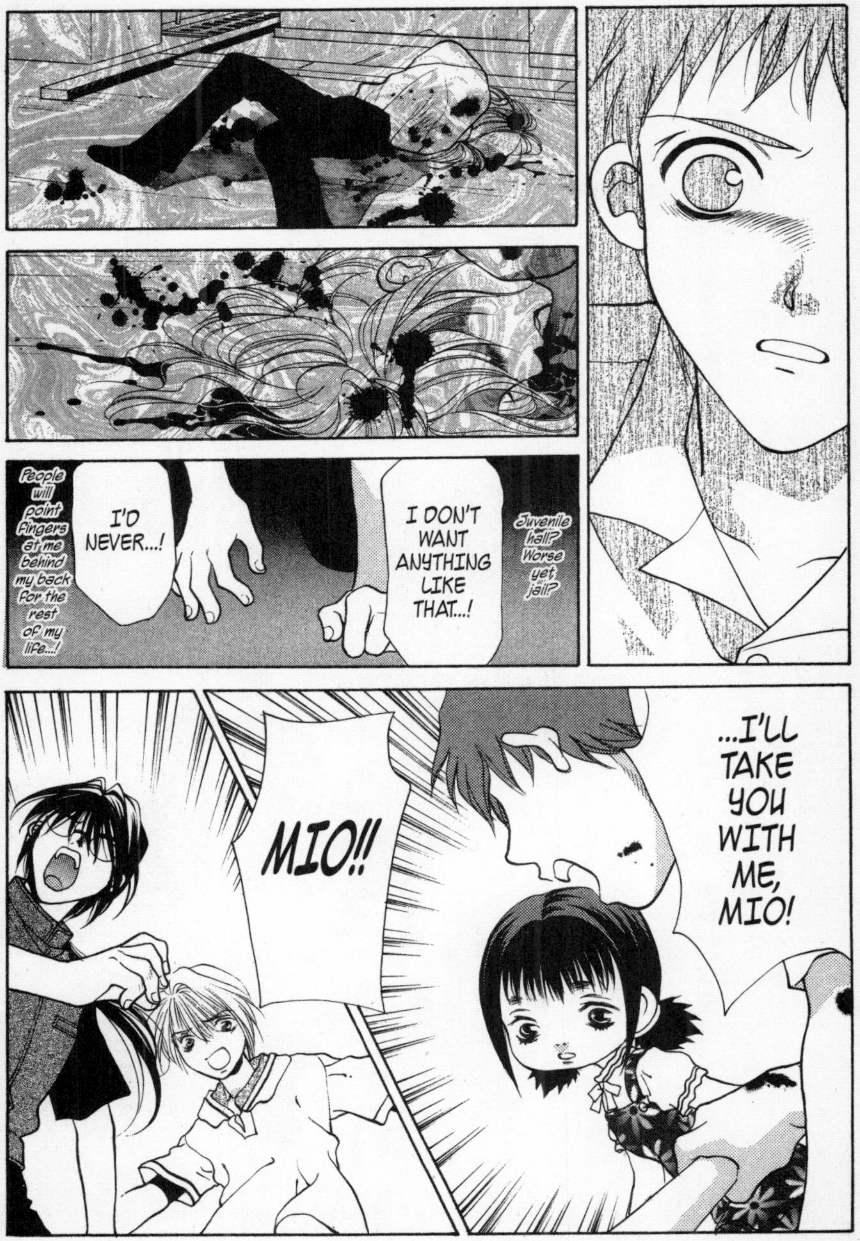
Juvenile hall? Worse yet jail?
I DON'T WANT ANYTHING LIKE THAT...!
I'D NEVER...!
People will point fingers at me behind my back for the rest of my life...!
...I'LL TAKE YOU WITH ME, MIO!
MIO!!

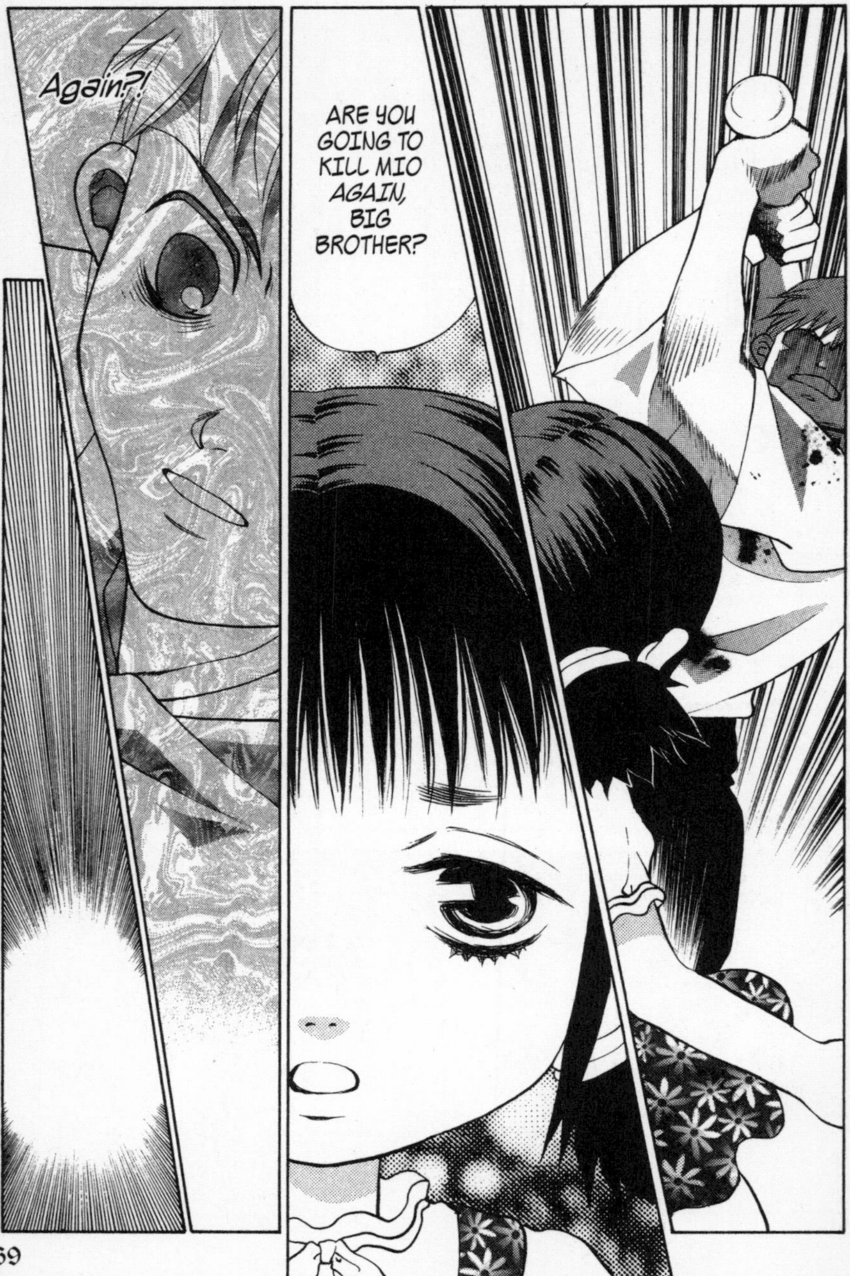
ARE YOU GOING TO KILL MIO AGAIN, BIG BROTHER?
Again?!

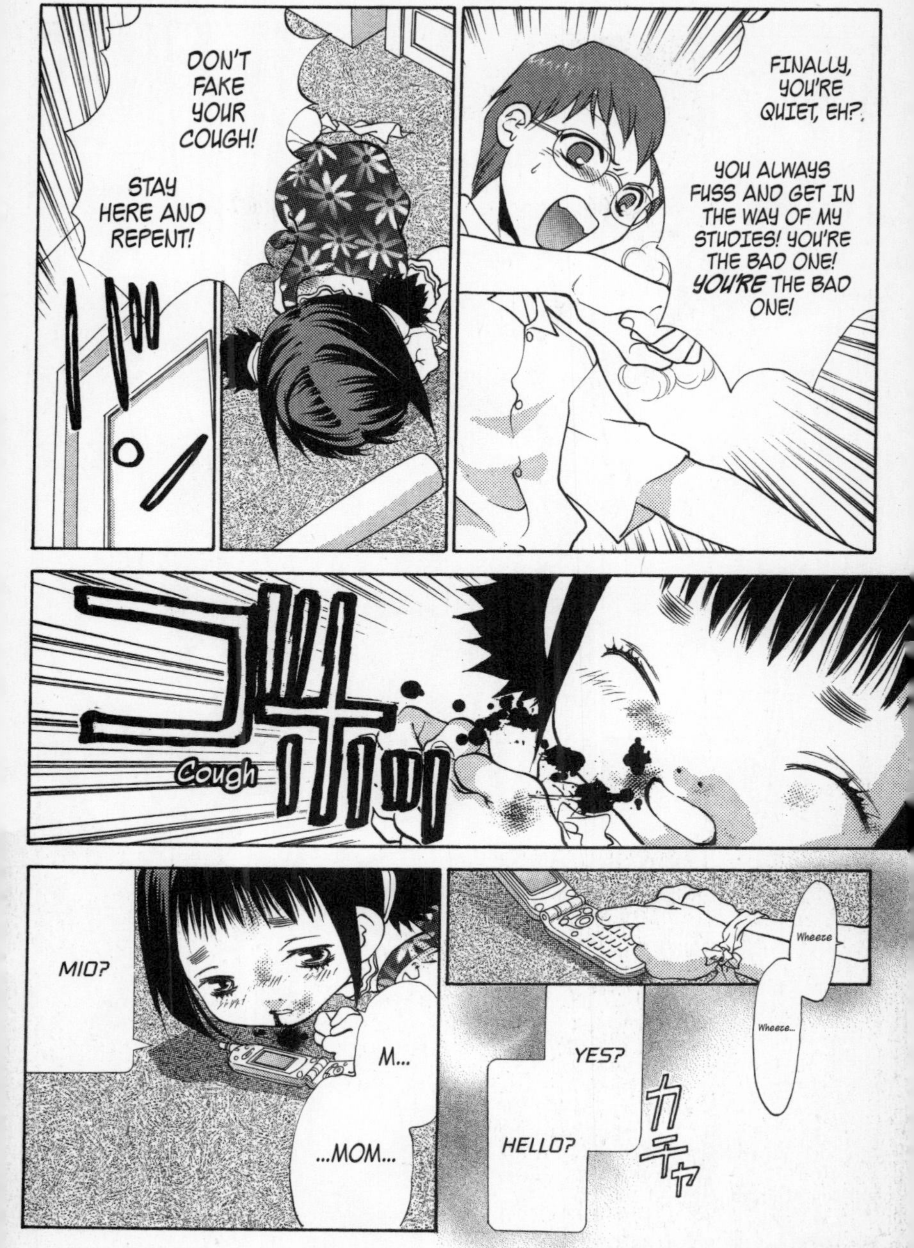
FINALLY, YOU'RE QUIET, EH?.
YOU ALWAYS FUSS AND GET IN THE WAY OF MY STUDIES! YOU'RE THE BAD ONE! *YOU'RE* THE BAD ONE!
DON'T FAKE YOUR COUGH!
STAY HERE AND REPENT!
Cough
Wheeze
Wheeze...
カチャ
YES?
HELLO?
MIO?
M...
...MOM...

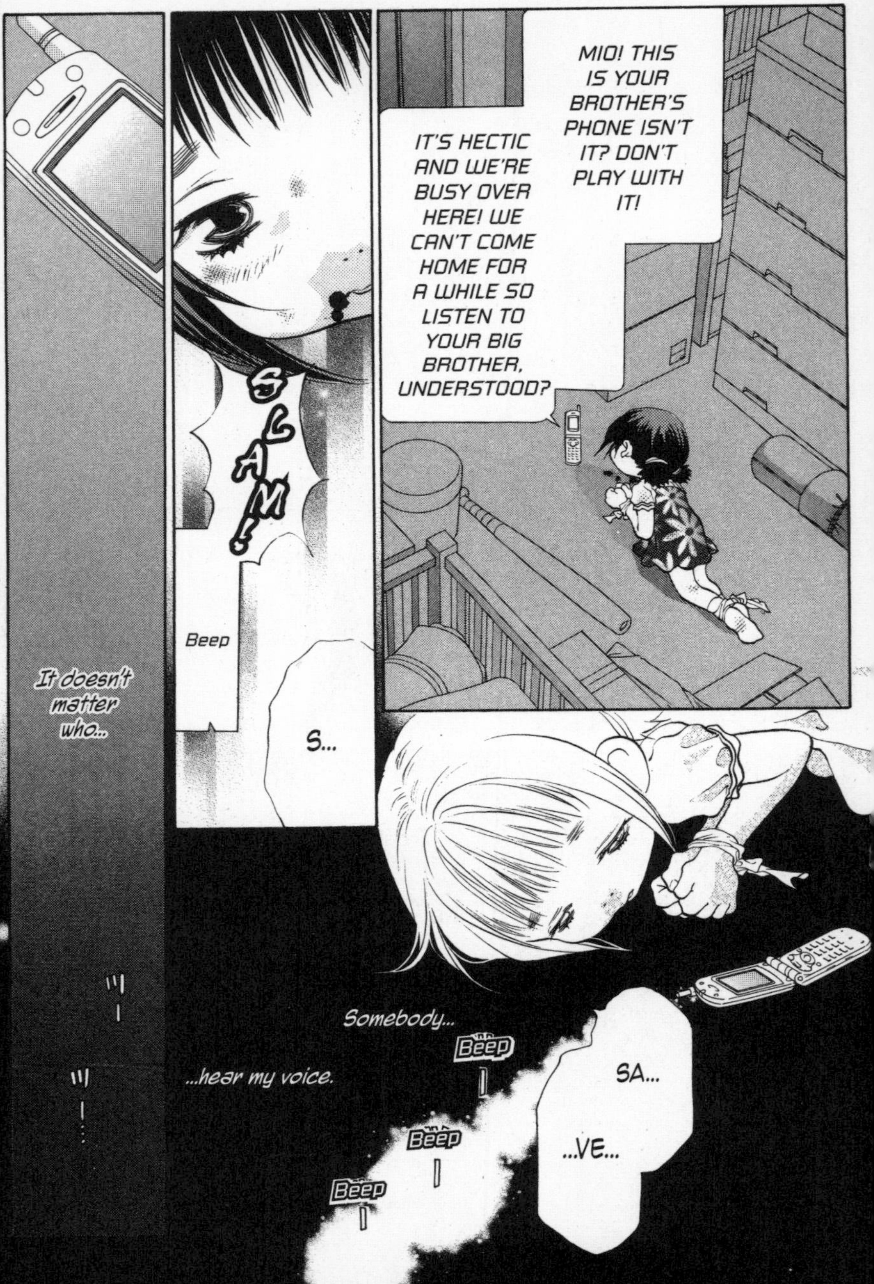
MIO! THIS IS YOUR BROTHER'S PHONE ISN'T IT? DON'T PLAY WITH IT!
IT'S HECTIC AND WE'RE BUSY OVER HERE! WE CAN'T COME HOME FOR A WHILE SO LISTEN TO YOUR BIG BROTHER, UNDERSTOOD?
SLAM!
Beep
S...
SA...
...VE...
Somebody...
Beep
Beep
Beep
...hear my voice.
It doesn't matter who...

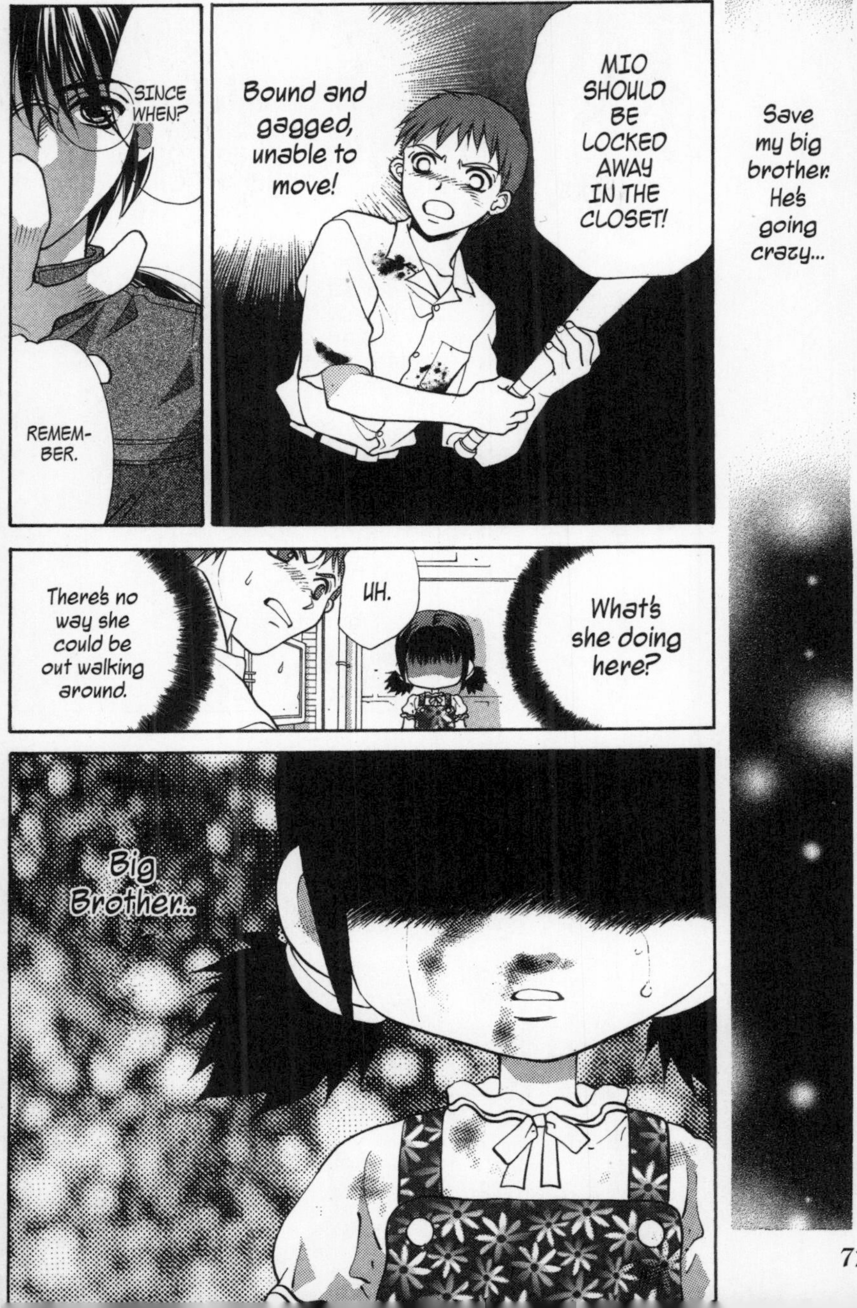

Save my big brother. He's going crazy...
MIO SHOULD BE LOCKED AWAY IN THE CLOSET!
Bound and gagged, unable to move!
SINCE WHEN?
REMEMBER.
What's she doing here?
UH.
There's no way she could be out walking around.
Big Brother...

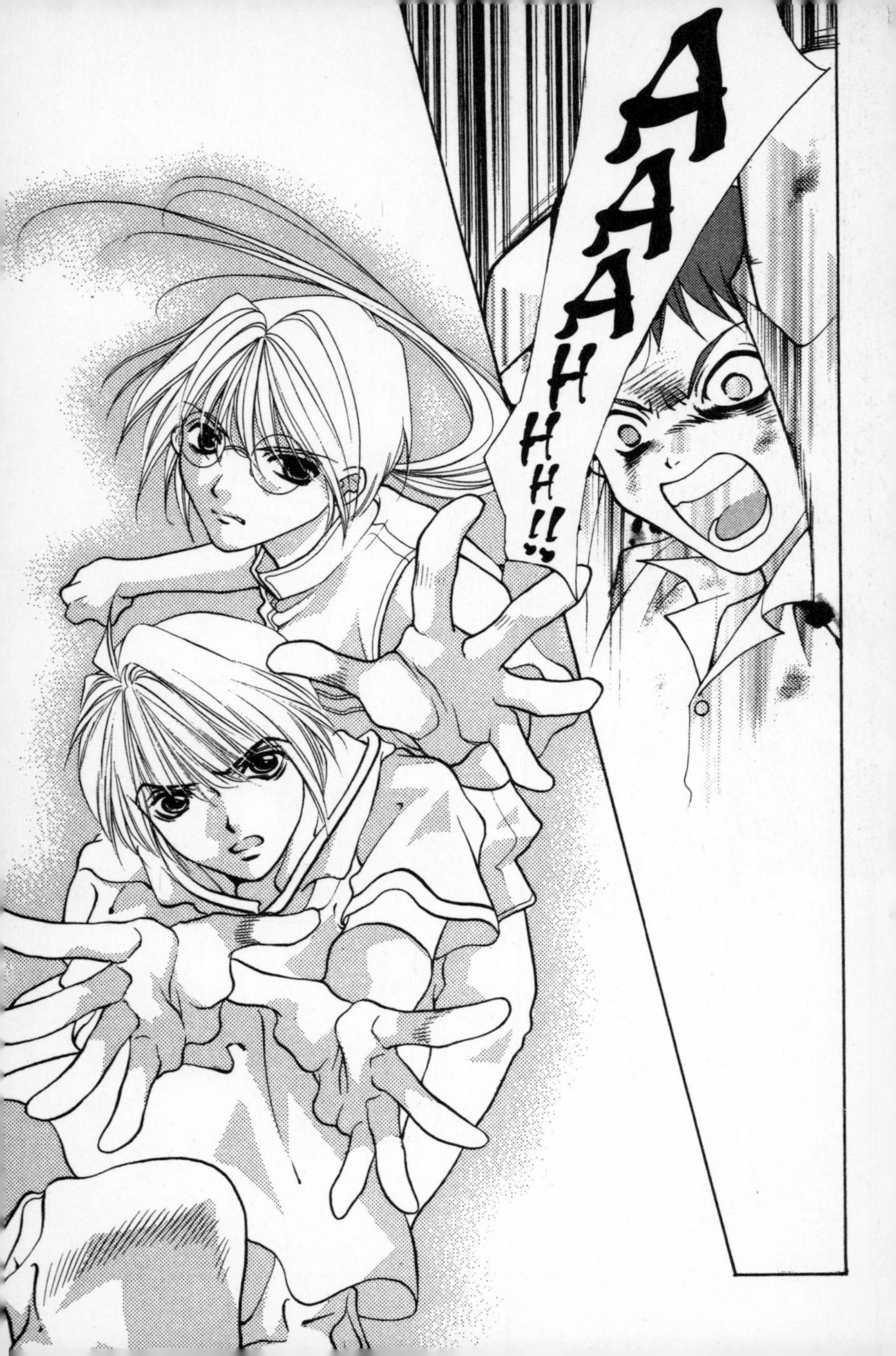
AAAAHHHH!!

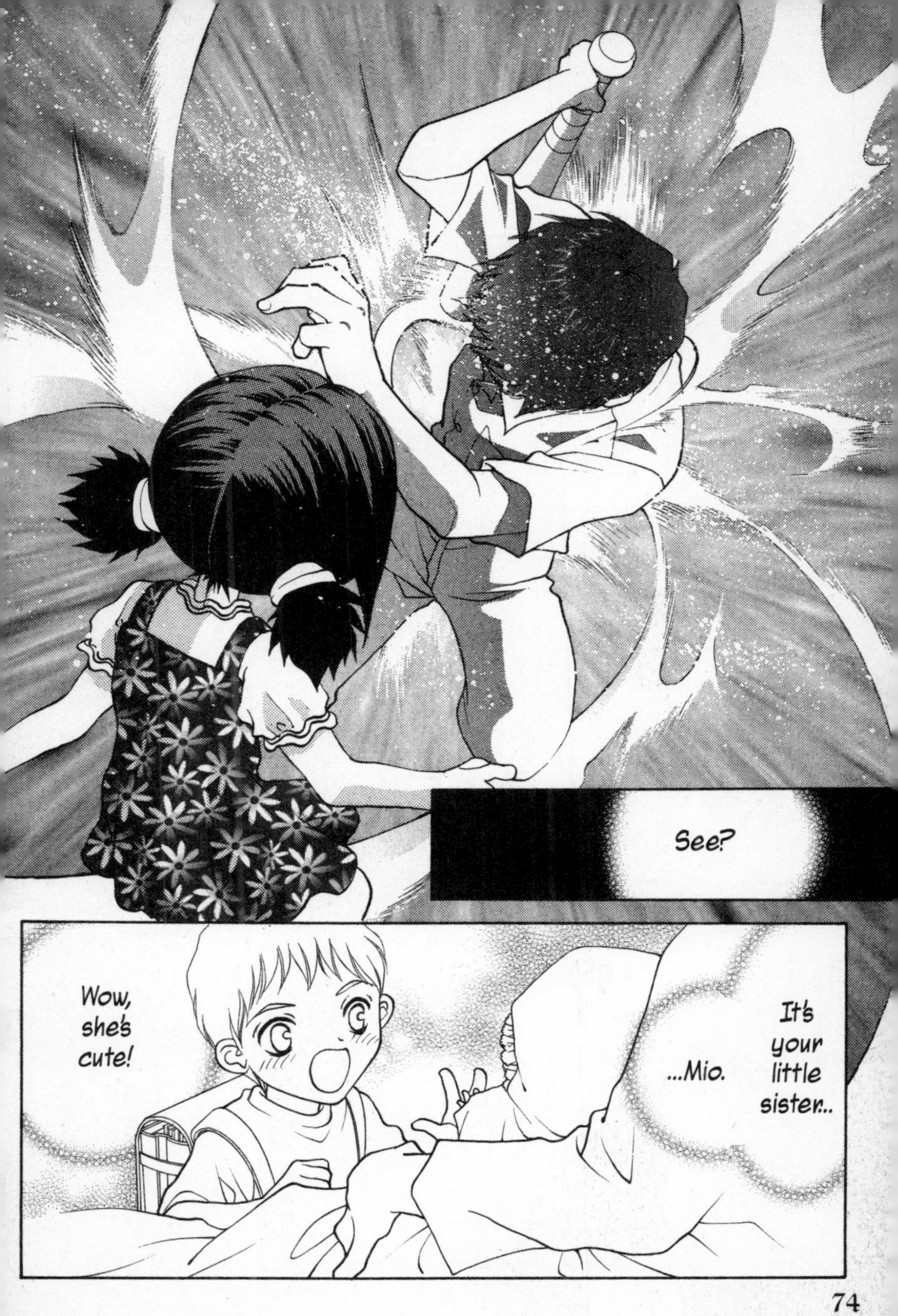
See?
It's your little sister..
...Mio.
Wow, she's cute!

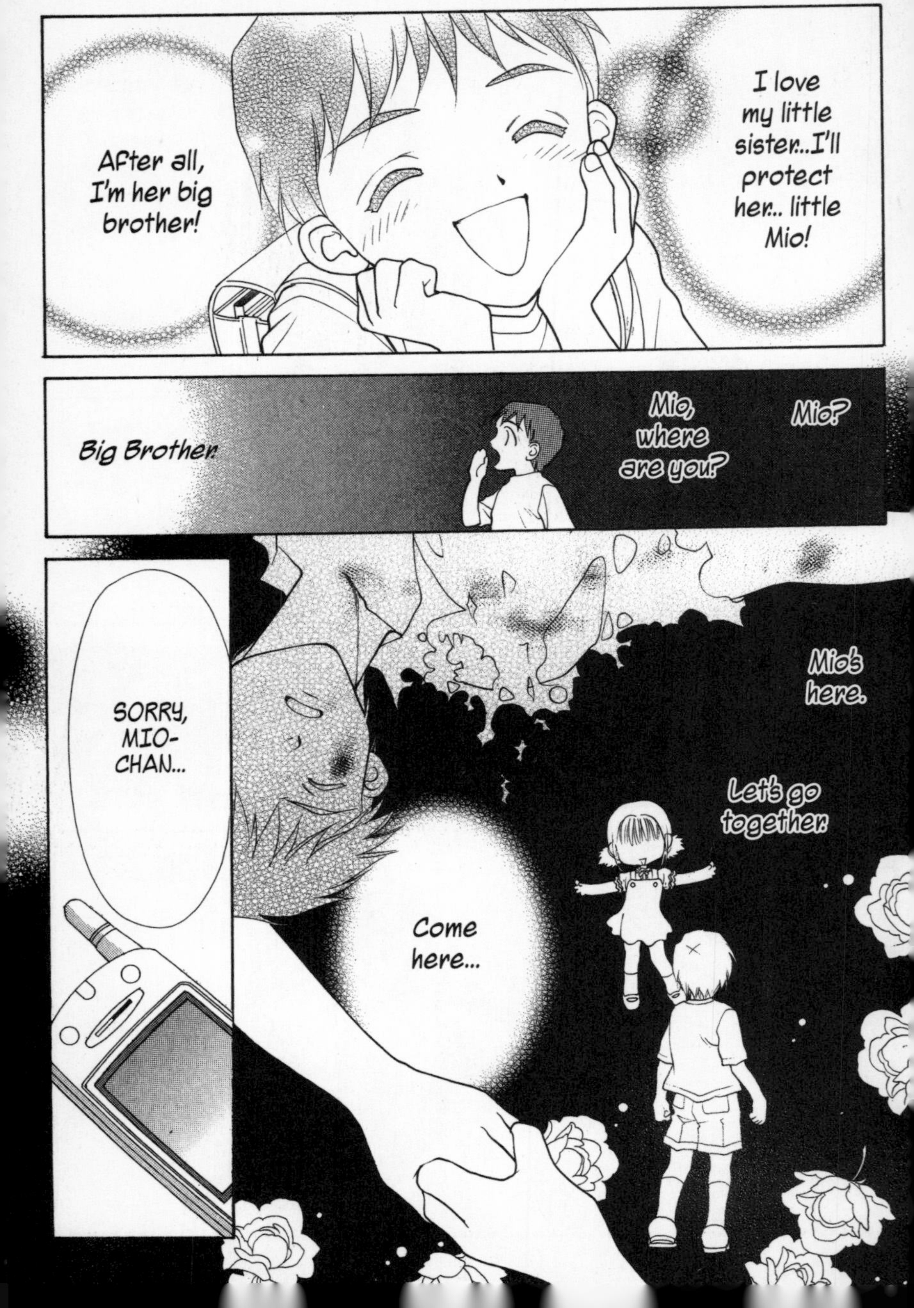
I love my little sister...I'll protect her.. little Mio!
After all, I'm her big brother!
Mio?
Mio, where are you?
Big Brother
Mio's here.
Let's go together
Come here...
SORRY, MIO-CHAN...

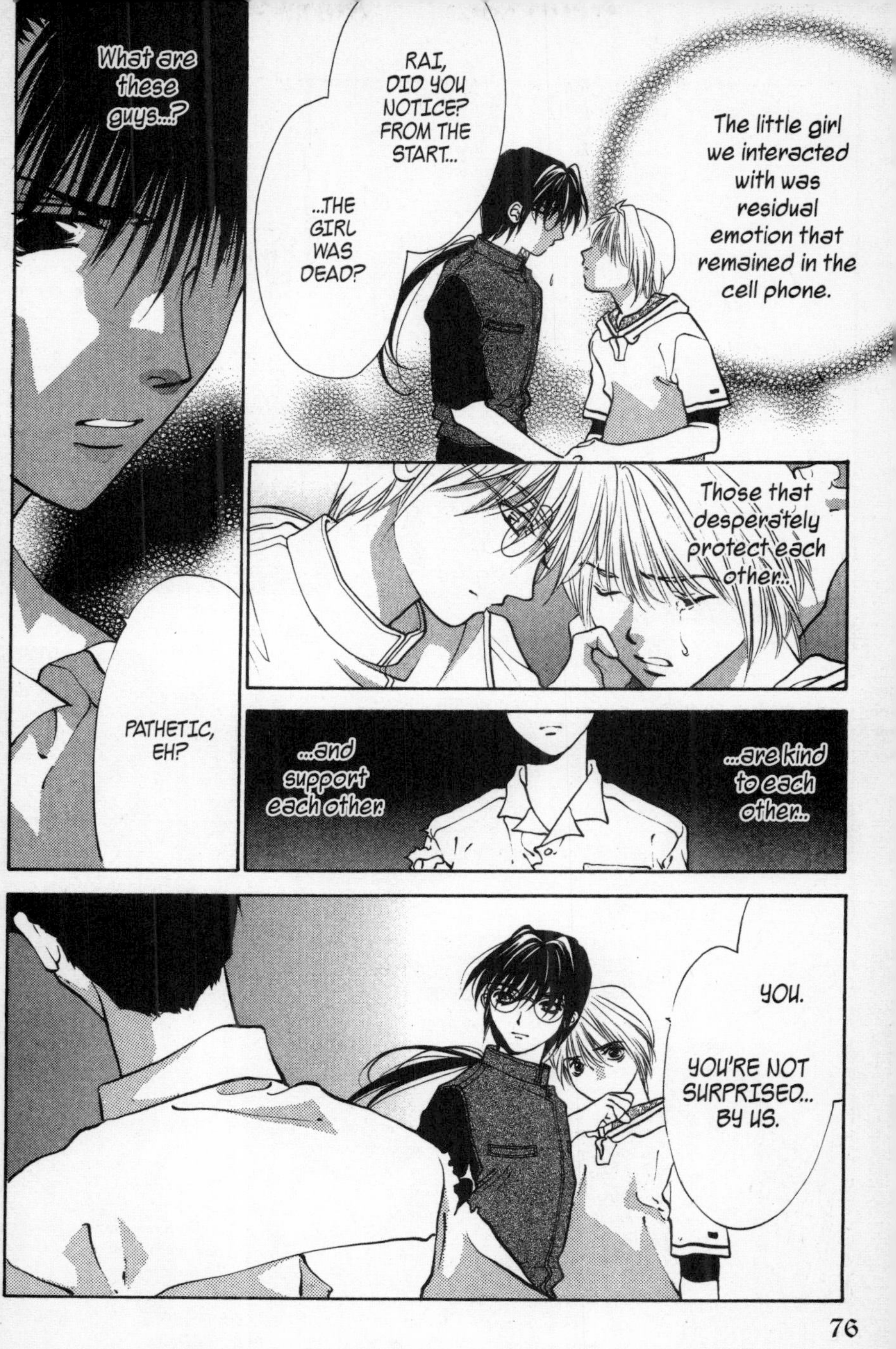
RAI, DID YOU NOTICE? FROM THE START...
...THE GIRL WAS DEAD?
The little girl we interacted with was residual emotion that remained in the cell phone.
Those that desperately protect each other..
...are kind to each other..
...and support each other.
What are these guys...?
PATHETIC, EH?
YOU.
YOU'RE NOT SURPRISED... BY US.

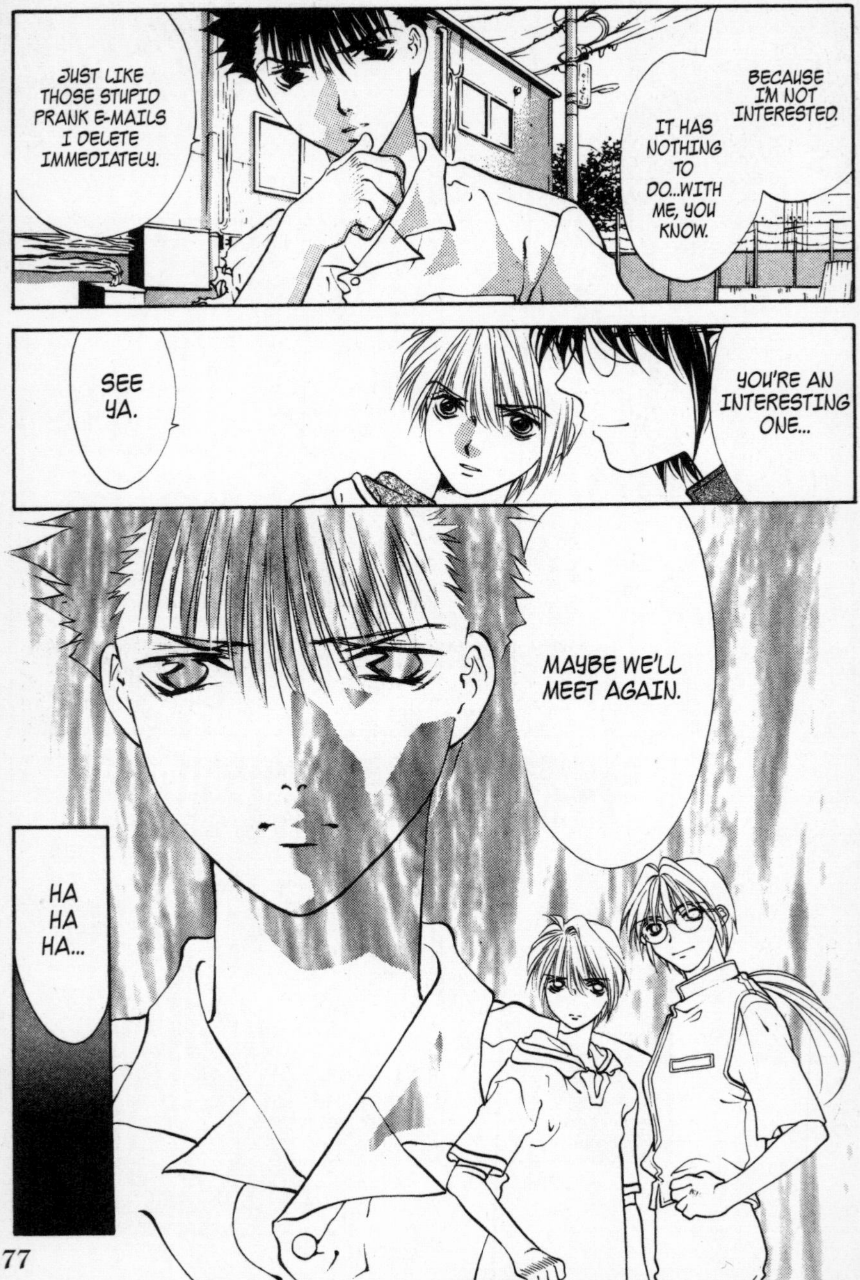
BECAUSE I'M NOT INTERESTED.
IT HAS NOTHING TO DO...WITH ME, YOU KNOW.
JUST LIKE THOSE STUPID PRANK E-MAILS I DELETE IMMEDIATELY.
YOU'RE AN INTERESTING ONE...
SEE YA.
MAYBE WE'LL MEET AGAIN.
HA HA HA...

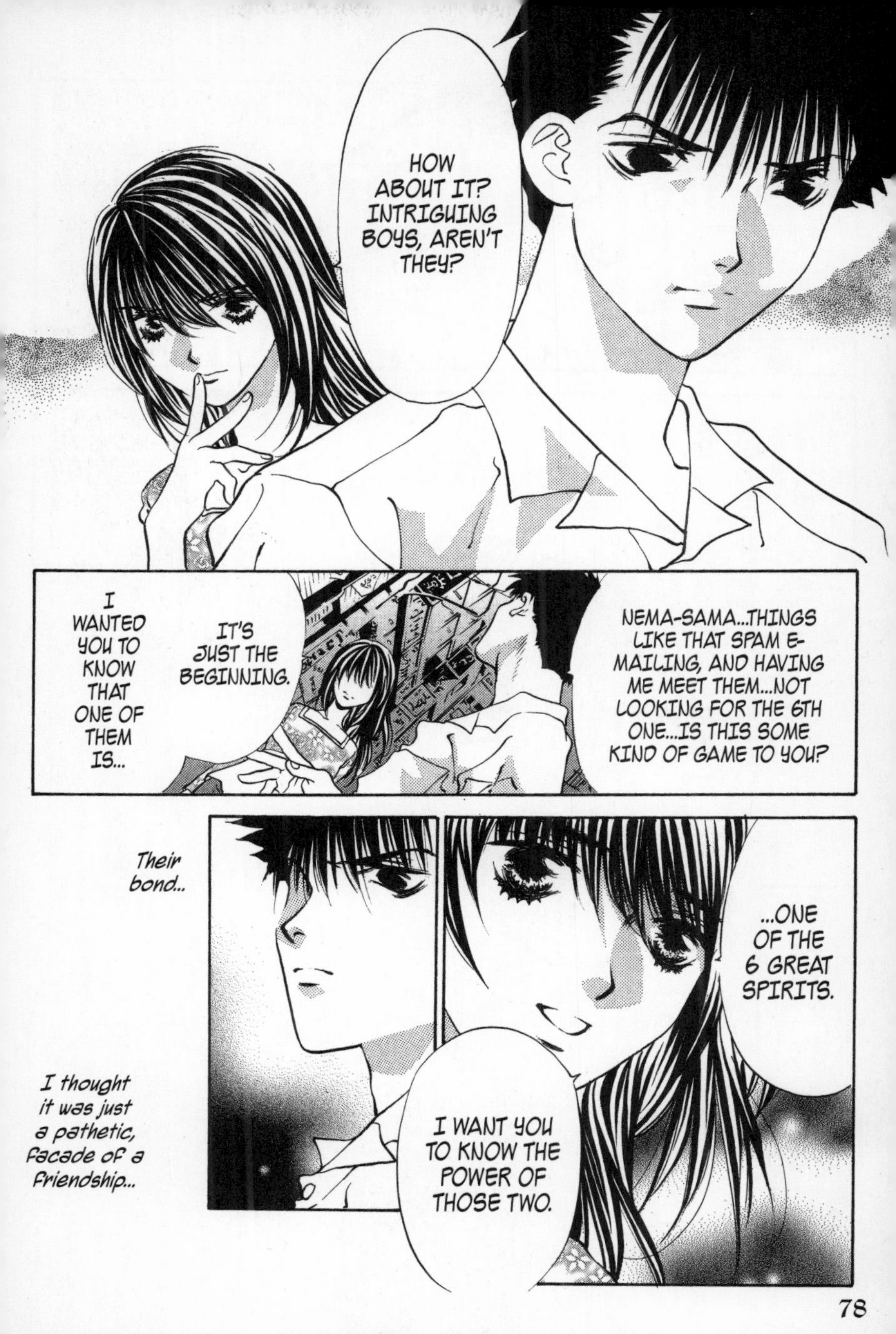
HOW ABOUT IT? INTRIGUING BOYS, AREN'T THEY?
NEMA-SAMA...THINGS LIKE THAT SPAM E-MAILING, AND HAVING ME MEET THEM...NOT LOOKING FOR THE 6TH ONE...IS THIS SOME KIND OF GAME TO YOU?
IT'S JUST THE BEGINNING.
I WANTED YOU TO KNOW THAT ONE OF THEM IS...
...ONE OF THE 6 GREAT SPIRITS.
I WANT YOU TO KNOW THE POWER OF THOSE TWO.
Their bond...
I thought it was just a pathetic, facade of a friendship...

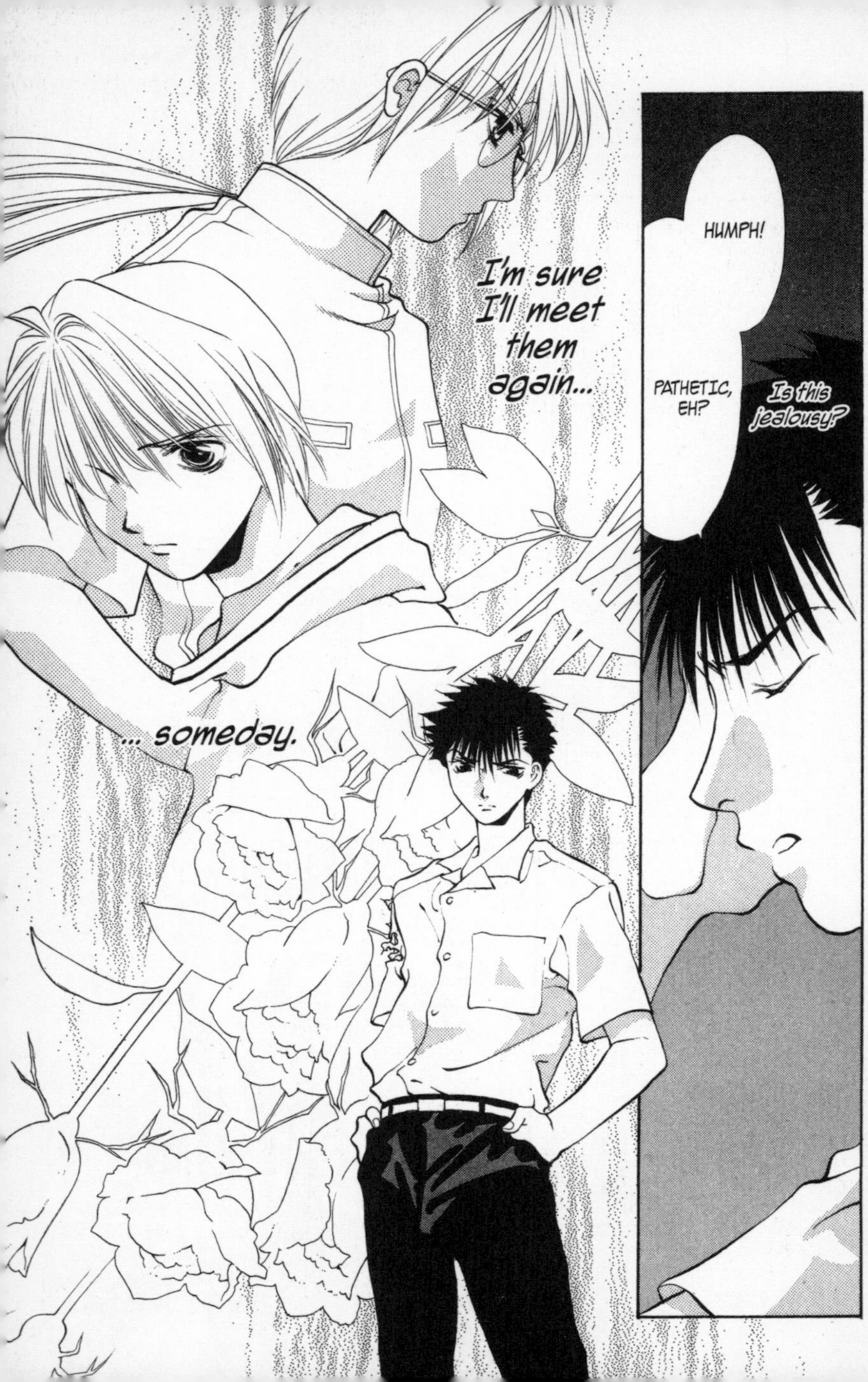
HUMPH!
Is this jealousy?
PATHETIC, EH?
I'm sure I'll meet them again...
... someday.

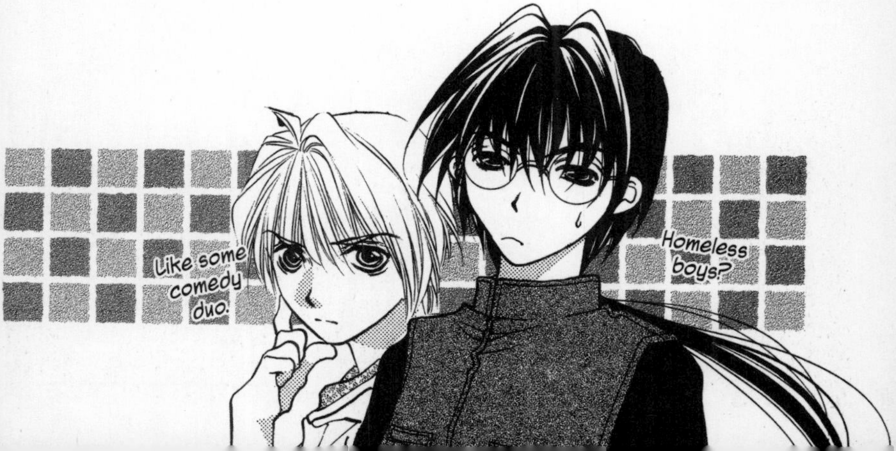
Homeless boys?
Like some comedy duo.

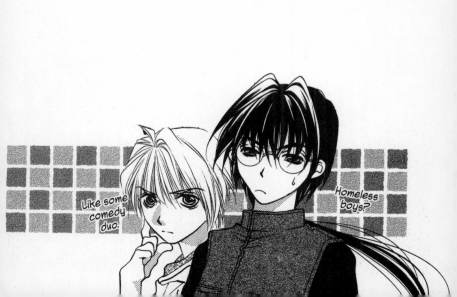

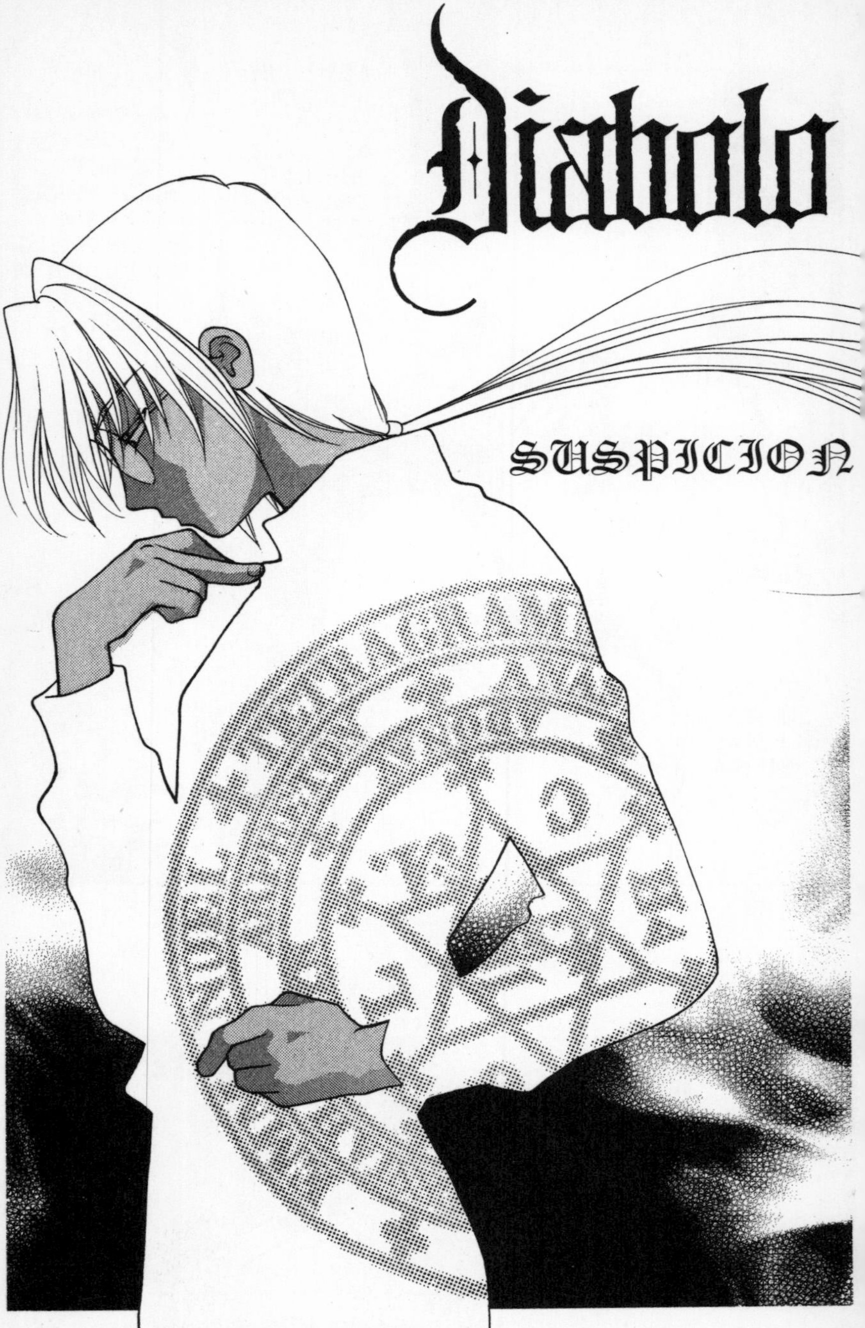
Diabolo
SUSPICION

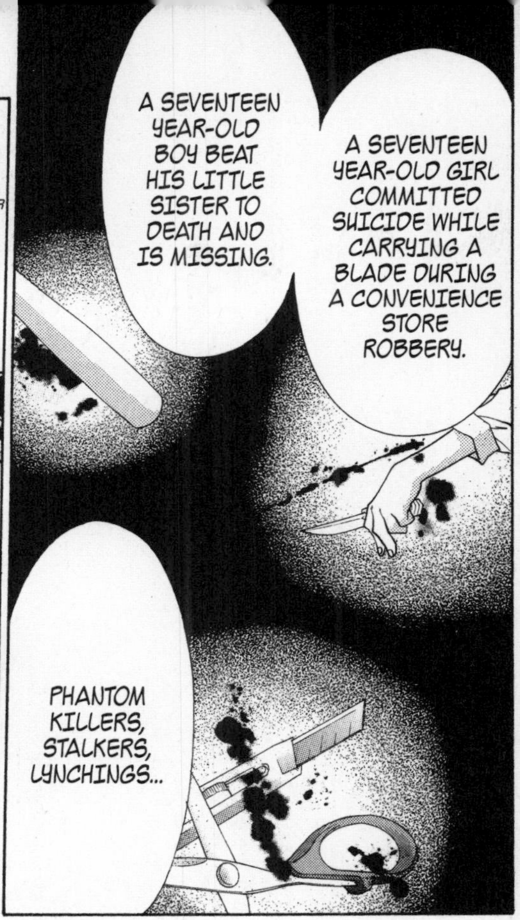
A SEVENTEEN YEAR-OLD GIRL COMMITTED SUICIDE WHILE CARRYING A BLADE DURING A CONVENIENCE STORE ROBBERY.
A SEVENTEEN YEAR-OLD BOY BEAT HIS LITTLE SISTER TO DEATH AND IS MISSING.
PHANTOM KILLERS, STALKERS, LYNCHINGS...

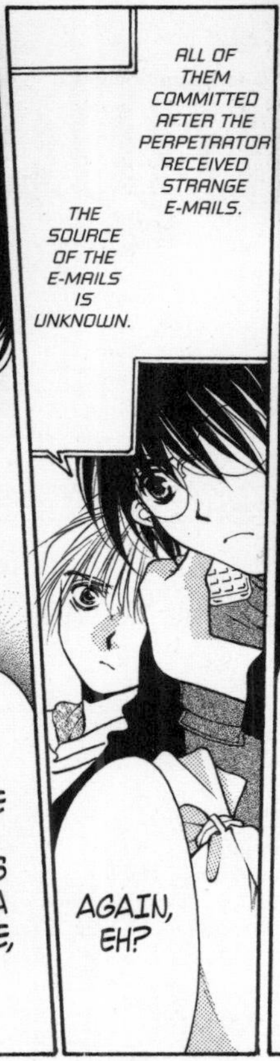
ALL OF THEM COMMITTED AFTER THE PERPETRATOR RECEIVED STRANGE E-MAILS.
THE SOURCE OF THE E-MAILS IS UNKNOWN.
AGAIN, EH?

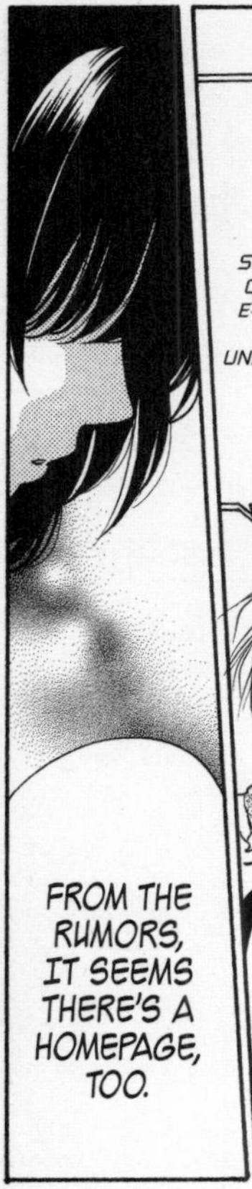
FROM THE RUMORS, IT SEEMS THERE'S A HOMEPAGE, TOO.

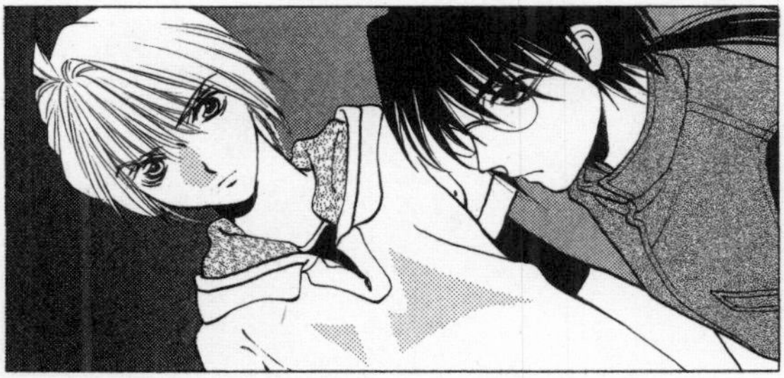

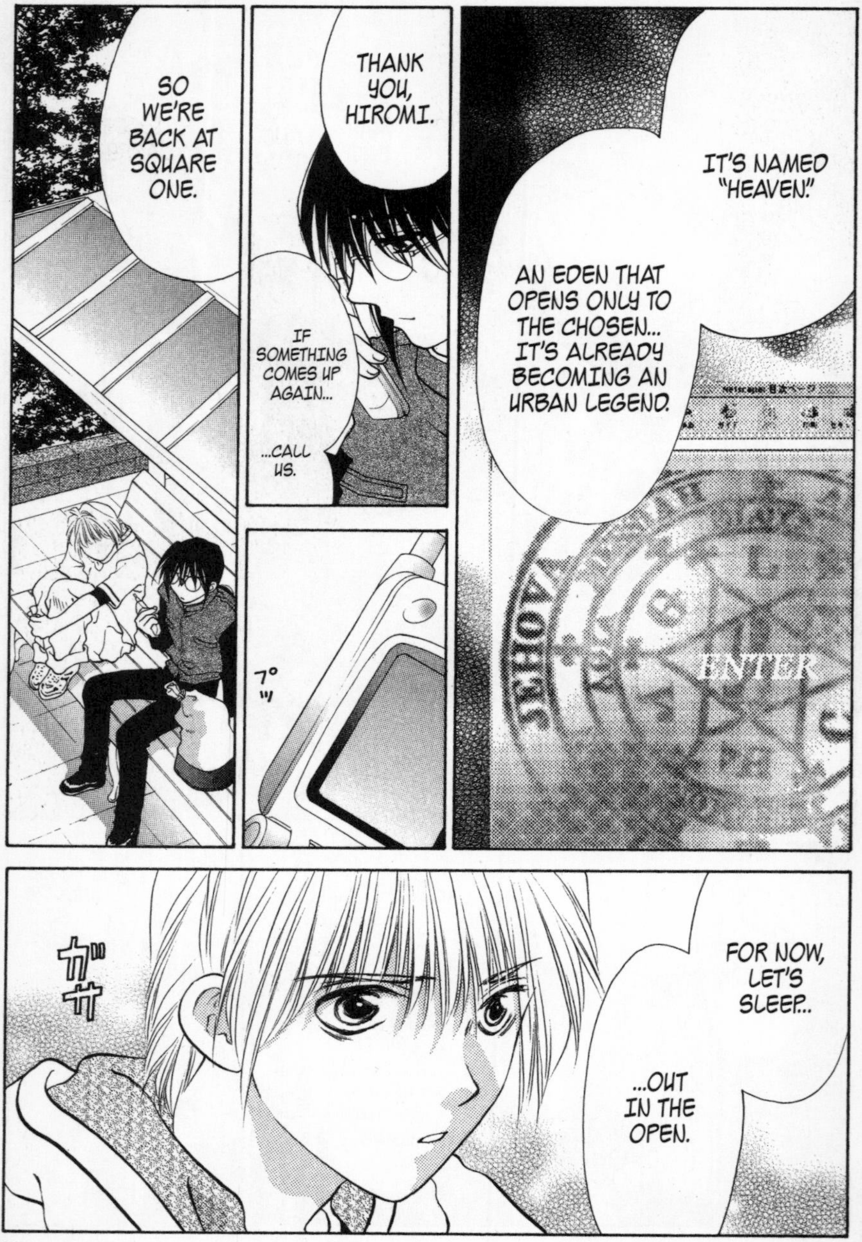
IT'S NAMED "HEAVEN."
AN EDEN THAT OPENS ONLY TO THE CHOSEN... IT'S ALREADY BECOMING AN URBAN LEGEND.
ENTER
THANK YOU, HIROMI.
IF SOMETHING COMES UP AGAIN...
...CALL US.
プツ
SO WE'RE BACK AT SQUARE ONE.
FOR NOW, LET'S SLEEP...
...OUT IN THE OPEN.
ガサ

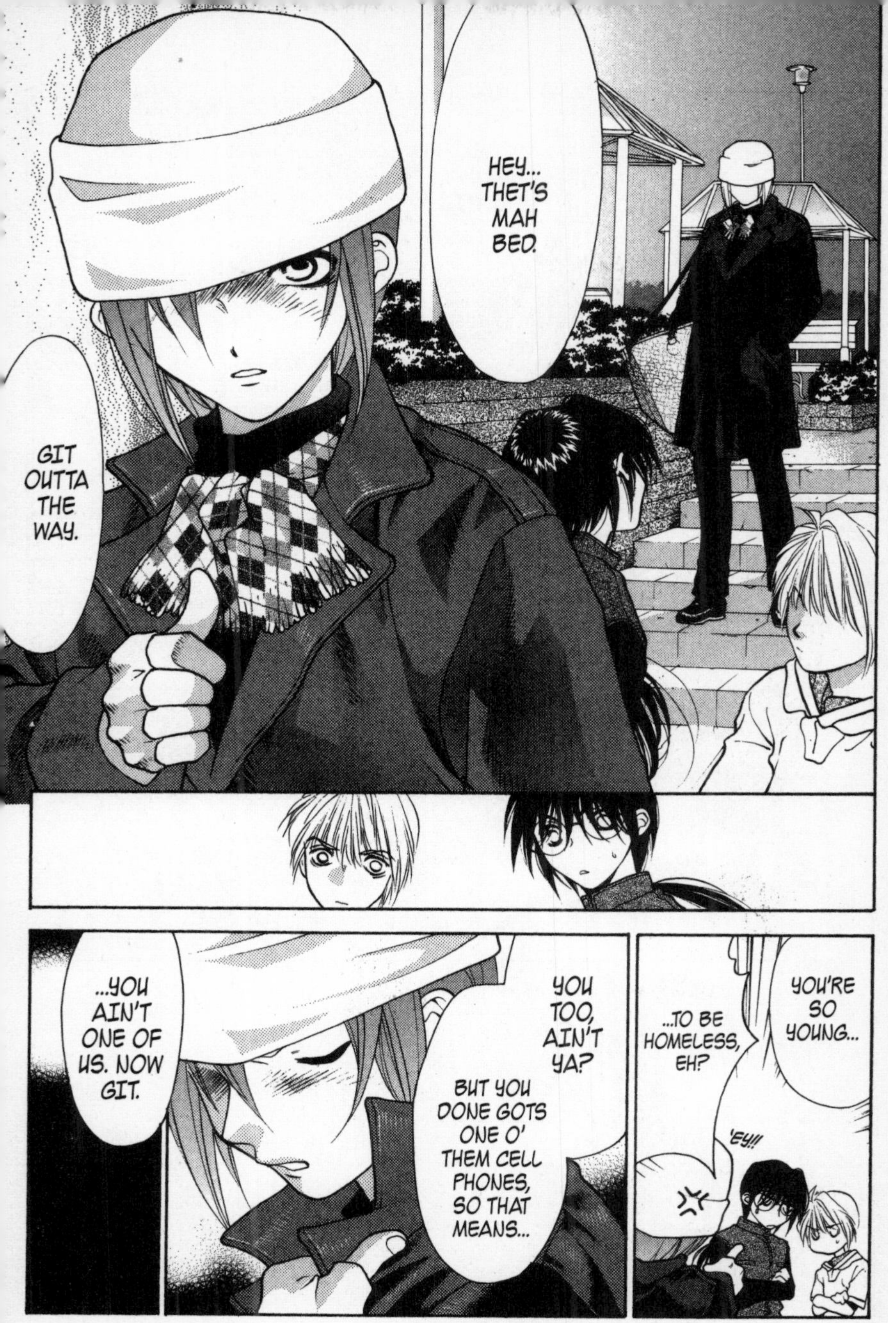
HEY... THET'S MAH BED.
GIT OUTTA THE WAY.
YOU'RE SO YOUNG...
...TO BE HOMELESS, EH?
'EY!!
YOU TOO, AIN'T YA?
BUT YOU DONE GOTS ONE O' THEM CELL PHONES, SO THAT MEANS...
...YOU AIN'T ONE OF US. NOW GIT.

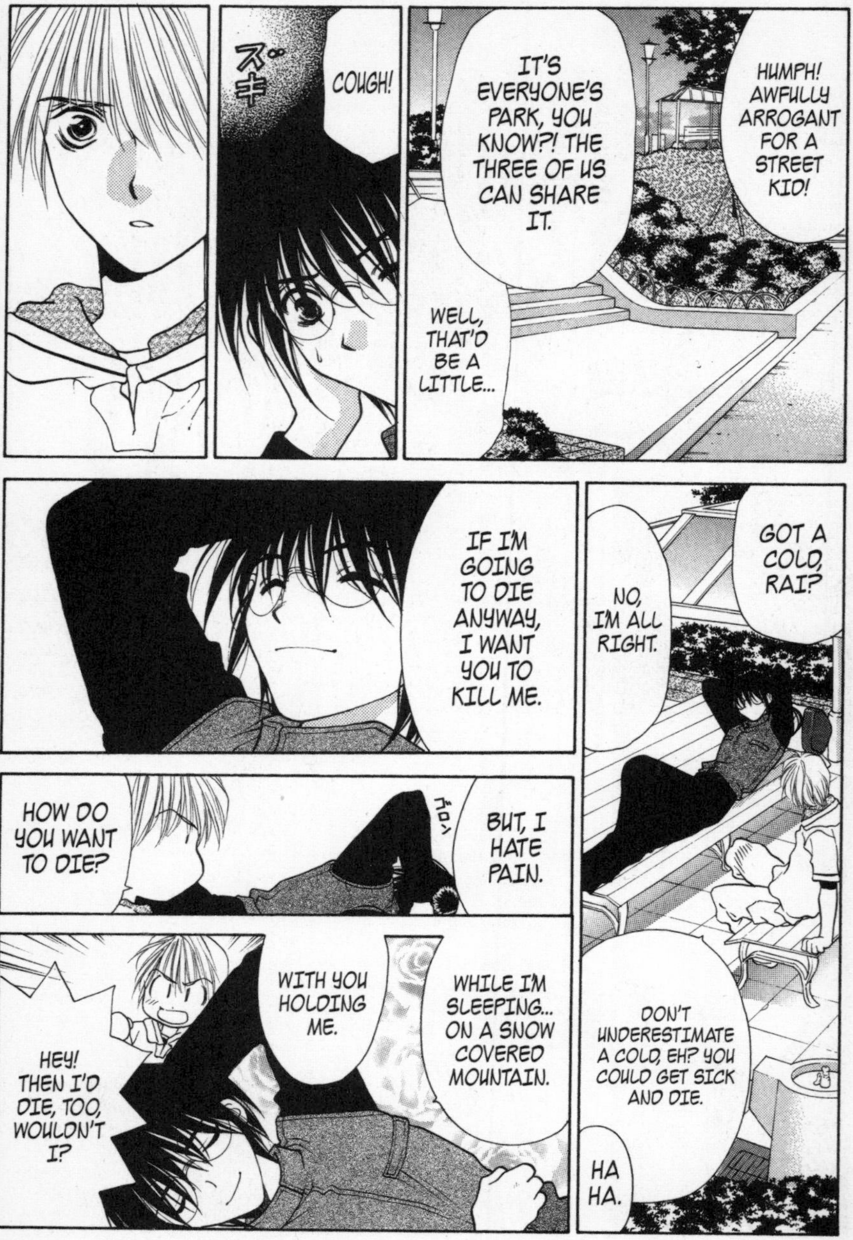
HUMPH! AWFULLY ARROGANT FOR A STREET KID!
IT'S EVERYONE'S PARK, YOU KNOW?! THE THREE OF US CAN SHARE IT.
WELL, THAT'D BE A LITTLE...
ズキ
COUGH!
GOT A COLD, RAI?
NO, I'M ALL RIGHT.
DON'T UNDERESTIMATE A COLD, EH? YOU COULD GET SICK AND DIE.
HA HA.
IF I'M GOING TO DIE ANYWAY, I WANT YOU TO KILL ME.
ゴロン
BUT, I HATE PAIN.
HOW DO YOU WANT TO DIE?
WHILE I'M SLEEPING... ON A SNOW COVERED MOUNTAIN.
WITH YOU HOLDING ME.
HEY! THEN I'D DIE, TOO, WOULDN'T I?

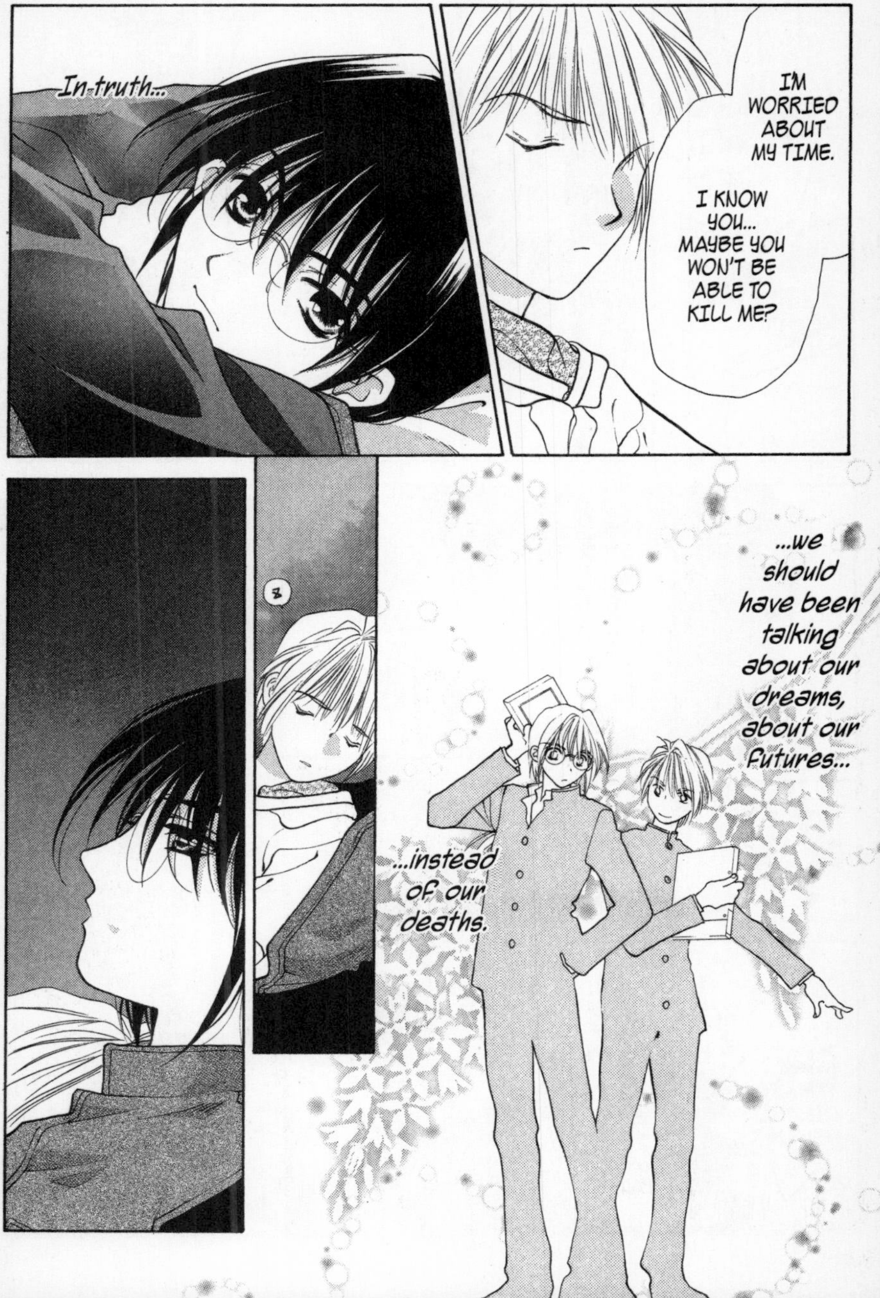
I'M WORRIED ABOUT MY TIME.
I KNOW YOU... MAYBE YOU WON'T BE ABLE TO KILL ME?
In truth...
...we should have been talking about our dreams, about our futures...
...instead of our deaths.

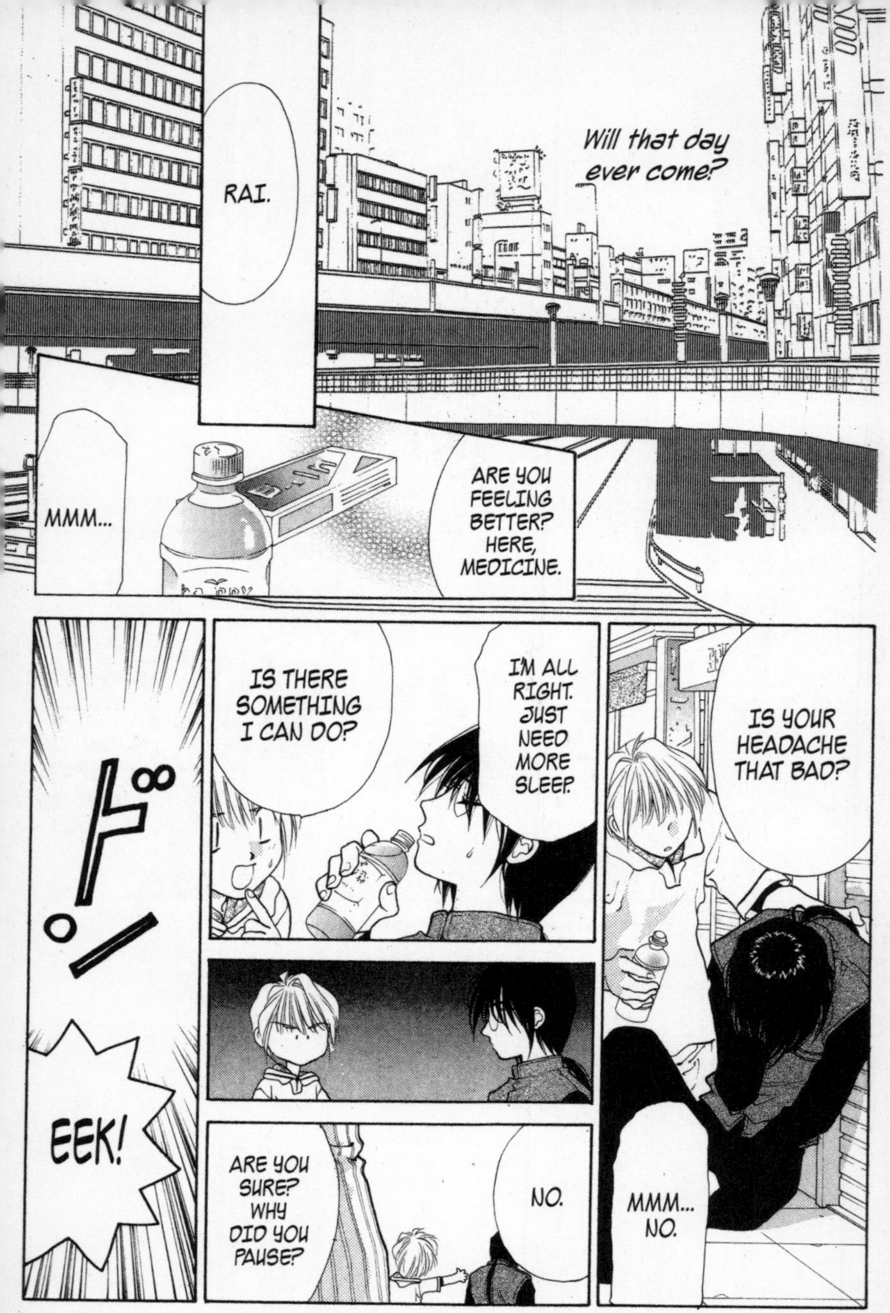
Will that day ever come?
RAI.
ARE YOU FEELING BETTER? HERE, MEDICINE.
MMM...
IS YOUR HEADACHE THAT BAD?
MMM... NO.
I'M ALL RIGHT. JUST NEED MORE SLEEP.
IS THERE SOMETHING I CAN DO?
NO.
ARE YOU SURE? WHY DID YOU PAUSE?
EEK!

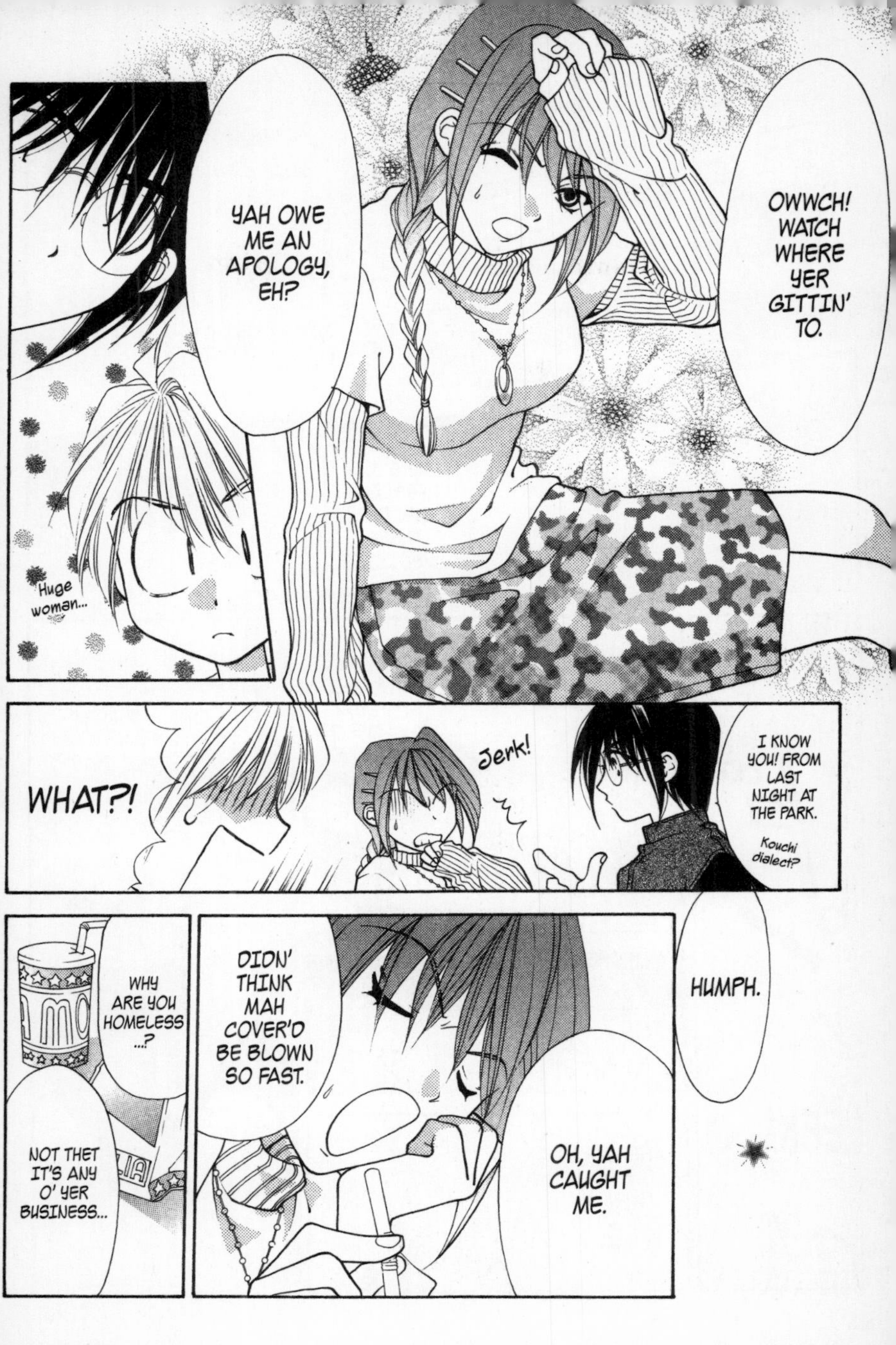
OWWCH! WATCH WHERE YER GITTIN' TO.
YAH OWE ME AN APOLOGY, EH?
Huge woman...
I KNOW YOU! FROM LAST NIGHT AT THE PARK.
Kouchi dialect?
Jerk!
WHAT?!
HUMPH.
OH, YAH CAUGHT ME.
DIDN' THINK MAH COVER'D BE BLOWN SO FAST.
WHY ARE YOU HOMELESS ...?
NOT THET IT'S ANY O' YER BUSINESS...

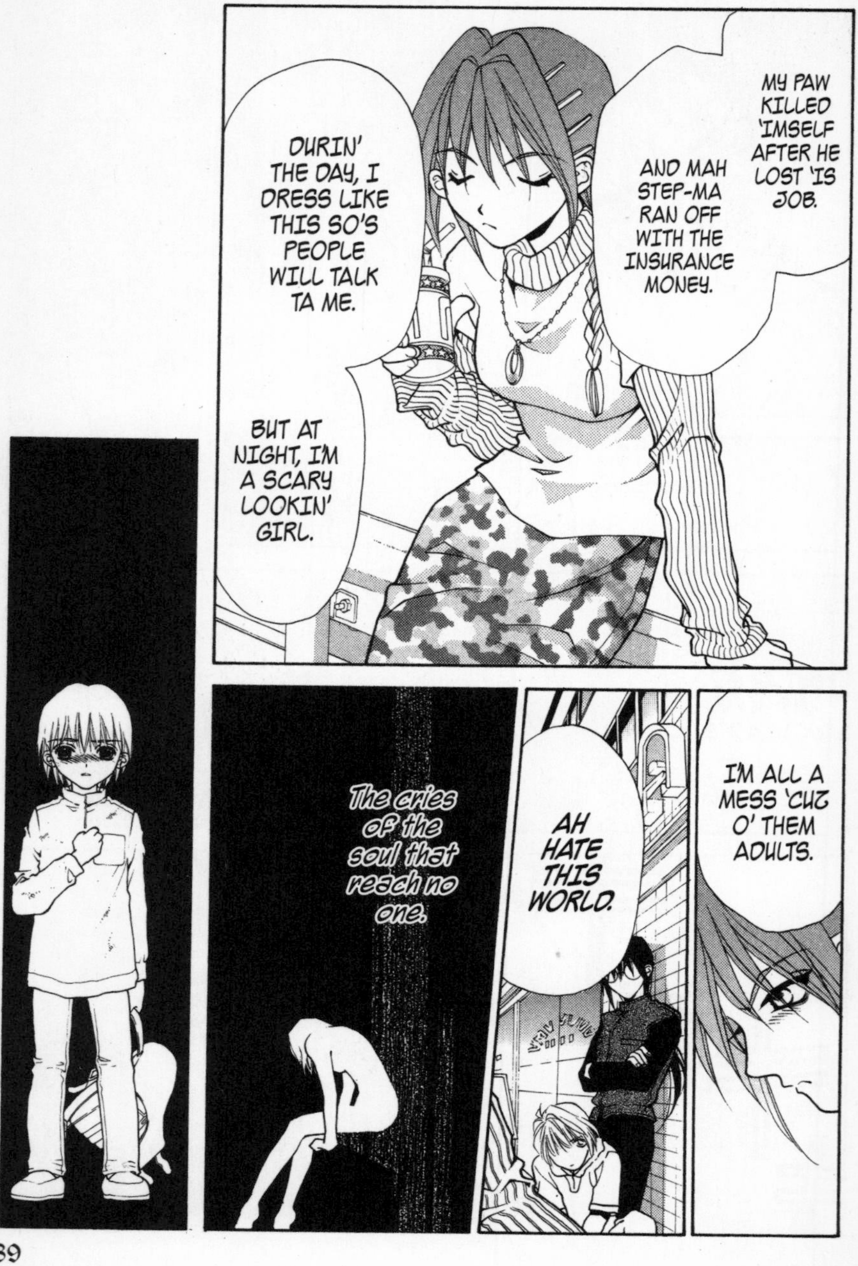
MY PAW KILLED 'IMSELF AFTER HE LOST 'IS JOB.
AND MAH STEP-MA RAN OFF WITH THE INSURANCE MONEY.
DURIN' THE DAY, I DRESS LIKE THIS SO'S PEOPLE WILL TALK TA ME.
BUT AT NIGHT, I'M A SCARY LOOKIN' GIRL.
I'M ALL A MESS 'CUZ O' THEM ADULTS.
AH HATE THIS WORLD.
The cries of the soul that reach no one.

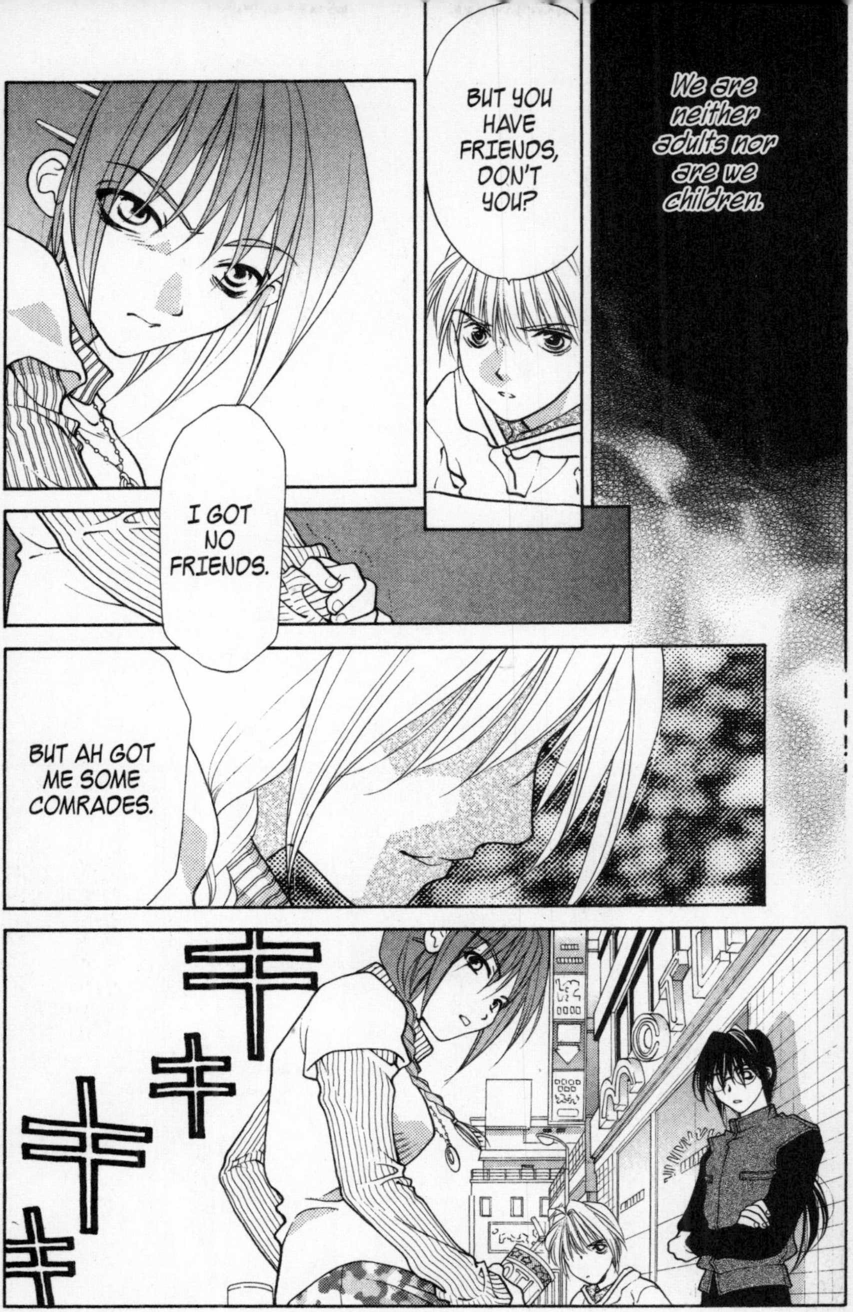
We are neither adults nor are we children.
BUT YOU HAVE FRIENDS, DON'T YOU?
I GOT NO FRIENDS.
BUT AH GOT ME SOME COMRADES.

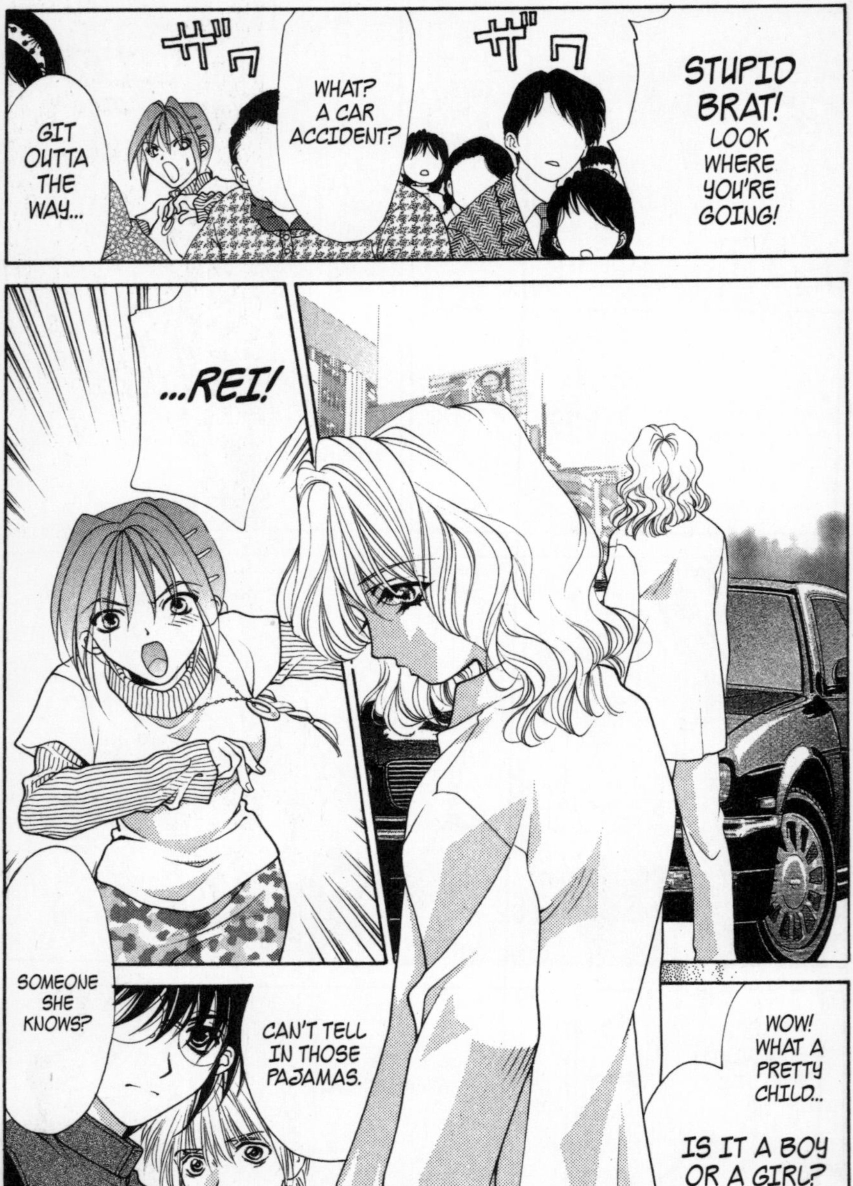
STUPID BRAT! LOOK WHERE YOU'RE GOING!
ザワ
WHAT? A CAR ACCIDENT?
ザワ
GIT OUTTA THE WAY...
...REI!
WOW! WHAT A PRETTY CHILD...
IS IT A BOY OR A GIRL?
CAN'T TELL IN THOSE PAJAMAS.
SOMEONE SHE KNOWS?

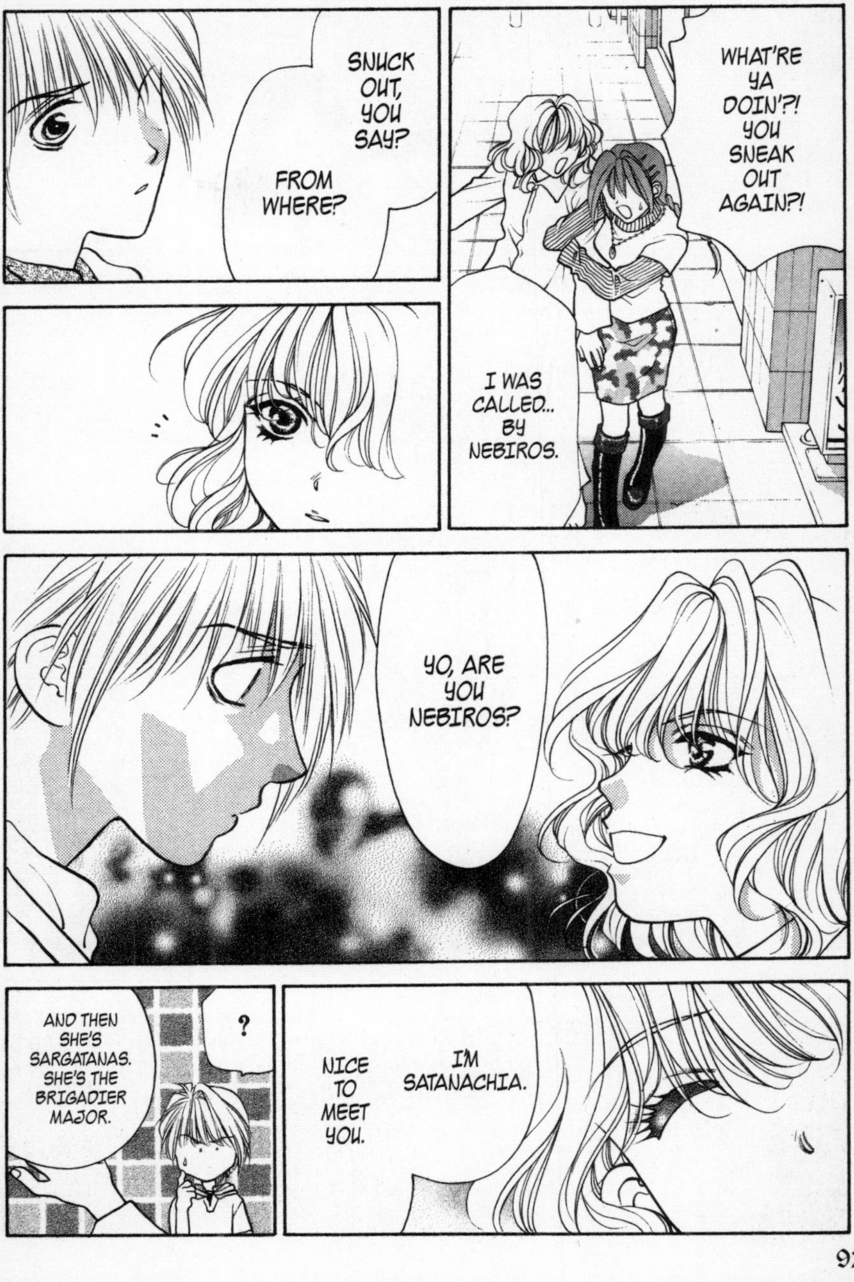
WHAT'RE YA DOIN'?! YOU SNEAK OUT AGAIN?!
I WAS CALLED... BY NEBIROS.
SNUCK OUT, YOU SAY?
FROM WHERE?
YO, ARE YOU NEBIROS?
I'M SATANACHIA.
NICE TO MEET YOU.
?
AND THEN SHE'S SARGATANAS. SHE'S THE BRIGADIER MAJOR.

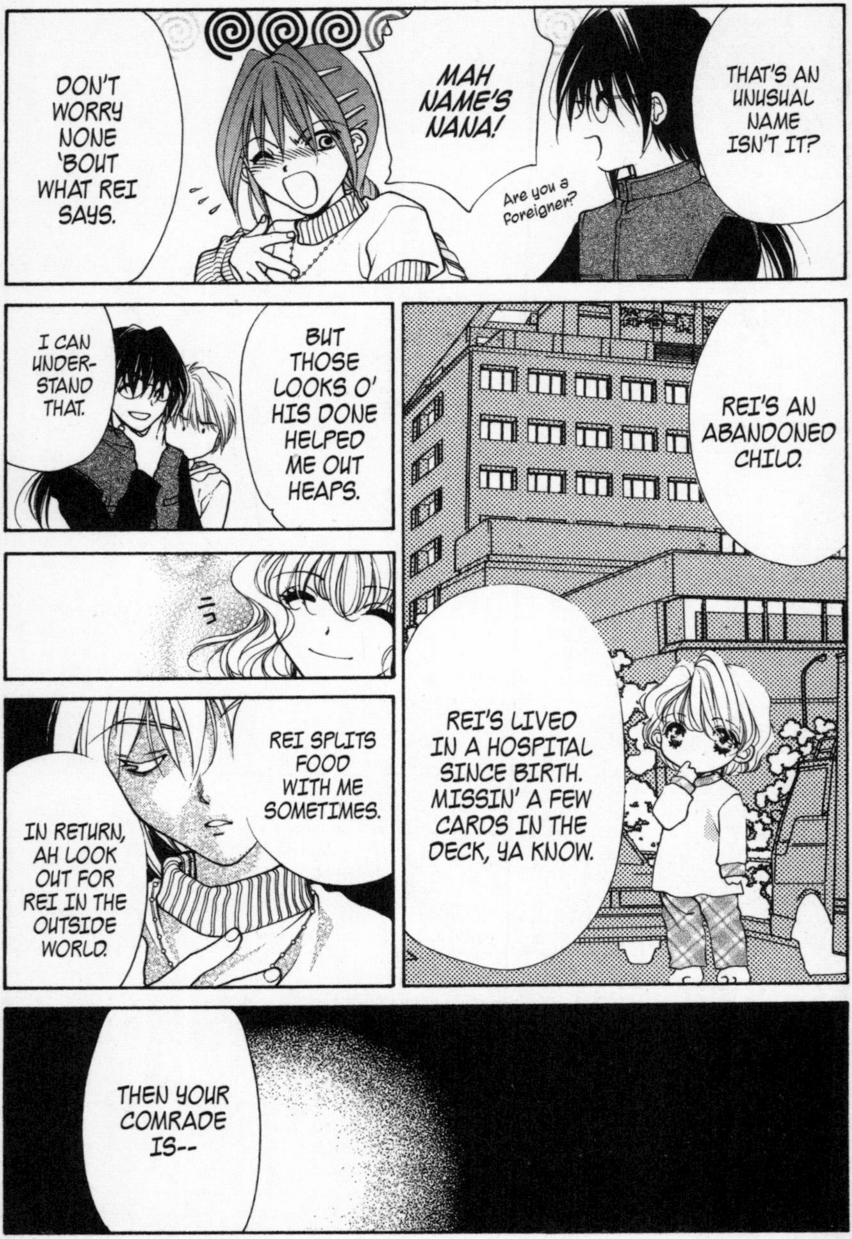
THAT'S AN UNUSUAL NAME ISN'T IT?
Are you a foreigner?
MAH NAME'S NANA!
DON'T WORRY NONE 'BOUT WHAT REI SAYS.
REI'S AN ABANDONED CHILD.
REI'S LIVED IN A HOSPITAL SINCE BIRTH. MISSIN' A FEW CARDS IN THE DECK, YA KNOW.
BUT THOSE LOOKS O' HIS DONE HELPED ME OUT HEAPS.
I CAN UNDER-STAND THAT.
REI SPLITS FOOD WITH ME SOMETIMES.
IN RETURN, AH LOOK OUT FOR REI IN THE OUTSIDE WORLD.
THEN YOUR COMRADE IS--

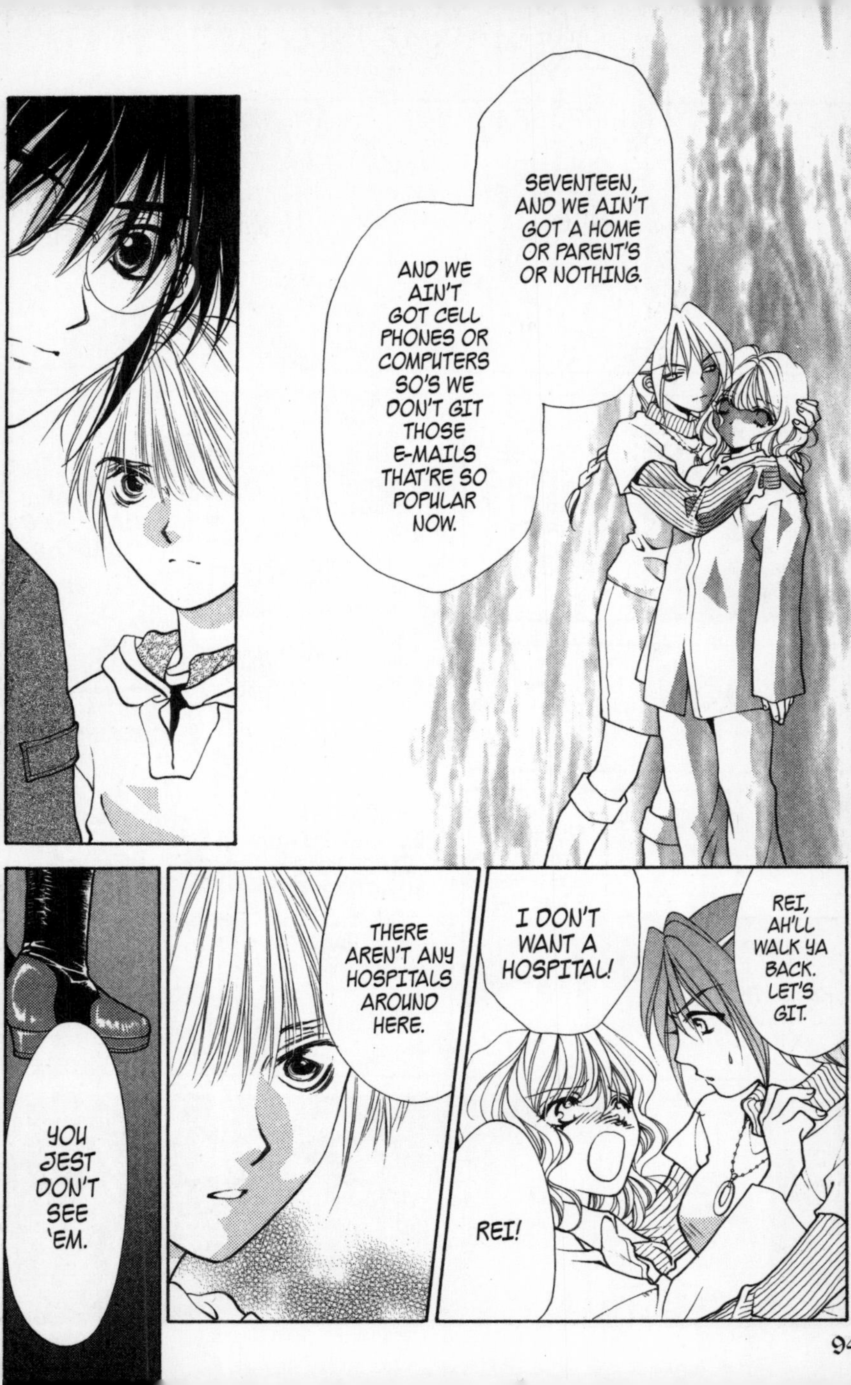
SEVENTEEN, AND WE AIN'T GOT A HOME OR PARENT'S OR NOTHING.
AND WE AIN'T GOT CELL PHONES OR COMPUTERS SO'S WE DON'T GIT THOSE E-MAILS THAT'RE SO POPULAR NOW.
REI, AH'LL WALK YA BACK. LET'S GIT.
I DON'T WANT A HOSPITAL!
REI!
THERE AREN'T ANY HOSPITALS AROUND HERE.
YOU JEST DON'T SEE 'EM.

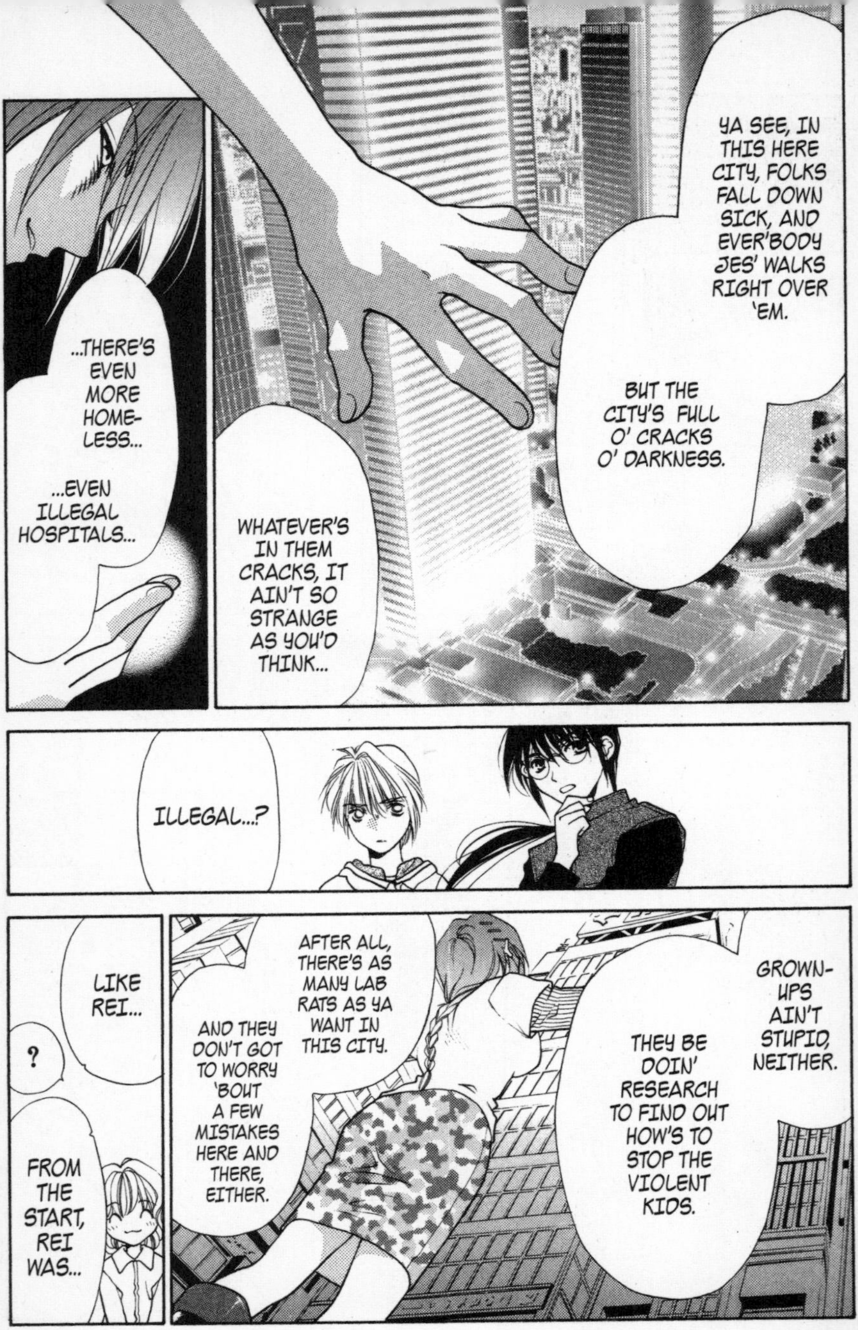
YA SEE, IN THIS HERE CITY, FOLKS FALL DOWN SICK, AND EVER'BODY JES' WALKS RIGHT OVER 'EM.
BUT THE CITY'S FULL O' CRACKS O' DARKNESS.
WHATEVER'S IN THEM CRACKS, IT AIN'T SO STRANGE AS YOU'D THINK...
...THERE'S EVEN MORE HOMELESS...
...EVEN ILLEGAL HOSPITALS...
ILLEGAL...?
GROWN-UPS AIN'T STUPID, NEITHER.
THEY BE DOIN' RESEARCH TO FIND OUT HOW'S TO STOP THE VIOLENT KIDS.
AFTER ALL, THERE'S AS MANY LAB RATS AS YA WANT IN THIS CITY.
AND THEY DON'T GOT TO WORRY 'BOUT A FEW MISTAKES HERE AND THERE, EITHER.
LIKE REI...
?
FROM THE START, REI WAS...

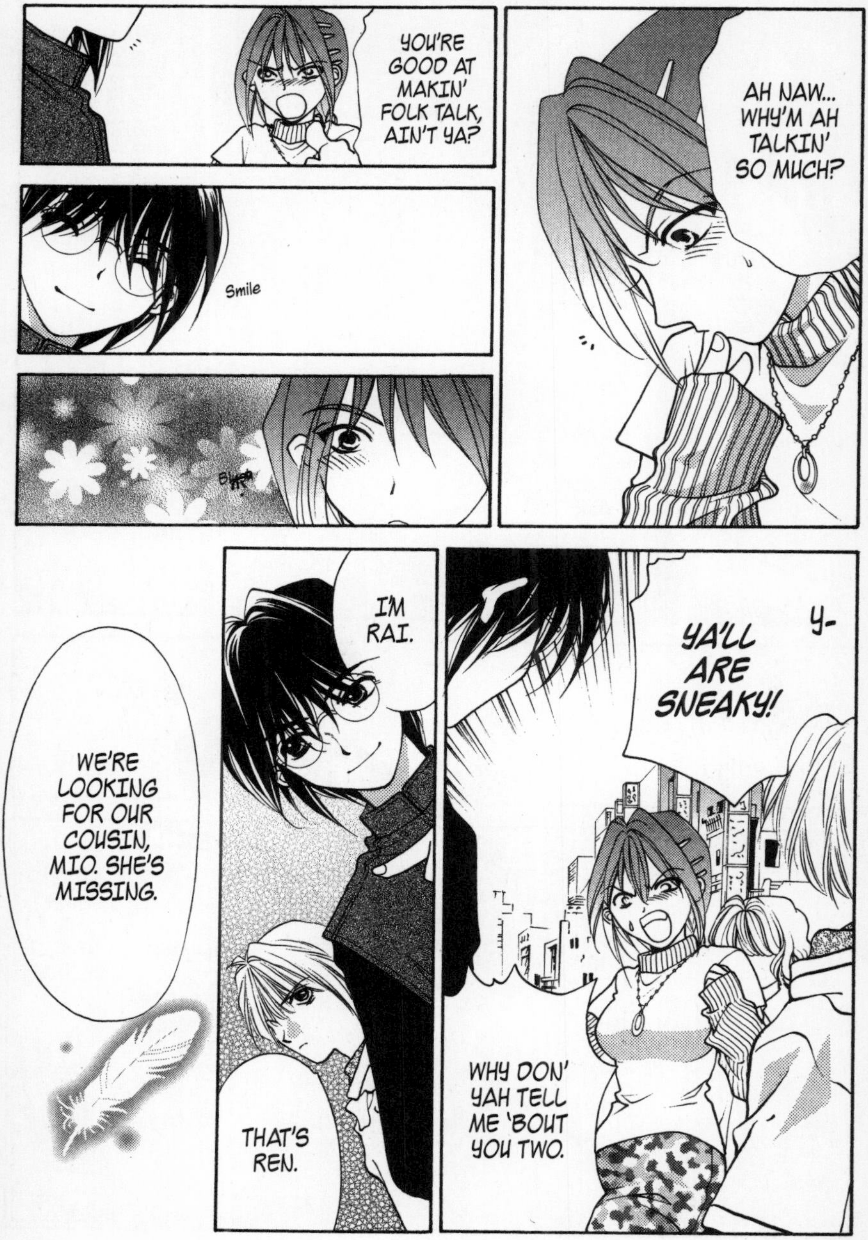
AH NAW... WHY'M AH TALKIN' SO MUCH?
YOU'RE GOOD AT MAKIN' FOLK TALK, AIN'T YA?
Smile
Y-
YA'LL ARE SNEAKY!
WHY DON' YAH TELL ME 'BOUT YOU TWO.
I'M RAI.
THAT'S REN.
WE'RE LOOKING FOR OUR COUSIN, MIO. SHE'S MISSING.

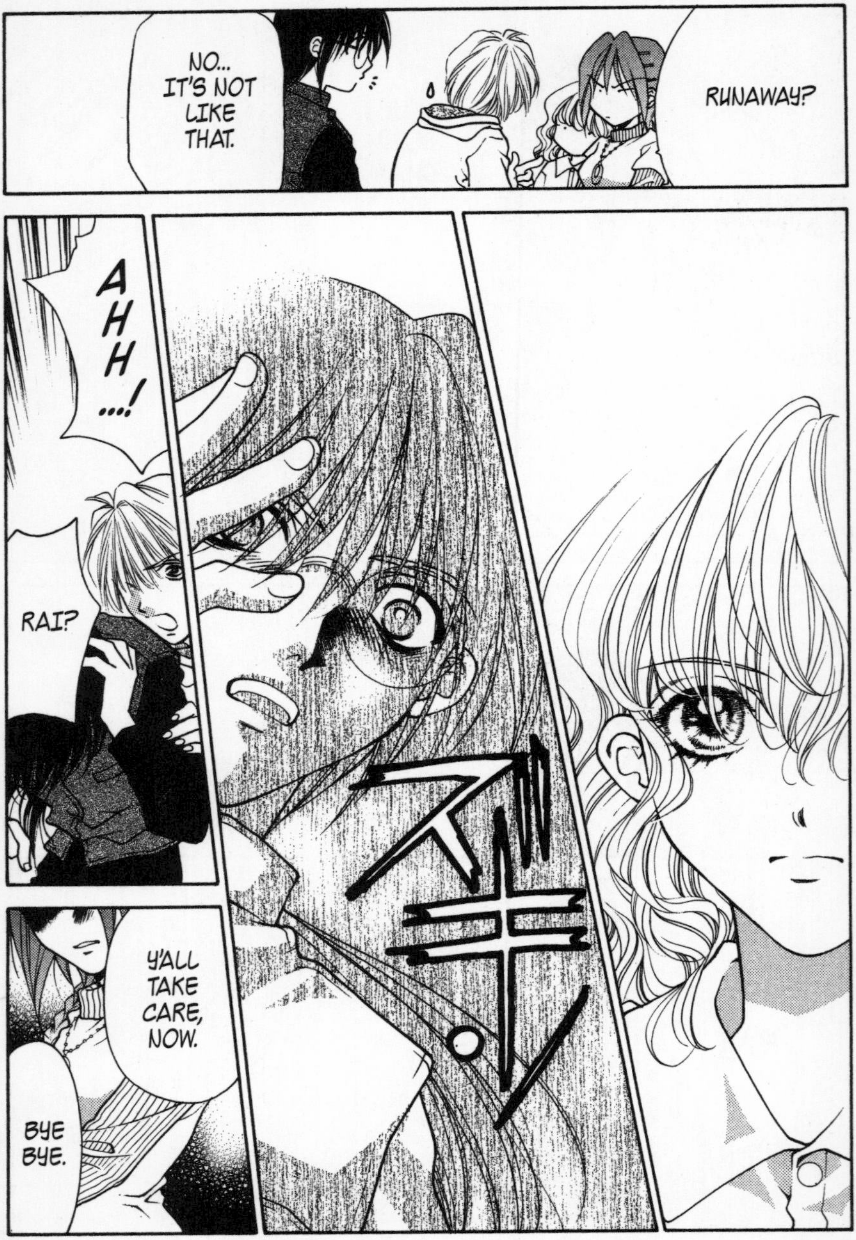
RUNAWAY?
NO... IT'S NOT LIKE THAT.
ズキン
AHH...!
RAI?
Y'ALL TAKE CARE, NOW.
BYE BYE.

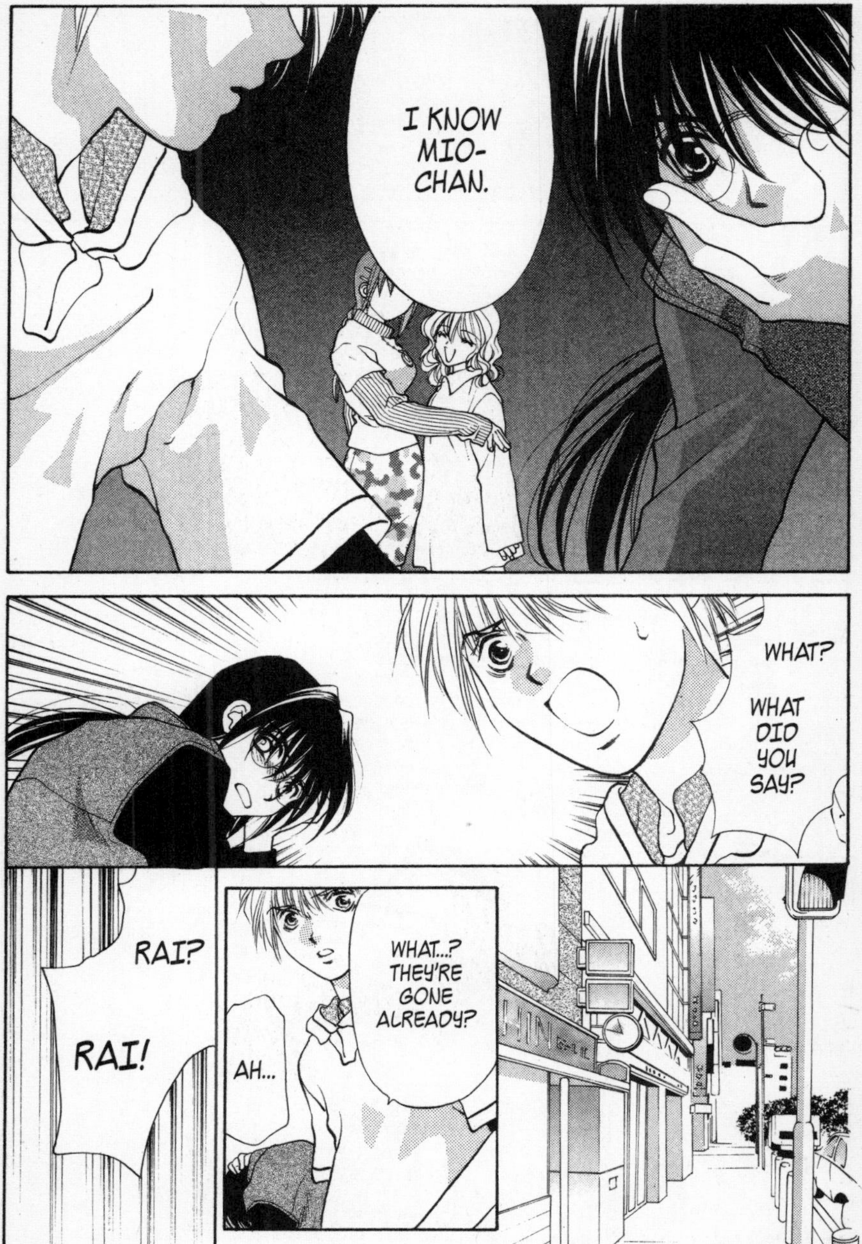
I KNOW MIO-CHAN.
WHAT?
WHAT DID YOU SAY?
WHAT...? THEY'RE GONE ALREADY?
AH...
RAI?
RAI!

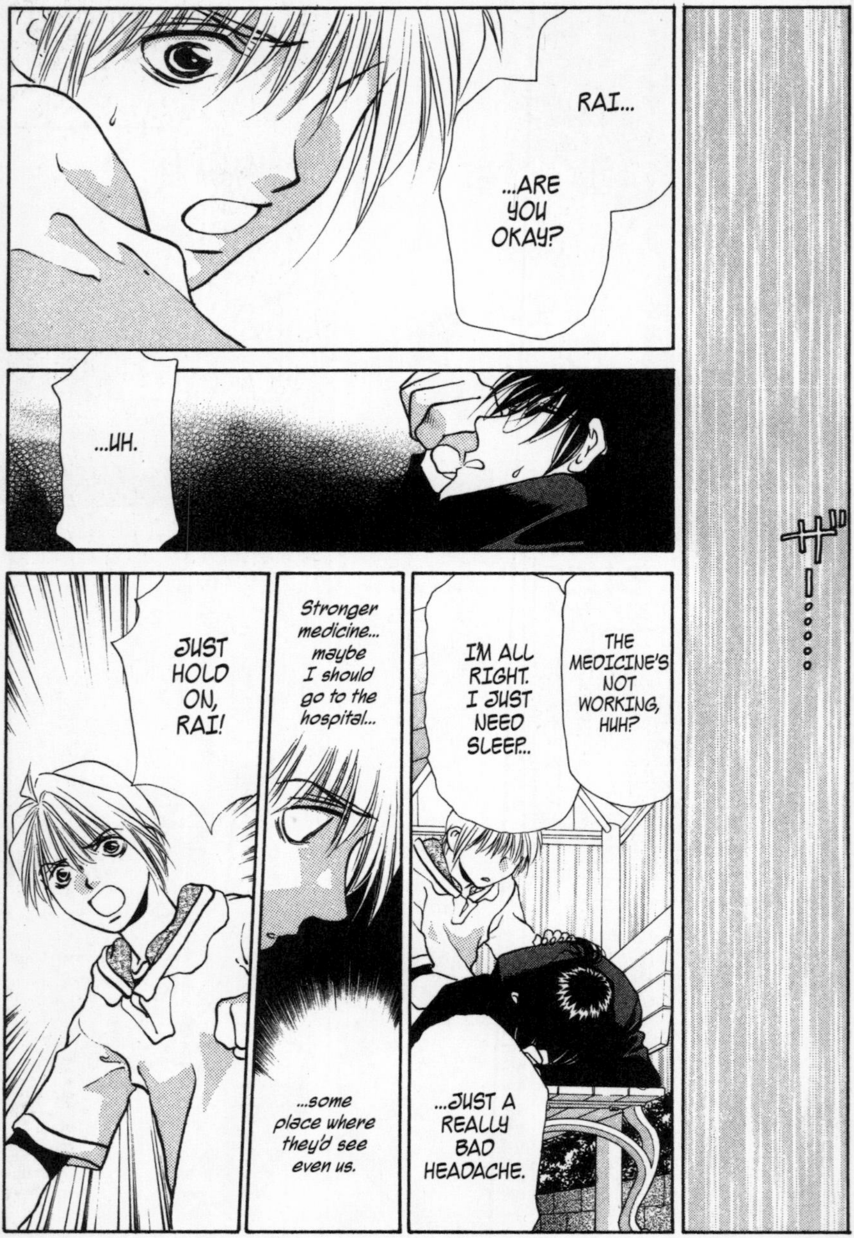
ザー・・・・・
RAI...
...ARE YOU OKAY?
...UH.
THE MEDICINE'S NOT WORKING, HUH?
I'M ALL RIGHT. I JUST NEED SLEEP...
...JUST A REALLY BAD HEADACHE.
Stronger medicine... maybe I should go to the hospital...
...some place where they'd see even us.
JUST HOLD ON, RAI!

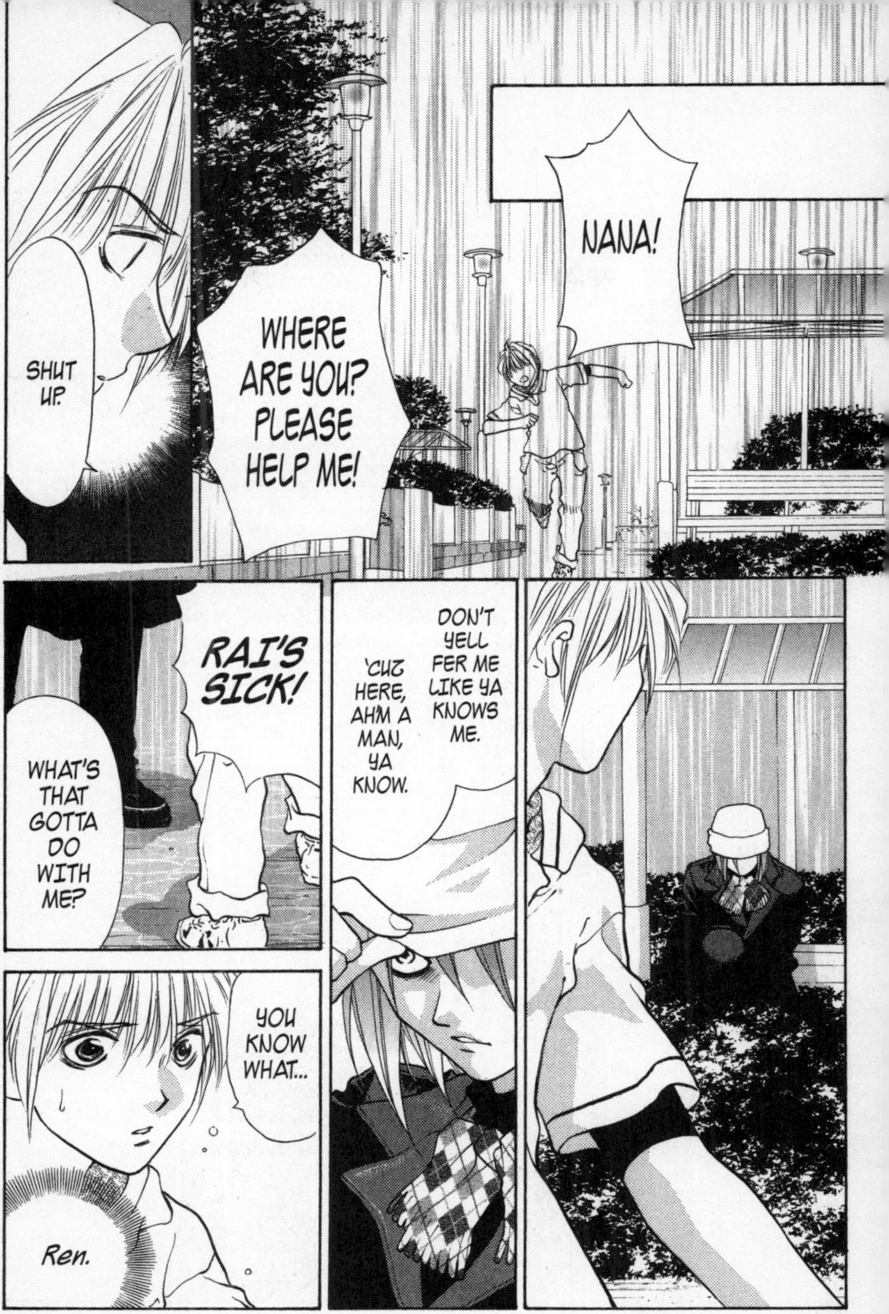
NANA!
WHERE ARE YOU? PLEASE HELP ME!
SHUT UP.
DON'T YELL FER ME LIKE YA KNOWS ME.
'CUZ HERE, AH'M A MAN, YA KNOW.
RAI'S SICK!
WHAT'S THAT GOTTA DO WITH ME?
YOU KNOW WHAT...
Ren.

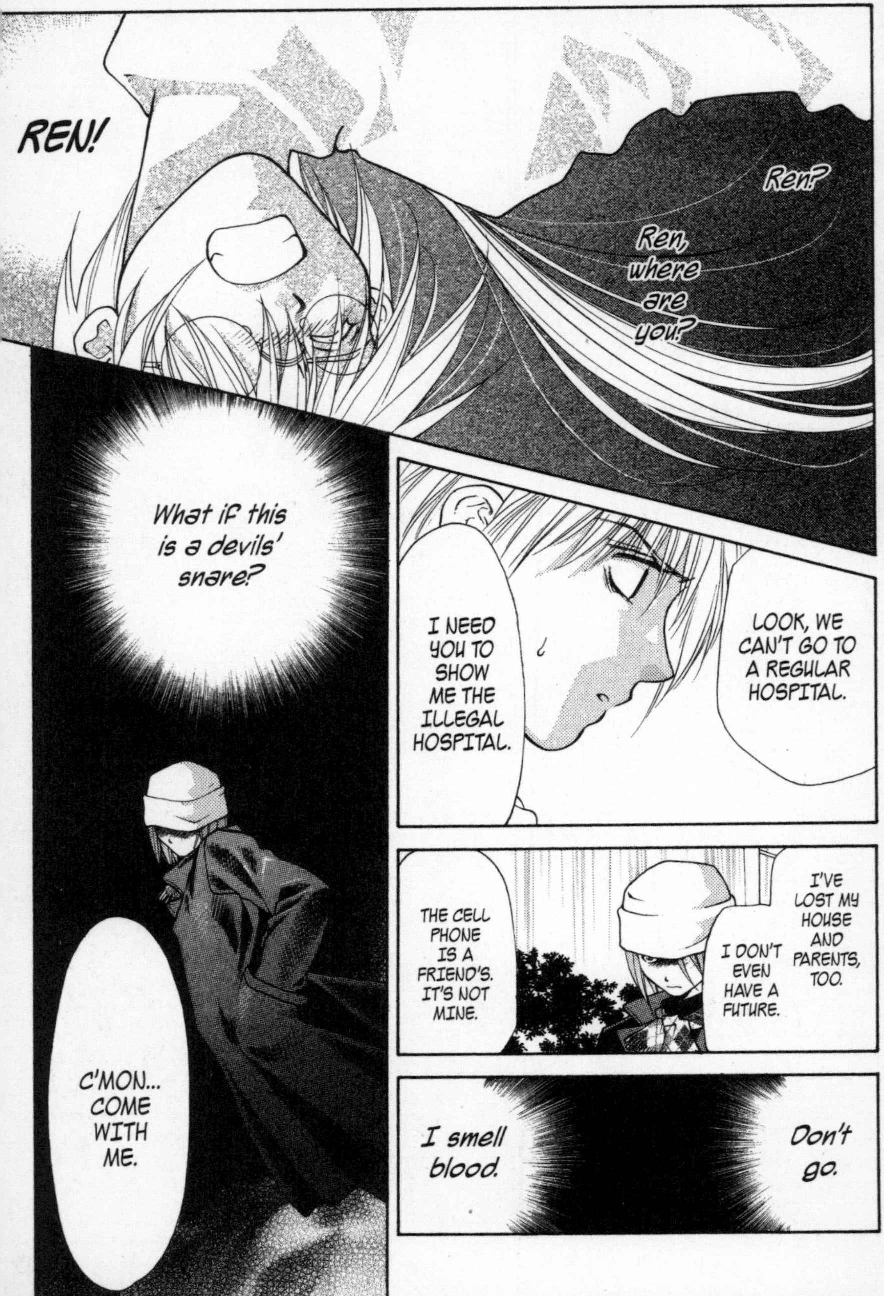
Ren?
Ren, where are you?
REN!
LOOK, WE CAN'T GO TO A REGULAR HOSPITAL.
I NEED YOU TO SHOW ME THE ILLEGAL HOSPITAL.
I'VE LOST MY HOUSE AND PARENTS, TOO.
I DON'T EVEN HAVE A FUTURE.
THE CELL PHONE IS A FRIEND'S. IT'S NOT MINE.
Don't go.
I smell blood.
What if this is a devils' snare?
C'MON... COME WITH ME.

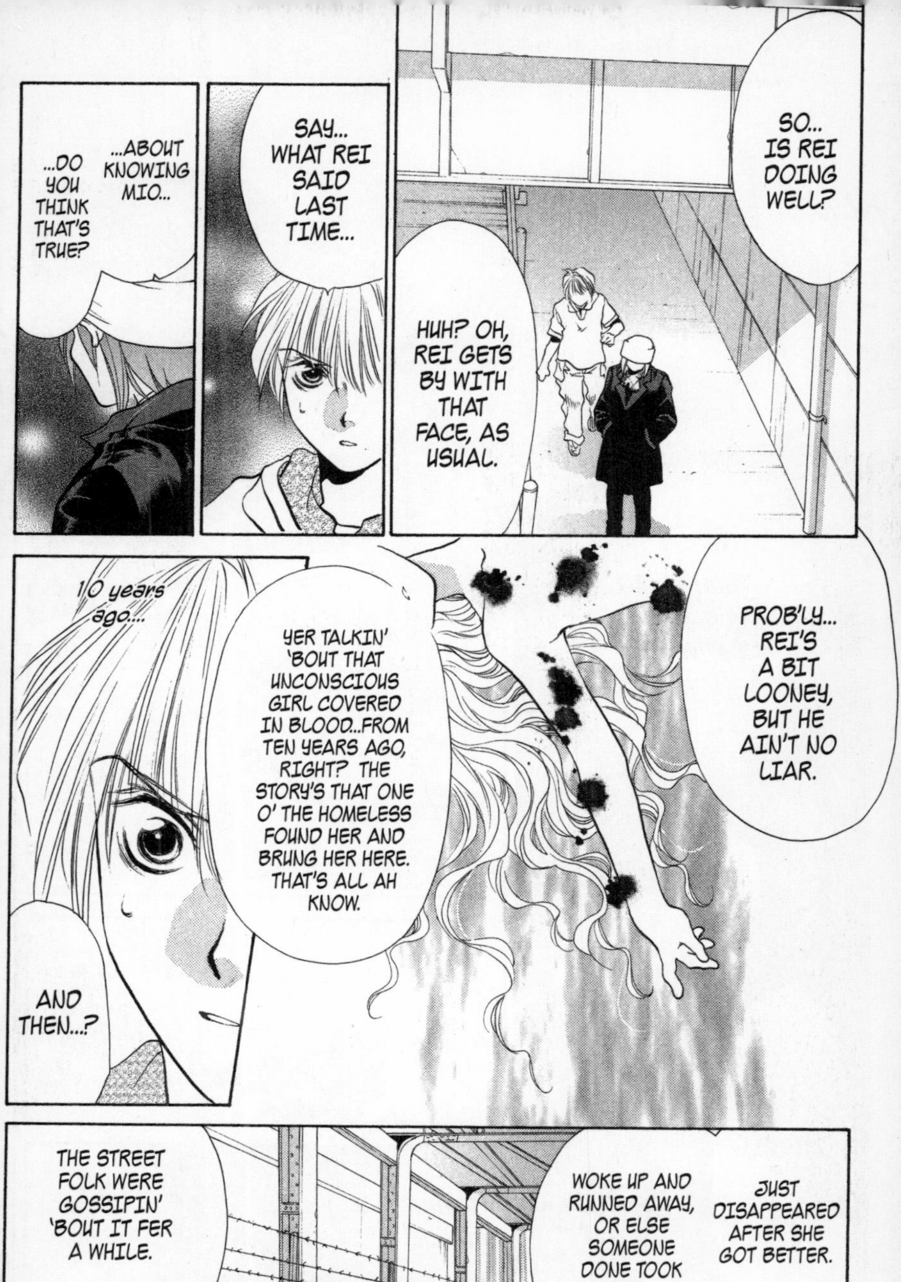
SO... IS REI DOING WELL?
HUH? OH, REI GETS BY WITH THAT FACE, AS USUAL.
SAY... WHAT REI SAID LAST TIME...
...ABOUT KNOWING MIO...
...DO YOU THINK THAT'S TRUE?
PROB'LY... REI'S A BIT LOONEY, BUT HE AIN'T NO LIAR.
YER TALKIN' 'BOUT THAT UNCONSCIOUS GIRL COVERED IN BLOOD...FROM TEN YEARS AGO, RIGHT? THE STORY'S THAT ONE O' THE HOMELESS FOUND HER AND BRUNG HER HERE. THAT'S ALL AH KNOW.
10 years ago....
AND THEN...?
JUST DISAPPEARED AFTER SHE GOT BETTER.
WOKE UP AND RUNNED AWAY, OR ELSE SOMEONE DONE TOOK HER.
THE STREET FOLK WERE GOSSIPIN' 'BOUT IT FER A WHILE.

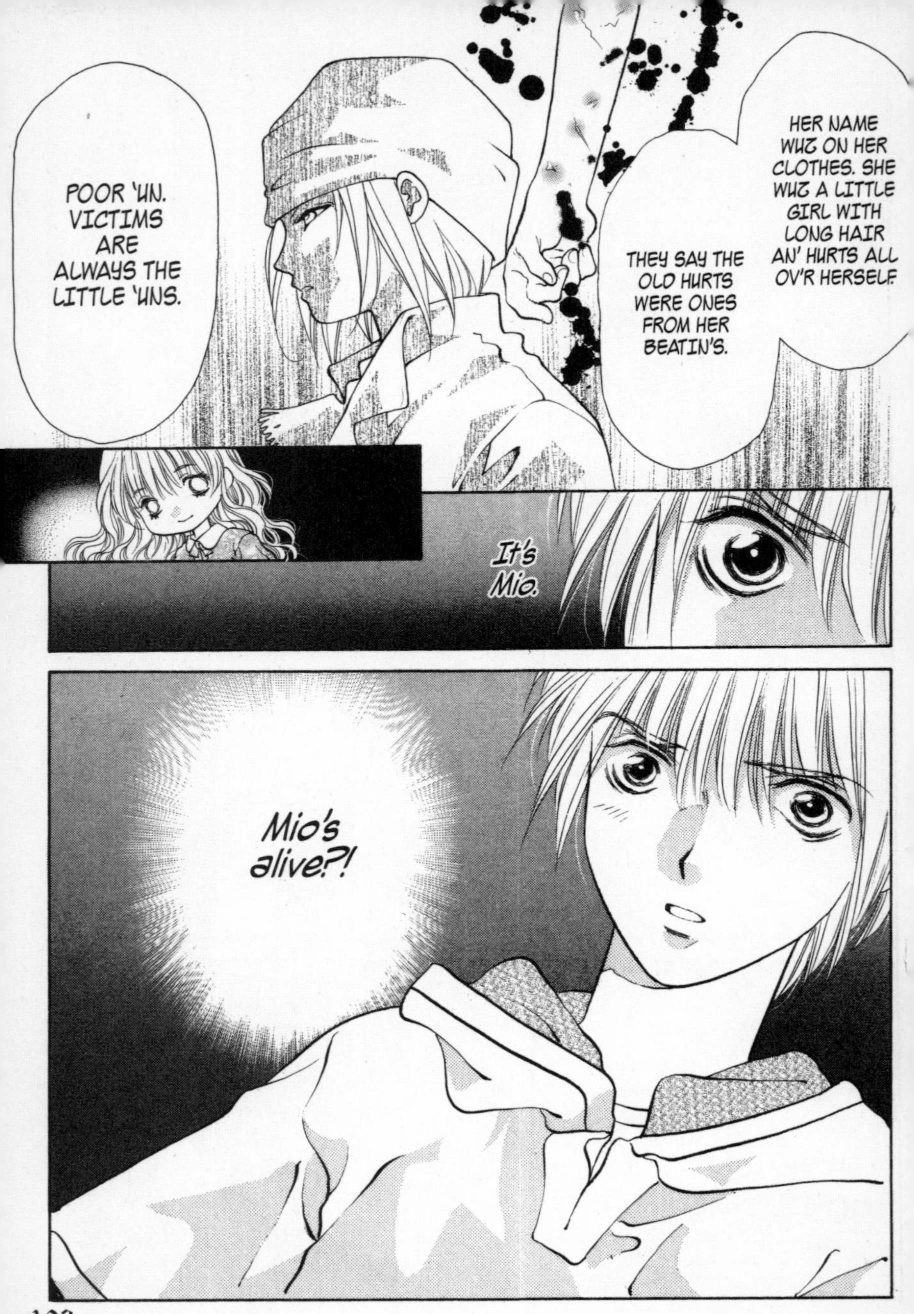
HER NAME WUZ ON HER CLOTHES. SHE WUZ A LITTLE GIRL WITH LONG HAIR AN' HURTS ALL OV'R HERSELF.
THEY SAY THE OLD HURTS WERE ONES FROM HER BEATIN'S.
POOR 'UN. VICTIMS ARE ALWAYS THE LITTLE 'UNS.
It's Mio.
Mio's alive?!

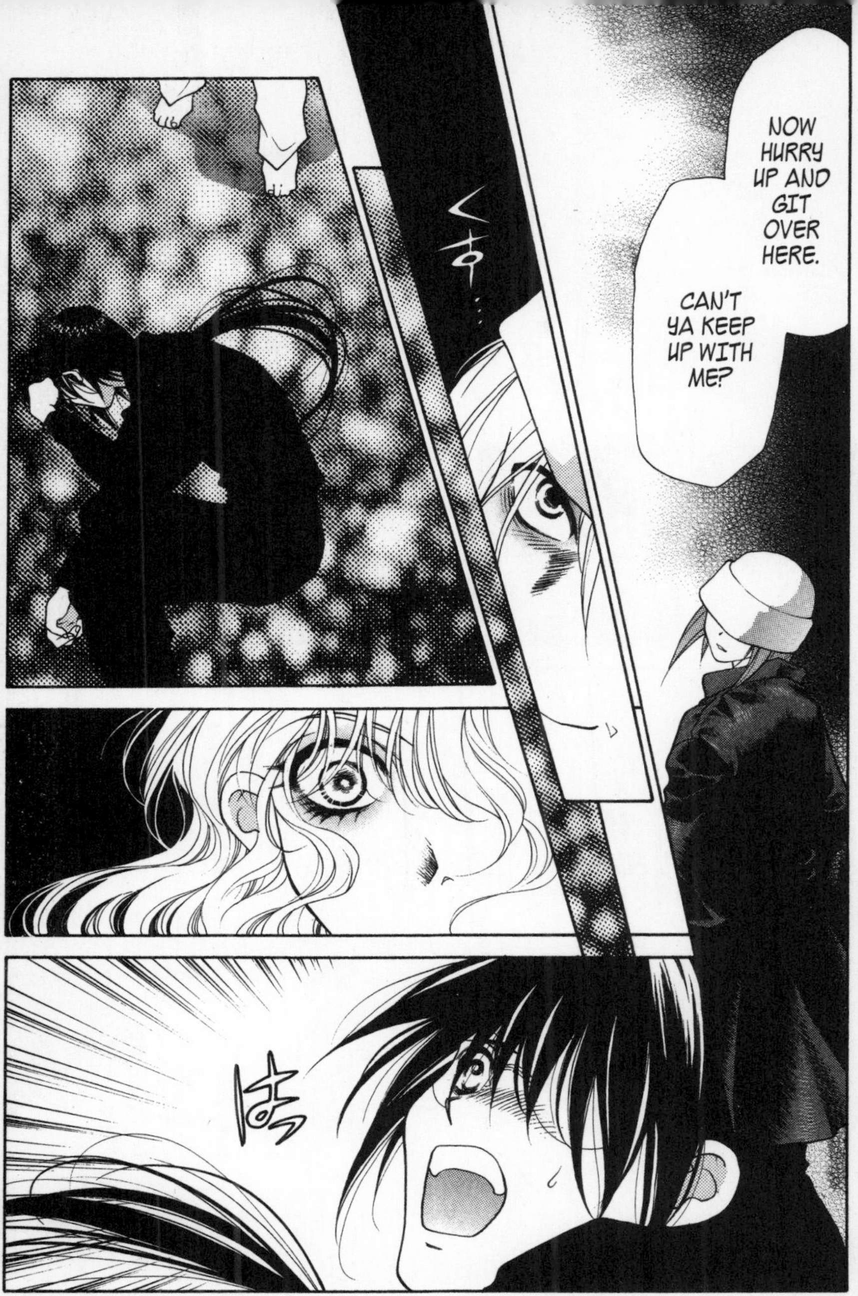

NOW HURRY UP AND GIT OVER HERE.
CAN'T YA KEEP UP WITH ME?
くすっ…
はっ

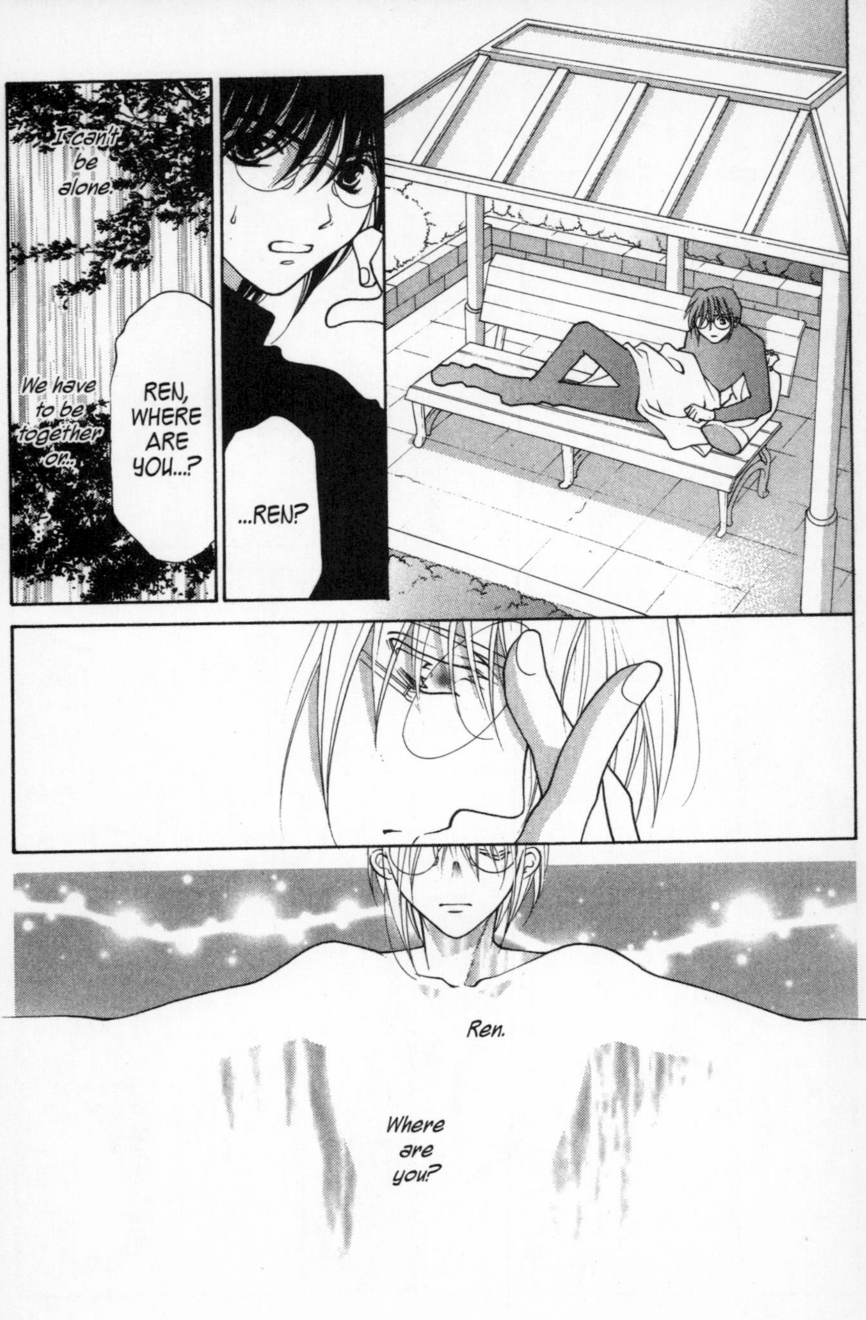
...REN?
I can't be alone.
REN, WHERE ARE YOU...?
We have to be together on...
Ren.
Where are you?

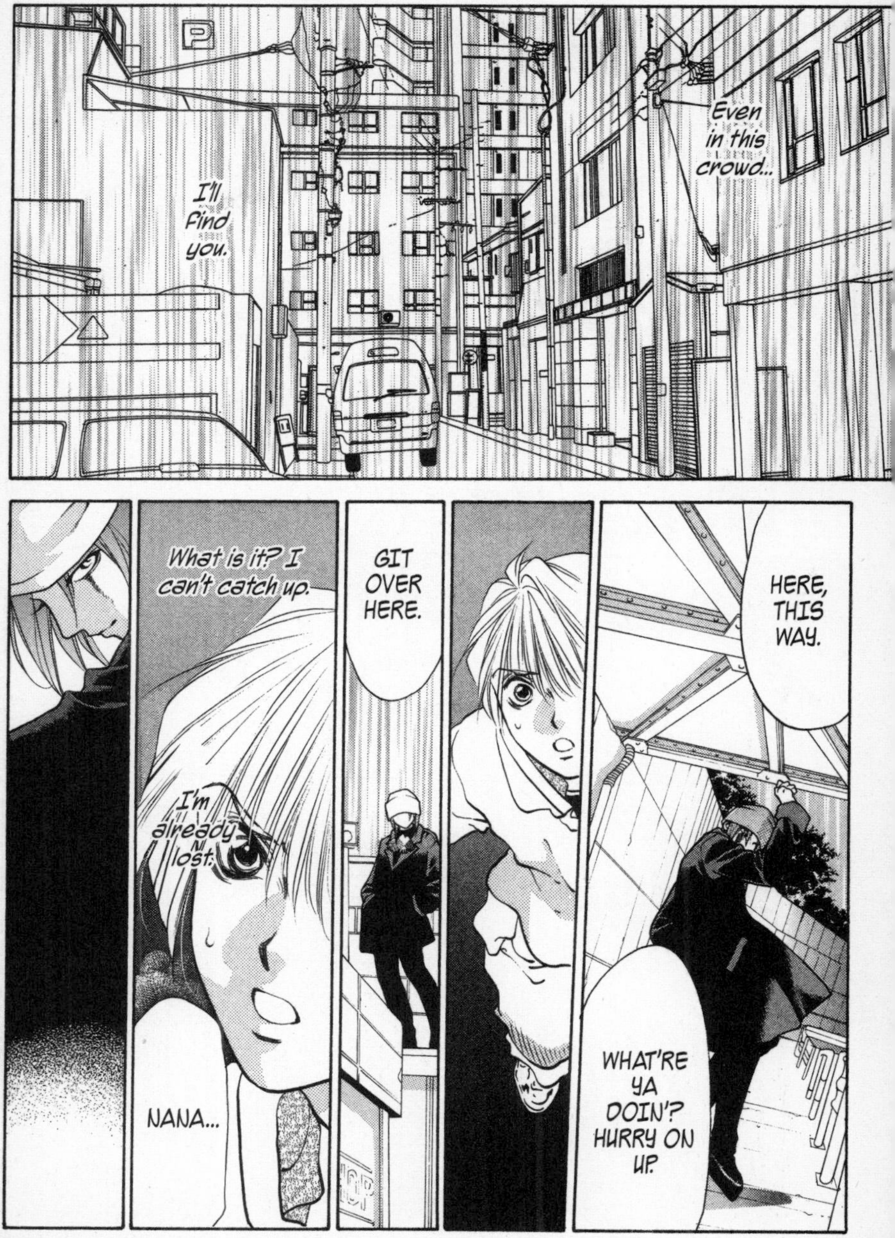
Even in this crowd...
I'll find you.
HERE, THIS WAY.
WHAT'RE YA DOIN'? HURRY ON UP.
GIT OVER HERE.
What is it? I can't catch up.
I'm already lost.
NANA...

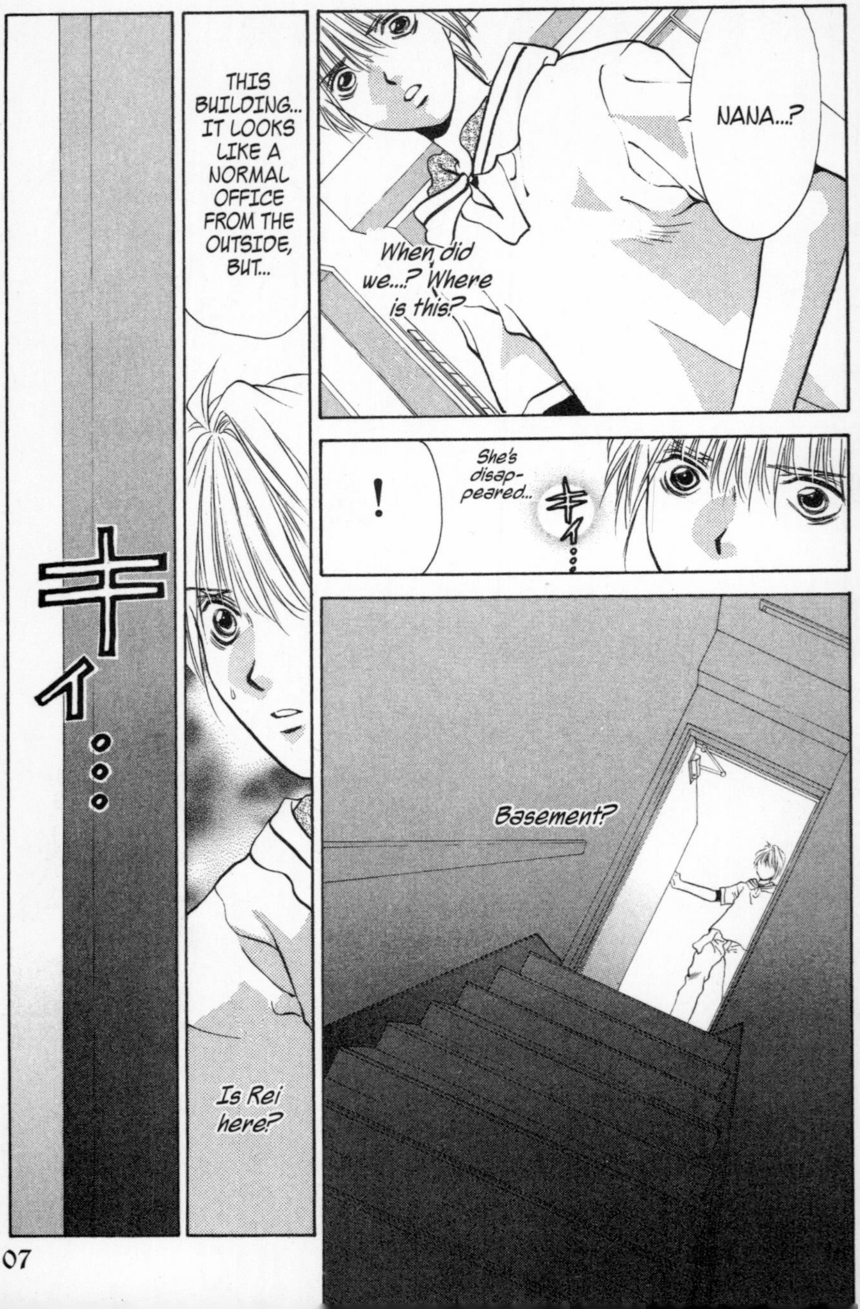

NANA...?
When did we...? Where is this?
!
She's disappeared...
キィ...
Basement?
THIS BUILDING... IT LOOKS LIKE A NORMAL OFFICE FROM THE OUTSIDE, BUT...
Is Rei here?
キィ...

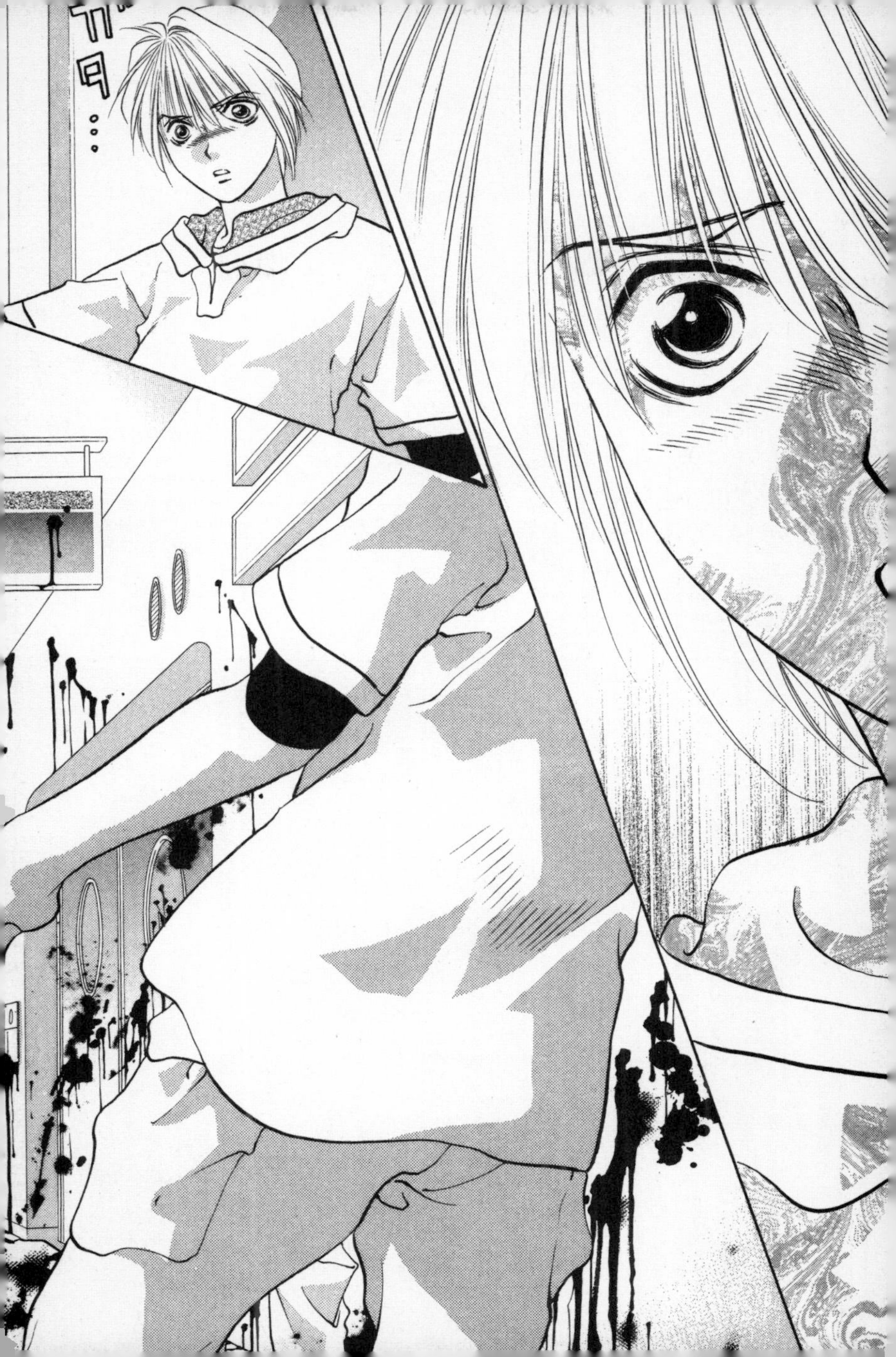
ガタ…

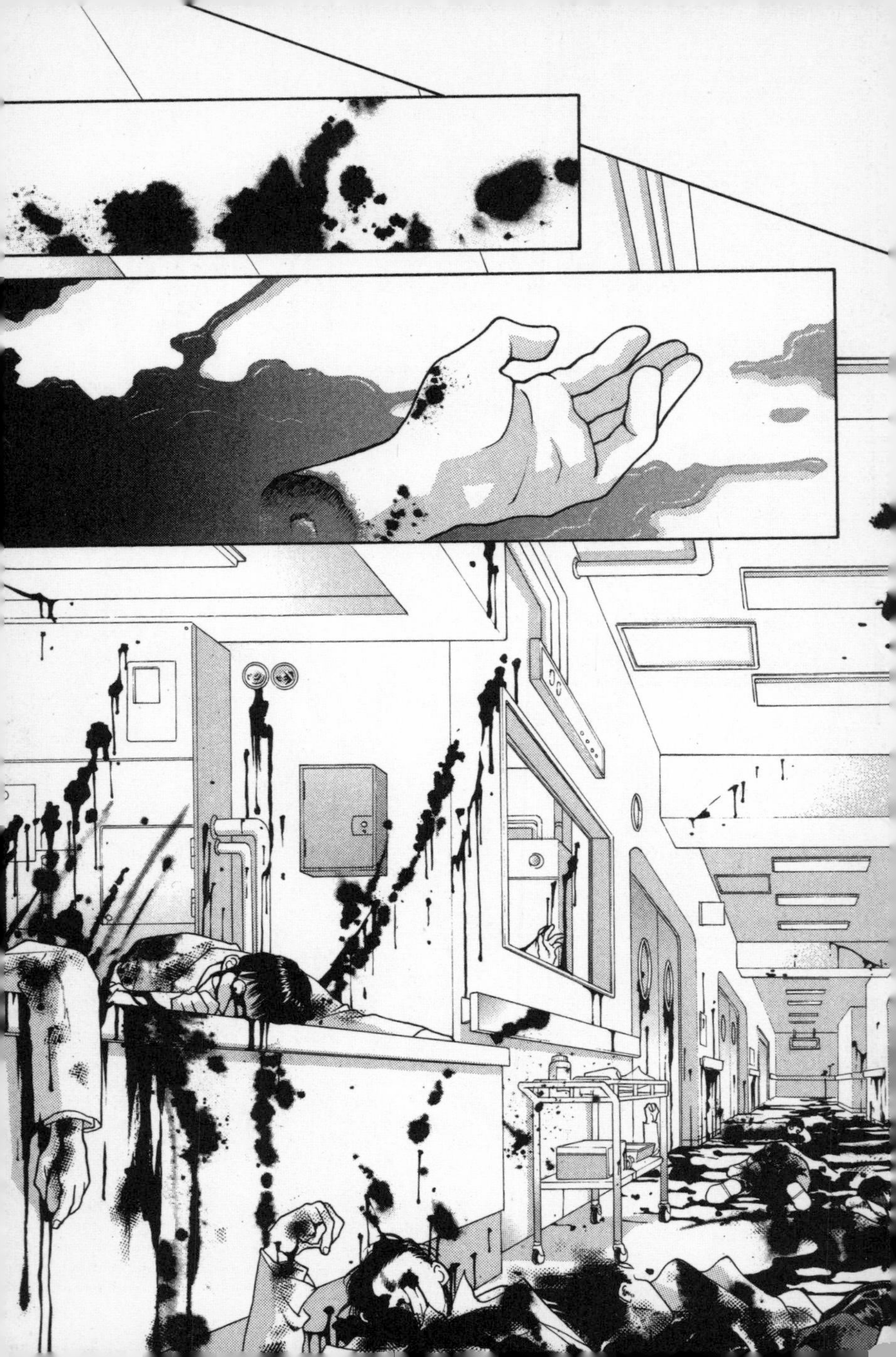

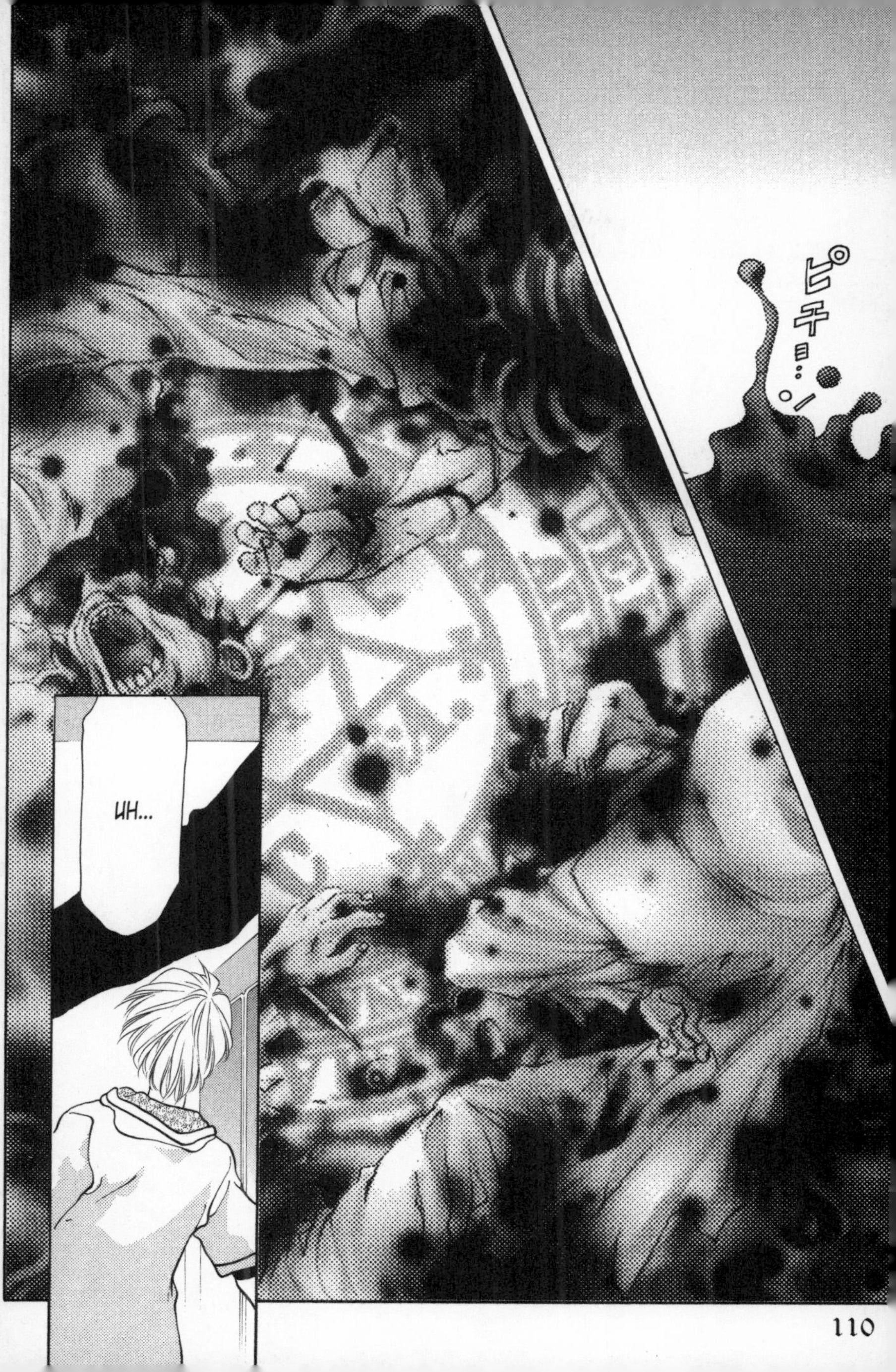
ピチョ・・ン
UH...

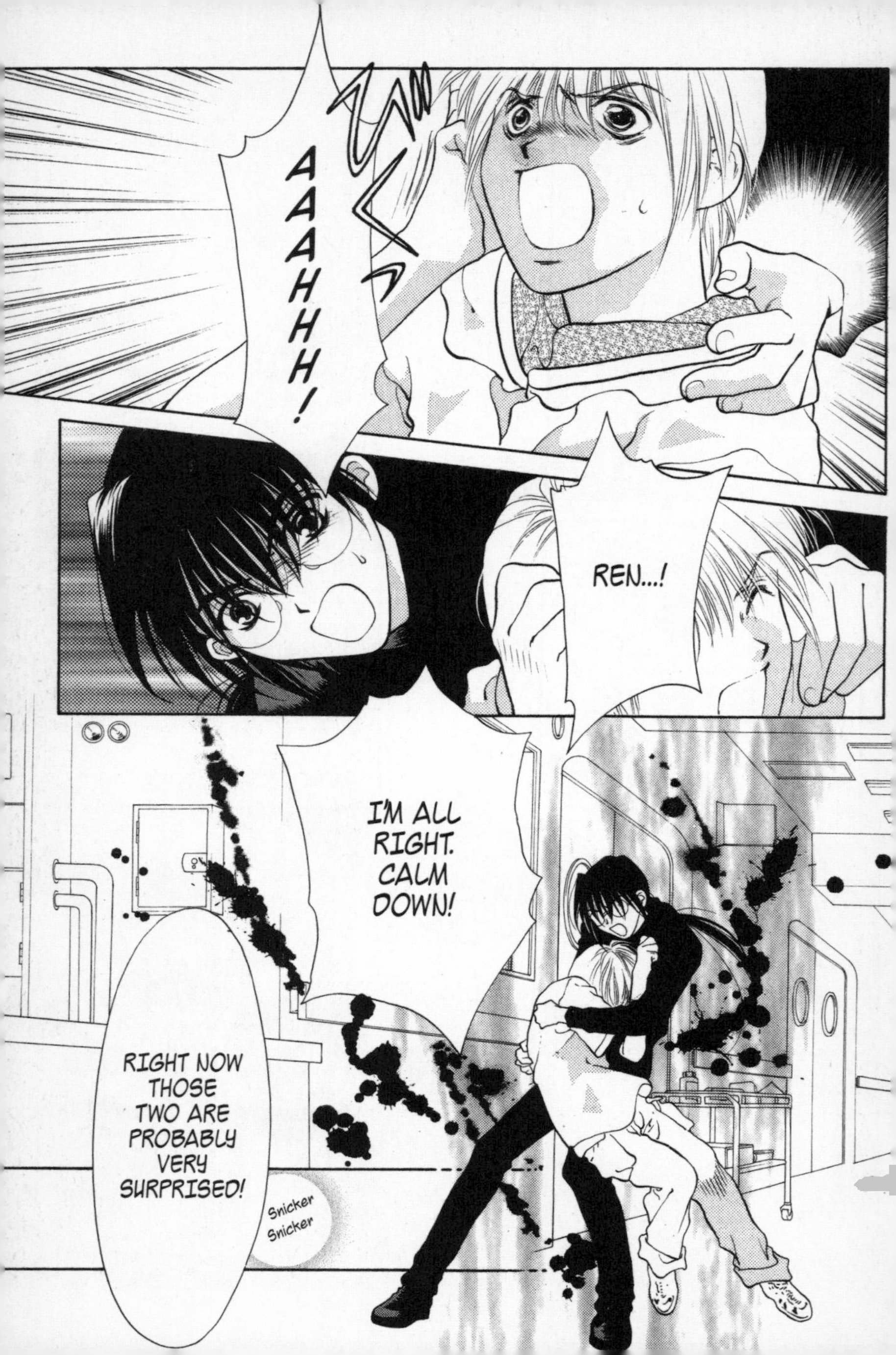
AAAAHHH!
REN...!
I'M ALL RIGHT. CALM DOWN!
RIGHT NOW THOSE TWO ARE PROBABLY VERY SURPRISED!
Snicker Snicker

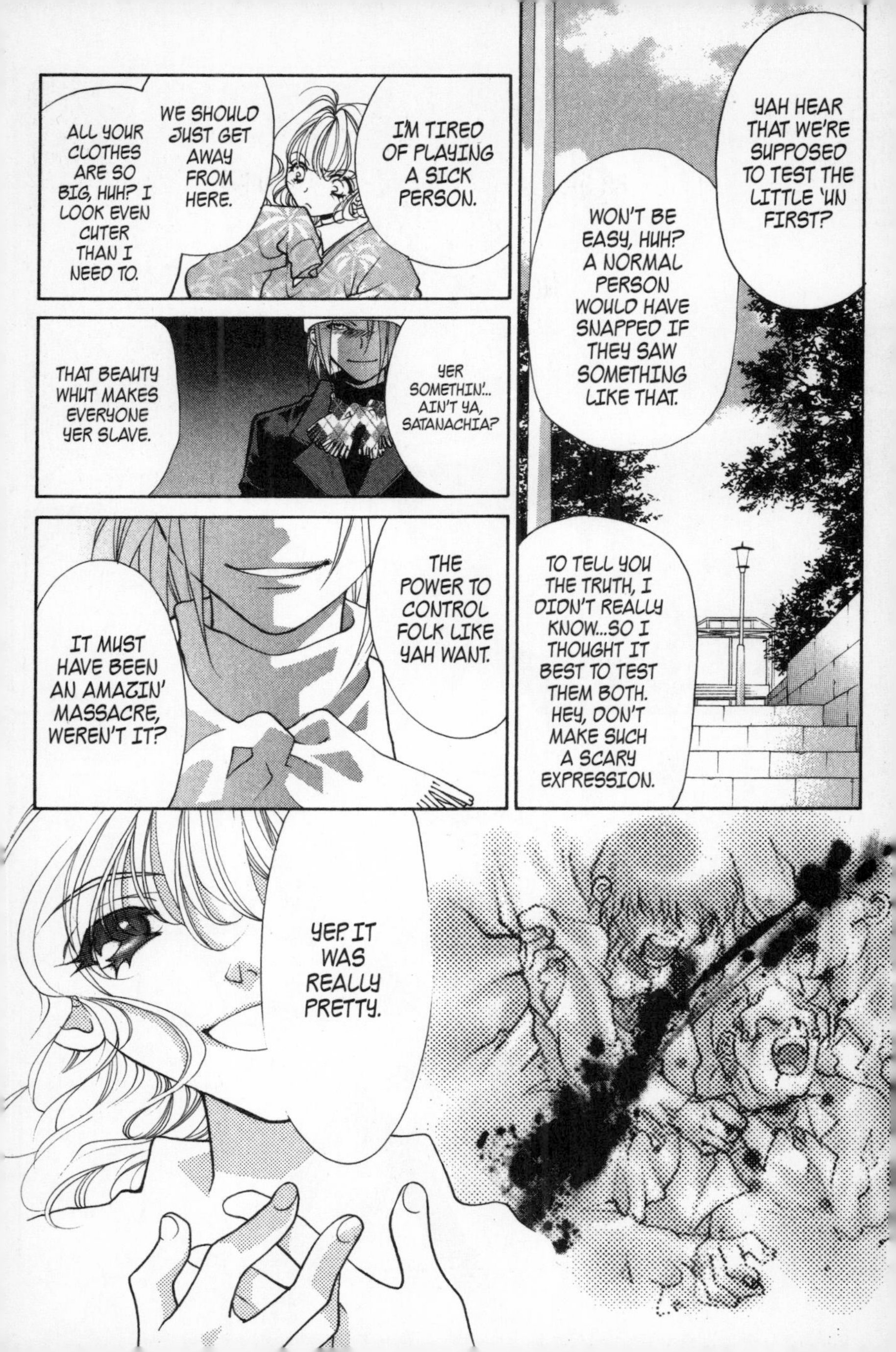

YAH HEAR THAT WE'RE SUPPOSED TO TEST THE LITTLE 'UN FIRST?
WON'T BE EASY, HUH? A NORMAL PERSON WOULD HAVE SNAPPED IF THEY SAW SOMETHING LIKE THAT.
TO TELL YOU THE TRUTH, I DIDN'T REALLY KNOW...SO I THOUGHT IT BEST TO TEST THEM BOTH. HEY, DON'T MAKE SUCH A SCARY EXPRESSION.
I'M TIRED OF PLAYING A SICK PERSON.
WE SHOULD JUST GET AWAY FROM HERE.
ALL YOUR CLOTHES ARE SO BIG, HUH? I LOOK EVEN CUTER THAN I NEED TO.
YER SOMETHIN'... AIN'T YA, SATANACHIA?
THAT BEAUTY WHUT MAKES EVERYONE YER SLAVE.
THE POWER TO CONTROL FOLK LIKE YAH WANT.
IT MUST HAVE BEEN AN AMAZIN' MASSACRE, WEREN'T IT?
YEP. IT WAS REALLY PRETTY.

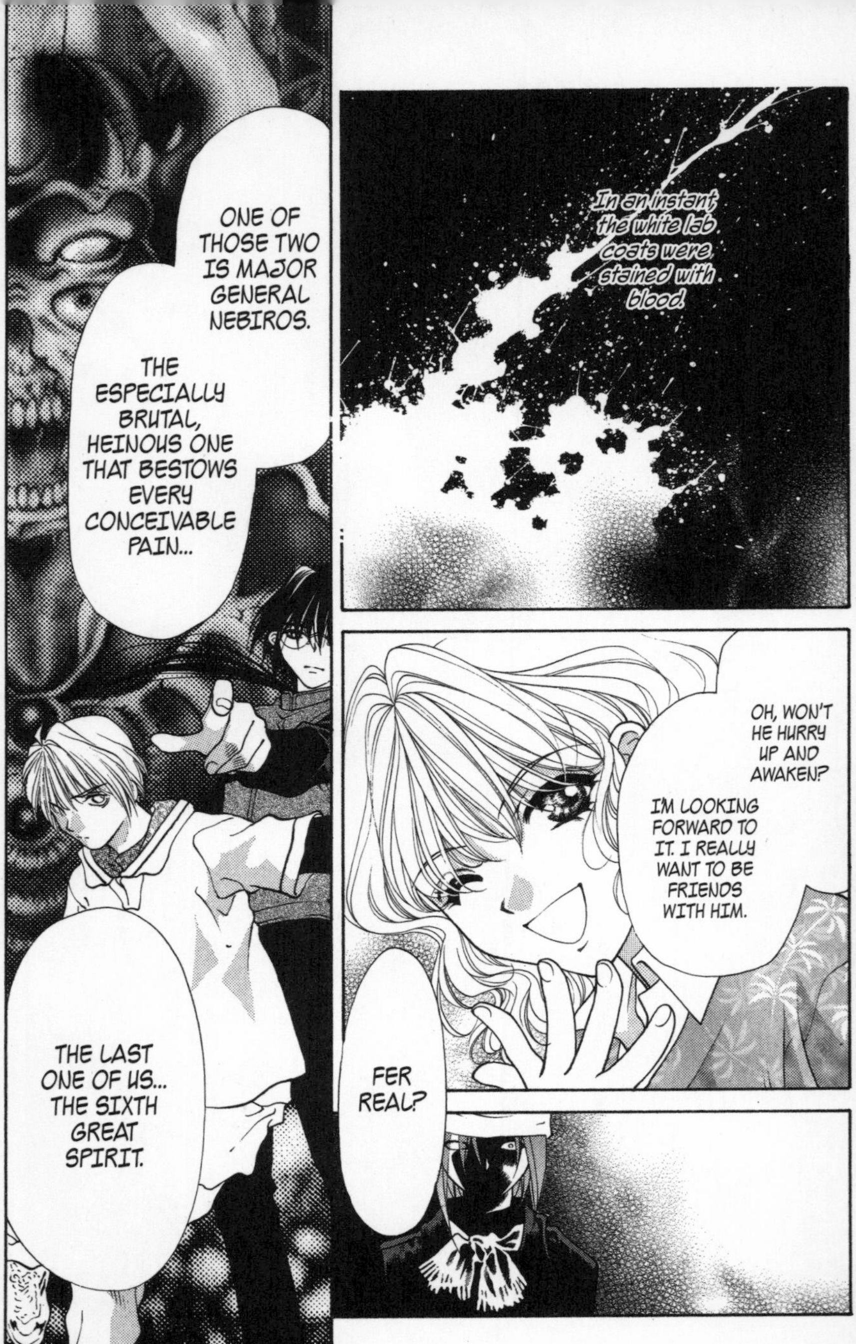
In an instant, the white lab coats were stained with blood.
OH, WON'T HE HURRY UP AND AWAKEN?
I'M LOOKING FORWARD TO IT. I REALLY WANT TO BE FRIENDS WITH HIM.
FER REAL?
ONE OF THOSE TWO IS MAJOR GENERAL NEBIROS.
THE ESPECIALLY BRUTAL, HEINOUS ONE THAT BESTOWS EVERY CONCEIVABLE PAIN...
THE LAST ONE OF US... THE SIXTH GREAT SPIRIT.

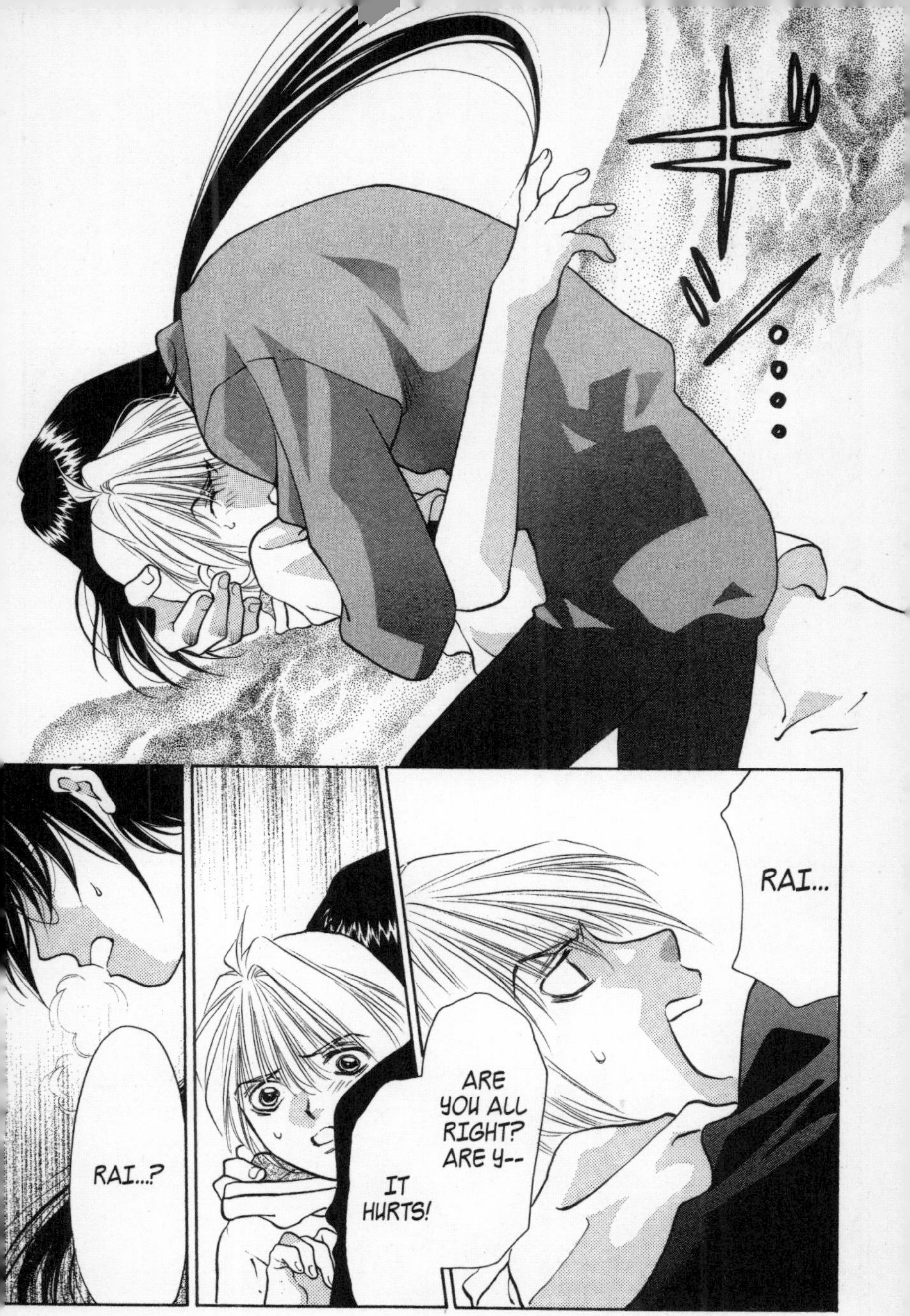
RAI...
ARE YOU ALL RIGHT? ARE Y--
IT HURTS!
RAI...?

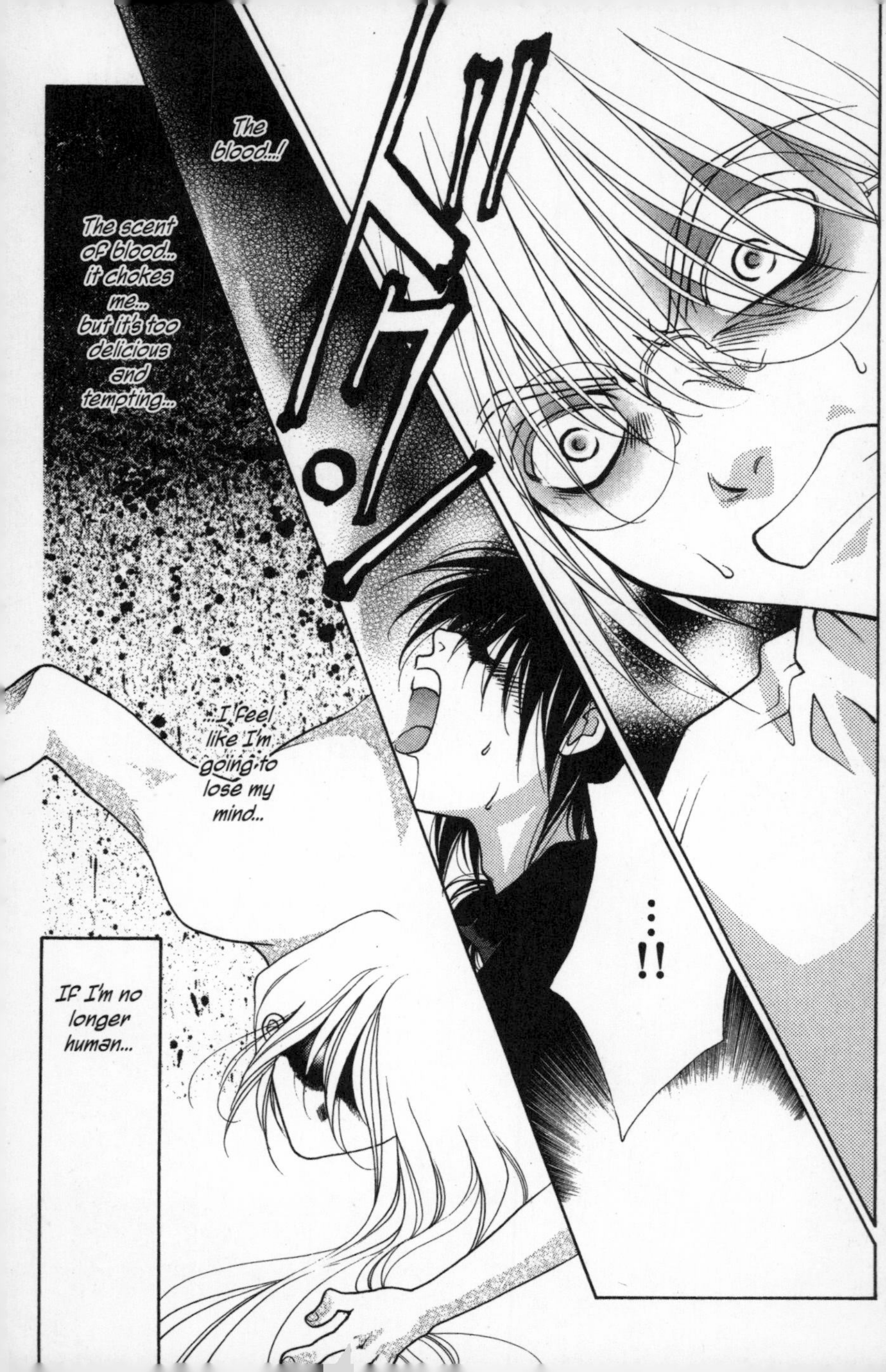
...!!
The blood..!
The scent of blood.. it chokes me... but it's too delicious and tempting...
...I feel like I'm going to lose my mind...
If I'm no longer human...

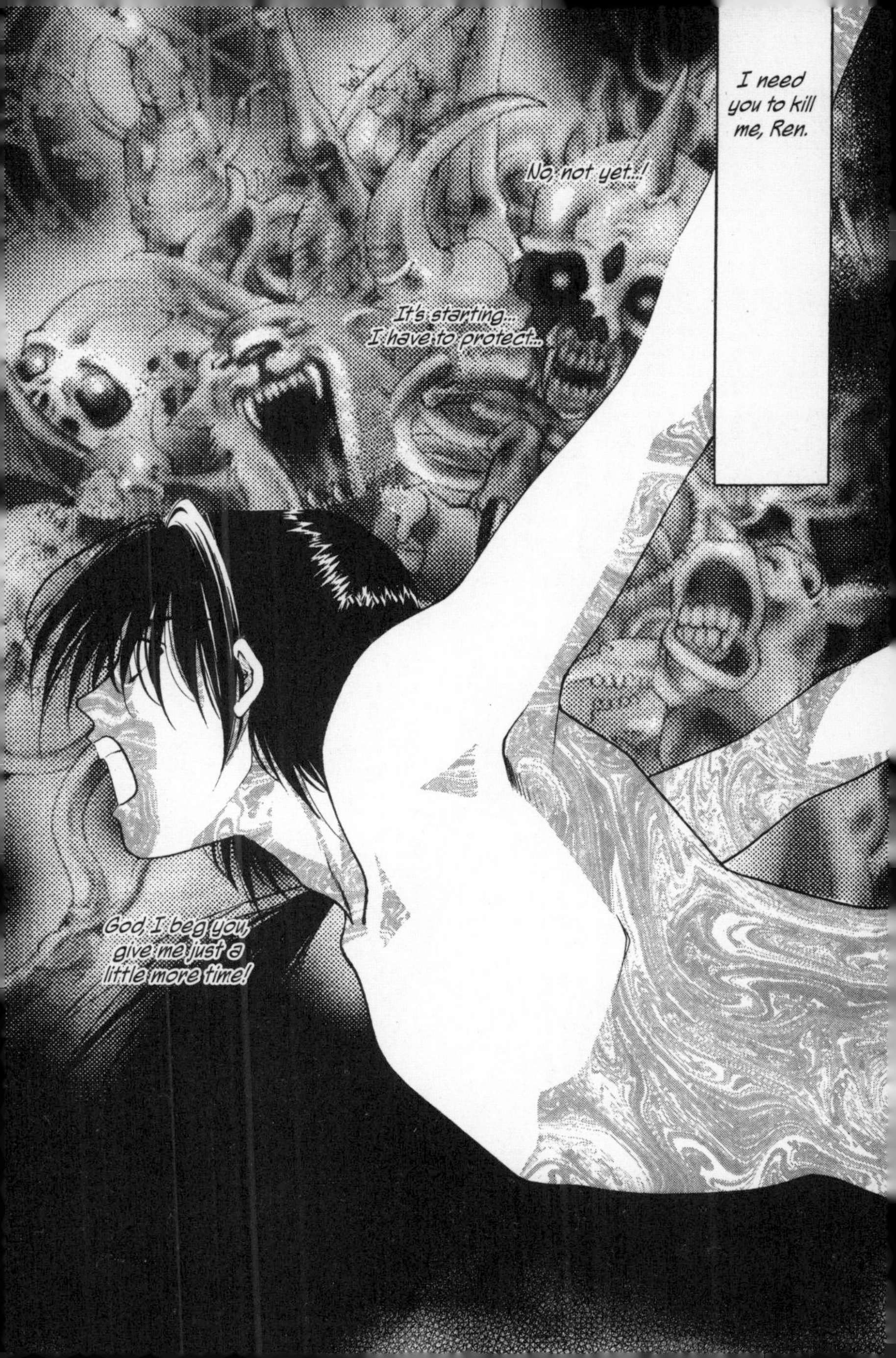
I need you to kill me, Ren.
No, not yet...!
It's starting... I have to protect...
God, I beg you, give me just a little more time!

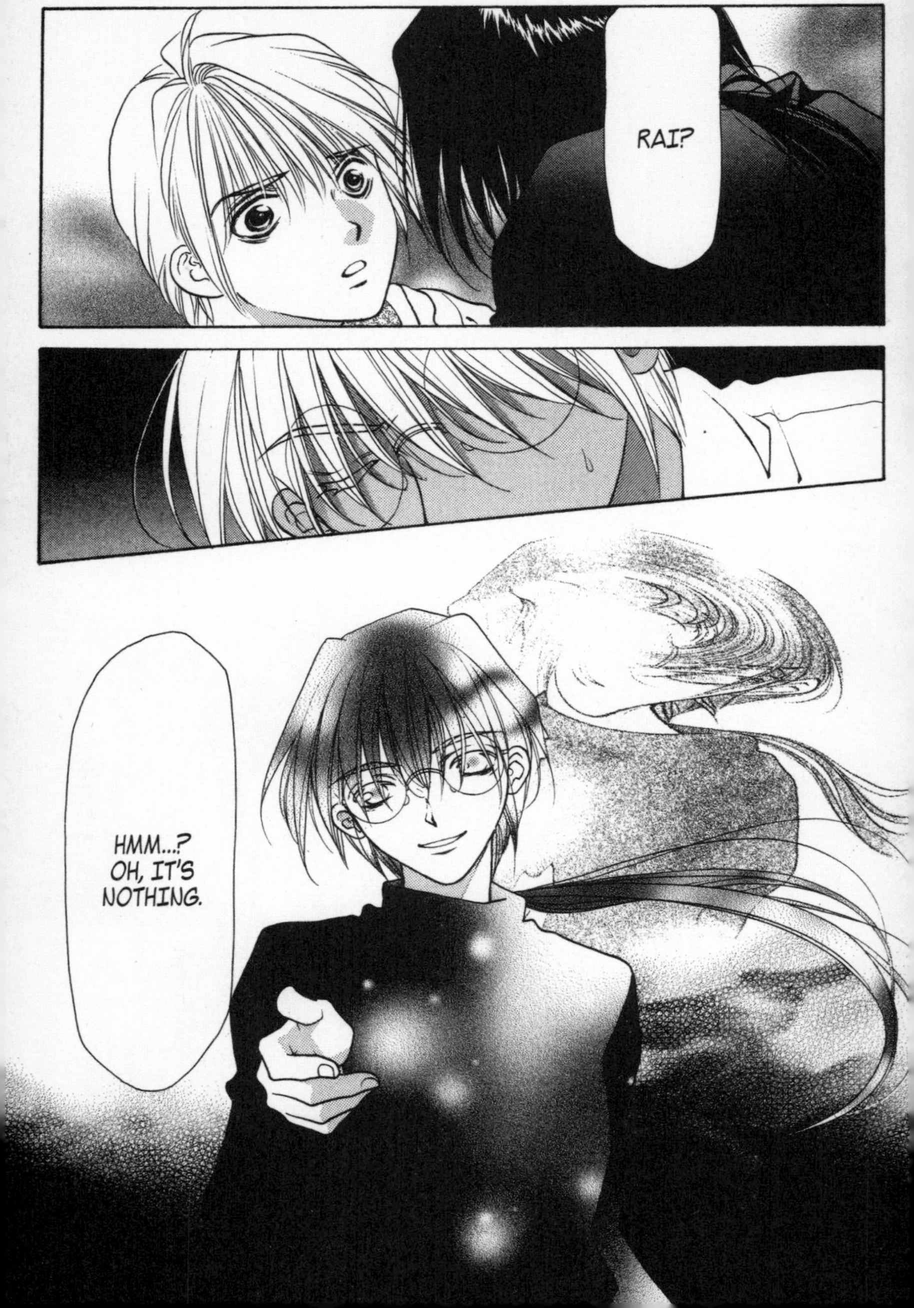
RAI?
HMM...? OH, IT'S NOTHING.

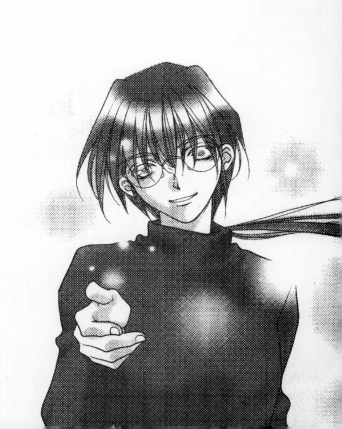

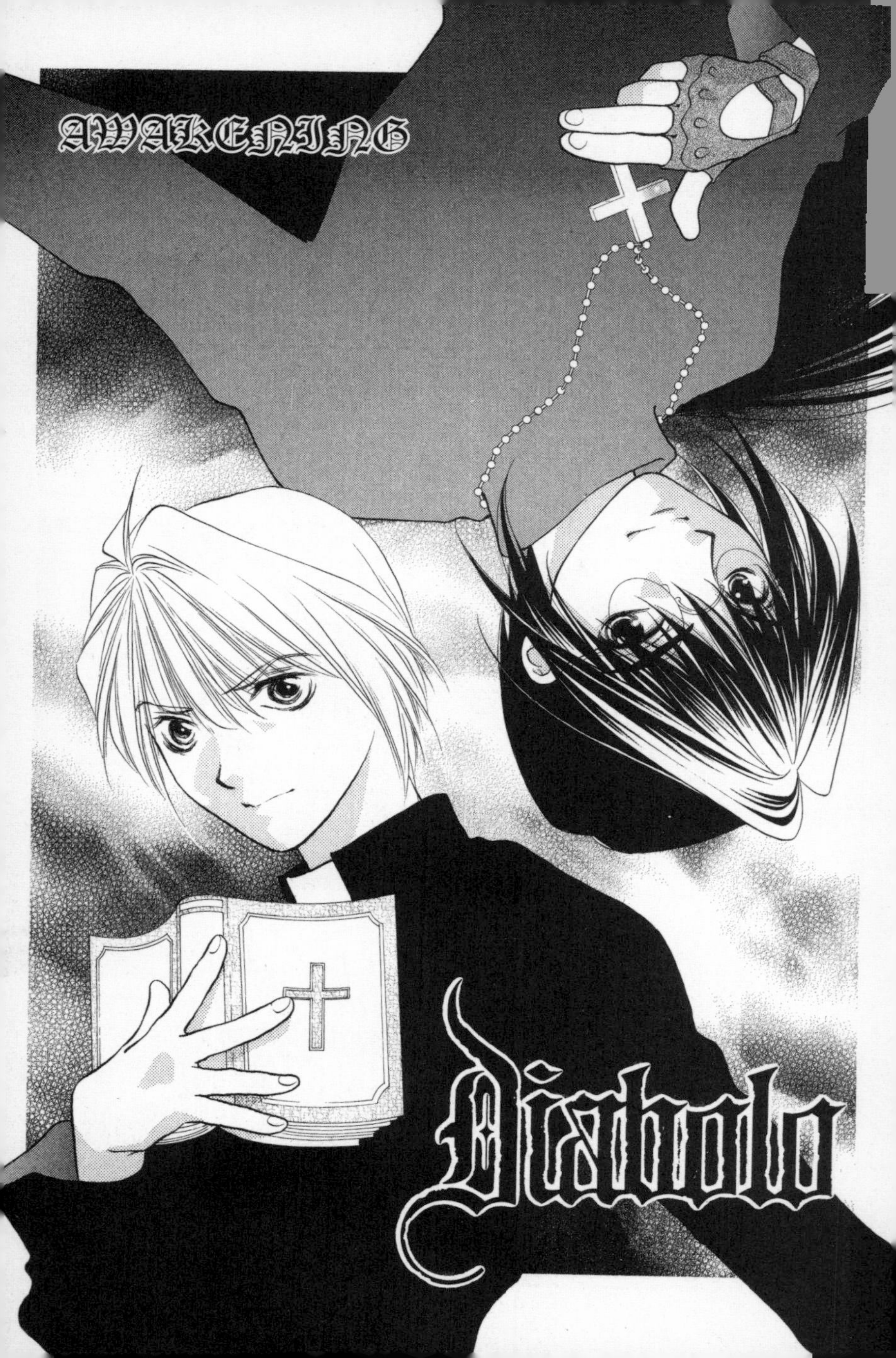
AWAKENING
Diabolo

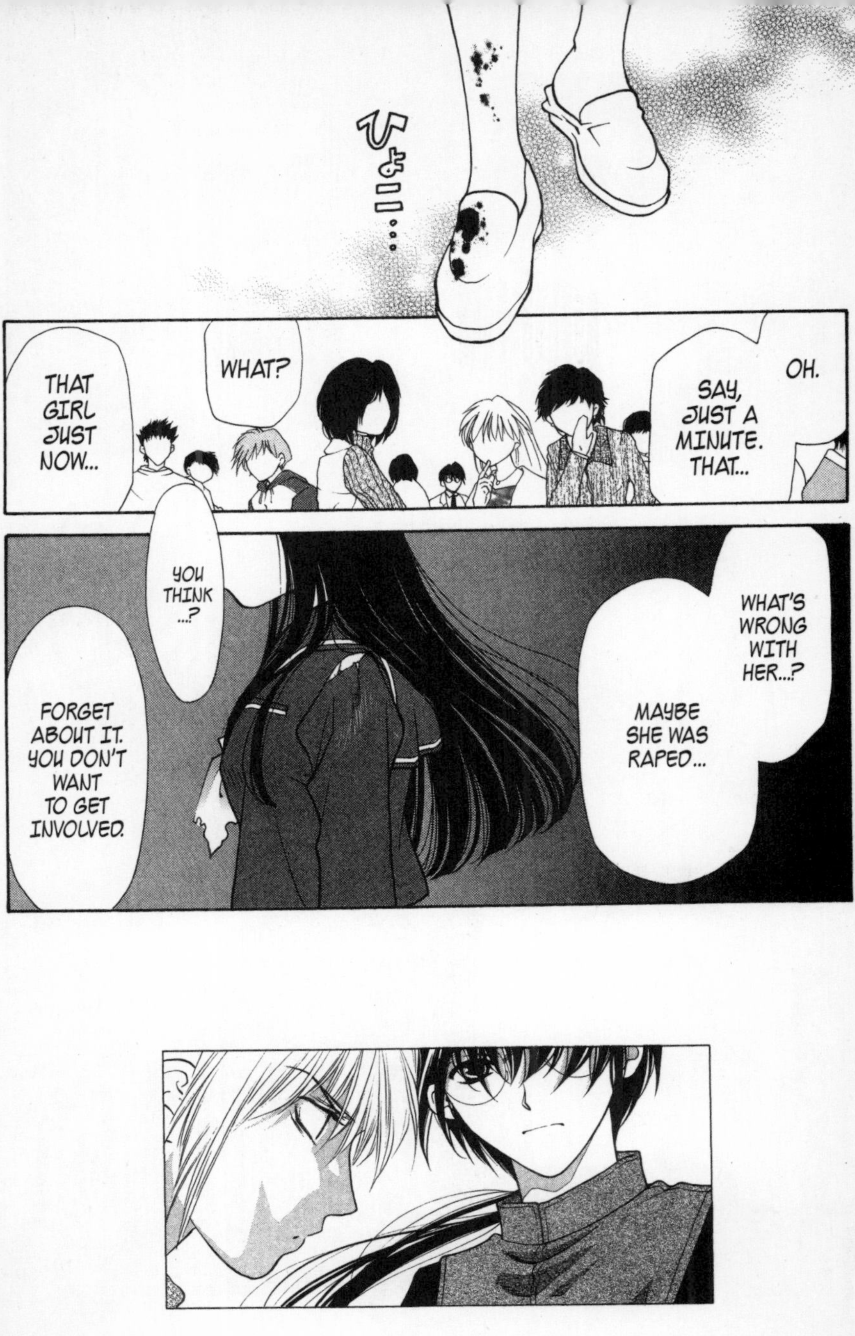
ひょーー…
OH.
SAY, JUST A MINUTE. THAT...
WHAT?
THAT GIRL JUST NOW...
WHAT'S WRONG WITH HER...?
MAYBE SHE WAS RAPED...
YOU THINK ...?
FORGET ABOUT IT. YOU DON'T WANT TO GET INVOLVED.

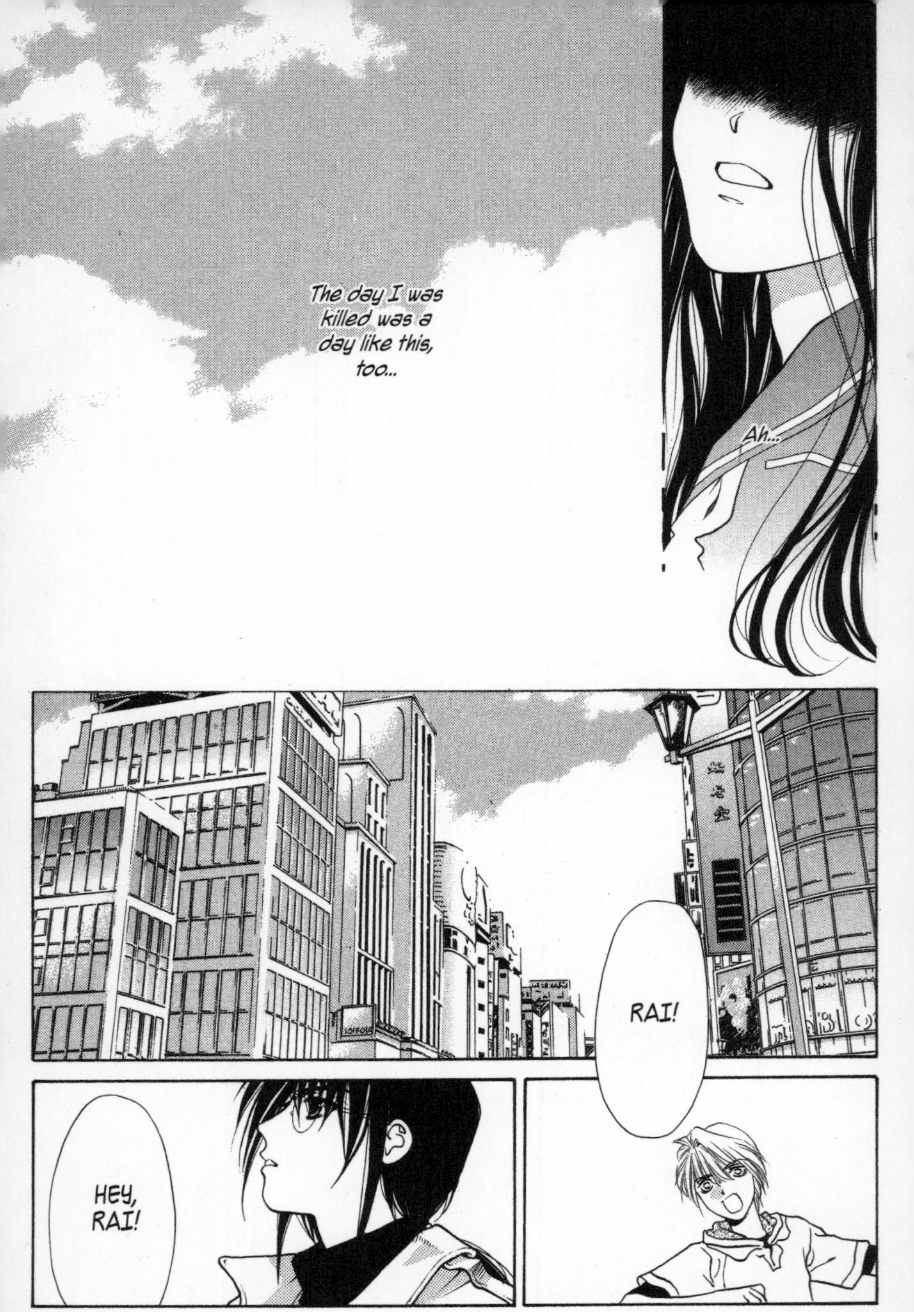

Ah...
The day I was killed was a day like this, too...
RAI!
HEY, RAI!

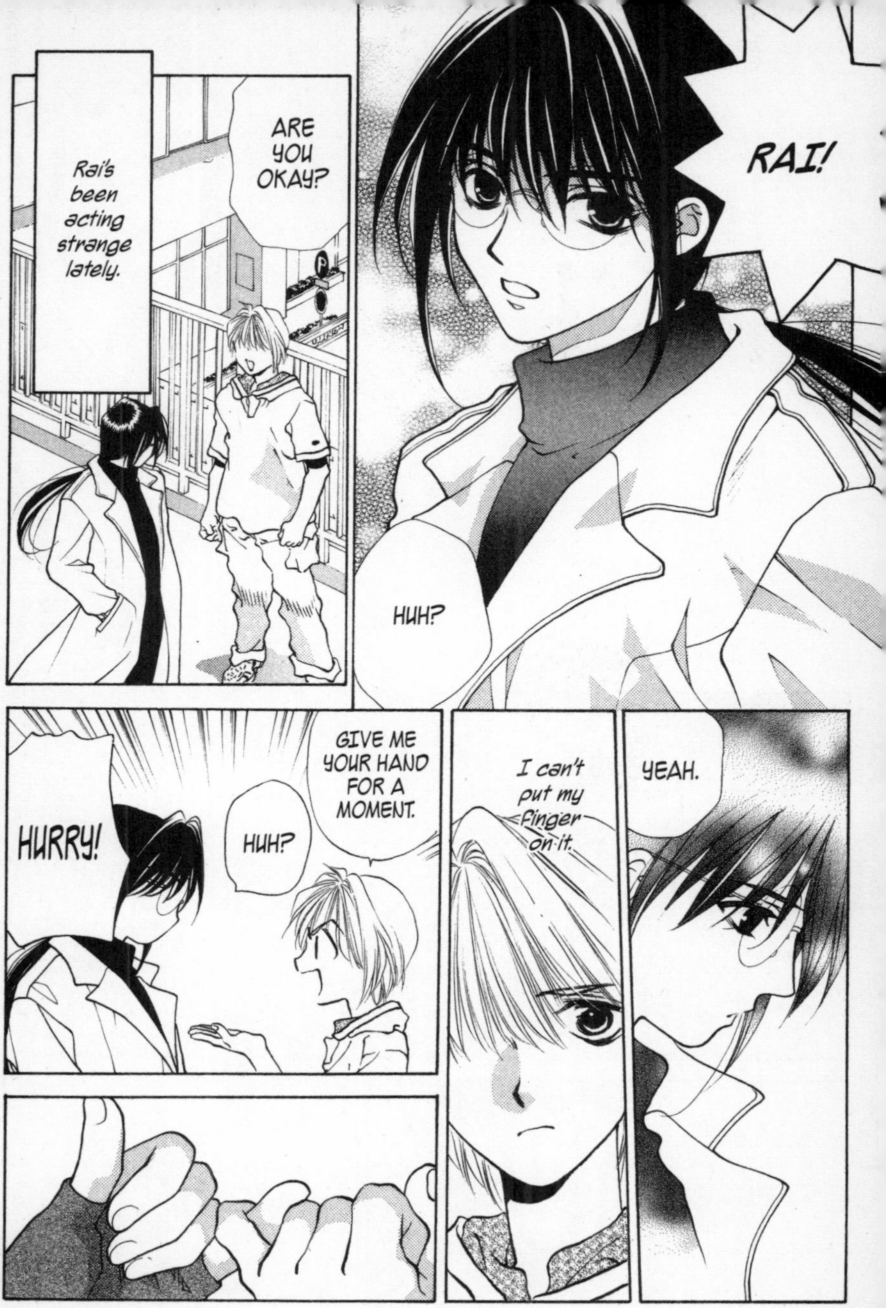
RAI!
HUH?
ARE YOU OKAY?
Rai's been acting strange lately.
YEAH.
I can't put my finger on it.
GIVE ME YOUR HAND FOR A MOMENT.
HUH?
HURRY!

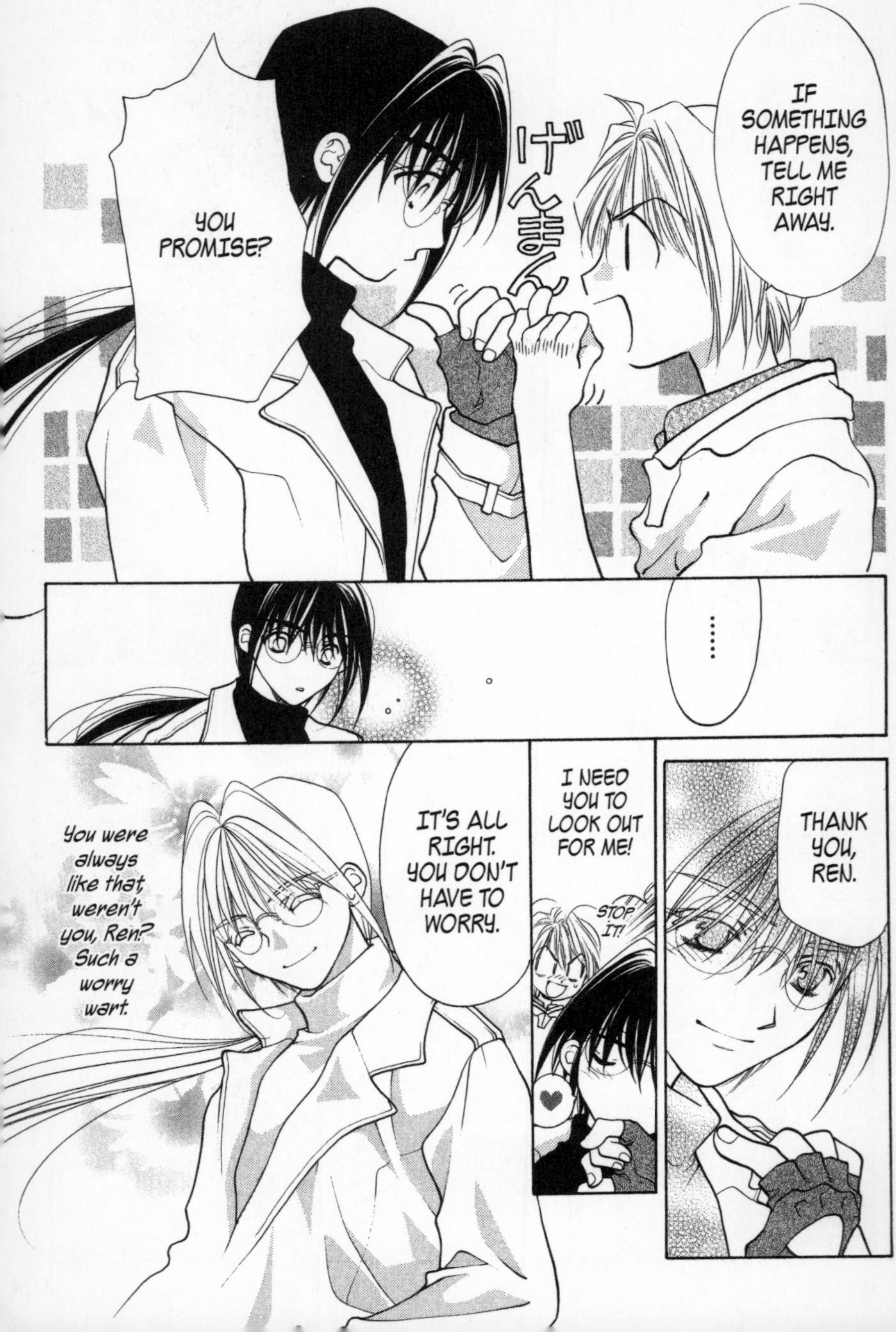

IF SOMETHING HAPPENS, TELL ME RIGHT AWAY.
げんまん
YOU PROMISE?
......
THANK YOU, REN.
I NEED YOU TO LOOK OUT FOR ME!
STOP IT!
IT'S ALL RIGHT. YOU DON'T HAVE TO WORRY.
You were always like that, weren't you, Ren? Such a worry wart.

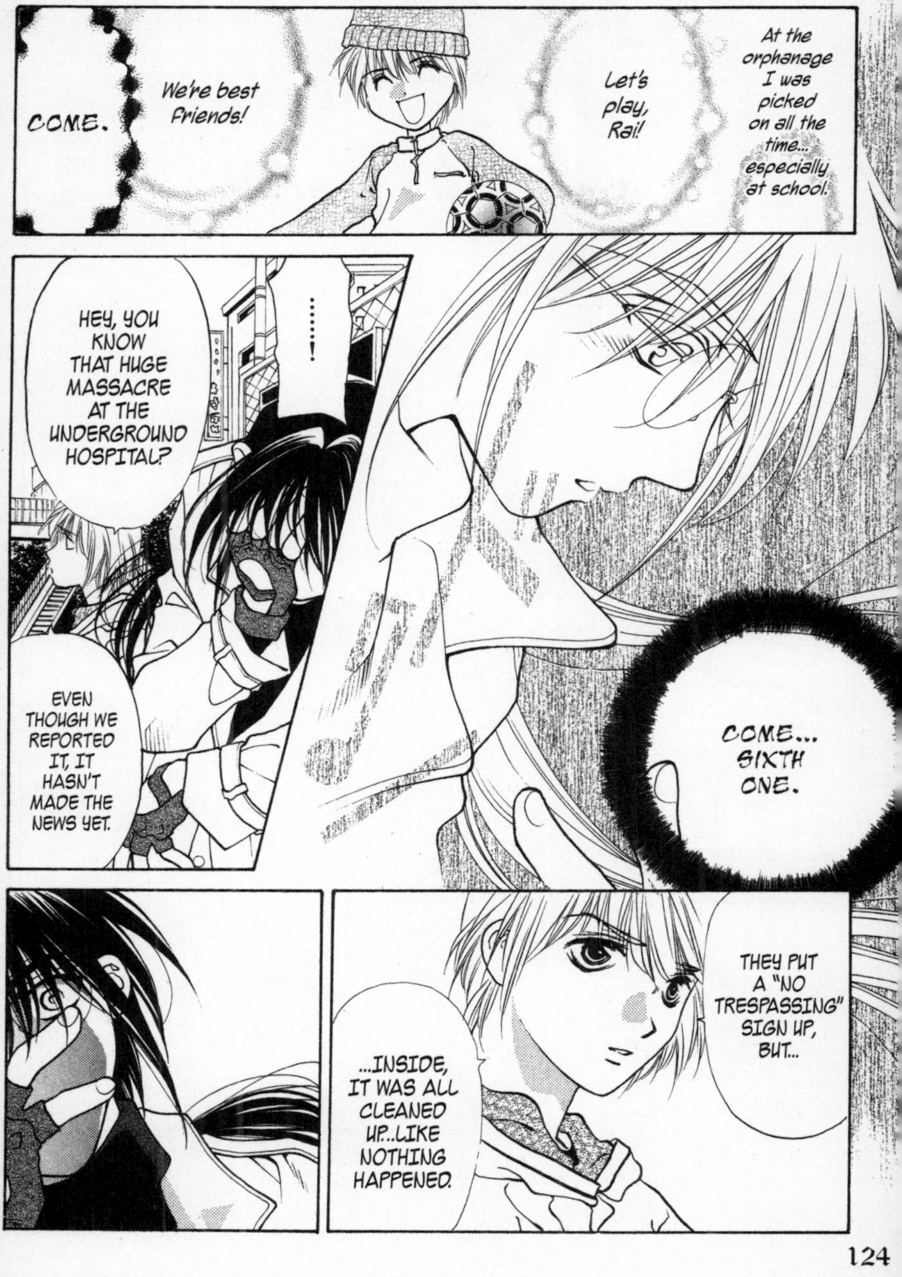
At the orphanage I was picked on all the time... especially at school.
Let's play, Rai!
We're best friends!
COME.
COME... SIXTH ONE.
......!
HEY, YOU KNOW THAT HUGE MASSACRE AT THE UNDERGROUND HOSPITAL?
EVEN THOUGH WE REPORTED IT, IT HASN'T MADE THE NEWS YET.
THEY PUT A "NO TRESPASSING" SIGN UP, BUT...
...INSIDE, IT WAS ALL CLEANED UP...LIKE NOTHING HAPPENED.

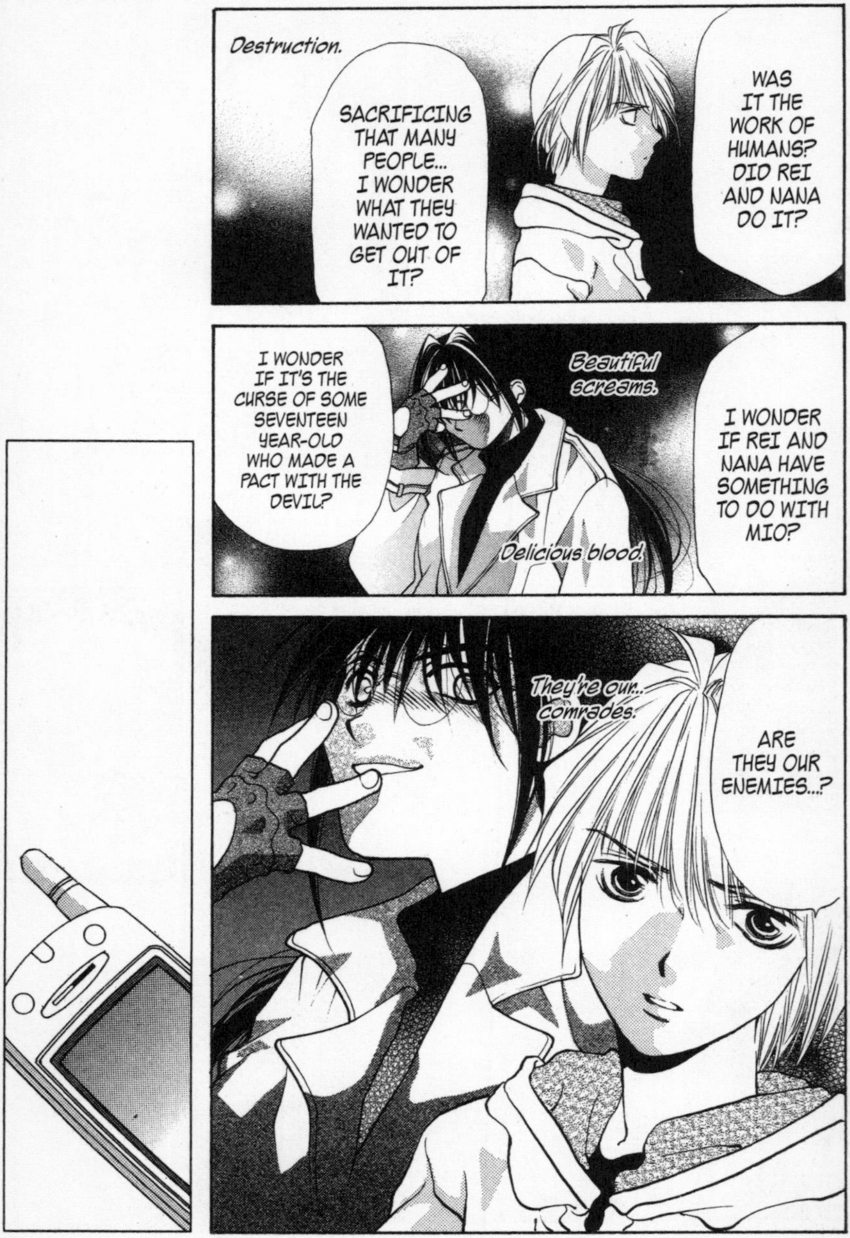
WAS IT THE WORK OF HUMANS? DID REI AND NANA DO IT?
Destruction.
SACRIFICING THAT MANY PEOPLE... I WONDER WHAT THEY WANTED TO GET OUT OF IT?
I WONDER IF REI AND NANA HAVE SOMETHING TO DO WITH MIO?
Beautiful screams.
I WONDER IF IT'S THE CURSE OF SOME SEVENTEEN YEAR-OLD WHO MADE A PACT WITH THE DEVIL?
Delicious blood.
ARE THEY OUR ENEMIES...?
They're our... comrades.

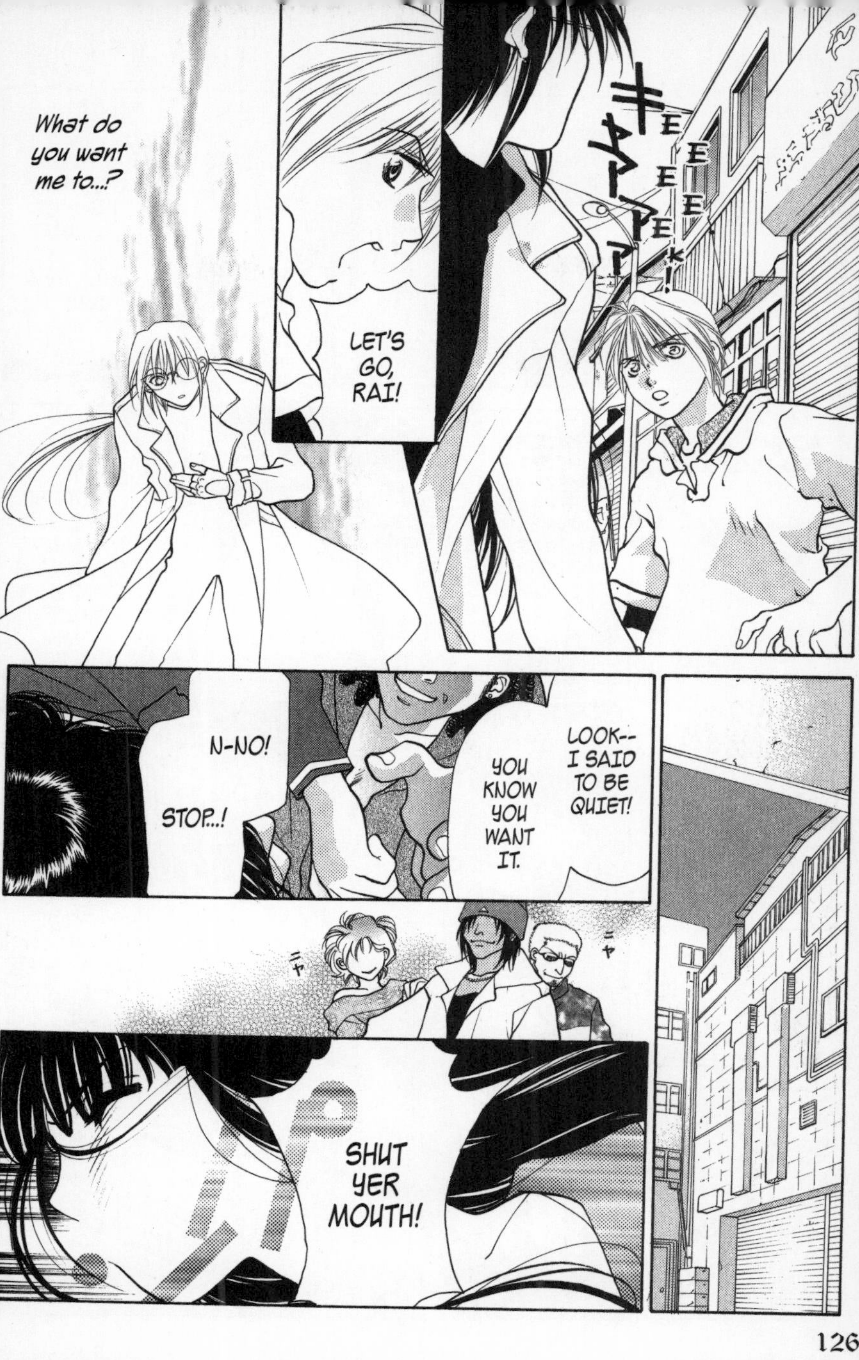
EEEEEEK!
キャーッ
LET'S GO, RAI!
What do you want me to...?
LOOK-- I SAID TO BE QUIET!
YOU KNOW YOU WANT IT.
N-NO!
STOP...!
ニャ
ニャ
SHUT YER MOUTH!

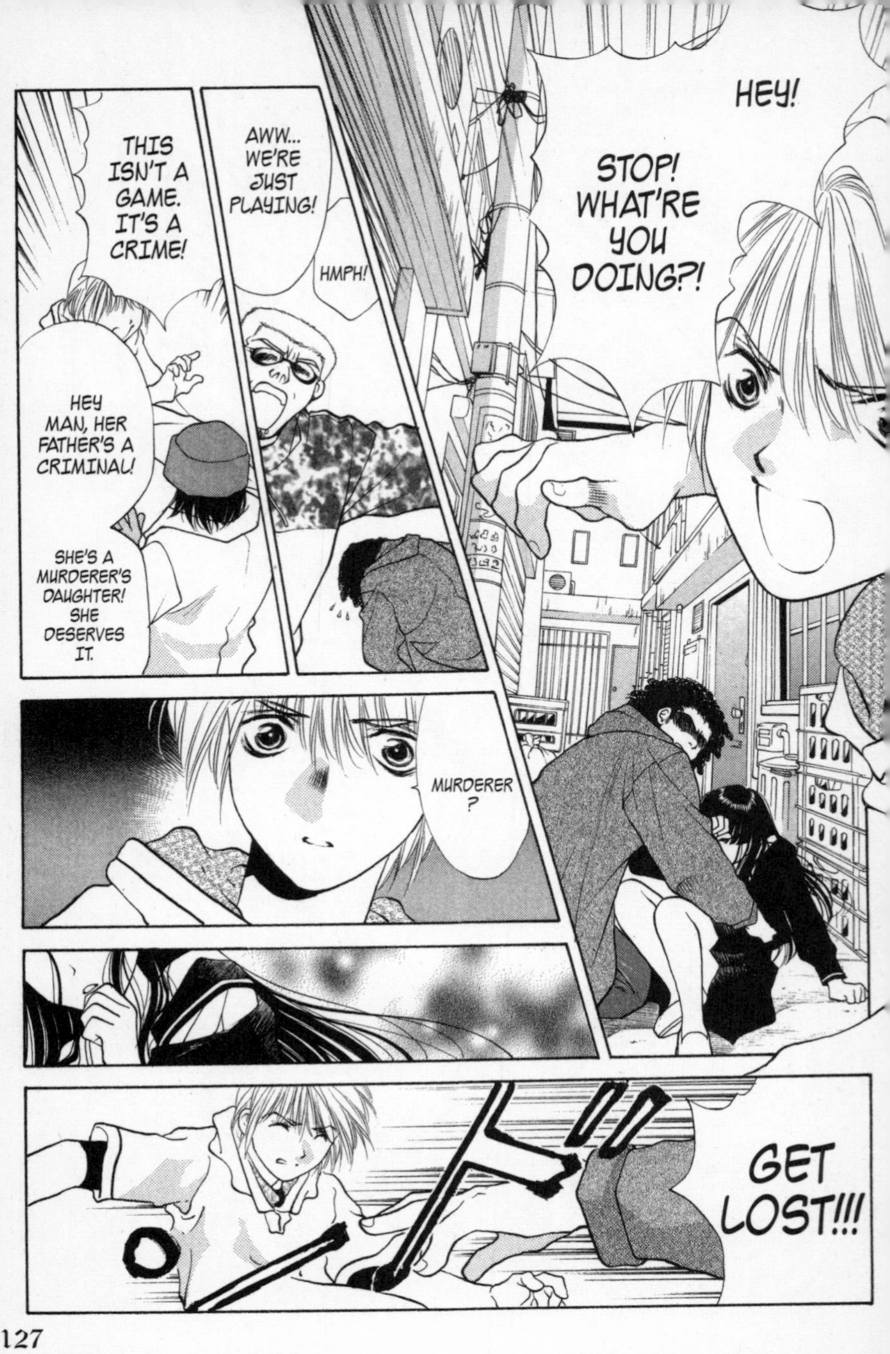
HEY!
STOP! WHAT'RE YOU DOING?!
AWW... WE'RE JUST PLAYING!
HMPH!
THIS ISN'T A GAME. IT'S A CRIME!
HEY MAN, HER FATHER'S A CRIMINAL!
SHE'S A MURDERER'S DAUGHTER! SHE DESERVES IT.
MURDERER?
GET LOST!!!

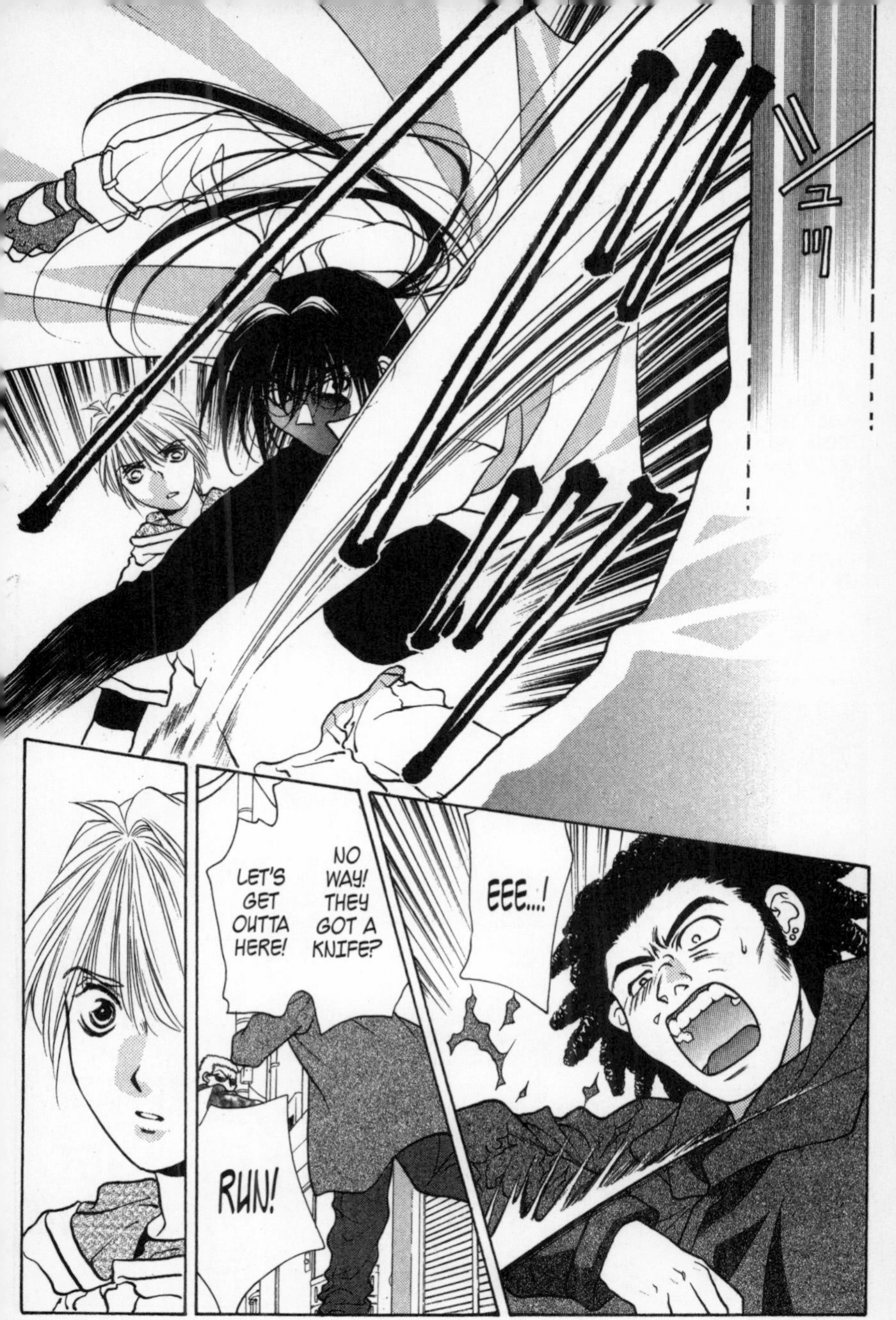
シュッ
EEE...!
NO WAY! THEY GOT A KNIFE?
LET'S GET OUTTA HERE!
RUN!

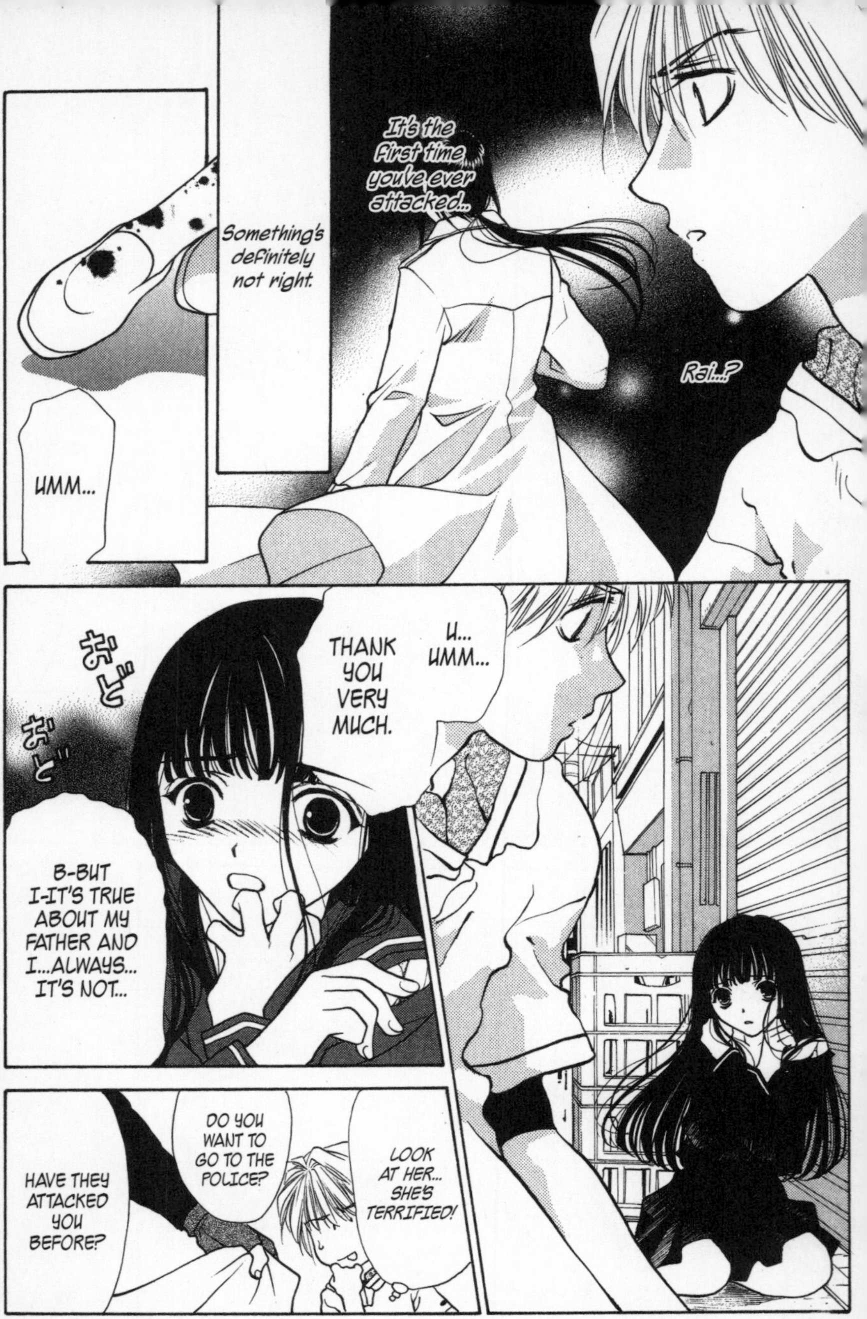
It's the first time you've ever attacked...
Rai...?
Something's definitely not right.
UMM...
U... UMM...
THANK YOU VERY MUCH.
おど
おど
B-BUT I-IT'S TRUE ABOUT MY FATHER AND I...ALWAYS... IT'S NOT...
LOOK AT HER... SHE'S TERRIFIED!
DO YOU WANT TO GO TO THE POLICE?
HAVE THEY ATTACKED YOU BEFORE?

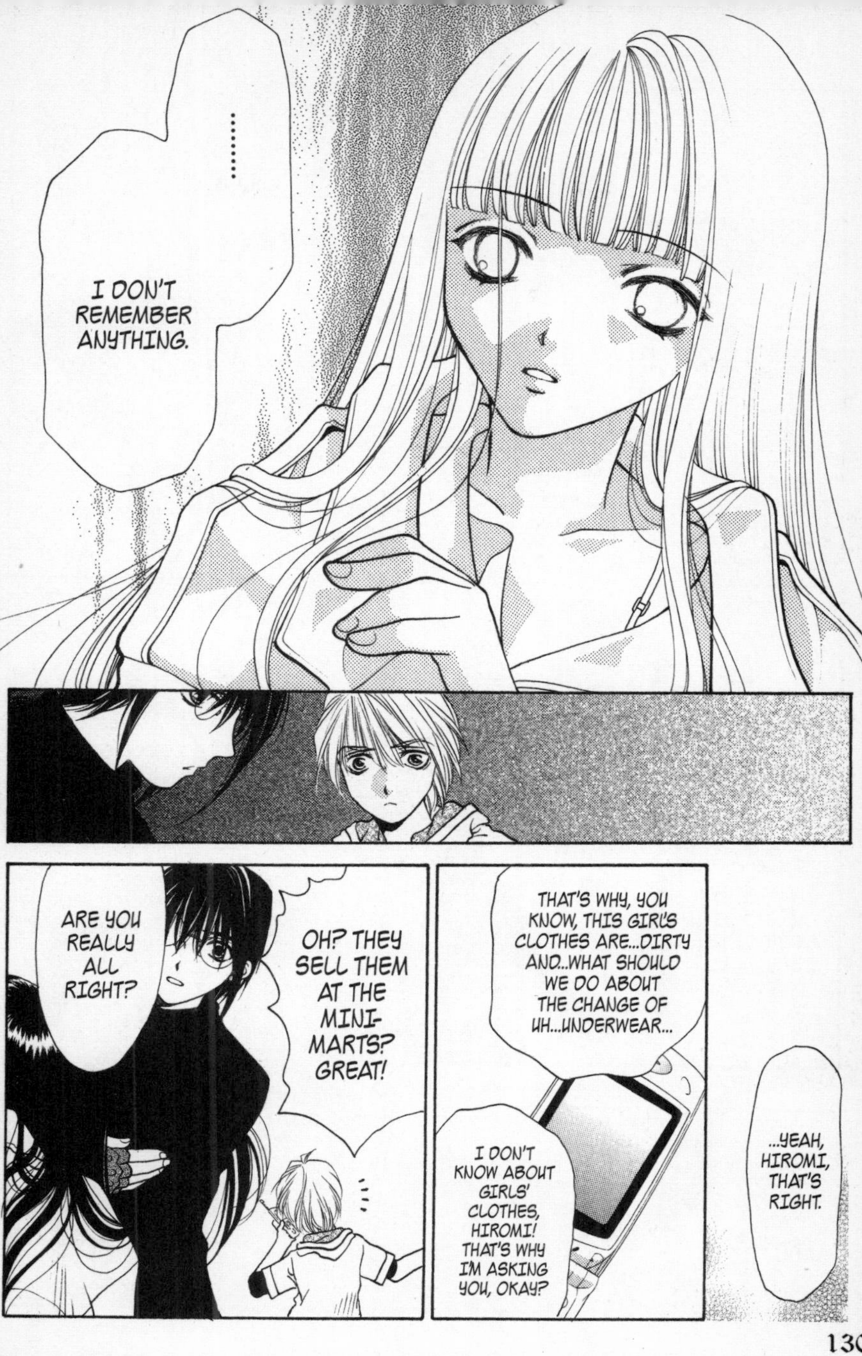
......
I DON'T REMEMBER ANYTHING.
THAT'S WHY, YOU KNOW, THIS GIRL'S CLOTHES ARE...DIRTY AND...WHAT SHOULD WE DO ABOUT THE CHANGE OF UH...UNDERWEAR...
...YEAH, HIROMI, THAT'S RIGHT.
I DON'T KNOW ABOUT GIRLS' CLOTHES, HIROMI! THAT'S WHY I'M ASKING YOU, OKAY?
OH? THEY SELL THEM AT THE MINI-MARTS? GREAT!
ARE YOU REALLY ALL RIGHT?

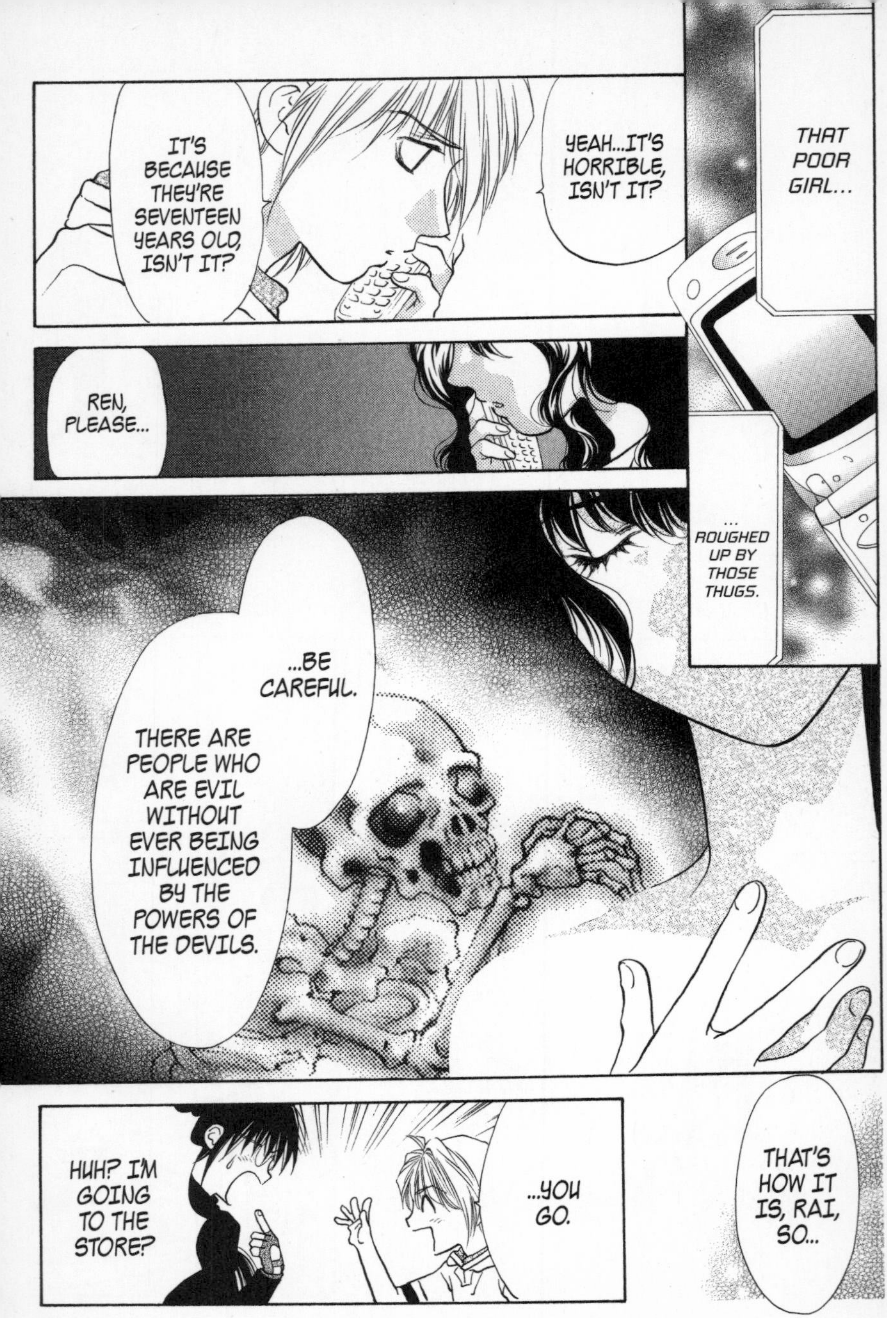
THAT POOR GIRL...
... ROUGHED UP BY THOSE THUGS.
YEAH...IT'S HORRIBLE, ISN'T IT?
IT'S BECAUSE THEY'RE SEVENTEEN YEARS OLD, ISN'T IT?
REN, PLEASE...
...BE CAREFUL.
THERE ARE PEOPLE WHO ARE EVIL WITHOUT EVER BEING INFLUENCED BY THE POWERS OF THE DEVILS.
THAT'S HOW IT IS, RAI, SO...
...YOU GO.
HUH? I'M GOING TO THE STORE?

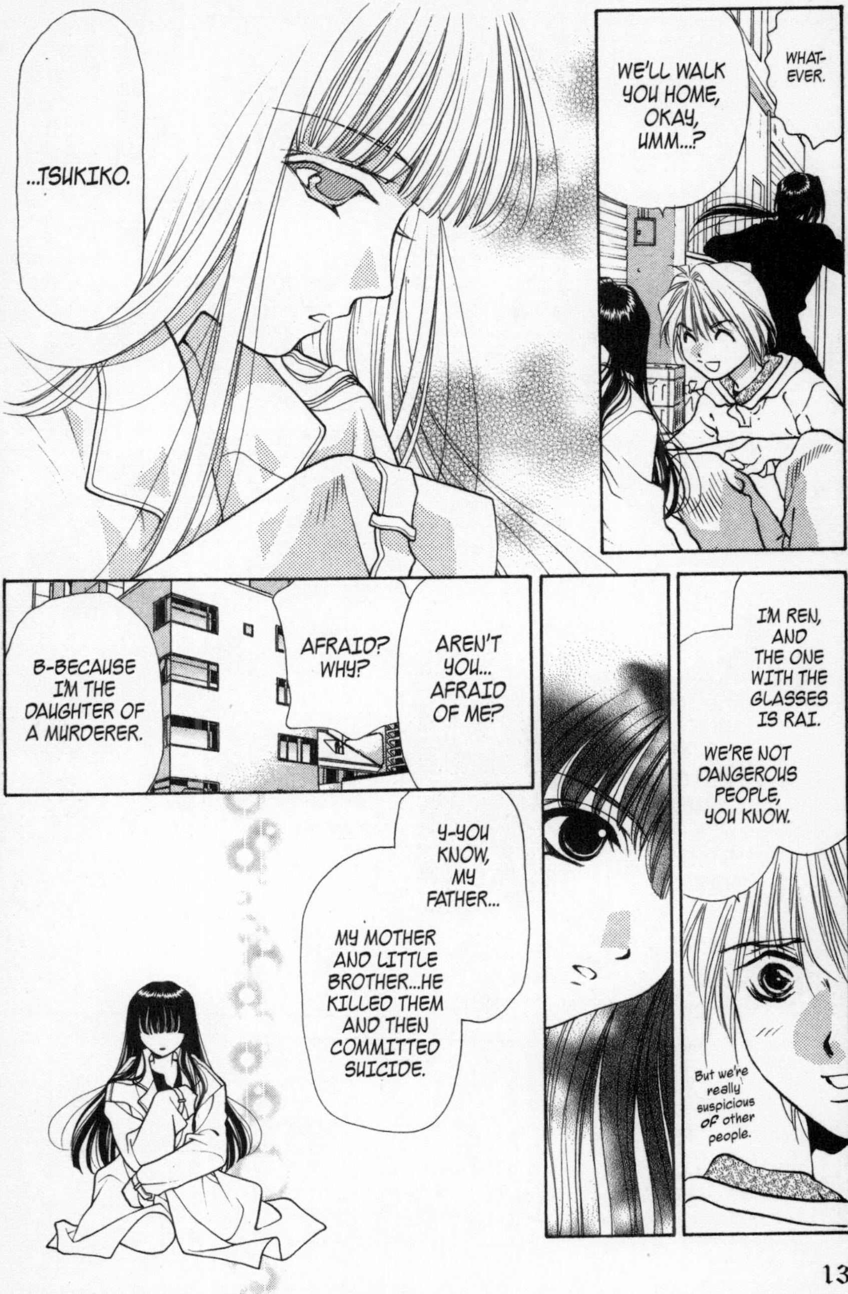
WHAT-EVER.
WE'LL WALK YOU HOME, OKAY, UMM...?
...TSUKIKO.
I'M REN, AND THE ONE WITH THE GLASSES IS RAI.
WE'RE NOT DANGEROUS PEOPLE, YOU KNOW.
But we're really suspicious of other people.
AREN'T YOU... AFRAID OF ME?
AFRAID? WHY?
B-BECAUSE I'M THE DAUGHTER OF A MURDERER.
Y-YOU KNOW, MY FATHER...
MY MOTHER AND LITTLE BROTHER...HE KILLED THEM AND THEN COMMITTED SUICIDE.

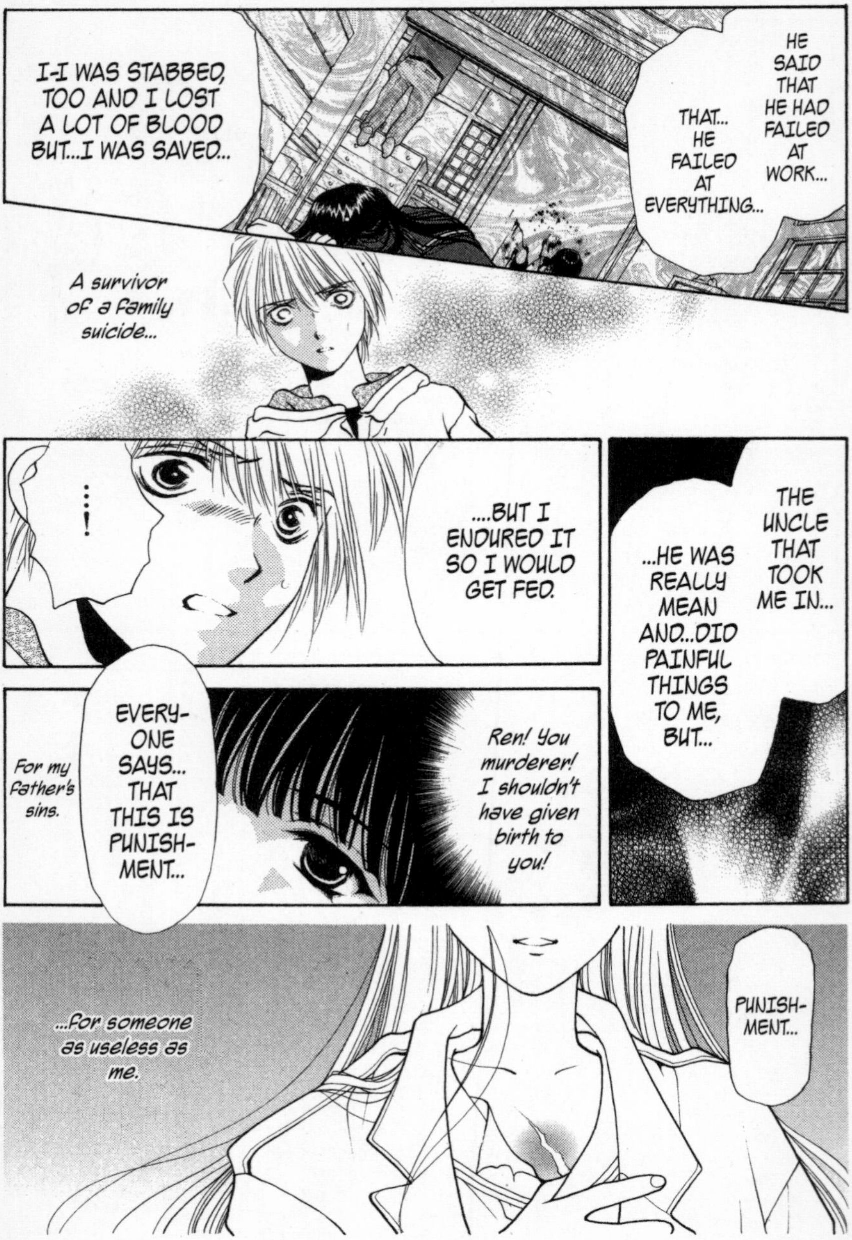
HE SAID THAT HE HAD FAILED AT WORK...
THAT... HE FAILED AT EVERYTHING...
I-I WAS STABBED, TOO AND I LOST A LOT OF BLOOD BUT...I WAS SAVED...
A survivor of a family suicide...
THE UNCLE THAT TOOK ME IN...
...HE WAS REALLY MEAN AND...DID PAINFUL THINGS TO ME, BUT...
....BUT I ENDURED IT SO I WOULD GET FED.
...!
Ren! You murderer! I shouldn't have given birth to you!
EVERY-ONE SAYS... THAT THIS IS PUNISH-MENT...
For my father's sins.
PUNISH-MENT...
...for someone as useless as me.

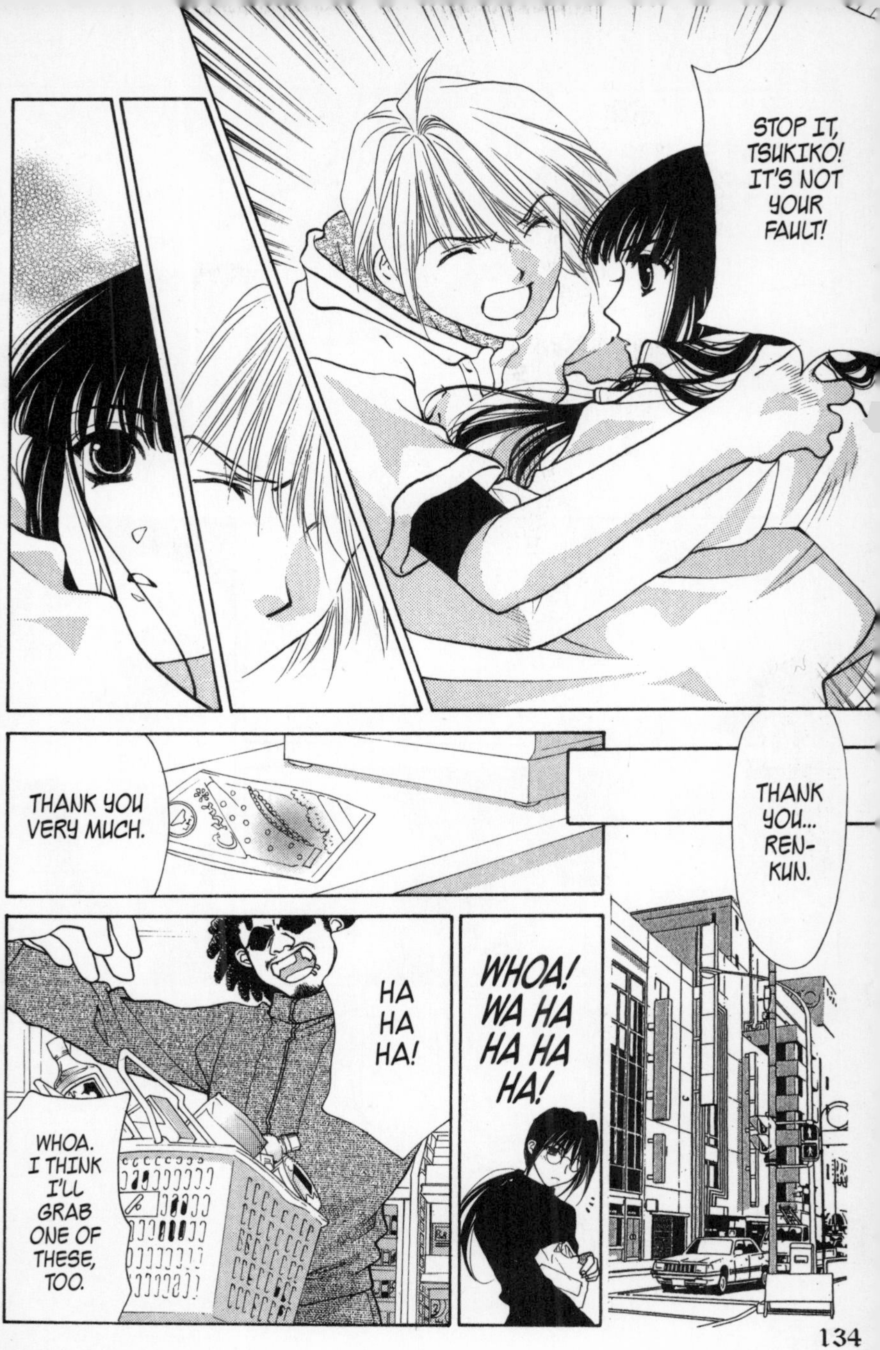
STOP IT, TSUKIKO! IT'S NOT YOUR FAULT!
THANK YOU... REN-KUN.
THANK YOU VERY MUCH.
WHOA! WA HA HA HA HA HA!
HA HA HA!
WHOA. I THINK I'LL GRAB ONE OF THESE, TOO.

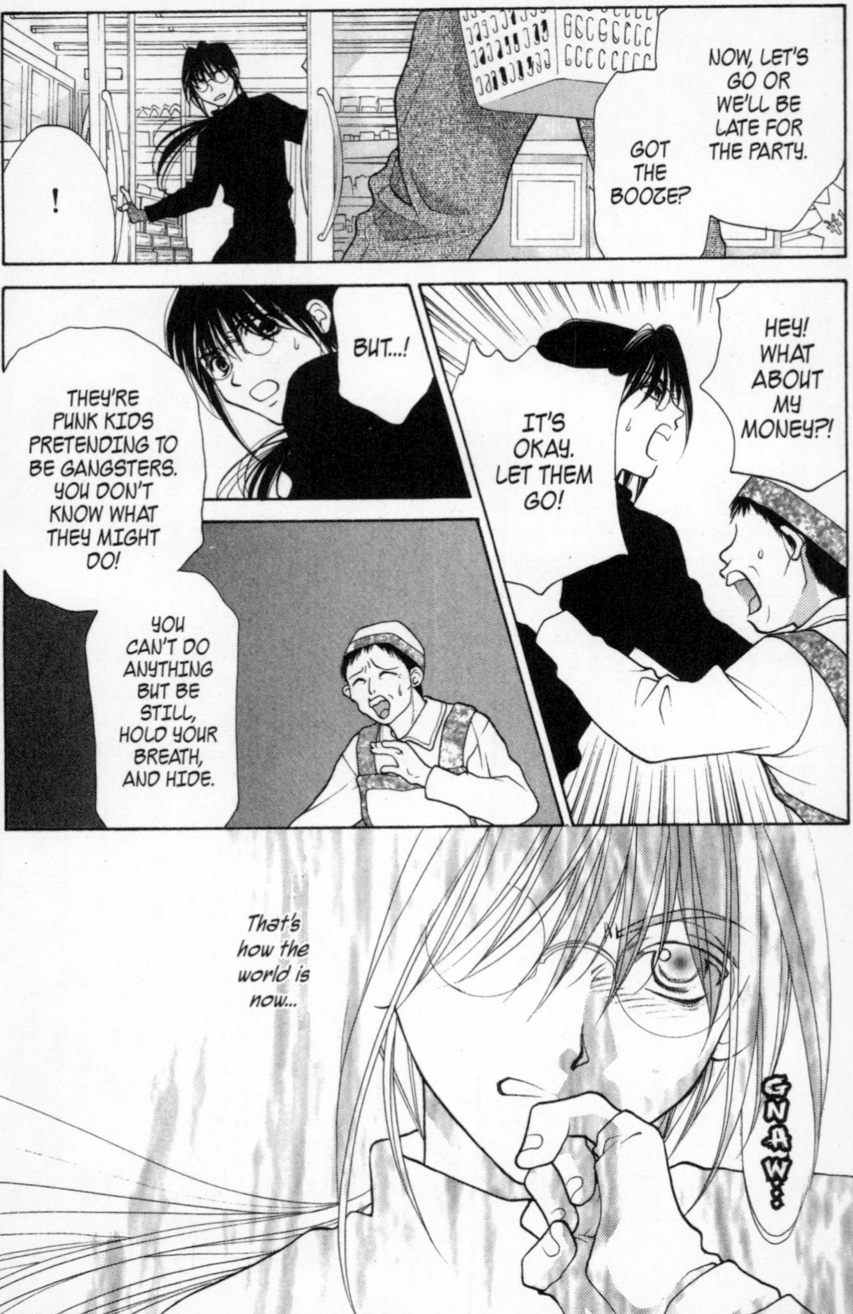
NOW, LET'S GO OR WE'LL BE LATE FOR THE PARTY.
GOT THE BOOZE?
!
HEY! WHAT ABOUT MY MONEY?!
IT'S OKAY. LET THEM GO!
BUT...!
THEY'RE PUNK KIDS PRETENDING TO BE GANGSTERS. YOU DON'T KNOW WHAT THEY MIGHT DO!
YOU CAN'T DO ANYTHING BUT BE STILL, HOLD YOUR BREATH, AND HIDE.
That's how the world is now...
GNAW...

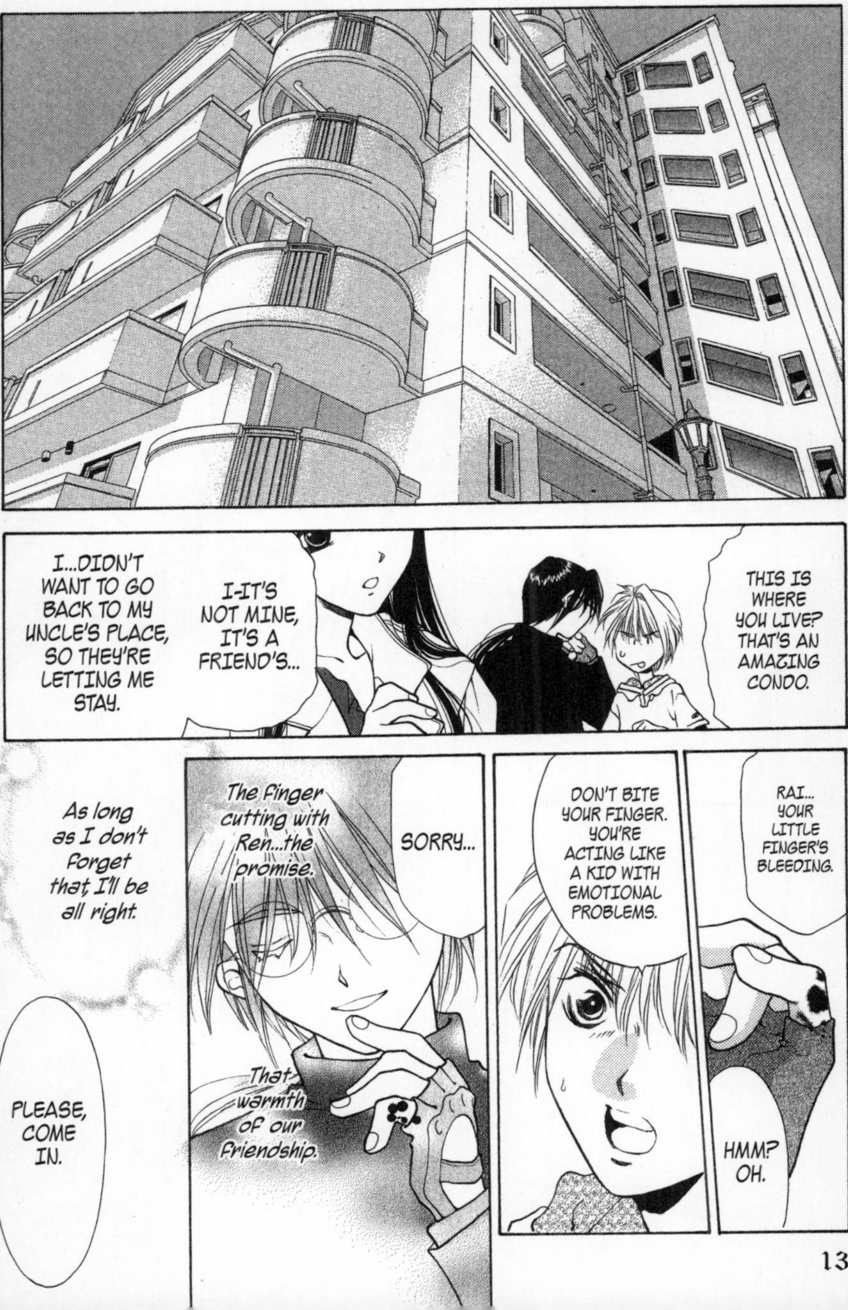
THIS IS WHERE YOU LIVE? THAT'S AN AMAZING CONDO.
I-IT'S NOT MINE, IT'S A FRIEND'S...
I...DIDN'T WANT TO GO BACK TO MY UNCLE'S PLACE, SO THEY'RE LETTING ME STAY.
RAI... YOUR LITTLE FINGER'S BLEEDING.
HMM? OH.
DON'T BITE YOUR FINGER. YOU'RE ACTING LIKE A KID WITH EMOTIONAL PROBLEMS.
SORRY...
The finger cutting with Ren...the promise.
That warmth of our friendship.
As long as I don't forget that, I'll be all right.
PLEASE, COME IN.

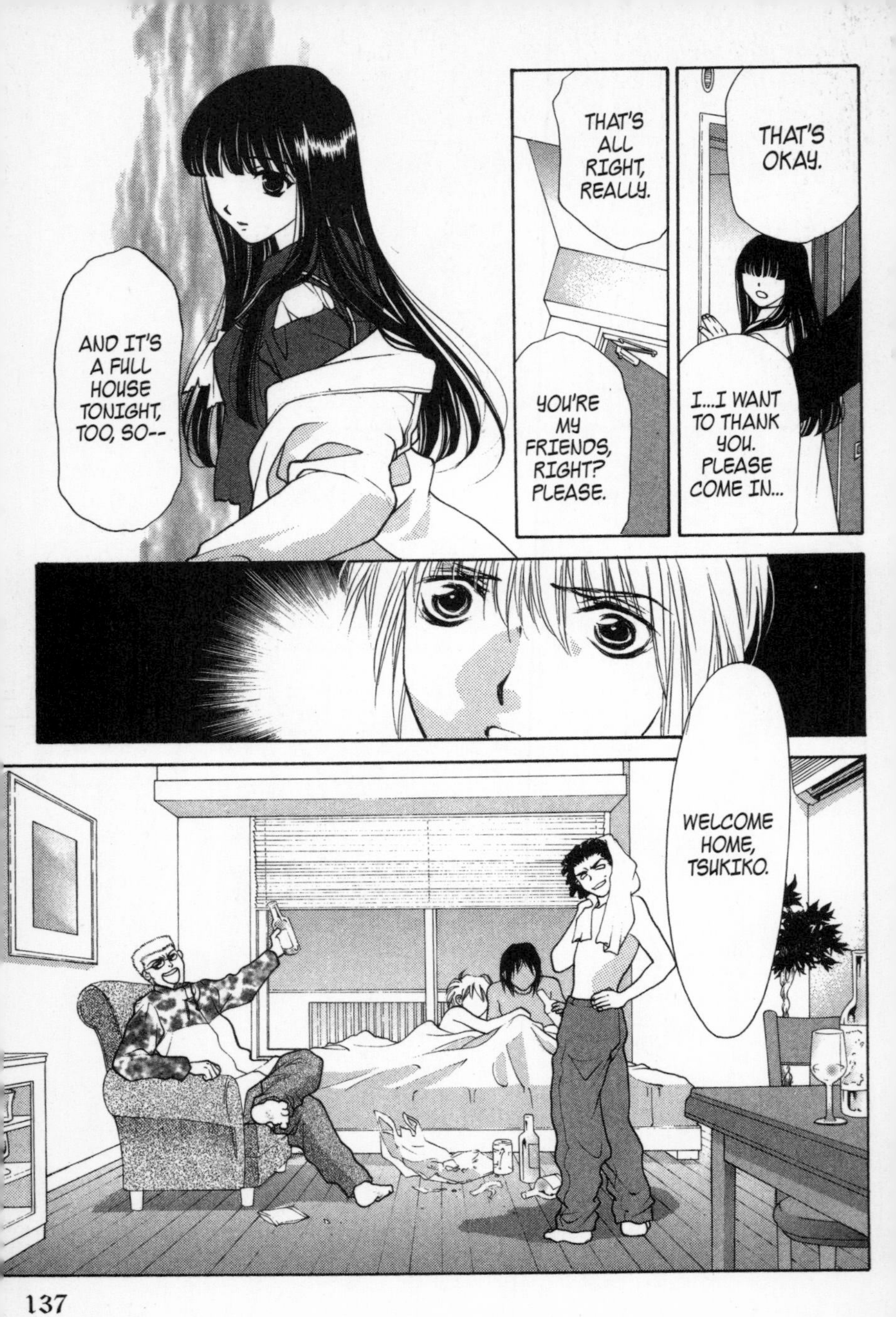
THAT'S OKAY.
I...I WANT TO THANK YOU. PLEASE COME IN...
THAT'S ALL RIGHT, REALLY.
YOU'RE MY FRIENDS, RIGHT? PLEASE.
AND IT'S A FULL HOUSE TONIGHT, TOO, SO--
WELCOME HOME, TSUKIKO.

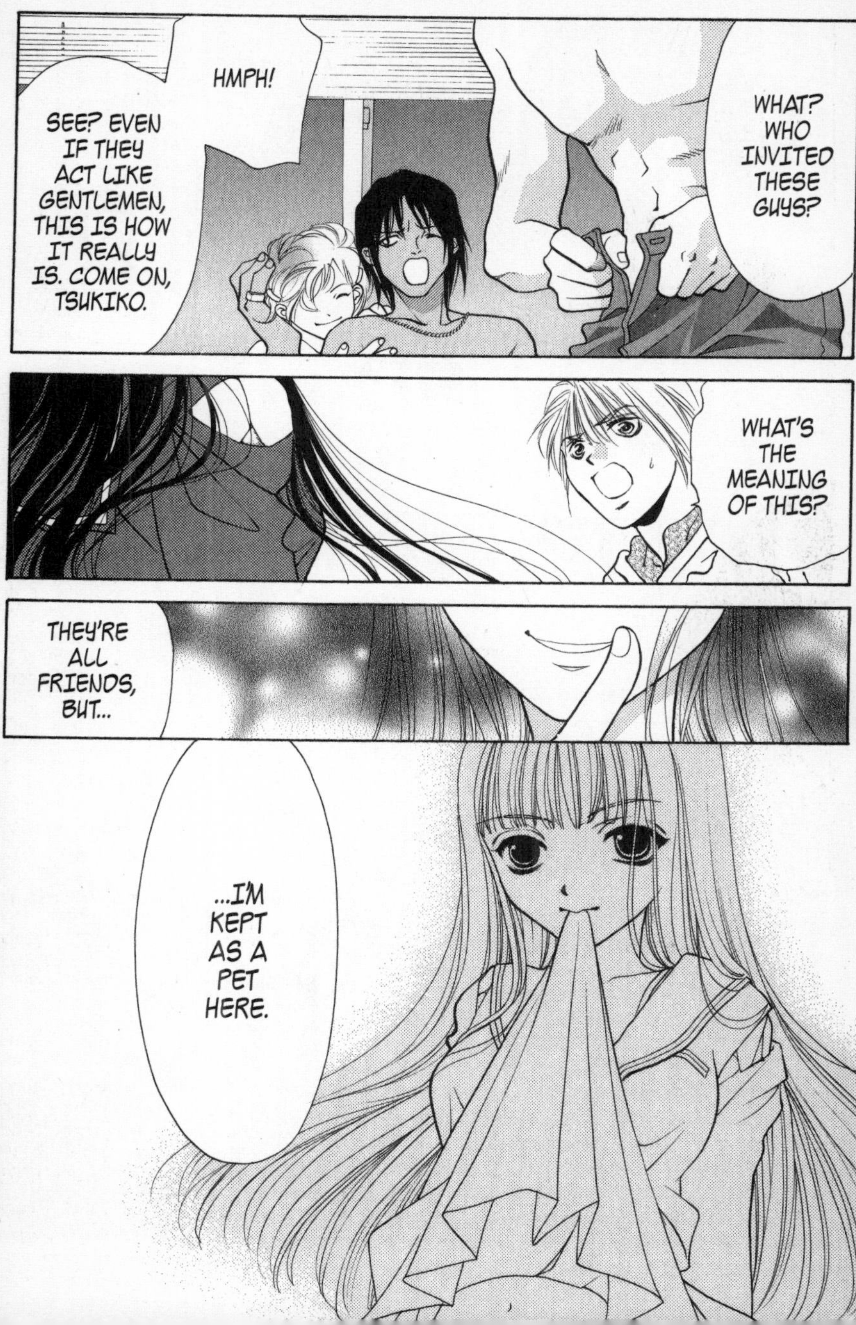
WHAT? WHO INVITED THESE GUYS?
HMPH!
SEE? EVEN IF THEY ACT LIKE GENTLEMEN, THIS IS HOW IT REALLY IS. COME ON, TSUKIKO.
WHAT'S THE MEANING OF THIS?
THEY'RE ALL FRIENDS, BUT...
...I'M KEPT AS A PET HERE.

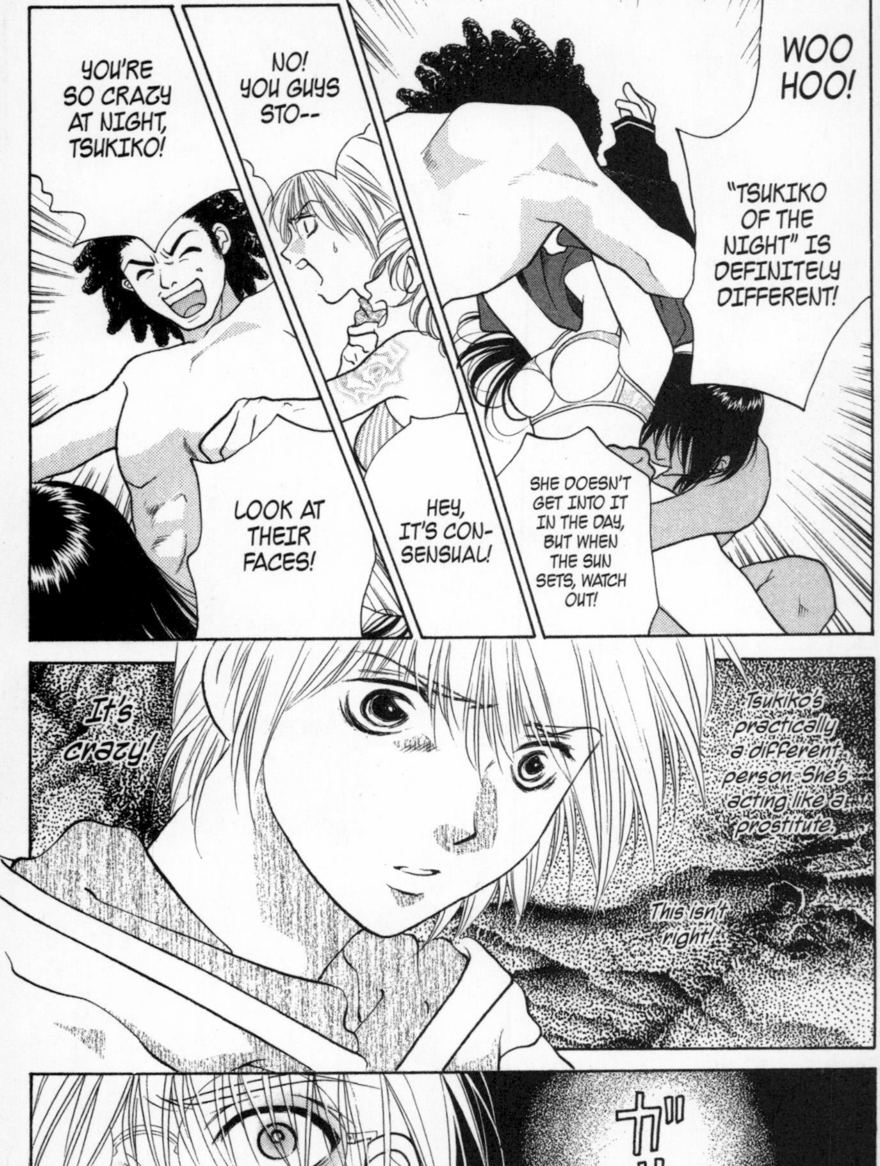
WOO HOO!
"TSUKIKO OF THE NIGHT" IS DEFINITELY DIFFERENT!
SHE DOESN'T GET INTO IT IN THE DAY, BUT WHEN THE SUN SETS, WATCH OUT!
NO! YOU GUYS STO--
HEY, IT'S CON-SENSUAL!
YOU'RE SO CRAZY AT NIGHT, TSUKIKO!
LOOK AT THEIR FACES!
Tsukiko's practically a different person. She's acting like a prostitute.
This isn't right!
It's crazy!
ガッ!

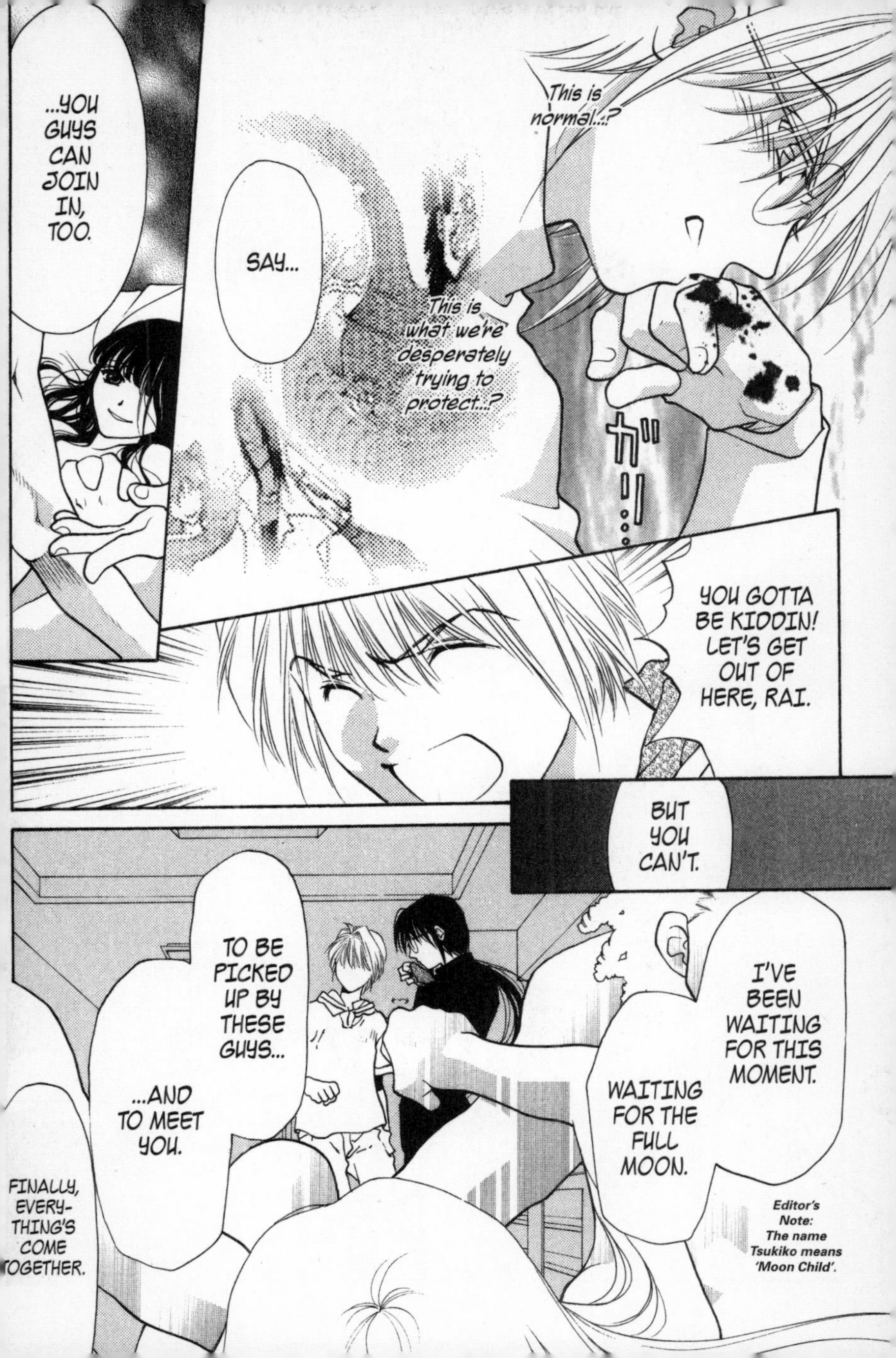

This is normal...?
This is what we're desperately trying to protect...?
SAY...
...YOU GUYS CAN JOIN IN, TOO.
YOU GOTTA BE KIDDIN! LET'S GET OUT OF HERE, RAI.
BUT YOU CAN'T.
I'VE BEEN WAITING FOR THIS MOMENT.
WAITING FOR THE FULL MOON.
TO BE PICKED UP BY THESE GUYS...
...AND TO MEET YOU.
FINALLY, EVERY-THING'S COME TOGETHER.

Editor's Note: The name Tsukiko means 'Moon Child'.

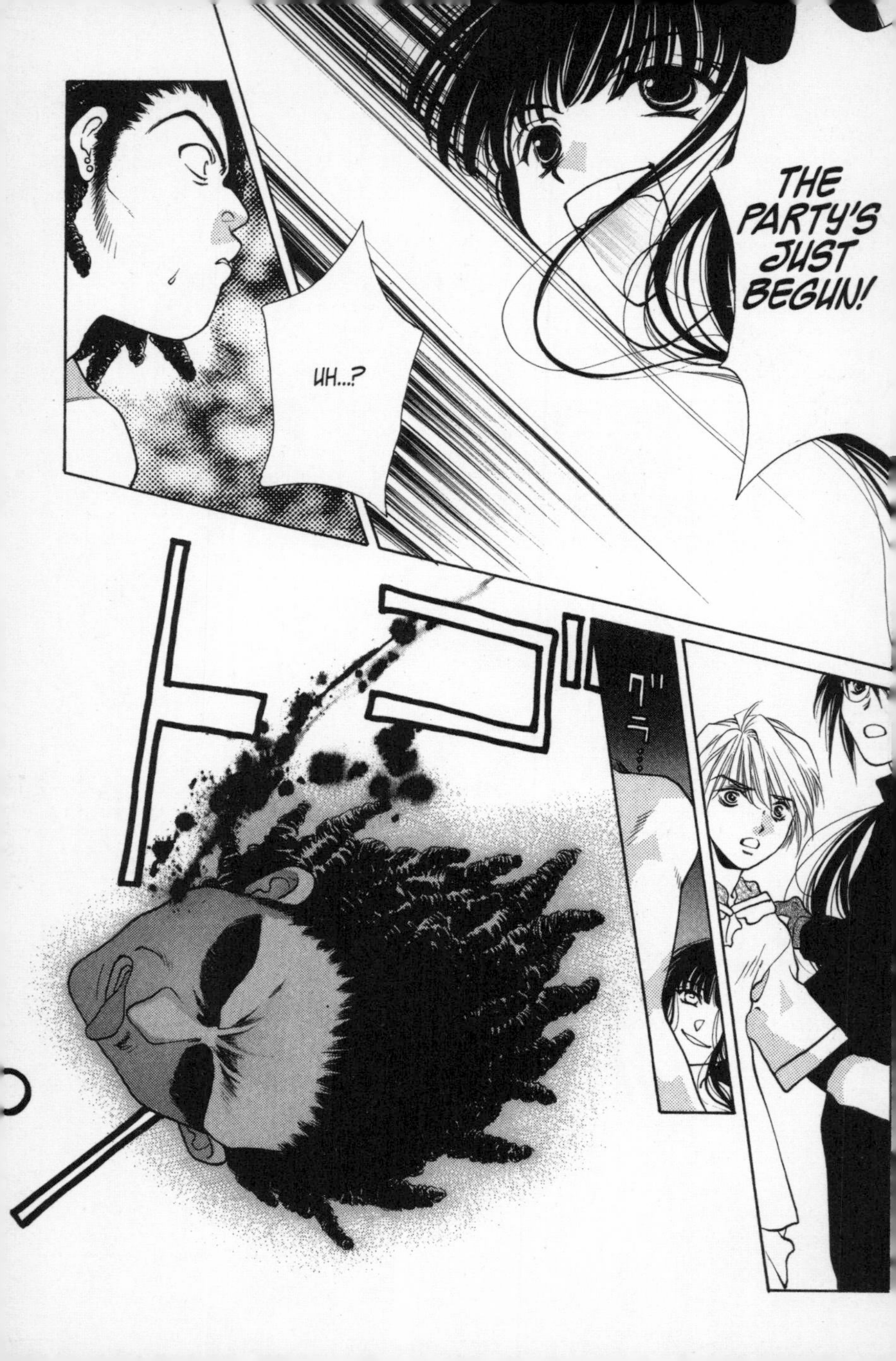
THE PARTY'S JUST BEGUN!
UH...?
グラ…

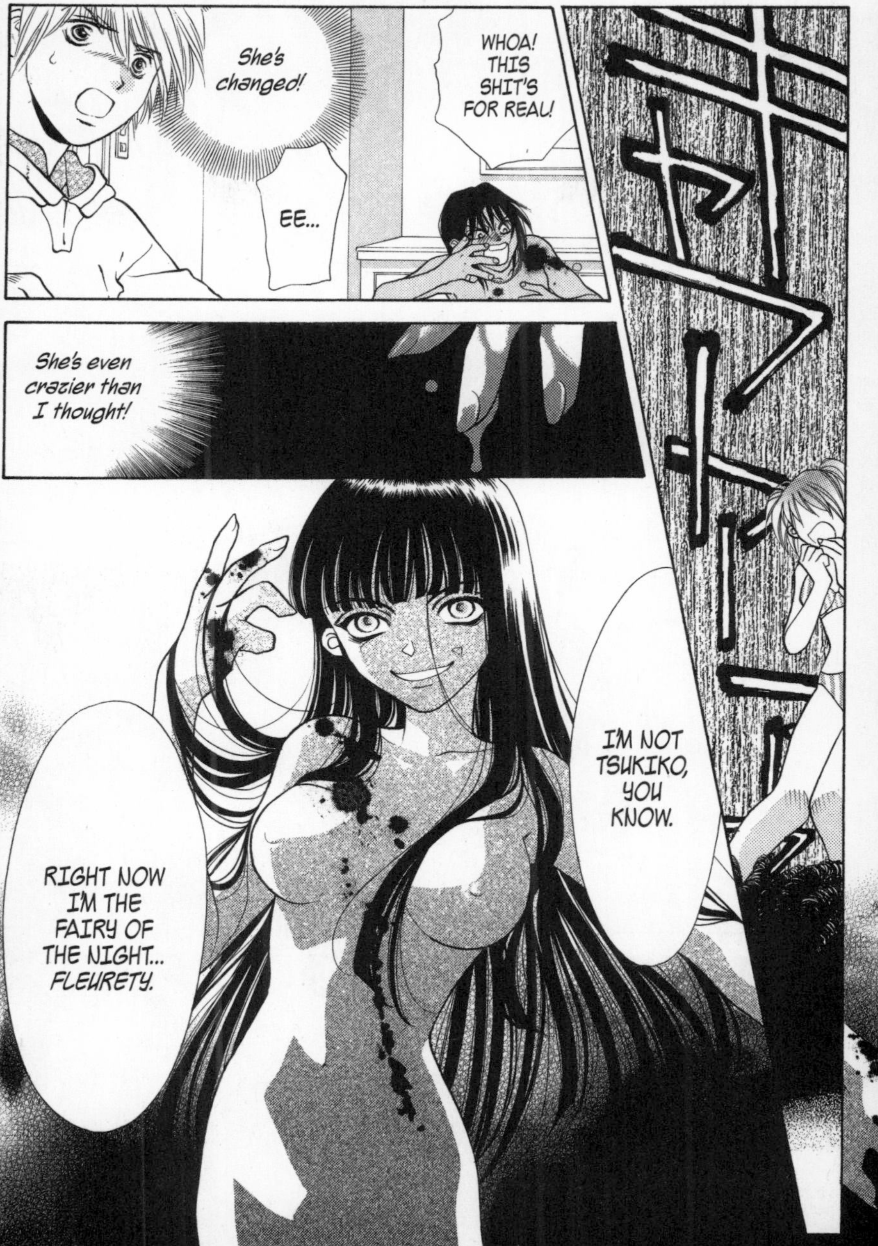
WHOA! THIS SHIT'S FOR REAL!
EE...
She's changed!
She's even crazier than I thought!
I'M NOT TSUKIKO, YOU KNOW.
RIGHT NOW I'M THE FAIRY OF THE NIGHT... FLEURETY.

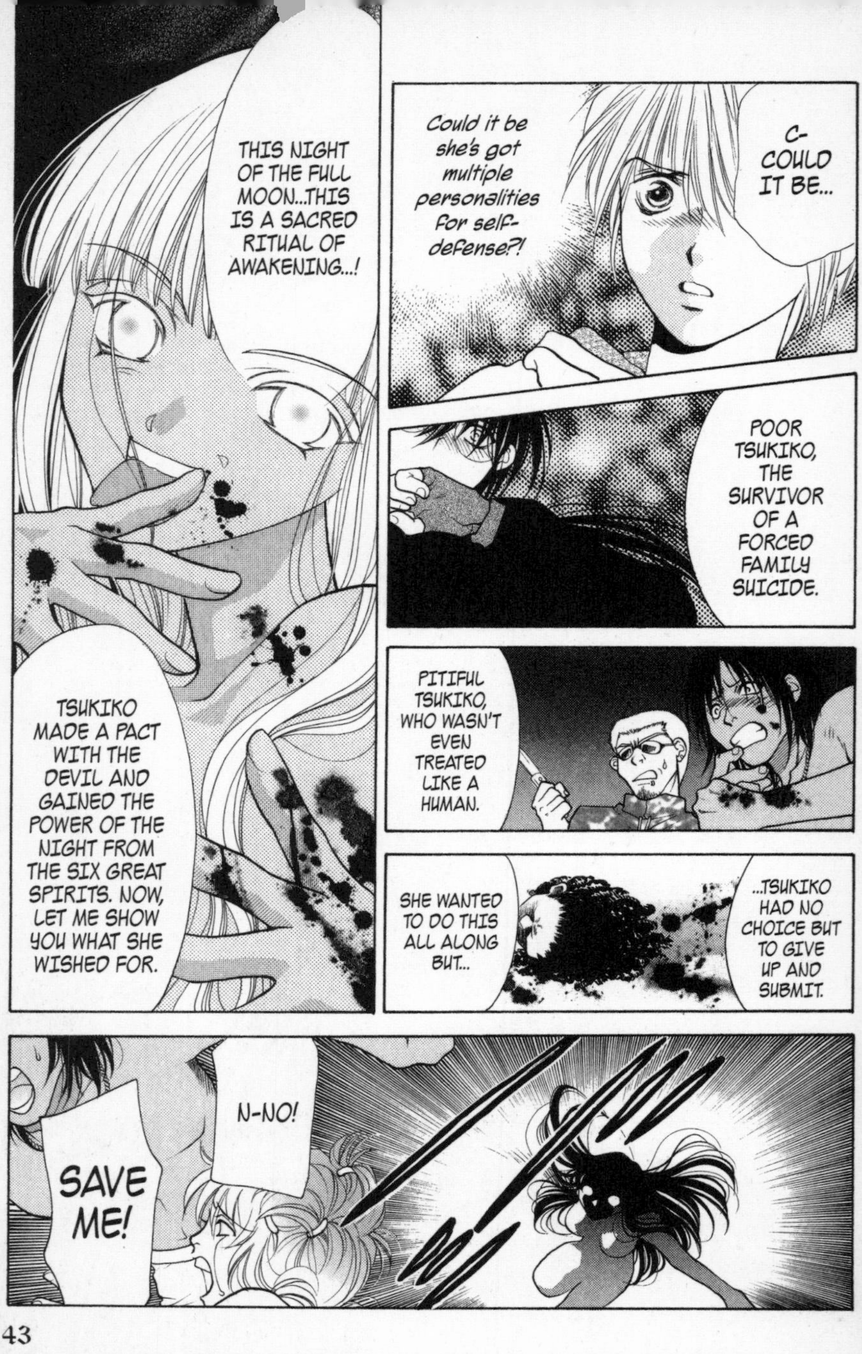
C-COULD IT BE...
Could it be she's got multiple personalities for self-defense?!
POOR TSUKIKO, THE SURVIVOR OF A FORCED FAMILY SUICIDE.
PITIFUL TSUKIKO, WHO WASN'T EVEN TREATED LIKE A HUMAN.
SHE WANTED TO DO THIS ALL ALONG BUT...
...TSUKIKO HAD NO CHOICE BUT TO GIVE UP AND SUBMIT.
THIS NIGHT OF THE FULL MOON...THIS IS A SACRED RITUAL OF AWAKENING...!
TSUKIKO MADE A PACT WITH THE DEVIL AND GAINED THE POWER OF THE NIGHT FROM THE SIX GREAT SPIRITS. NOW, LET ME SHOW YOU WHAT SHE WISHED FOR.
N-NO!
SAVE ME!

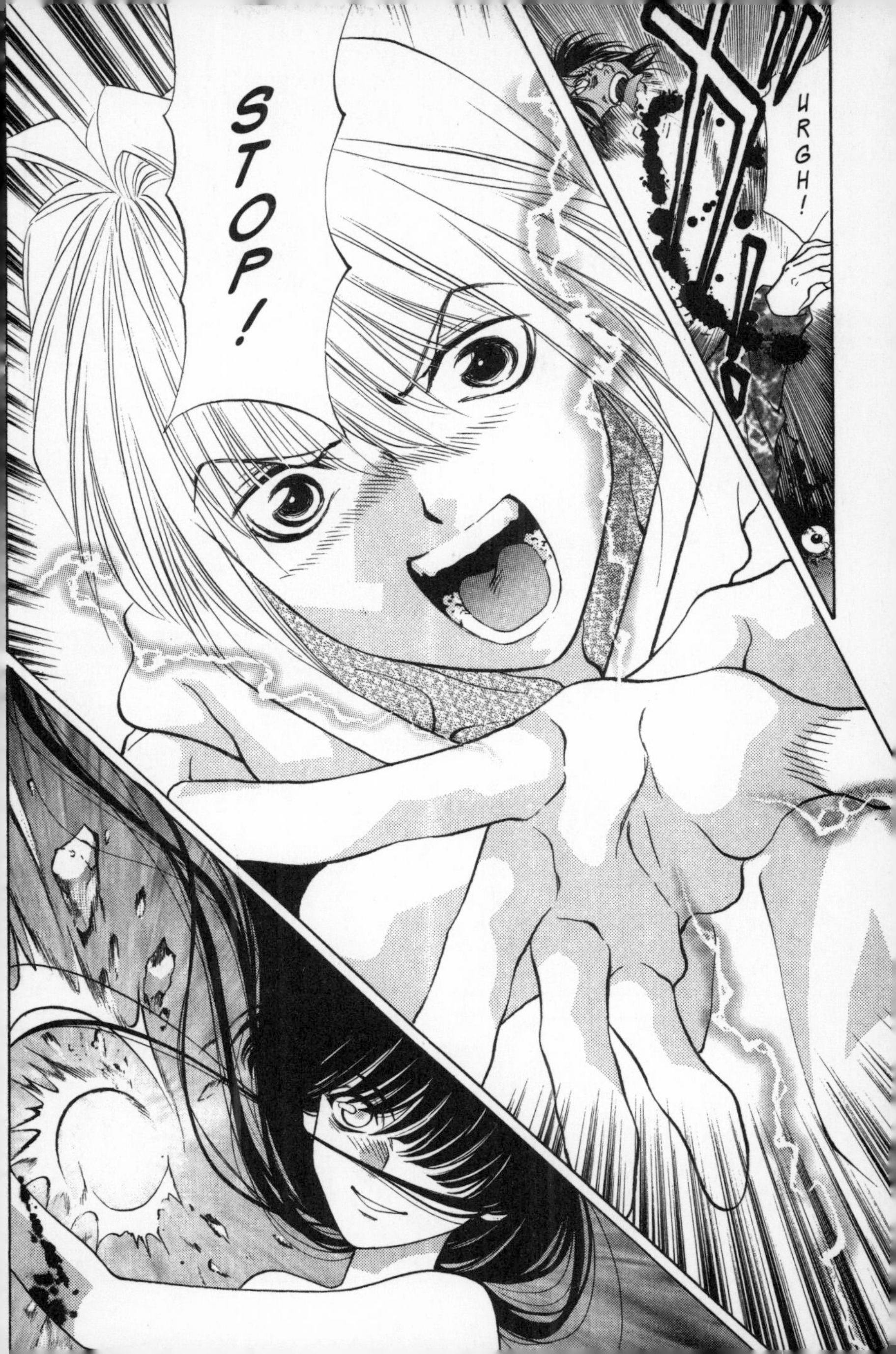
URGH!
STOP!

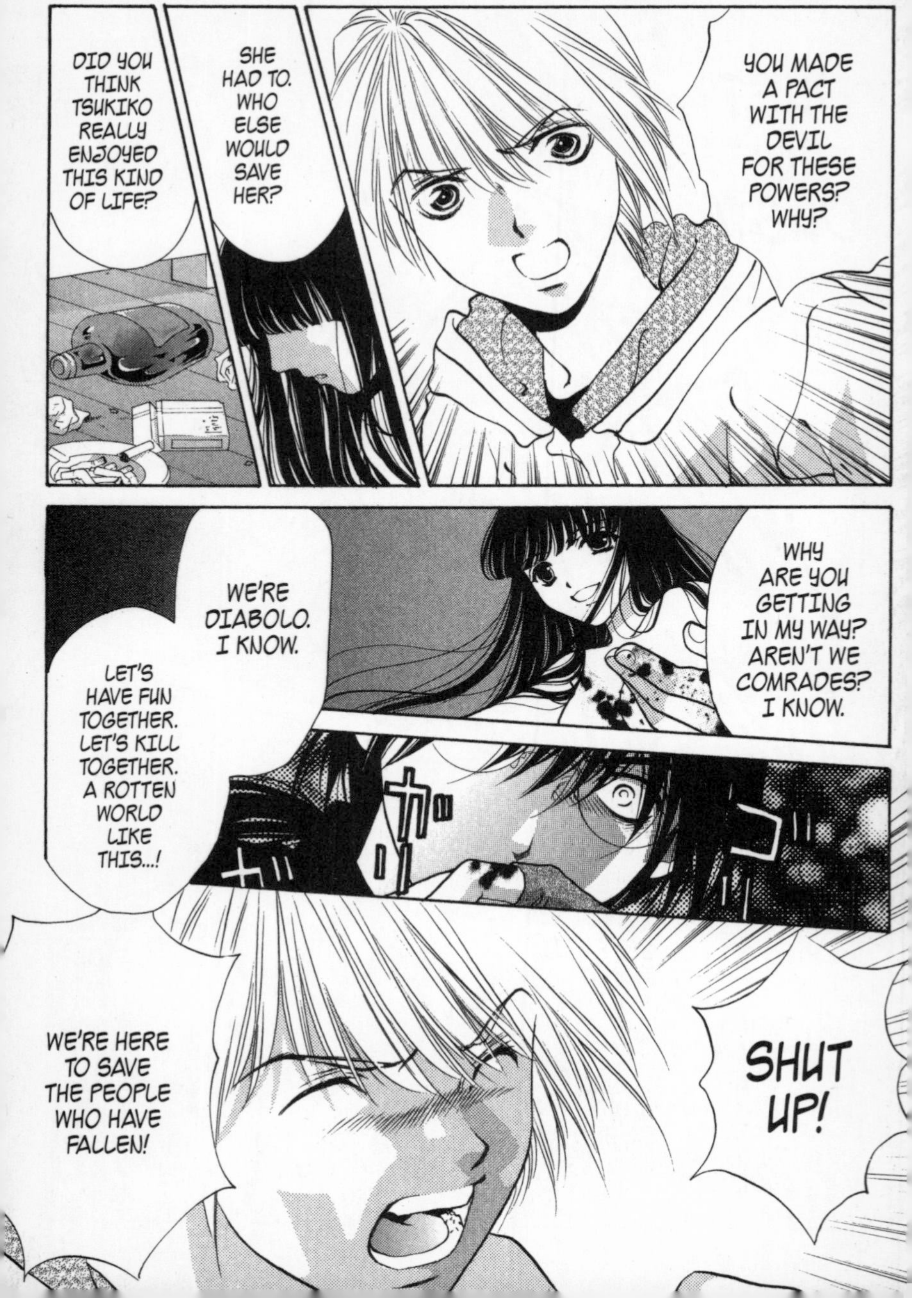
YOU MADE A PACT WITH THE DEVIL FOR THESE POWERS? WHY?
SHE HAD TO. WHO ELSE WOULD SAVE HER?
DID YOU THINK TSUKIKO REALLY ENJOYED THIS KIND OF LIFE?
WHY ARE YOU GETTING IN MY WAY? AREN'T WE COMRADES? I KNOW.
WE'RE DIABOLO. I KNOW.
LET'S HAVE FUN TOGETHER. LET'S KILL TOGETHER. A ROTTEN WORLD LIKE THIS...!
SHUT UP!
WE'RE HERE TO SAVE THE PEOPLE WHO HAVE FALLEN!

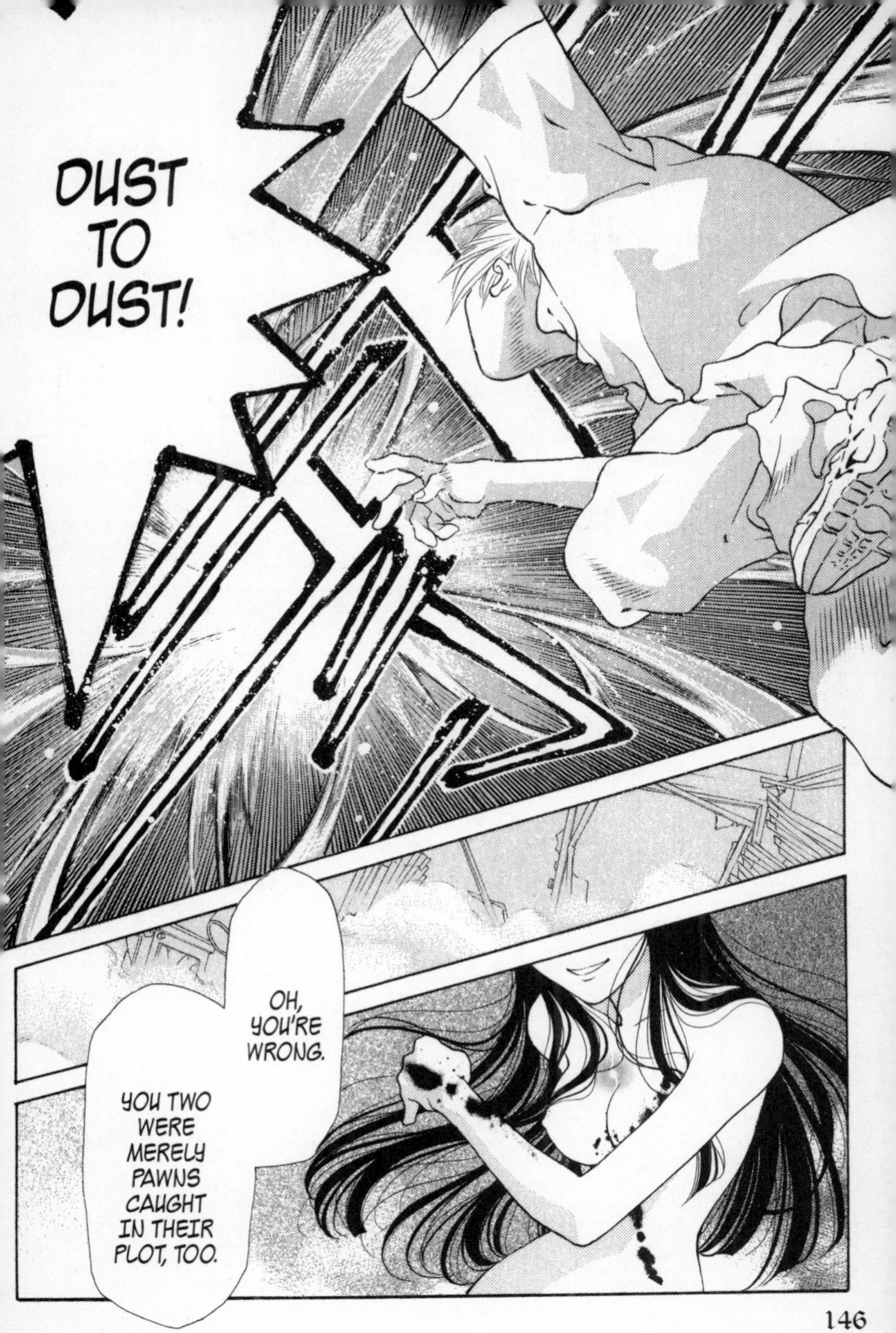
DUST TO DUST!
OH, YOU'RE WRONG.
YOU TWO WERE MERELY PAWNS CAUGHT IN THEIR PLOT, TOO.

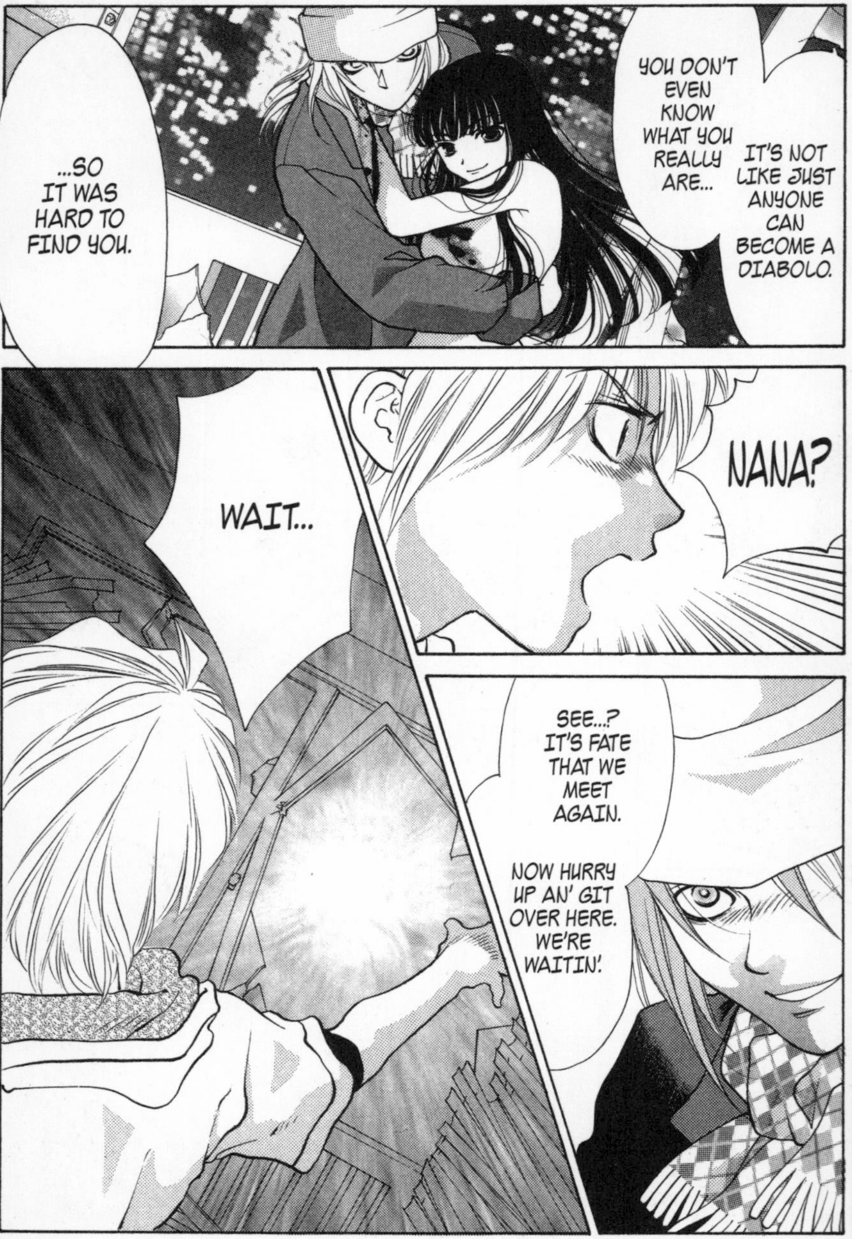
YOU DON'T EVEN KNOW WHAT YOU REALLY ARE...
IT'S NOT LIKE JUST ANYONE CAN BECOME A DIABOLO.
...SO IT WAS HARD TO FIND YOU.
NANA?
SEE...? IT'S FATE THAT WE MEET AGAIN.
NOW HURRY UP AN' GIT OVER HERE. WE'RE WAITIN'.
WAIT...

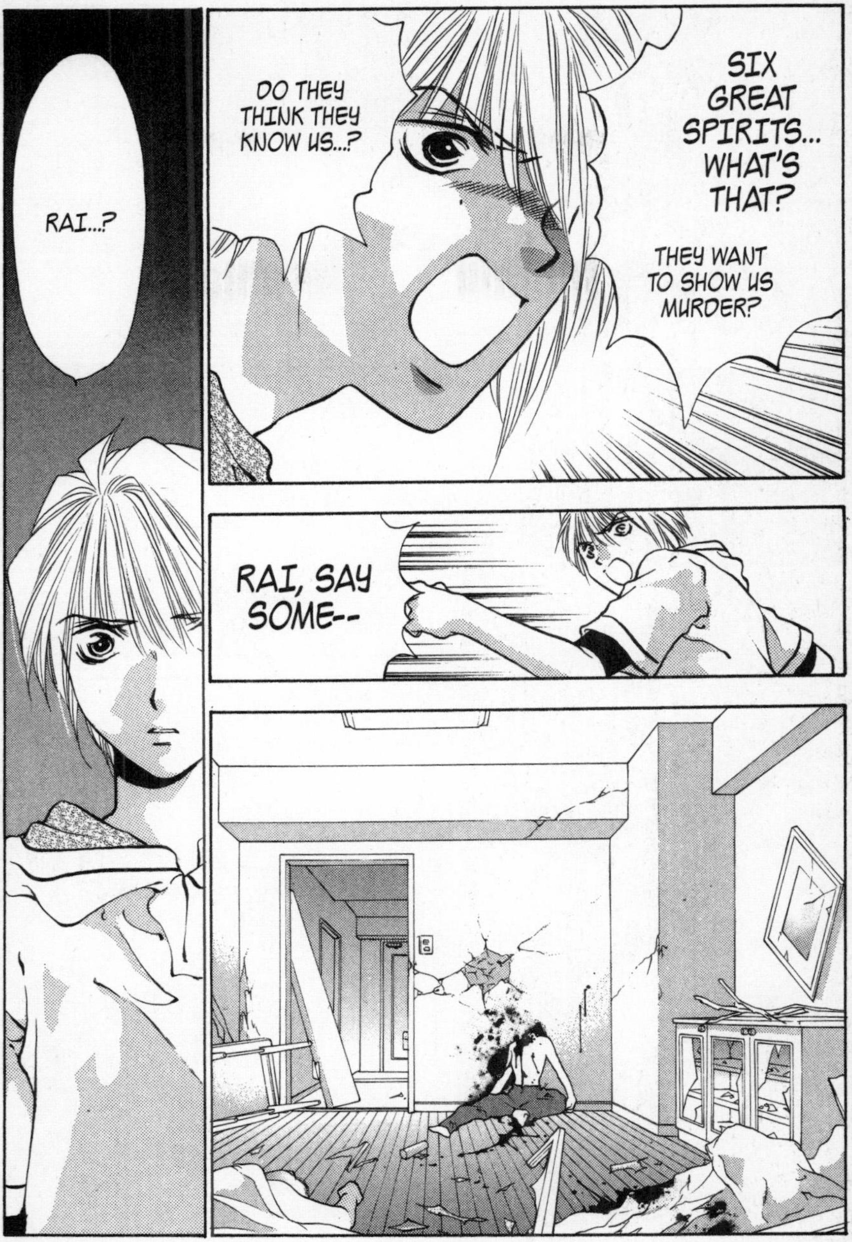
SIX GREAT SPIRITS... WHAT'S THAT?
THEY WANT TO SHOW US MURDER?
DO THEY THINK THEY KNOW US...?
RAI, SAY SOME--
RAI...?

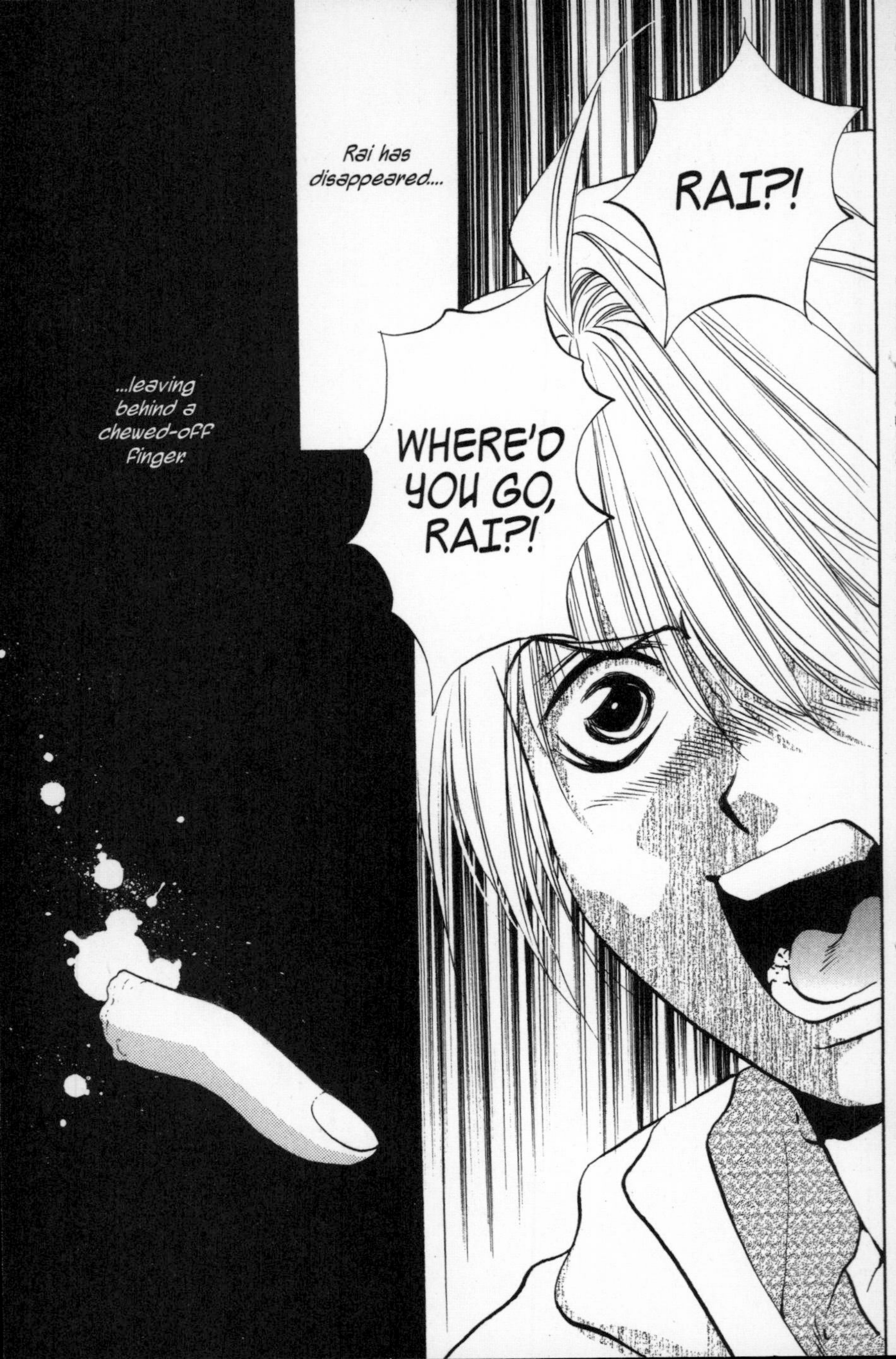
RAI?!
WHERE'D YOU GO, RAI?!
Rai has disappeared....
...leaving behind a chewed-off finger.

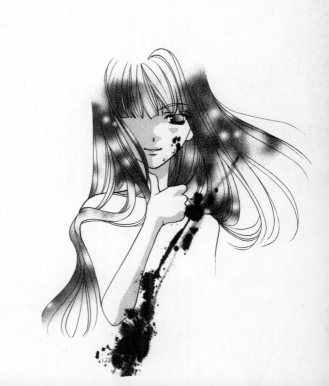

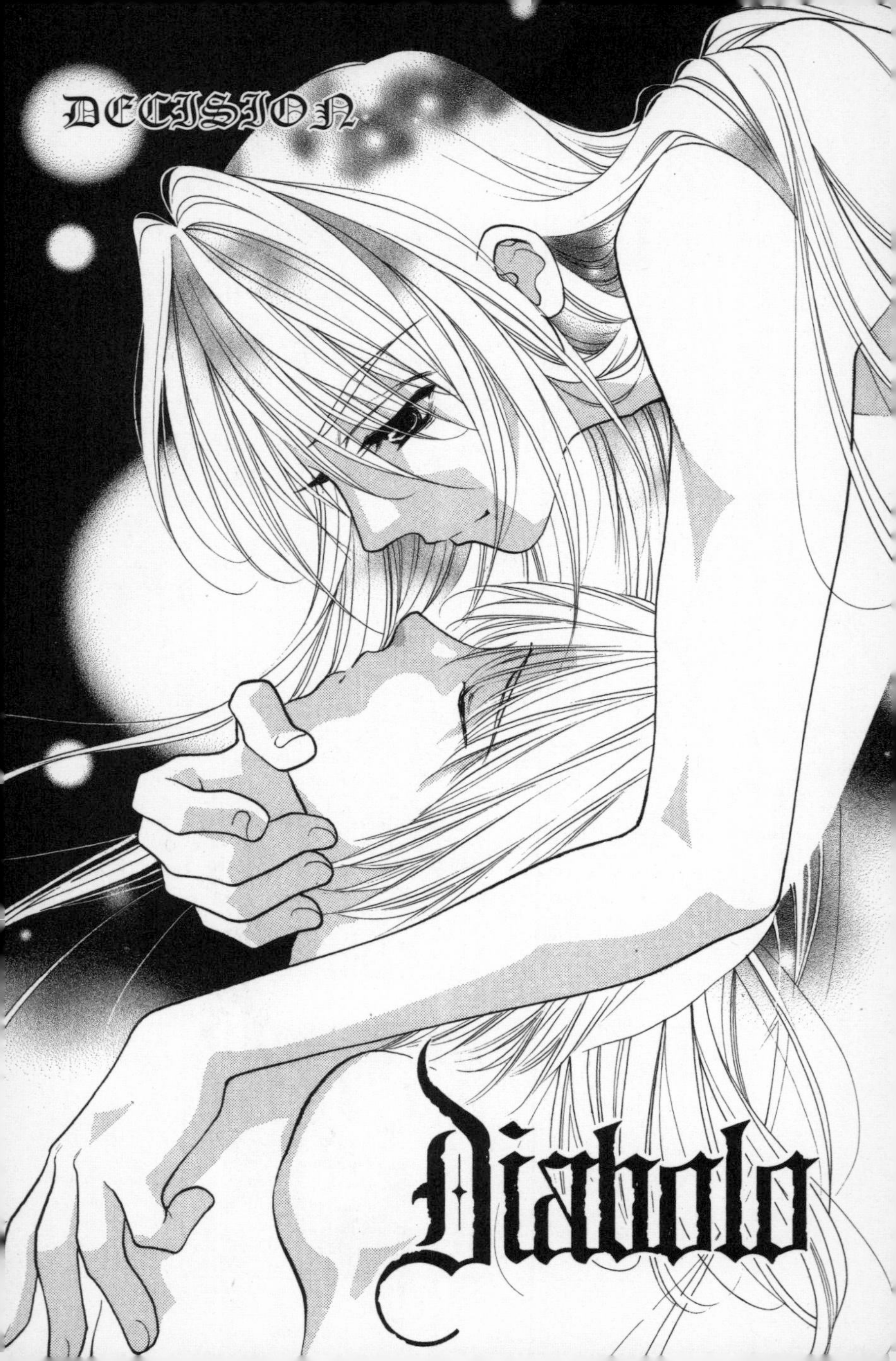
DECISION
Diabolo

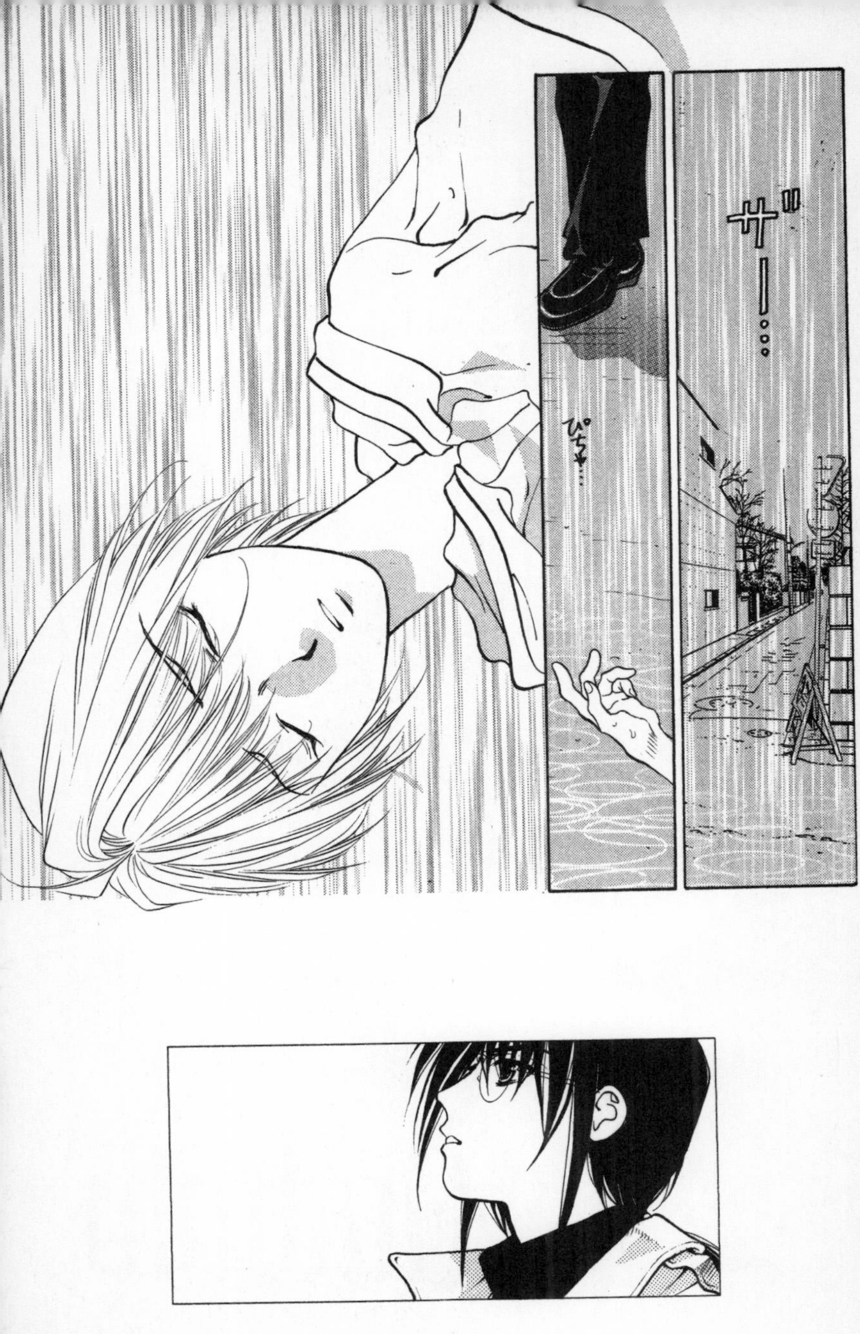
ザー…
ぴちゃ…

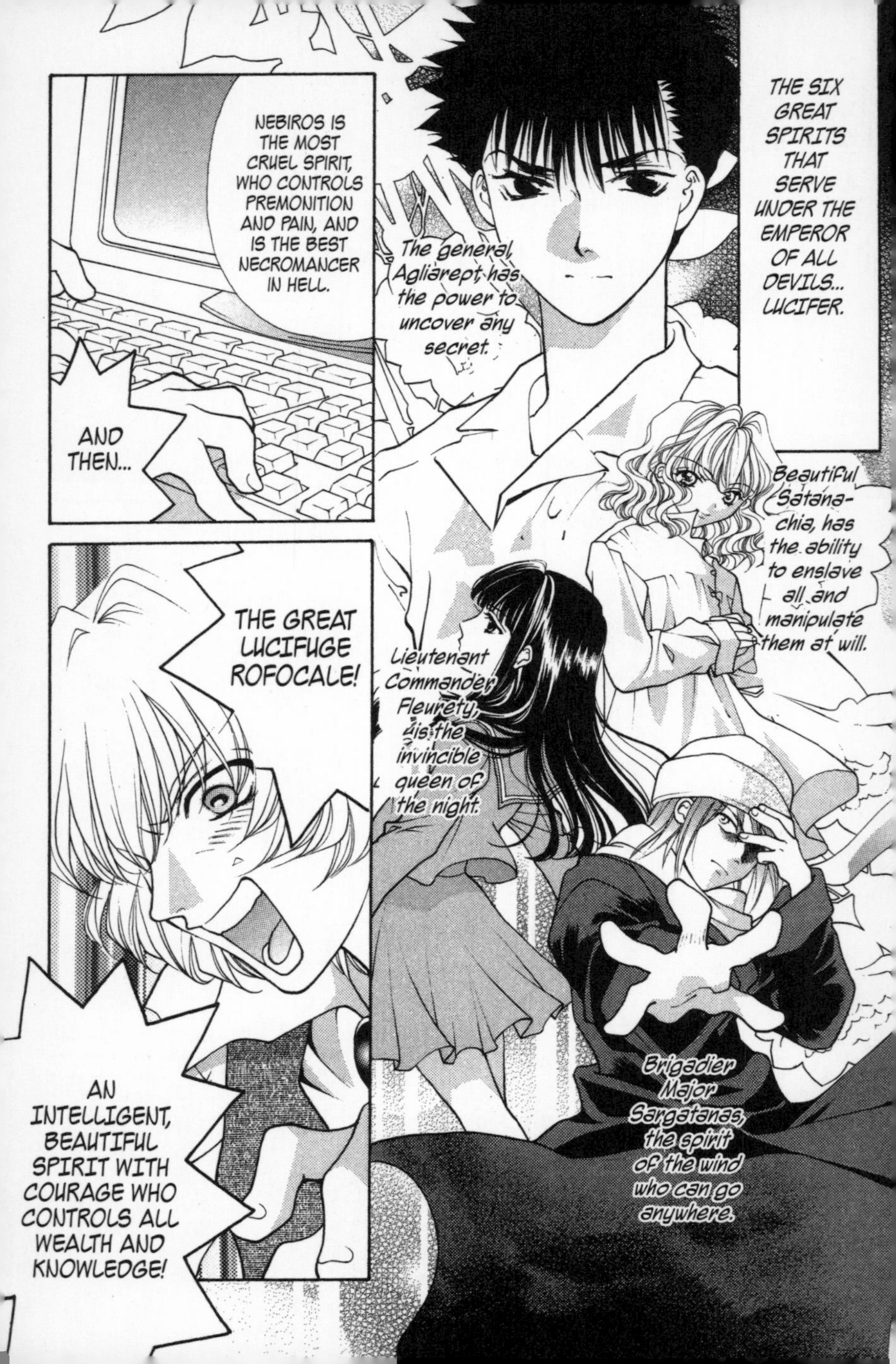
THE SIX GREAT SPIRITS THAT SERVE UNDER THE EMPEROR OF ALL DEVILS... LUCIFER.
The general, Agliarept, has the power to uncover any secret.
Beautiful Satanachia, has the ability to enslave all and manipulate them at will.
Lieutenant Commander Fleurety, is the invincible queen of the night.
Brigadier Major Sargatanas, the spirit of the wind who can go anywhere.
NEBIROS IS THE MOST CRUEL SPIRIT, WHO CONTROLS PREMONITION AND PAIN, AND IS THE BEST NECROMANCER IN HELL.
AND THEN...
THE GREAT LUCIFUGE ROFOCALE!
AN INTELLIGENT, BEAUTIFUL SPIRIT WITH COURAGE WHO CONTROLS ALL WEALTH AND KNOWLEDGE!

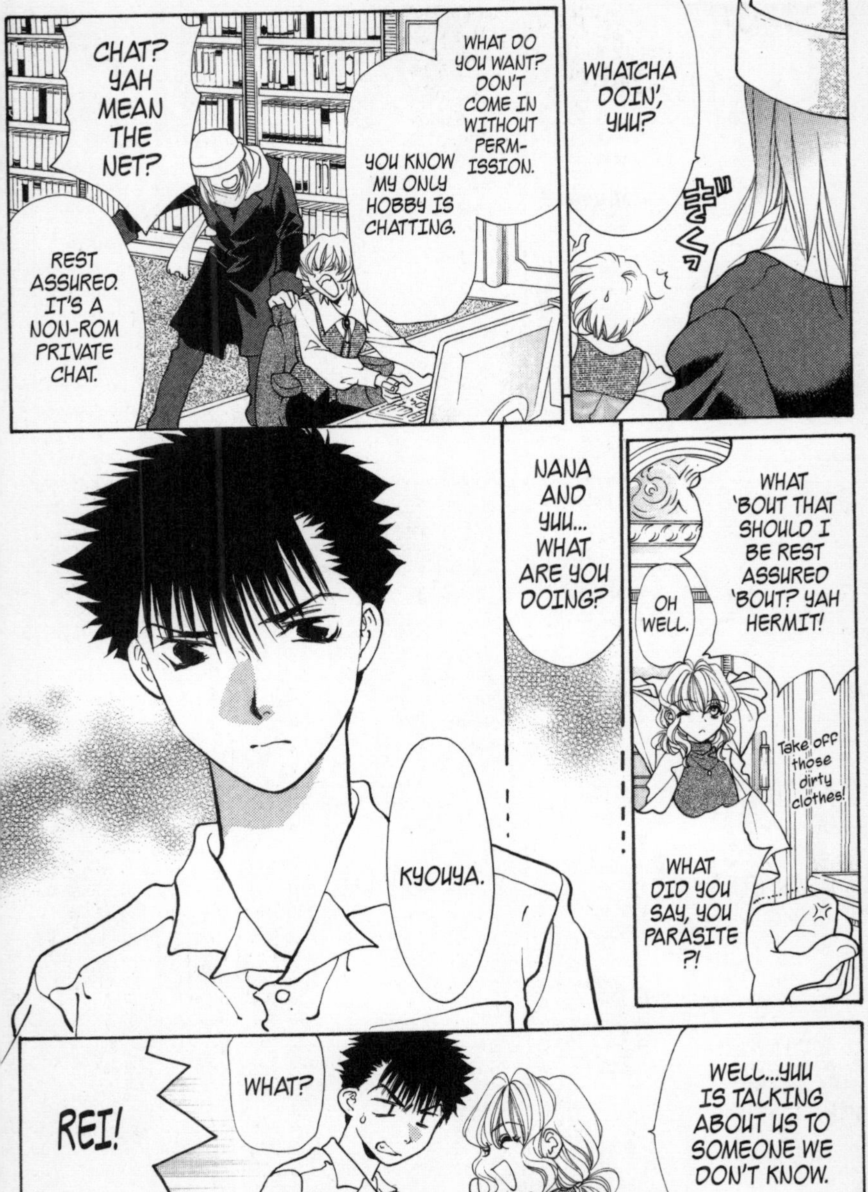
WHATCHA DOIN', YUU?
ぎくっ
WHAT DO YOU WANT? DON'T COME IN WITHOUT PERM-ISSION.
YOU KNOW MY ONLY HOBBY IS CHATTING.
CHAT? YAH MEAN THE NET?
REST ASSURED. IT'S A NON-ROM PRIVATE CHAT.
WHAT 'BOUT THAT SHOULD I BE REST ASSURED 'BOUT? YAH HERMIT!
OH WELL.
Take off those dirty clothes!
WHAT DID YOU SAY, YOU PARASITE ?!
NANA AND YUU... WHAT ARE YOU DOING?
KYOUYA.
WELL...YUU IS TALKING ABOUT US TO SOMEONE WE DON'T KNOW.
WHAT?
REI!

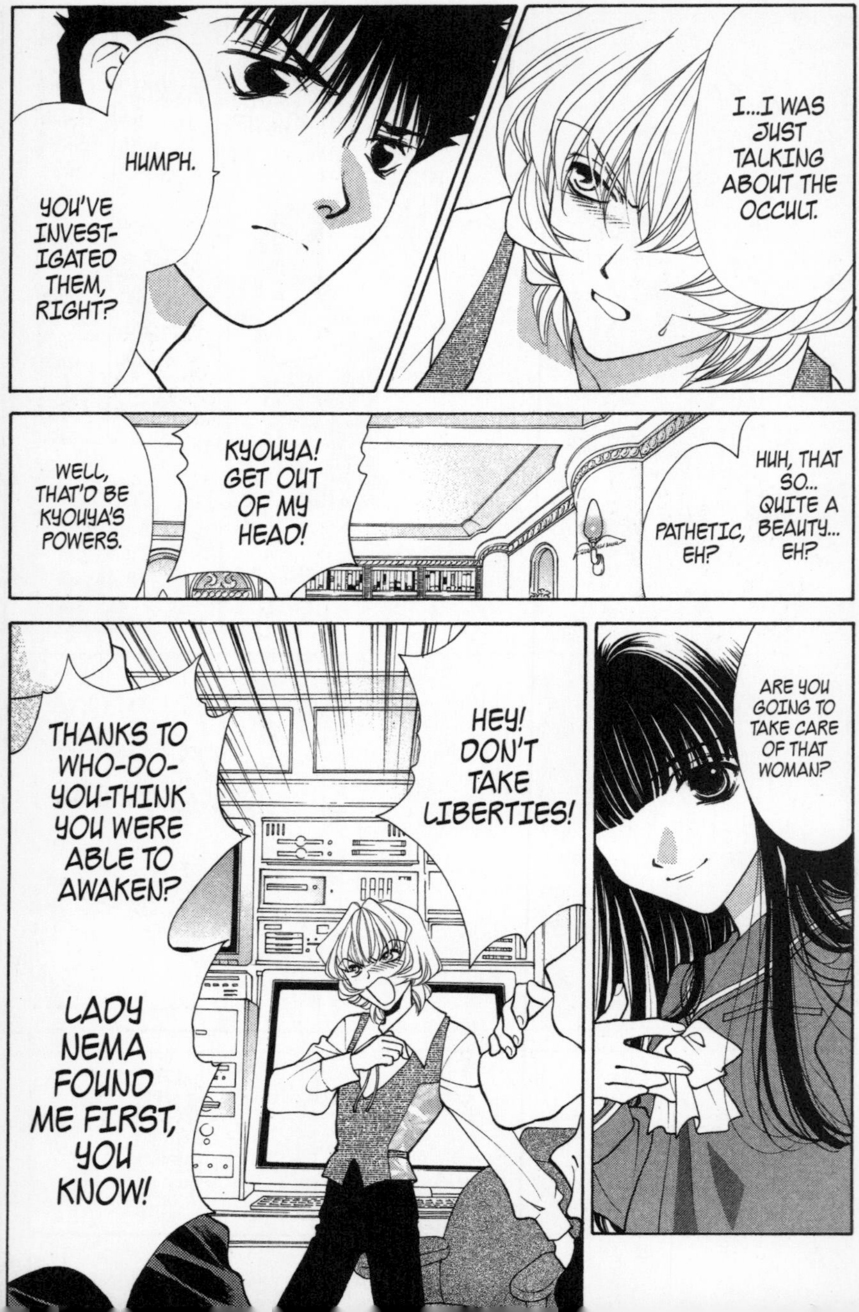
I...I WAS JUST TALKING ABOUT THE OCCULT.
HUMPH.
YOU'VE INVEST-IGATED THEM, RIGHT?
HUH, THAT SO... QUITE A BEAUTY... EH?
PATHETIC, EH?
KYOUYA! GET OUT OF MY HEAD!
WELL, THAT'D BE KYOUYA'S POWERS.
ARE YOU GOING TO TAKE CARE OF THAT WOMAN?
HEY! DON'T TAKE LIBERTIES!
THANKS TO WHO-DO-YOU-THINK YOU WERE ABLE TO AWAKEN?
LADY NEMA FOUND ME FIRST, YOU KNOW!

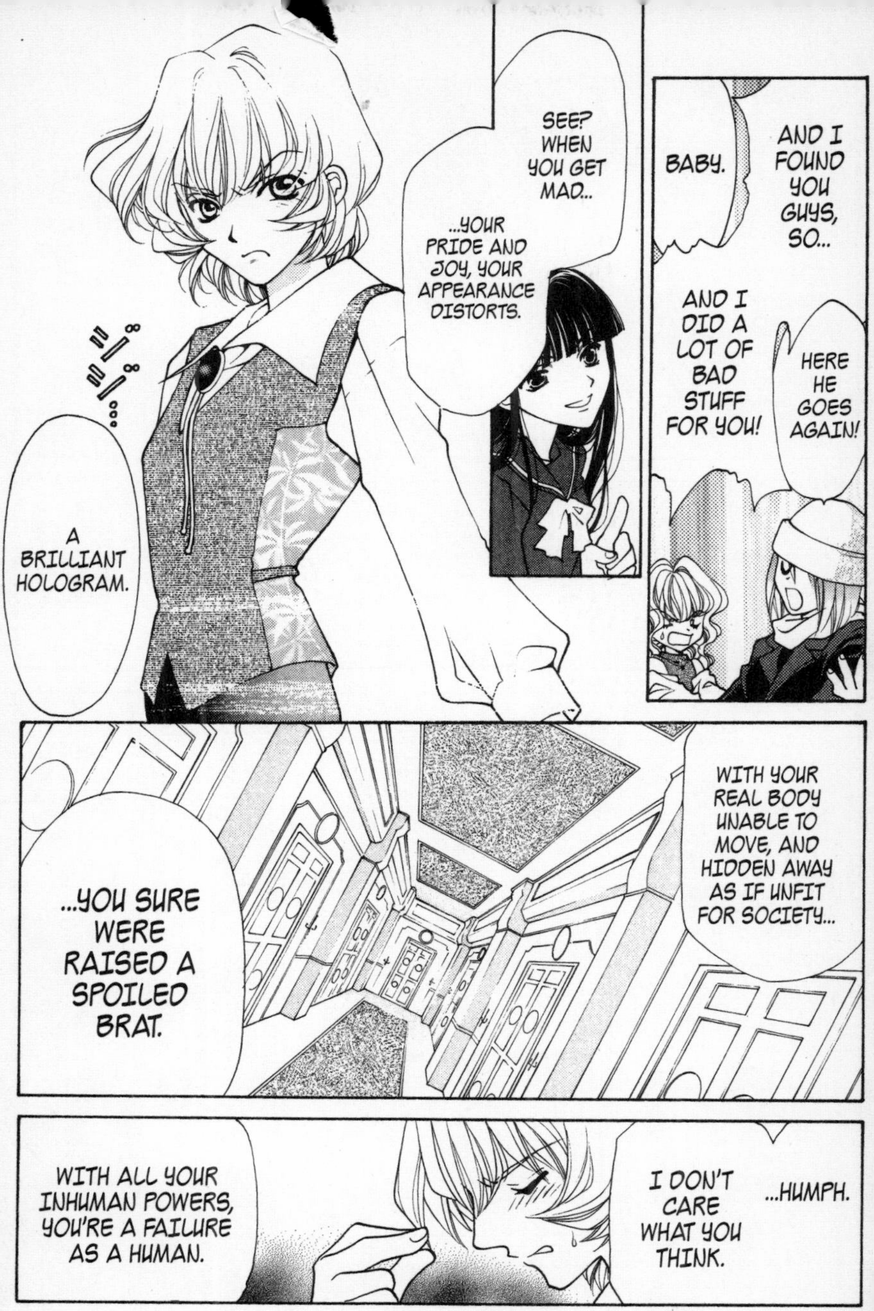
AND I FOUND YOU GUYS, SO...
BABY.
AND I DID A LOT OF BAD STUFF FOR YOU!
HERE HE GOES AGAIN!
SEE? WHEN YOU GET MAD...
...YOUR PRIDE AND JOY, YOUR APPEARANCE DISTORTS.
A BRILLIANT HOLOGRAM.
WITH YOUR REAL BODY UNABLE TO MOVE, AND HIDDEN AWAY AS IF UNFIT FOR SOCIETY...
...YOU SURE WERE RAISED A SPOILED BRAT.
...HUMPH.
I DON'T CARE WHAT YOU THINK.
WITH ALL YOUR INHUMAN POWERS, YOU'RE A FAILURE AS A HUMAN.

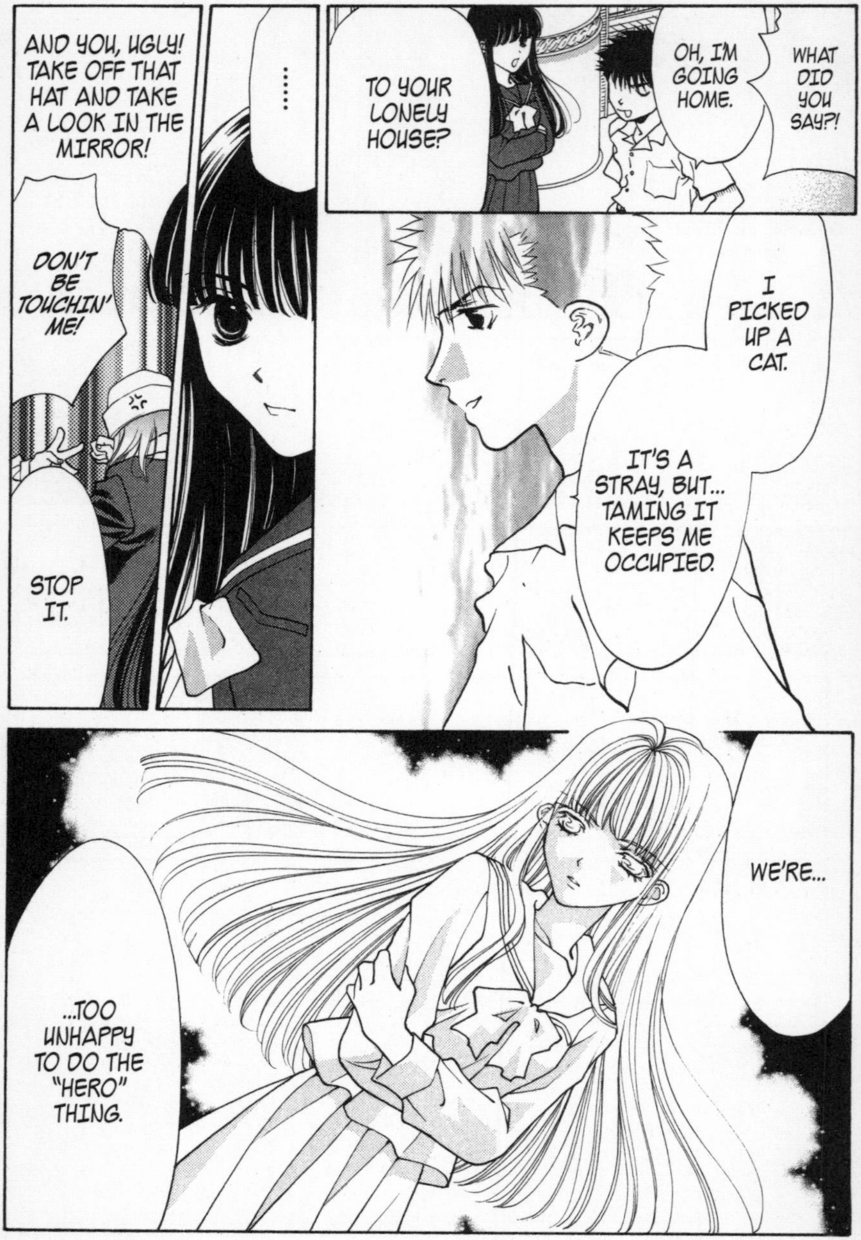
WHAT DID YOU SAY?!
OH, I'M GOING HOME.
TO YOUR LONELY HOUSE?
I PICKED UP A CAT.
IT'S A STRAY, BUT... TAMING IT KEEPS ME OCCUPIED.
......
AND YOU, UGLY! TAKE OFF THAT HAT AND TAKE A LOOK IN THE MIRROR!
DON'T BE TOUCHIN' ME!
STOP IT.
WE'RE...
...TOO UNHAPPY TO DO THE "HERO" THING.

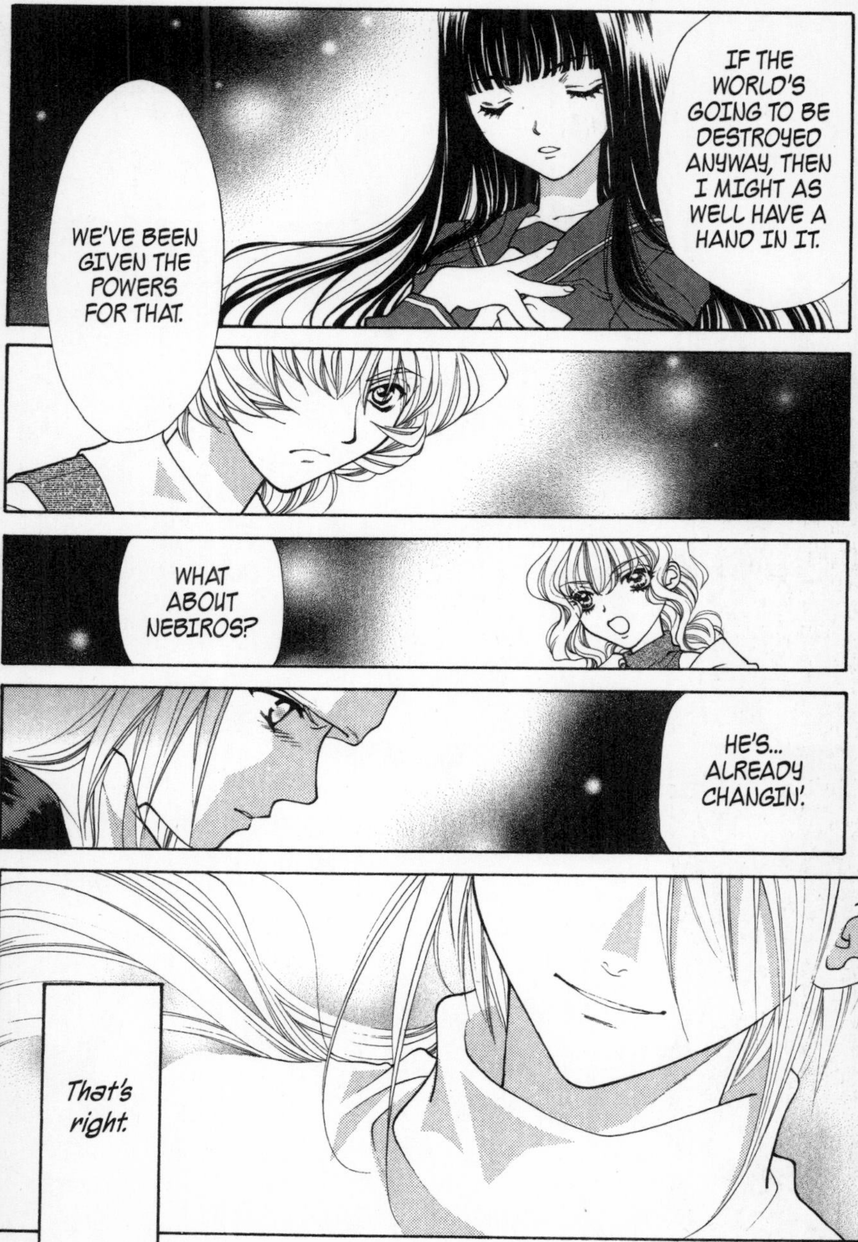
IF THE WORLD'S GOING TO BE DESTROYED ANYWAY, THEN I MIGHT AS WELL HAVE A HAND IN IT.
WE'VE BEEN GIVEN THE POWERS FOR THAT.
WHAT ABOUT NEBIROS?
HE'S... ALREADY CHANGIN'.
That's right.

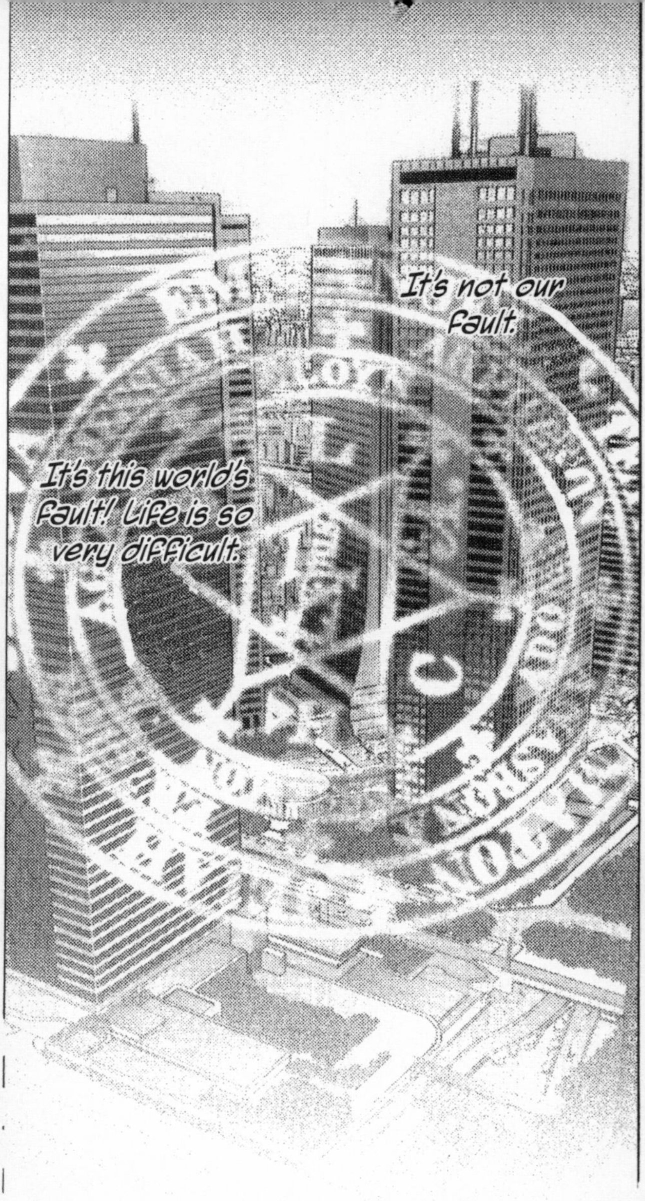
It's not our fault.
It's this world's fault! Life is so very difficult.
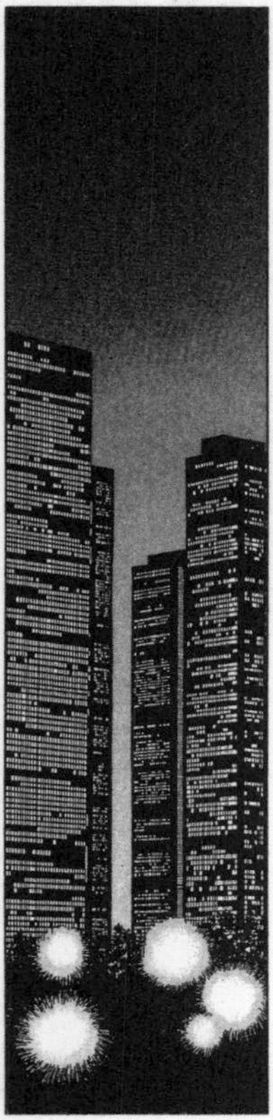

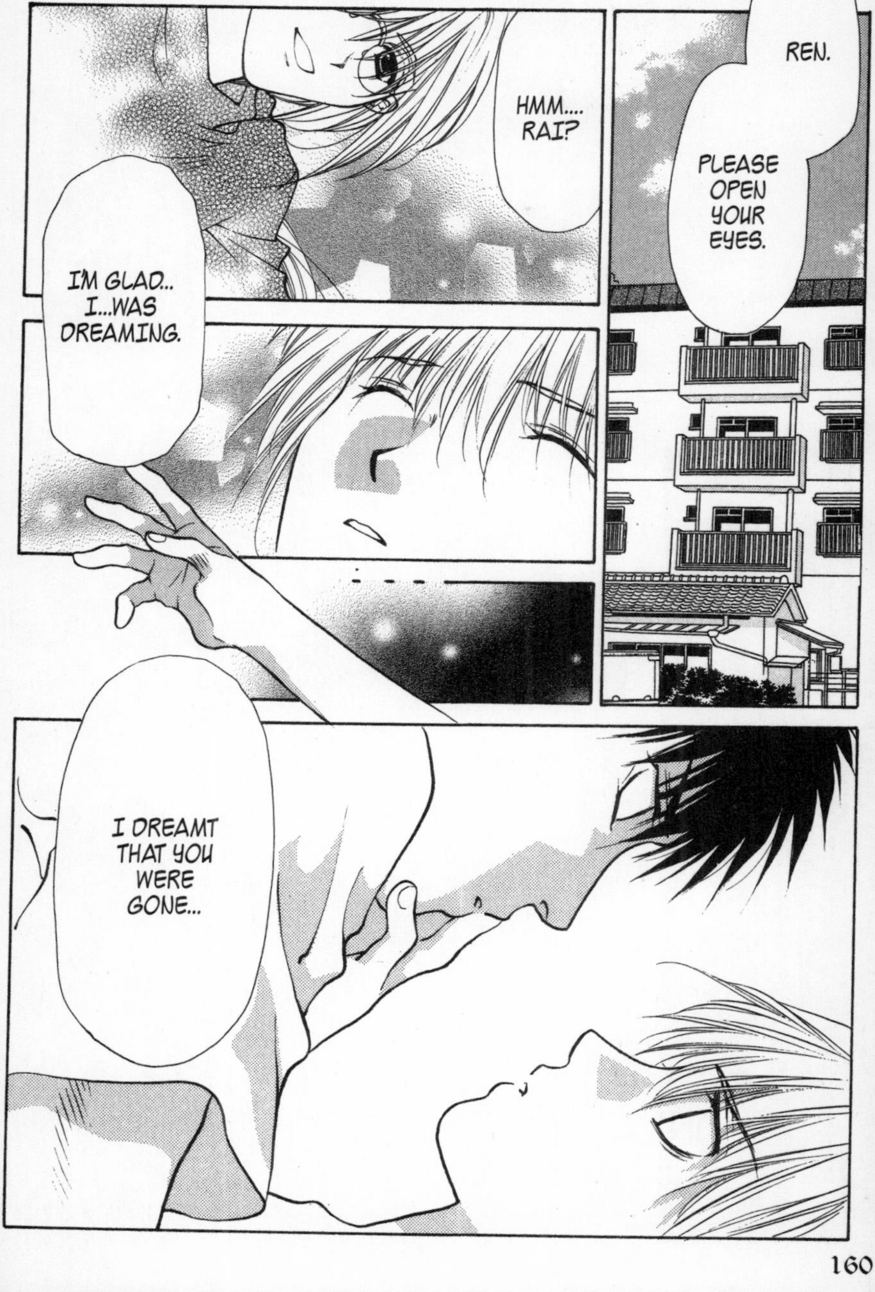
REN.
PLEASE OPEN YOUR EYES.
HMM.... RAI?
I'M GLAD... I...WAS DREAMING.
I DREAMT THAT YOU WERE GONE...

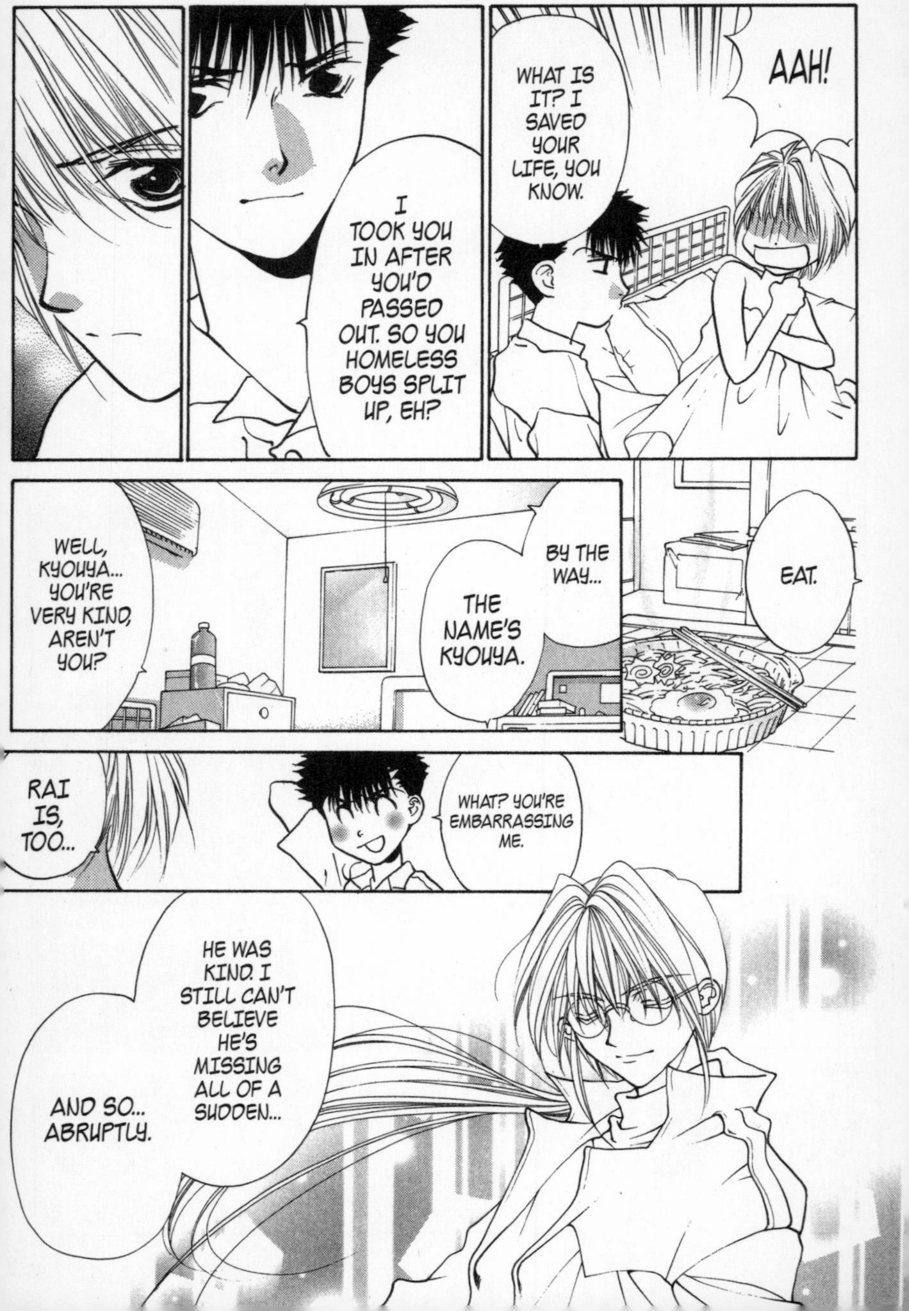

AAH!
WHAT IS IT? I SAVED YOUR LIFE, YOU KNOW.
I TOOK YOU IN AFTER YOU'D PASSED OUT. SO YOU HOMELESS BOYS SPLIT UP, EH?
EAT.
BY THE WAY...
THE NAME'S KYOUYA.
WELL, KYOUYA... YOU'RE VERY KIND, AREN'T YOU?
WHAT? YOU'RE EMBARRASSING ME.
RAI IS, TOO...
HE WAS KIND. I STILL CAN'T BELIEVE HE'S MISSING ALL OF A SUDDEN...
AND SO... ABRUPTLY.

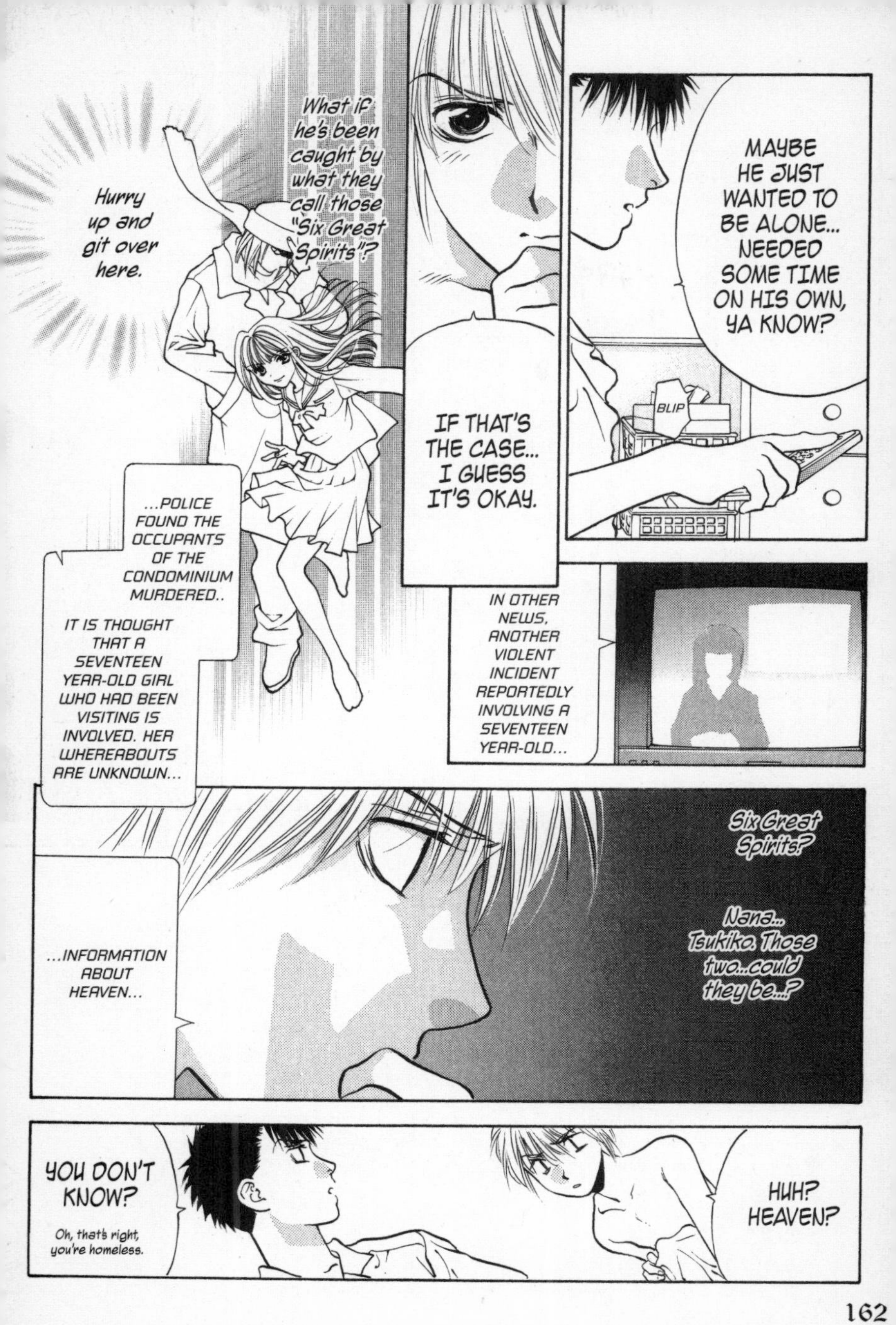
MAYBE HE JUST WANTED TO BE ALONE... NEEDED SOME TIME ON HIS OWN, YA KNOW?
BLIP
IF THAT'S THE CASE... I GUESS IT'S OKAY.
What if he's been caught by what they call those "Six Great Spirits"?
Hurry up and git over here.
IN OTHER NEWS, ANOTHER VIOLENT INCIDENT REPORTEDLY INVOLVING A SEVENTEEN YEAR-OLD...
...POLICE FOUND THE OCCUPANTS OF THE CONDOMINIUM MURDERED..
IT IS THOUGHT THAT A SEVENTEEN YEAR-OLD GIRL WHO HAD BEEN VISITING IS INVOLVED. HER WHEREABOUTS ARE UNKNOWN...
Six Great Spirits?
Nana... Tsukiko. Those two...could they be...?
...INFORMATION ABOUT HEAVEN...
HUH? HEAVEN?
YOU DON'T KNOW?
Oh, that's right, you're homeless.

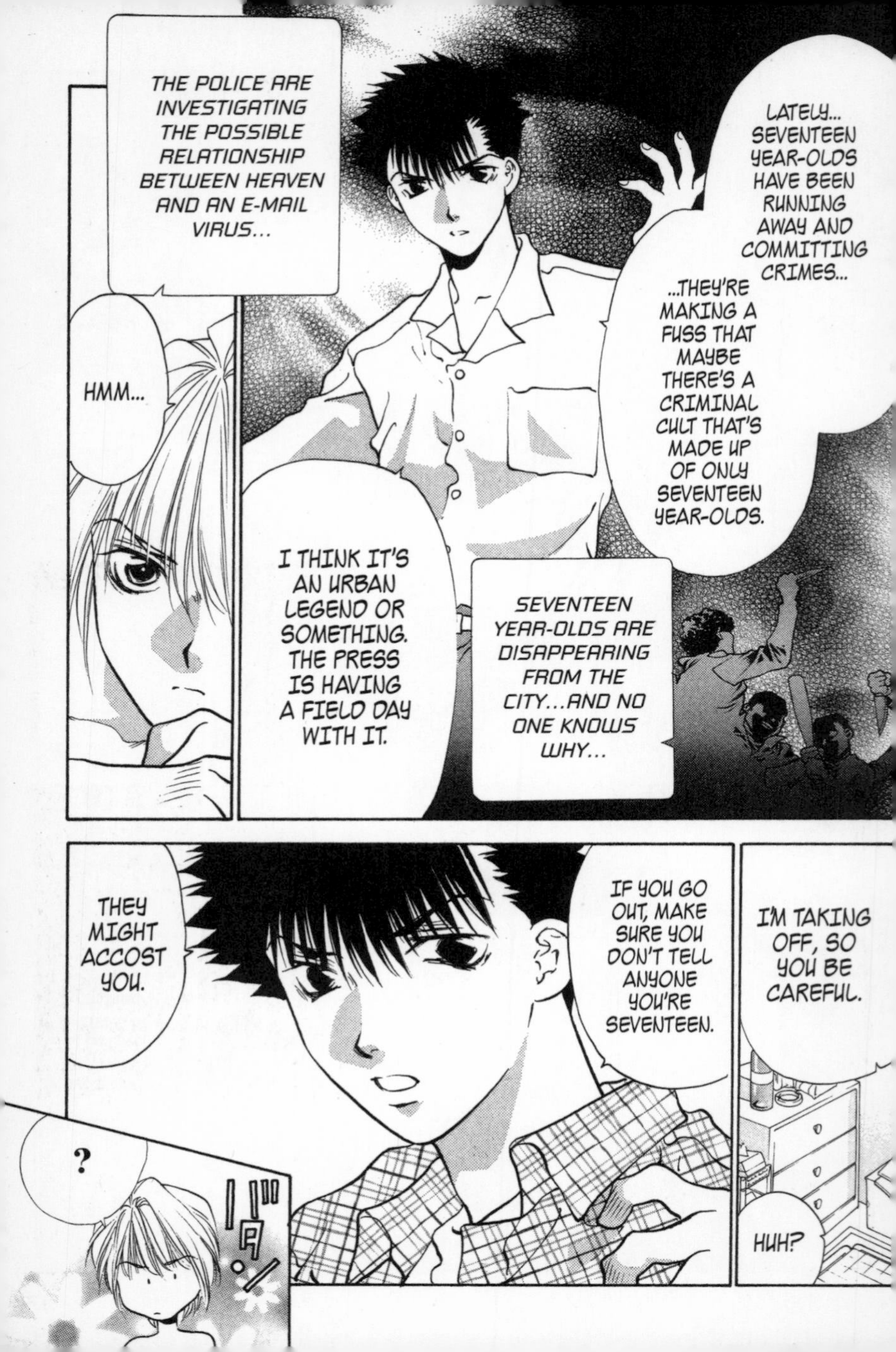
LATELY... SEVENTEEN YEAR-OLDS HAVE BEEN RUNNING AWAY AND COMMITTING CRIMES...
...THEY'RE MAKING A FUSS THAT MAYBE THERE'S A CRIMINAL CULT THAT'S MADE UP OF ONLY SEVENTEEN YEAR-OLDS.
SEVENTEEN YEAR-OLDS ARE DISAPPEARING FROM THE CITY...AND NO ONE KNOWS WHY...
I THINK IT'S AN URBAN LEGEND OR SOMETHING. THE PRESS IS HAVING A FIELD DAY WITH IT.
THE POLICE ARE INVESTIGATING THE POSSIBLE RELATIONSHIP BETWEEN HEAVEN AND AN E-MAIL VIRUS...
HMM...
I'M TAKING OFF, SO YOU BE CAREFUL.
HUH?
IF YOU GO OUT, MAKE SURE YOU DON'T TELL ANYONE YOU'RE SEVENTEEN.
THEY MIGHT ACCOST YOU.
?

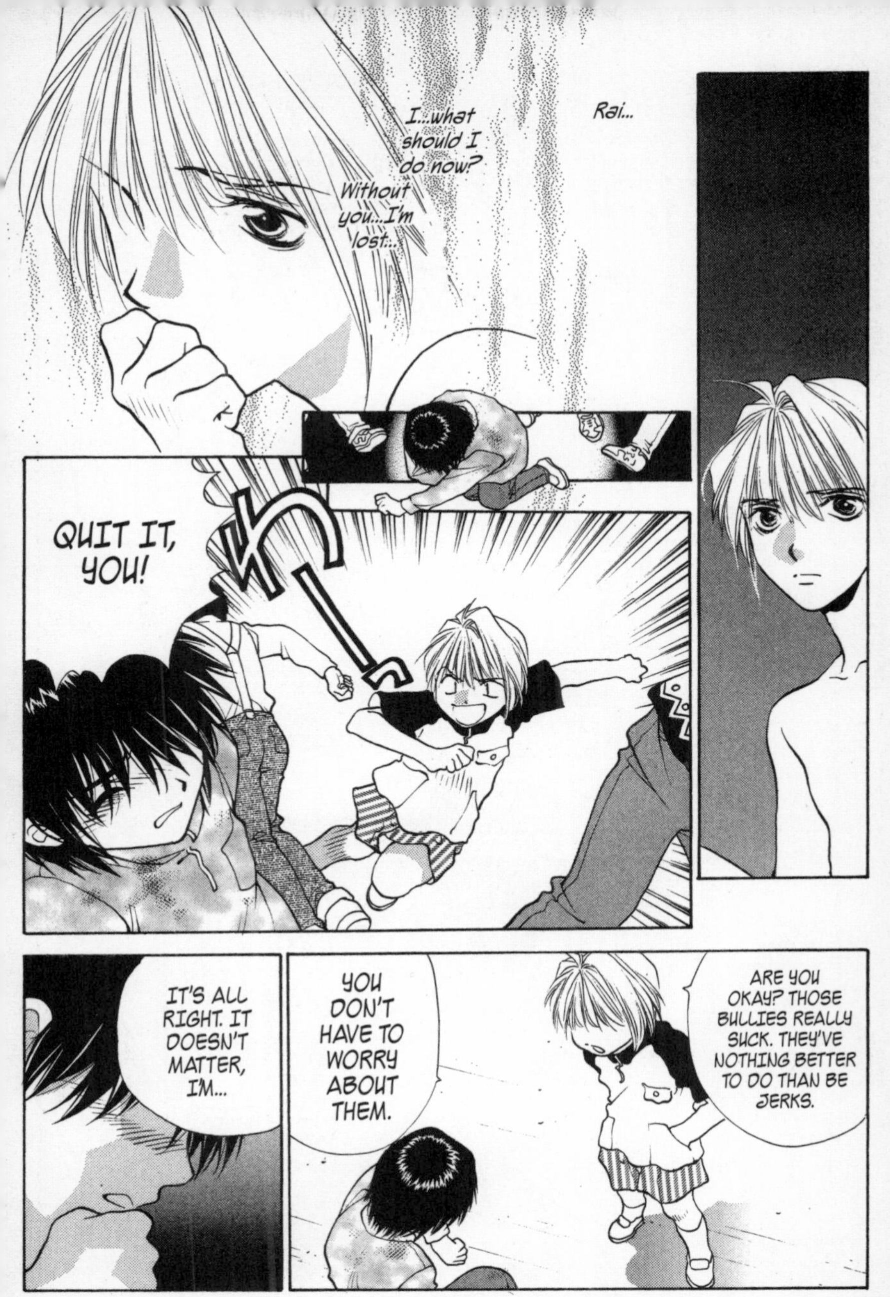
Rai...
I...what should I do now?
Without you...I'm lost...
QUIT IT, YOU!
ARE YOU OKAY? THOSE BULLIES REALLY SUCK. THEY'VE NOTHING BETTER TO DO THAN BE JERKS.
YOU DON'T HAVE TO WORRY ABOUT THEM.
IT'S ALL RIGHT. IT DOESN'T MATTER, I'M...

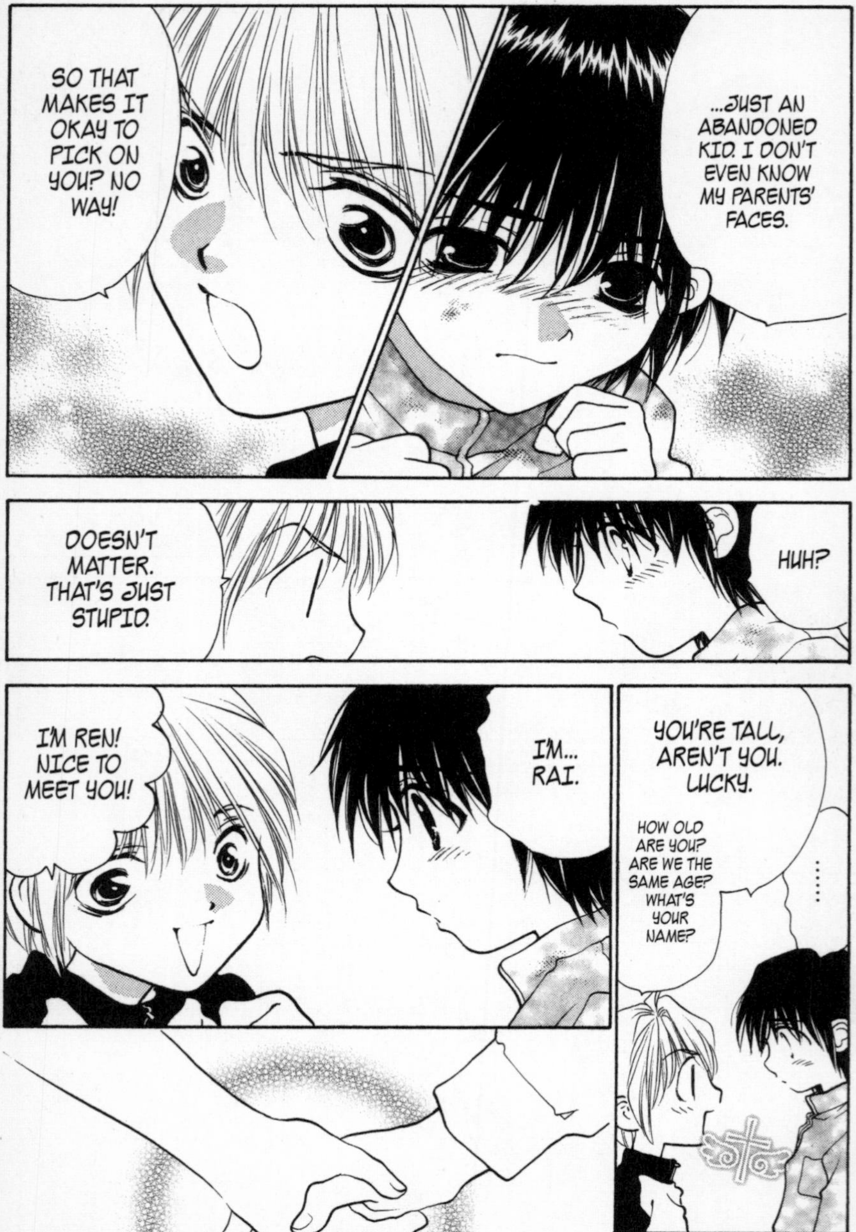
...JUST AN ABANDONED KID. I DON'T EVEN KNOW MY PARENTS' FACES.
SO THAT MAKES IT OKAY TO PICK ON YOU? NO WAY!
HUH?
DOESN'T MATTER. THAT'S JUST STUPID.
YOU'RE TALL, AREN'T YOU. LUCKY.
HOW OLD ARE YOU? ARE WE THE SAME AGE? WHAT'S YOUR NAME?
......
I'M... RAI.
I'M REN! NICE TO MEET YOU!

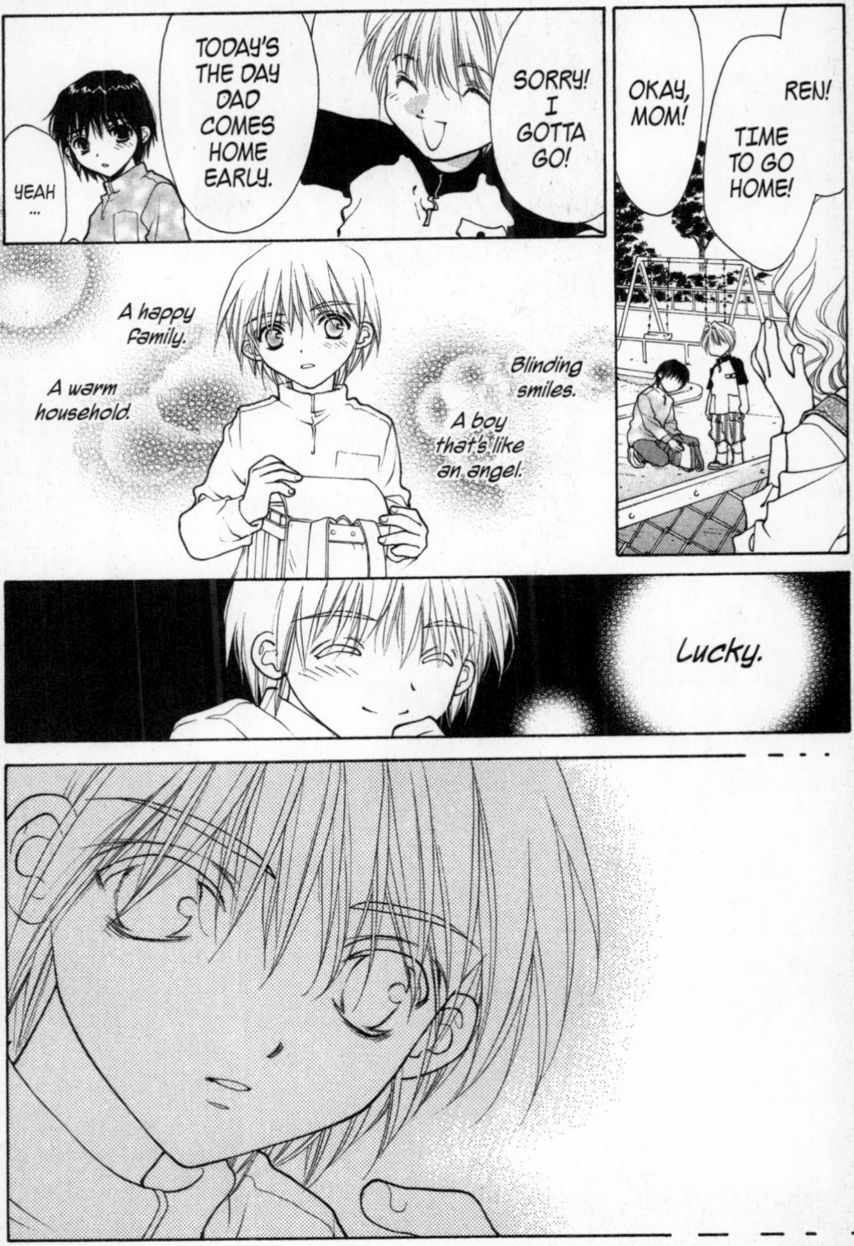
REN!
TIME TO GO HOME!
OKAY, MOM!
SORRY! I GOTTA GO!
TODAY'S THE DAY DAD COMES HOME EARLY.
YEAH ...
Blinding smiles.
A boy that's like an angel.
A happy family.
A warm household.
Lucky.

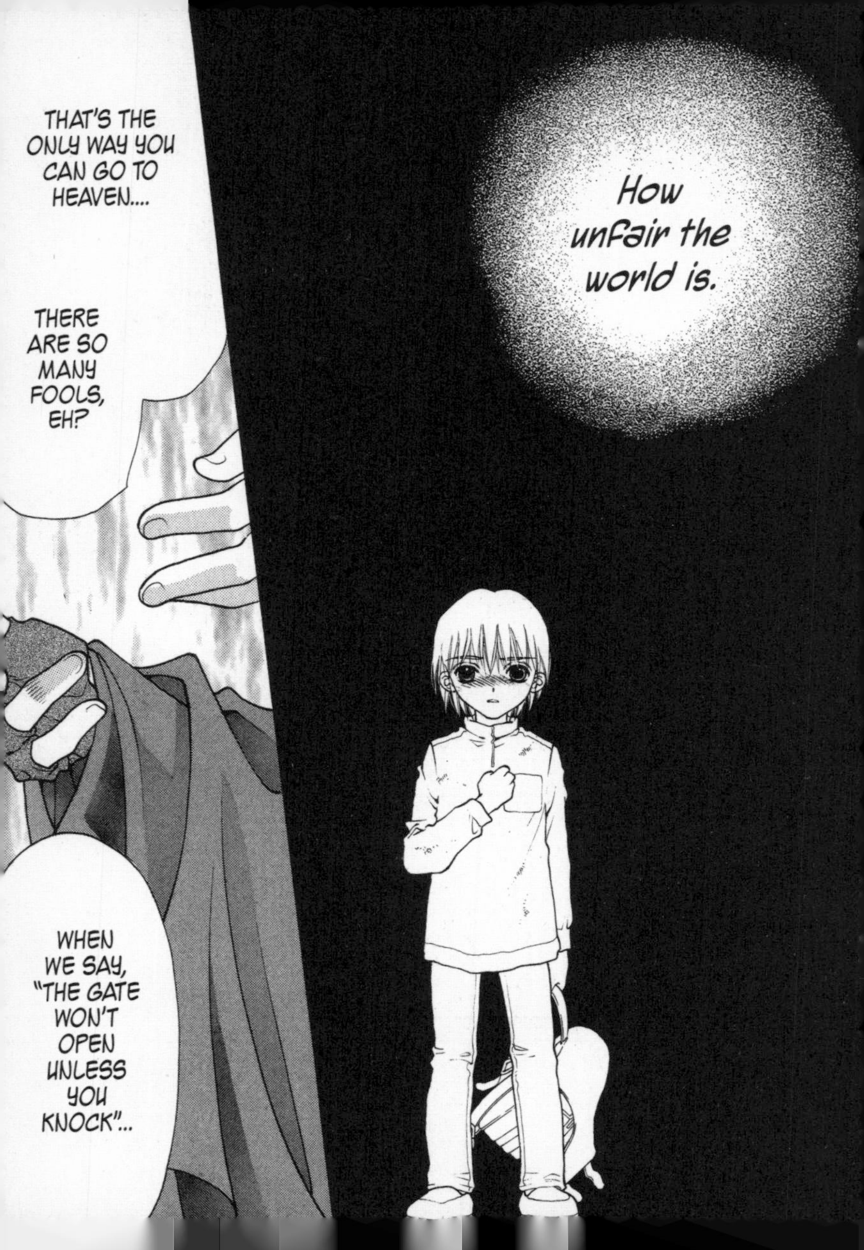
How unfair the world is.
THAT'S THE ONLY WAY YOU CAN GO TO HEAVEN....
THERE ARE SO MANY FOOLS, EH?
WHEN WE SAY, "THE GATE WON'T OPEN UNLESS YOU KNOCK"...

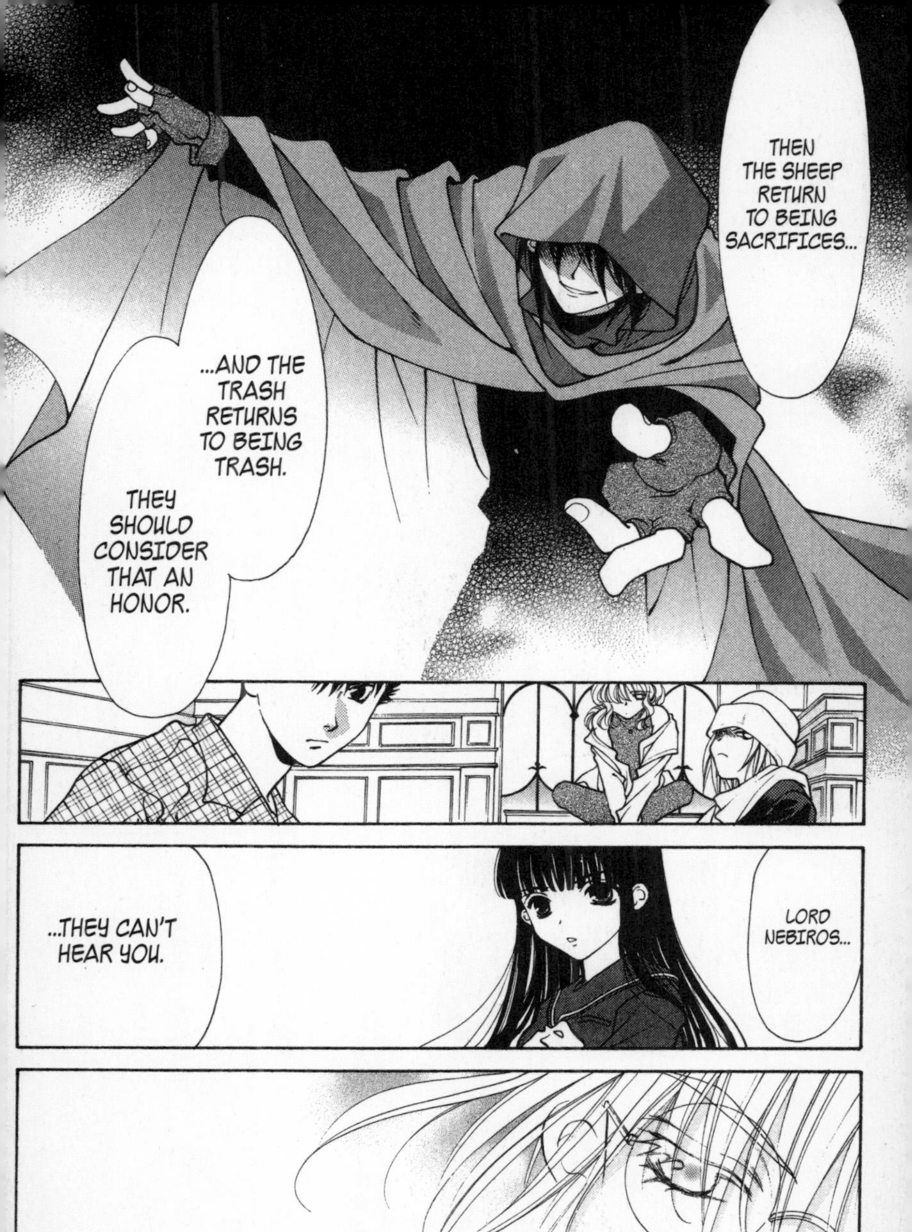
THEN THE SHEEP RETURN TO BEING SACRIFICES...
...AND THE TRASH RETURNS TO BEING TRASH.
THEY SHOULD CONSIDER THAT AN HONOR.
LORD NEBIROS...
...THEY CAN'T HEAR YOU.

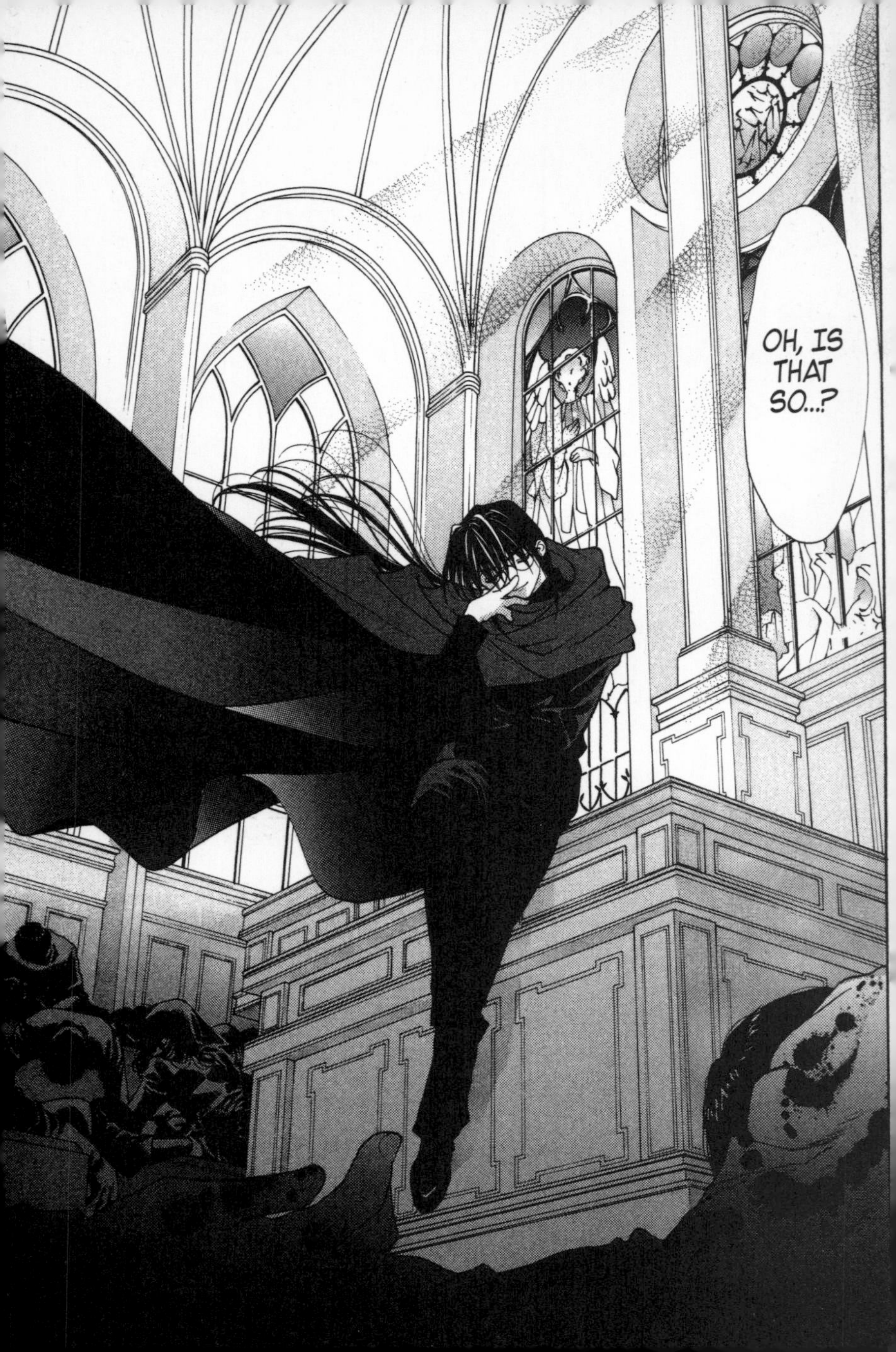
OH, IS THAT SO...?

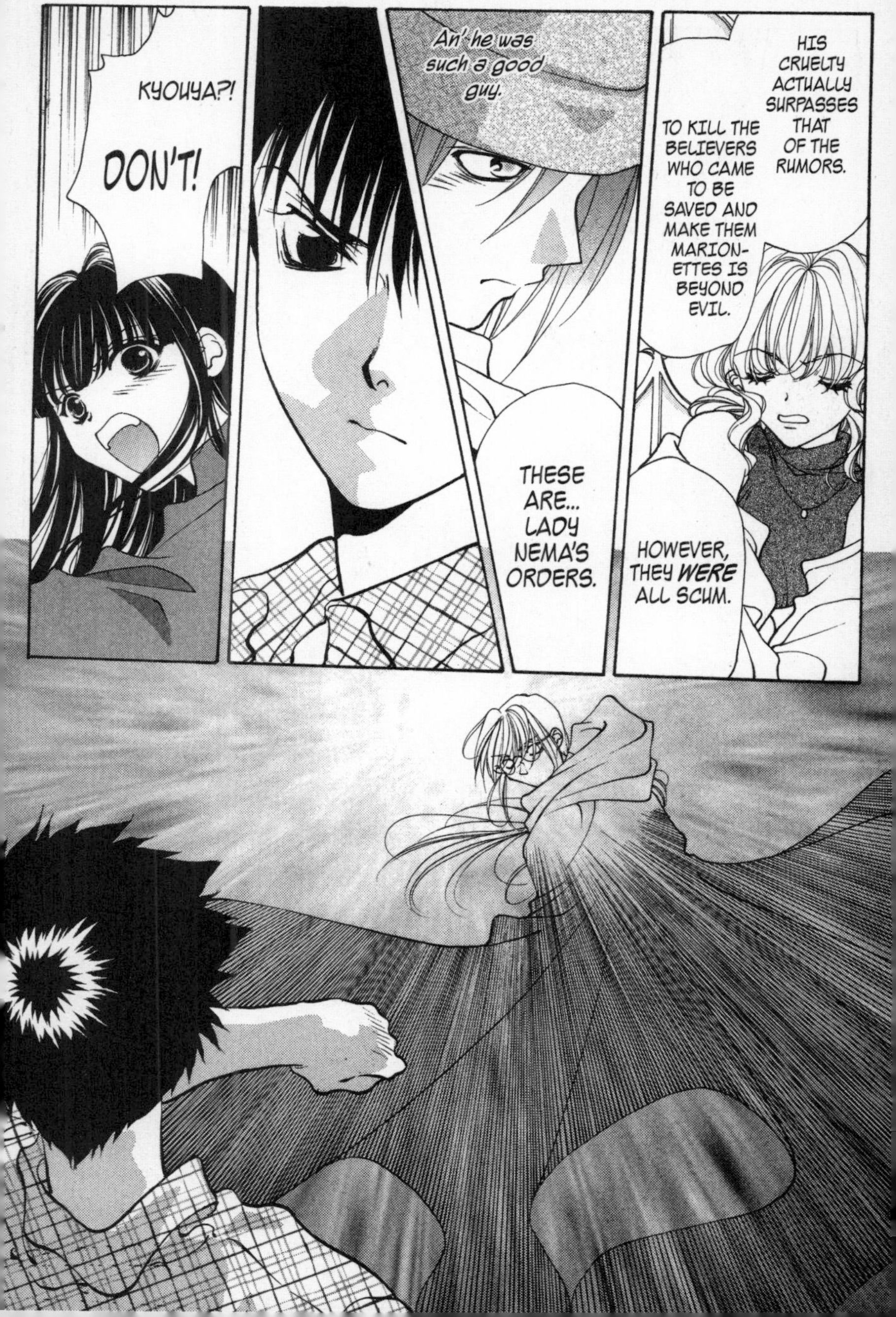
HIS CRUELTY ACTUALLY SURPASSES THAT OF THE RUMORS.
TO KILL THE BELIEVERS WHO CAME TO BE SAVED AND MAKE THEM MARIONETTES IS BEYOND EVIL.
HOWEVER, THEY *WERE* ALL SCUM.
An' he was such a good guy.
THESE ARE... LADY NEMA'S ORDERS.
KYOUYA?!
DON'T!

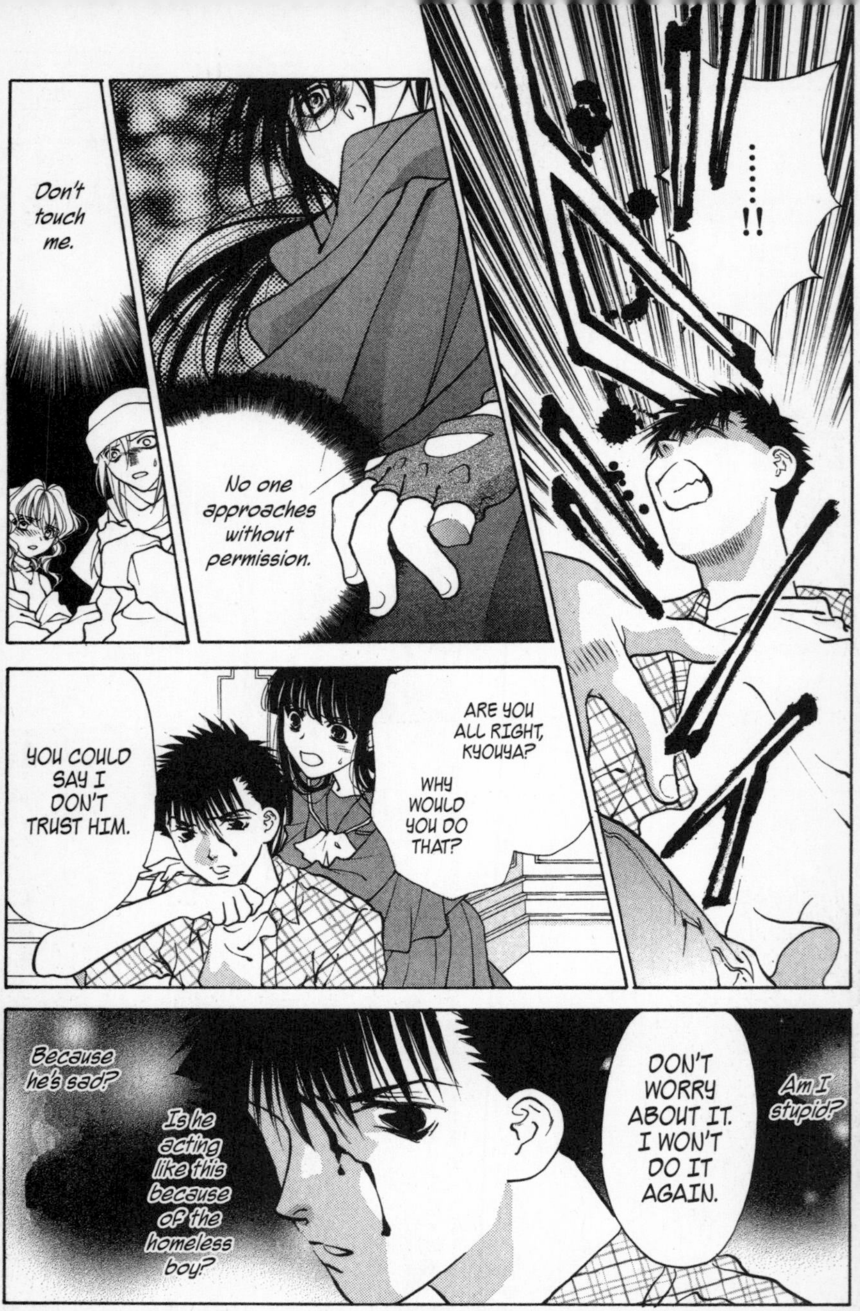
……!!
No one approaches without permission.
Don't touch me.
ARE YOU ALL RIGHT, KYOUYA?
WHY WOULD YOU DO THAT?
YOU COULD SAY I DON'T TRUST HIM.
DON'T WORRY ABOUT IT. I WON'T DO IT AGAIN.
Am I stupid?
Because he's sad?
Is he acting like this because of the homeless boy?

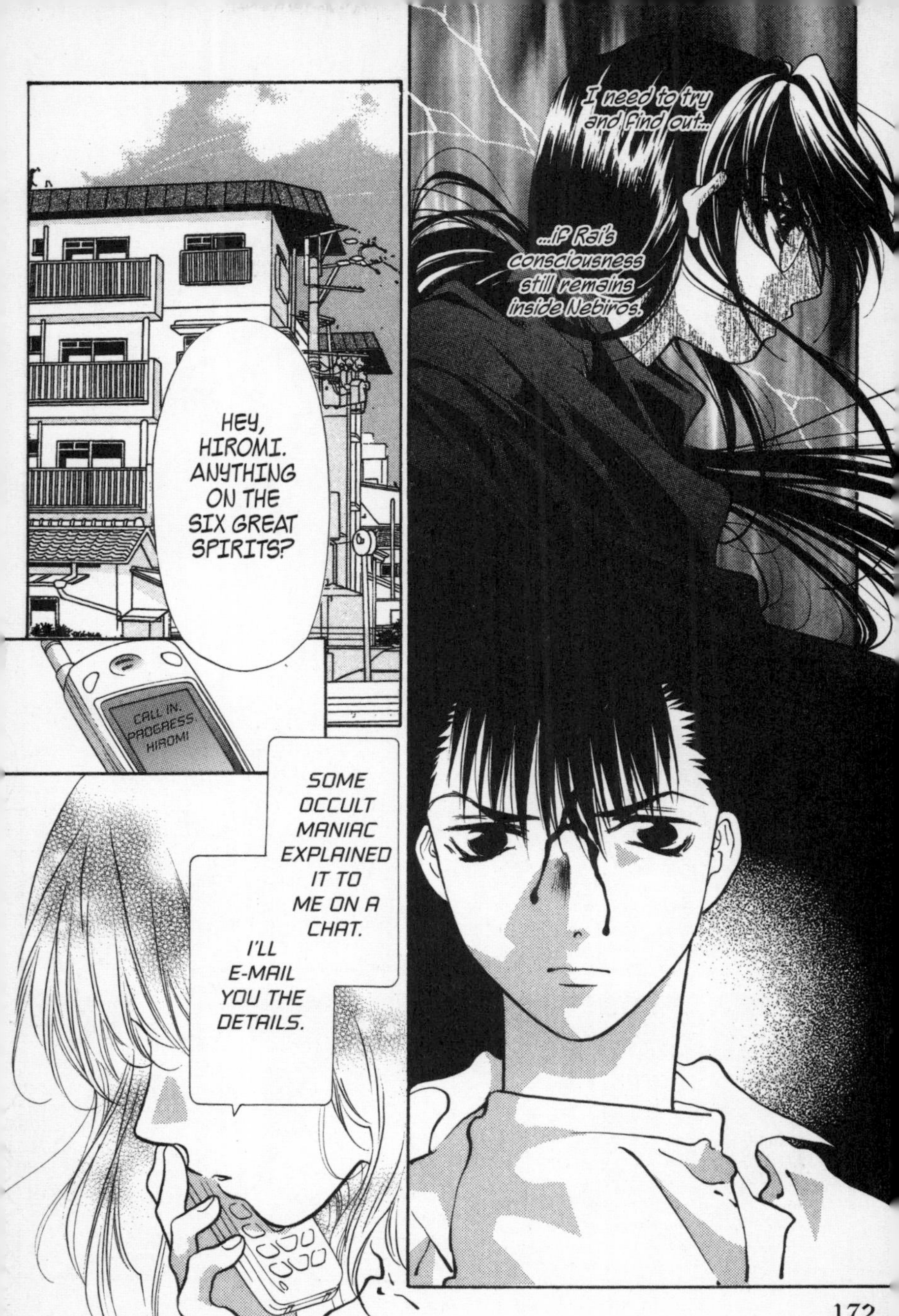
I need to try and find out...
...if Rai's consciousness still remains inside Nebiros.
HEY, HIROMI. ANYTHING ON THE SIX GREAT SPIRITS?
CALL IN PROGRESS HIROMI
SOME OCCULT MANIAC EXPLAINED IT TO ME ON A CHAT.
I'LL E-MAIL YOU THE DETAILS.

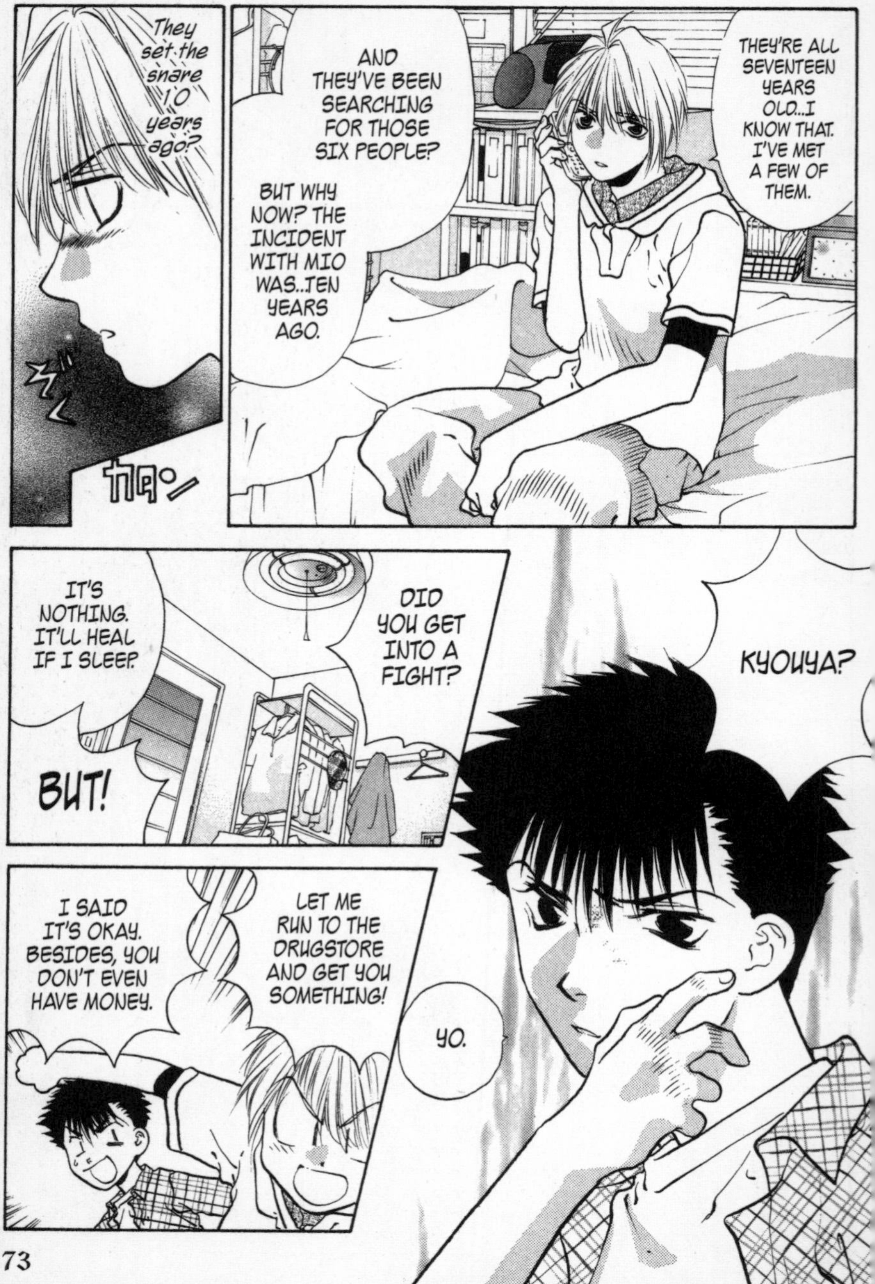
THEY'RE ALL SEVENTEEN YEARS OLD...I KNOW THAT. I'VE MET A FEW OF THEM.
AND THEY'VE BEEN SEARCHING FOR THOSE SIX PEOPLE?
BUT WHY NOW? THE INCIDENT WITH MIO WAS...TEN YEARS AGO.
They set the snare 10 years ago?
カタン
KYOUYA?
YO.
DID YOU GET INTO A FIGHT?
IT'S NOTHING. IT'LL HEAL IF I SLEEP.
BUT!
LET ME RUN TO THE DRUGSTORE AND GET YOU SOMETHING!
I SAID IT'S OKAY. BESIDES, YOU DON'T EVEN HAVE MONEY.

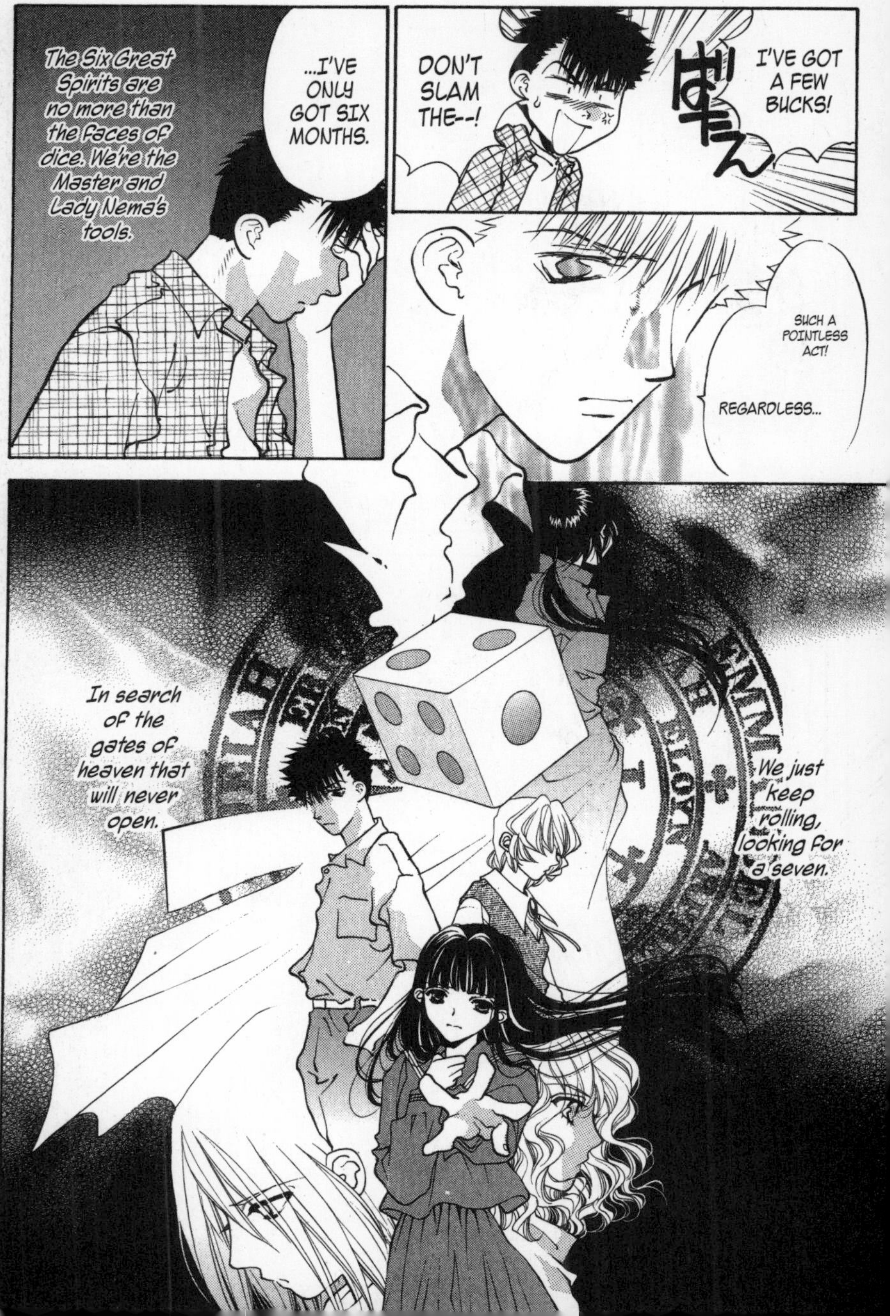

I'VE GOT A FEW BUCKS!
ばたん
DON'T SLAM THE--!
...I'VE ONLY GOT SIX MONTHS.
The Six Great Spirits are no more than the faces of dice. We're the Master and Lady Nema's tools.
SUCH A POINTLESS ACT!
REGARDLESS...
We just keep rolling, looking for a seven.
In search of the gates of heaven that will never open.

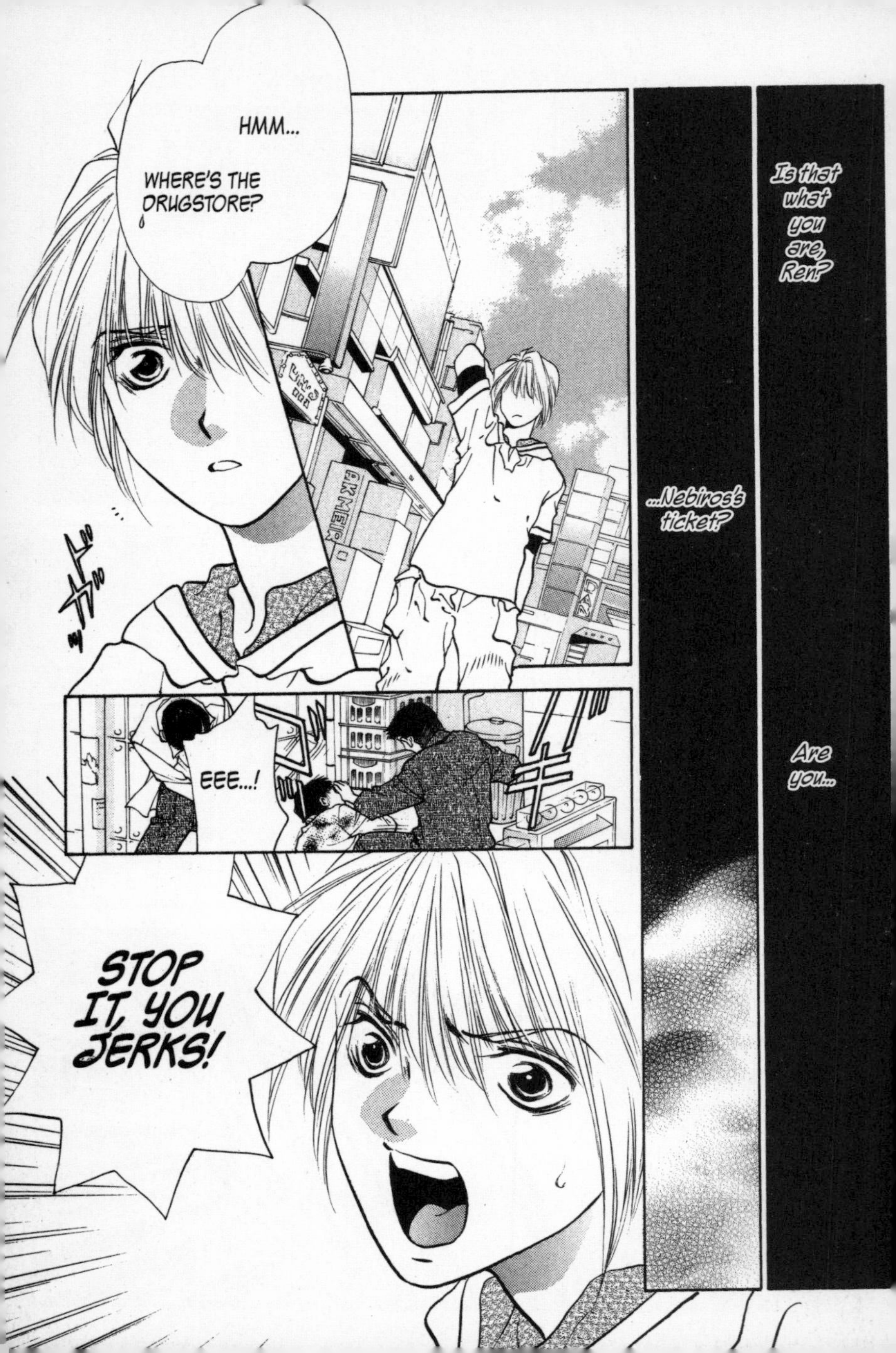

Is that what you are, Ren?
Are you...
...Nebiros's ticket?
HMM...
WHERE'S THE DRUGSTORE?
EEE...!
STOP IT, YOU JERKS!

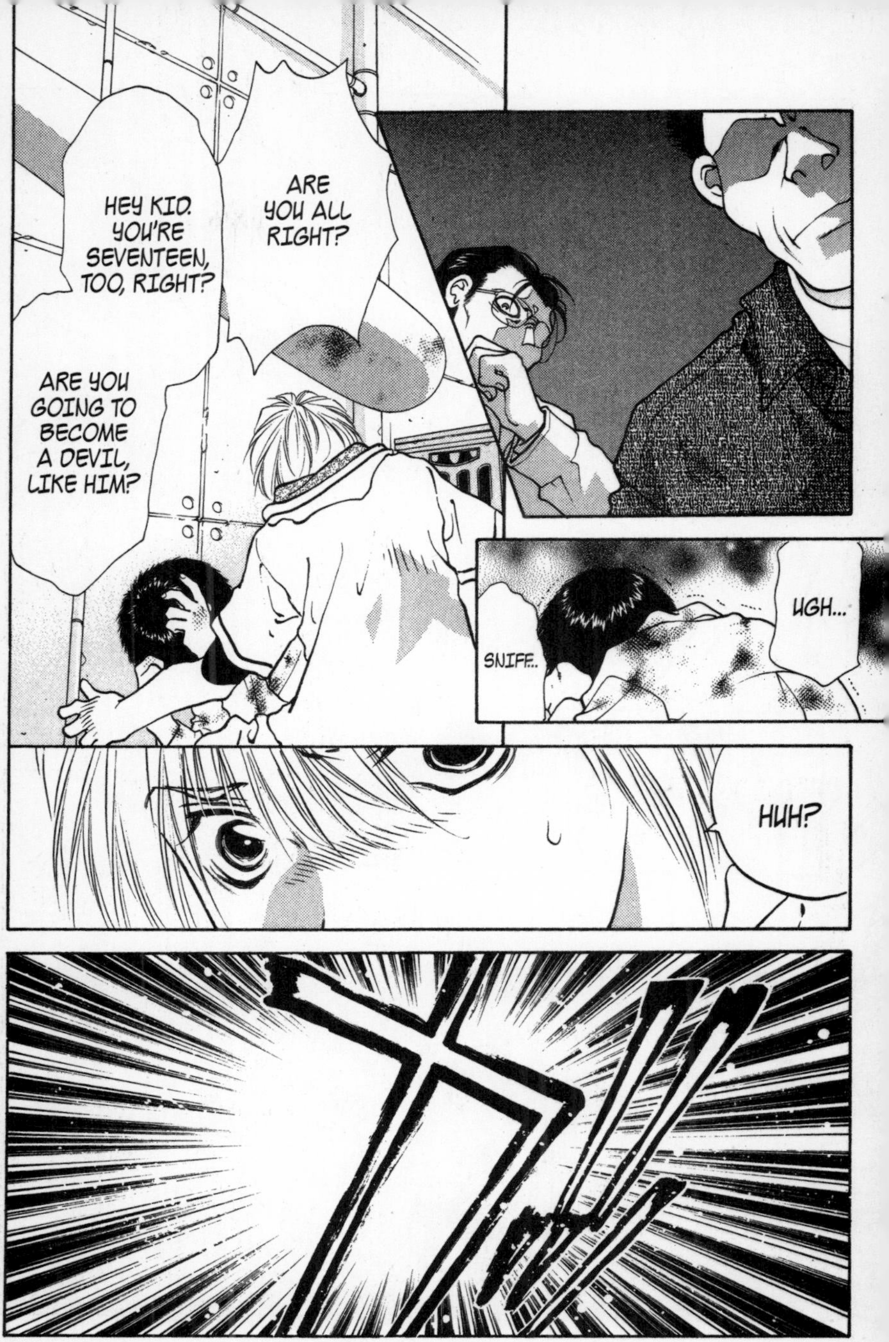
UGH...
SNIFF...
ARE YOU ALL RIGHT?
HEY KID. YOU'RE SEVENTEEN, TOO, RIGHT?
ARE YOU GOING TO BECOME A DEVIL, LIKE HIM?
HUH?

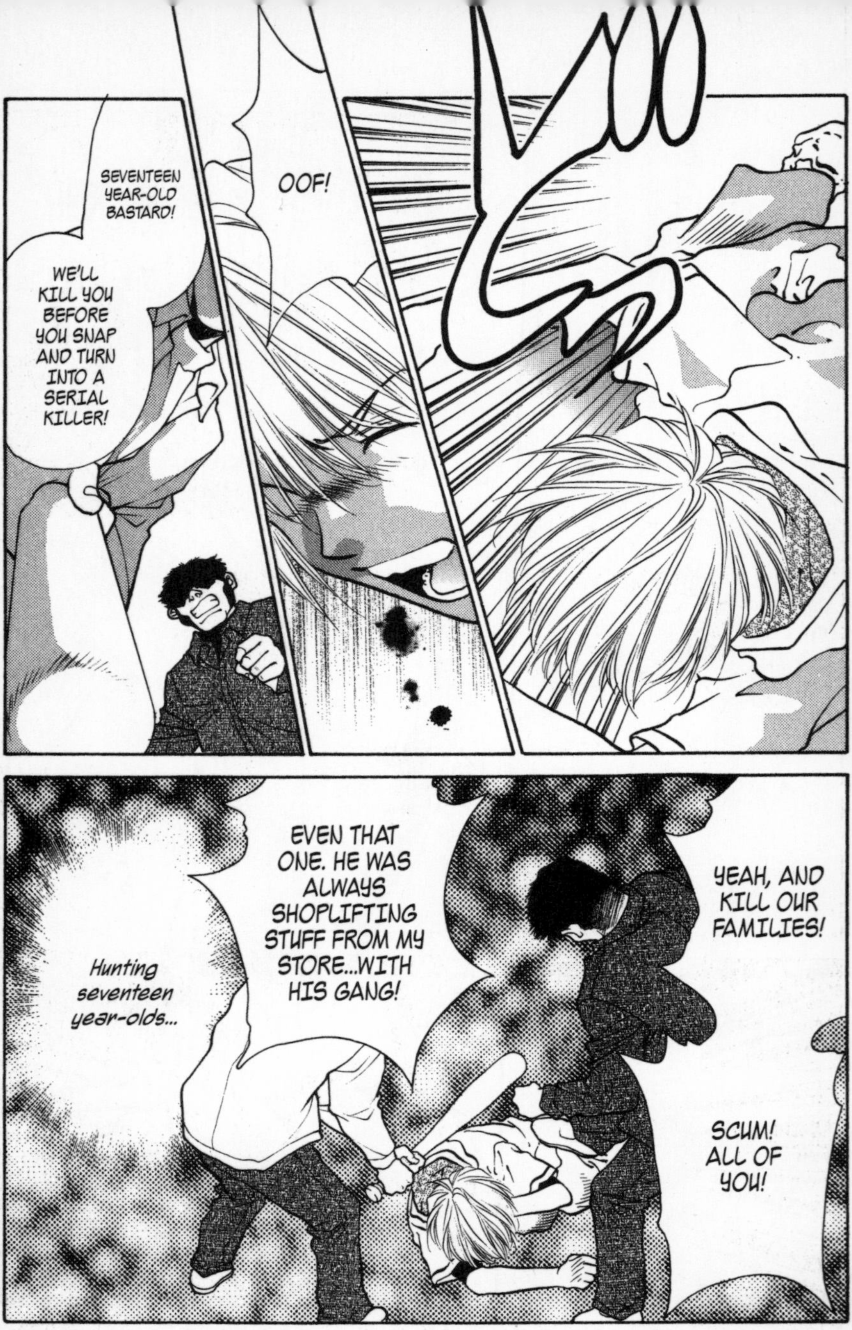
OOF!
SEVENTEEN YEAR-OLD BASTARD!
WE'LL KILL YOU BEFORE YOU SNAP AND TURN INTO A SERIAL KILLER!
YEAH, AND KILL OUR FAMILIES!
EVEN THAT ONE. HE WAS ALWAYS SHOPLIFTING STUFF FROM MY STORE...WITH HIS GANG!
SCUM! ALL OF YOU!
Hunting seventeen year-olds...

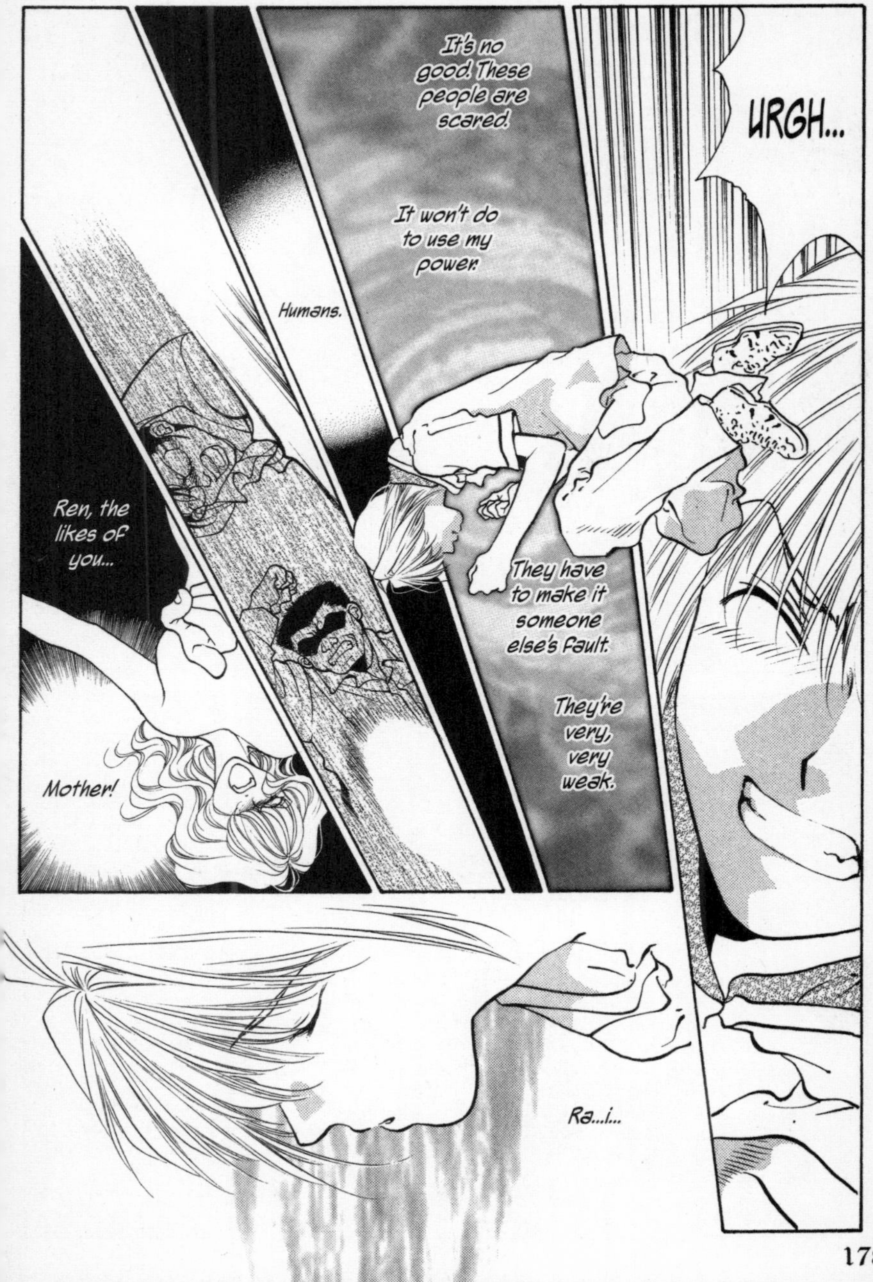
URGH...
It's no good. These people are scared.
It won't do to use my power.
They have to make it someone else's fault.
They're very, very weak.
Humans.
Ren, the likes of you...
Mother!
Ra...i...

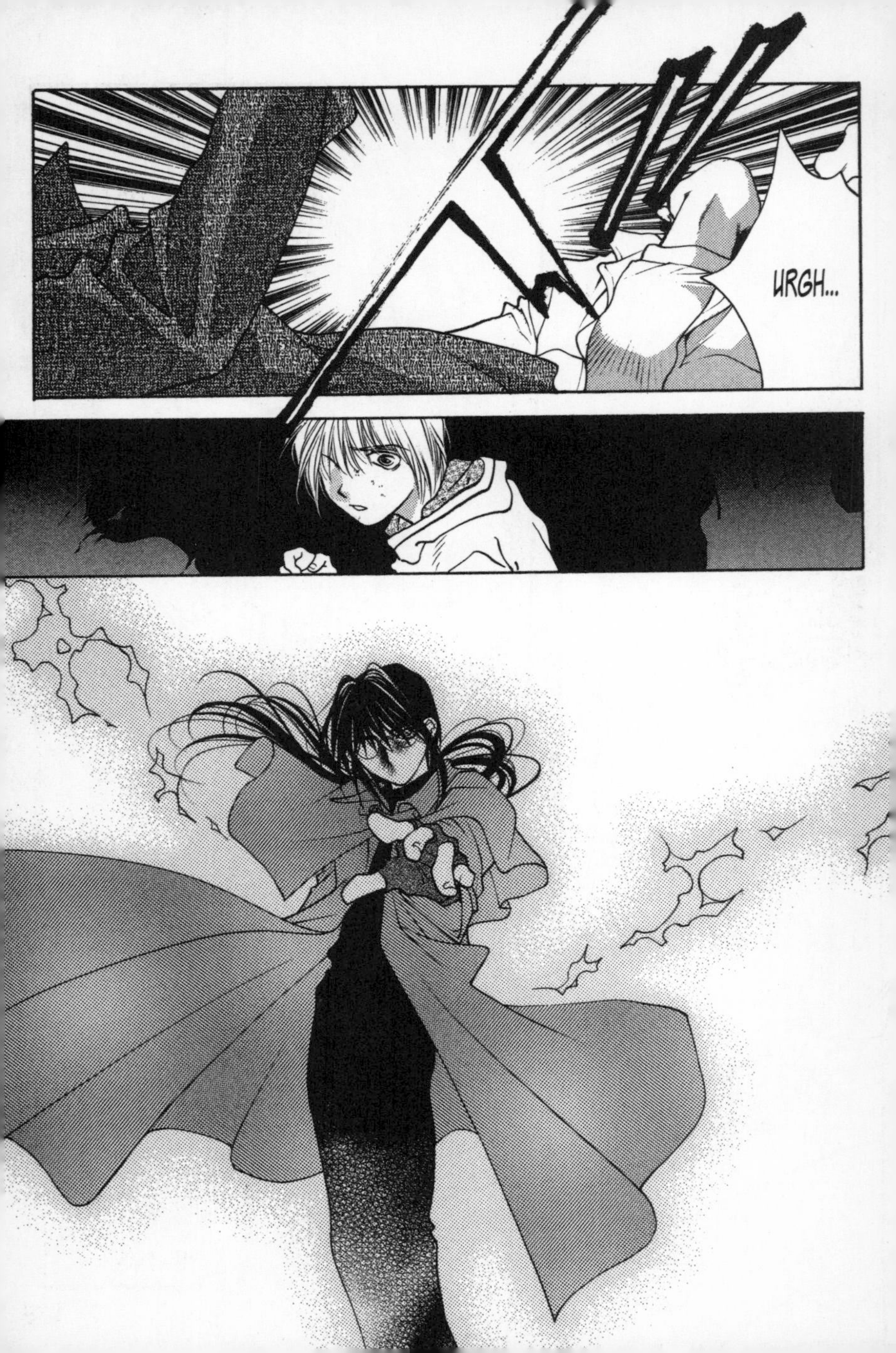
URGH...

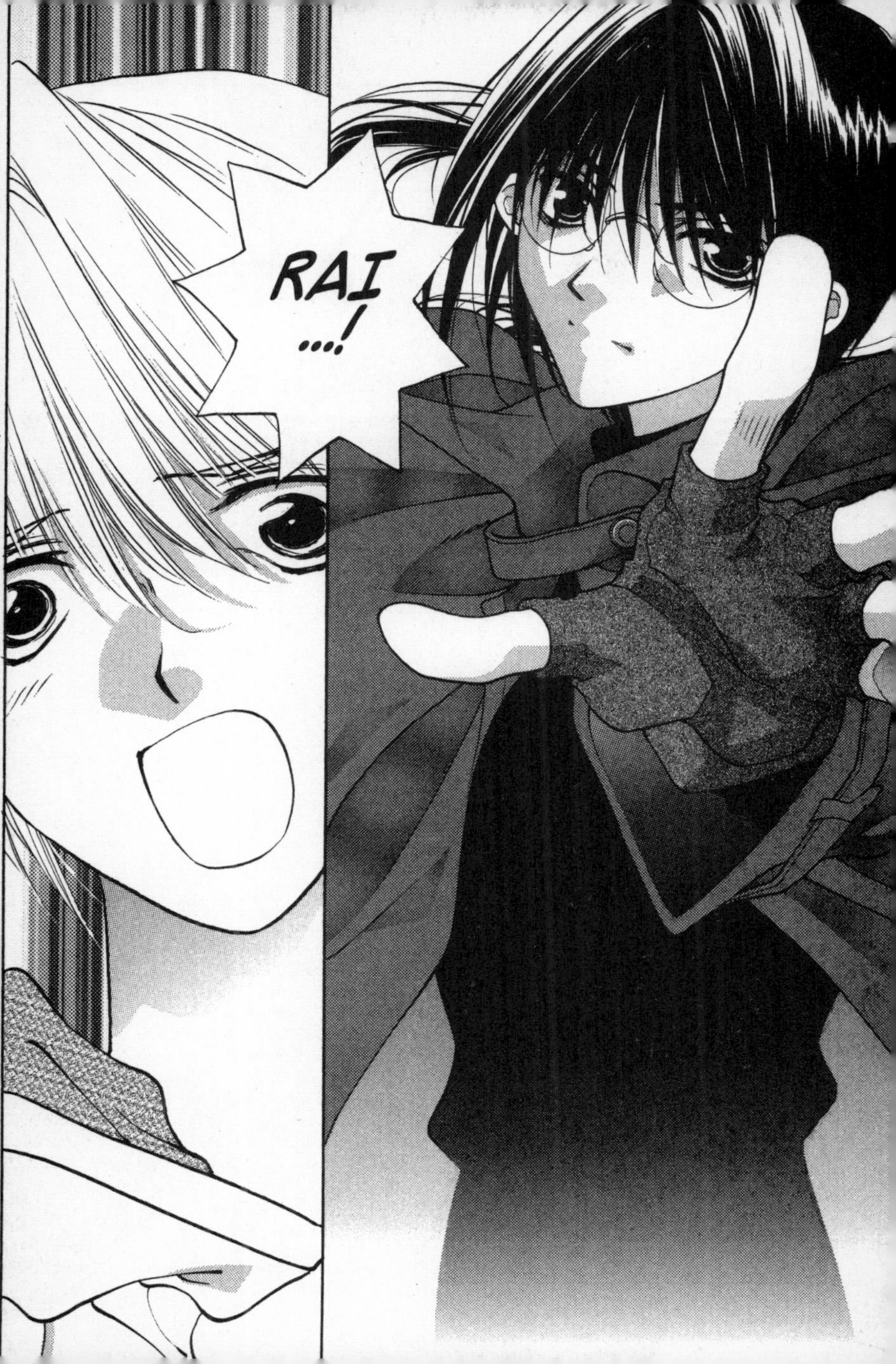
RAI ...!

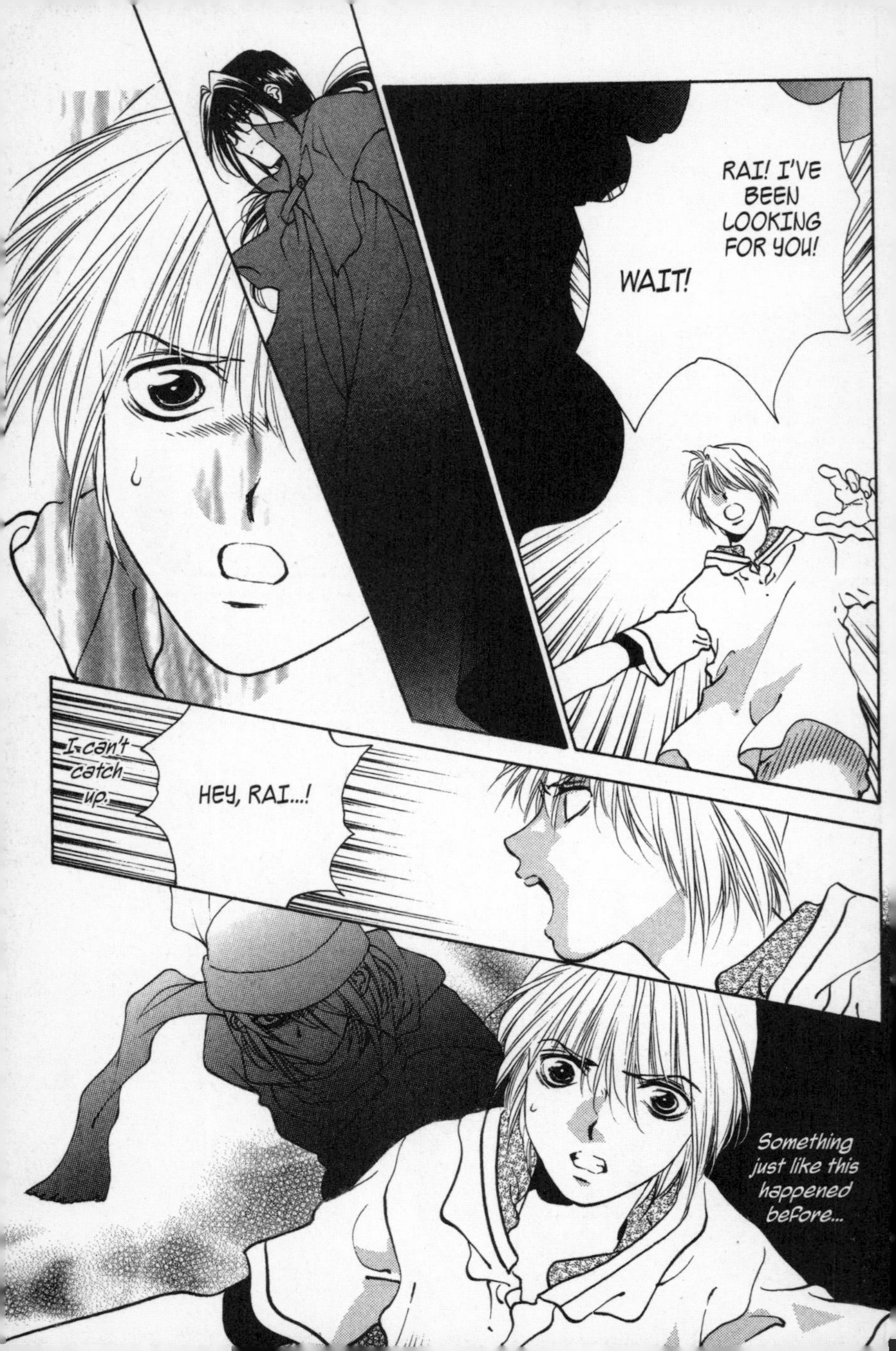
RAI! I'VE BEEN LOOKING FOR YOU!
WAIT!
HEY, RAI...!
I can't catch up.
Something just like this happened before...

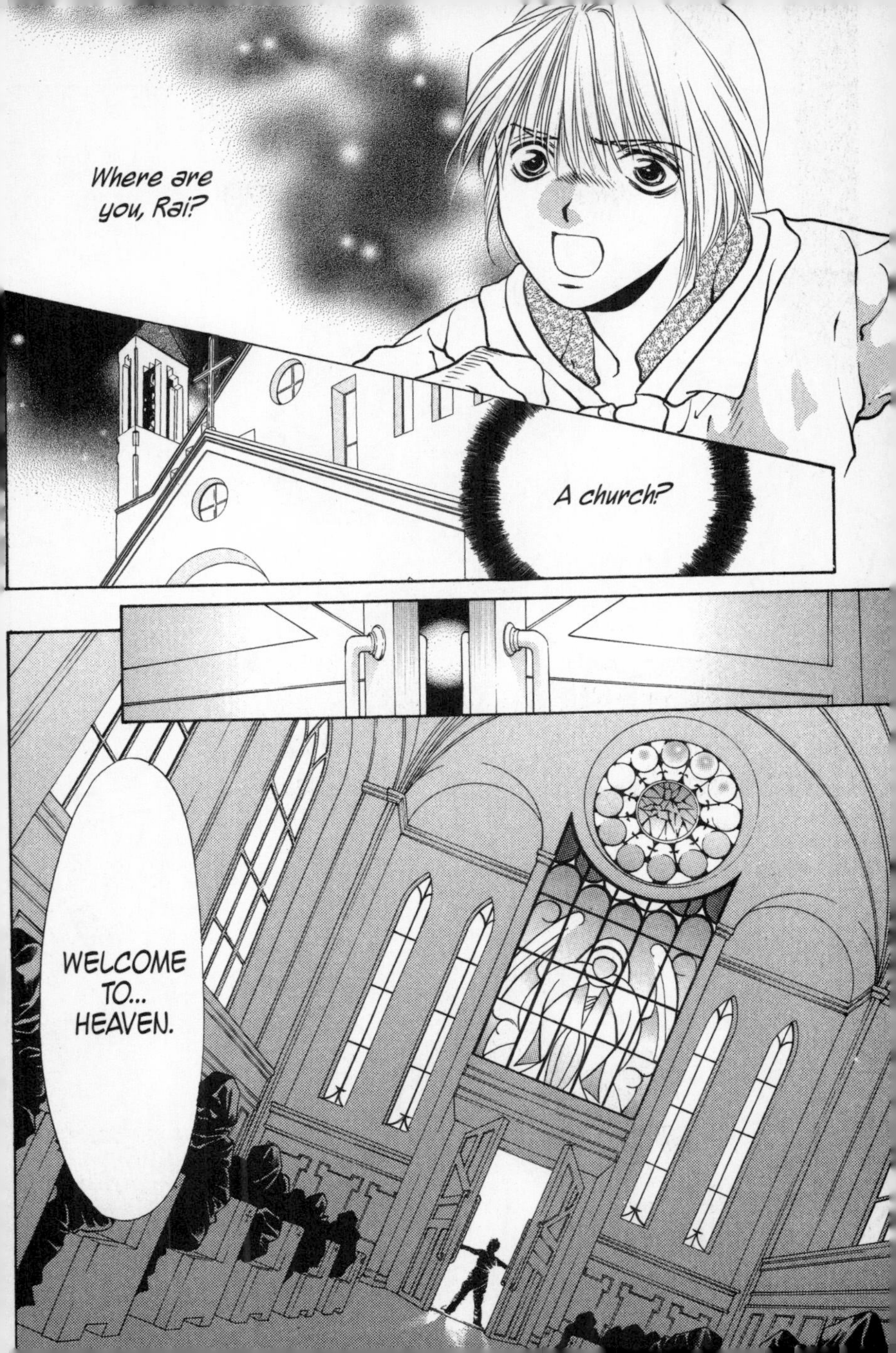
Where are you, Rai?
A church?
WELCOME TO... HEAVEN.

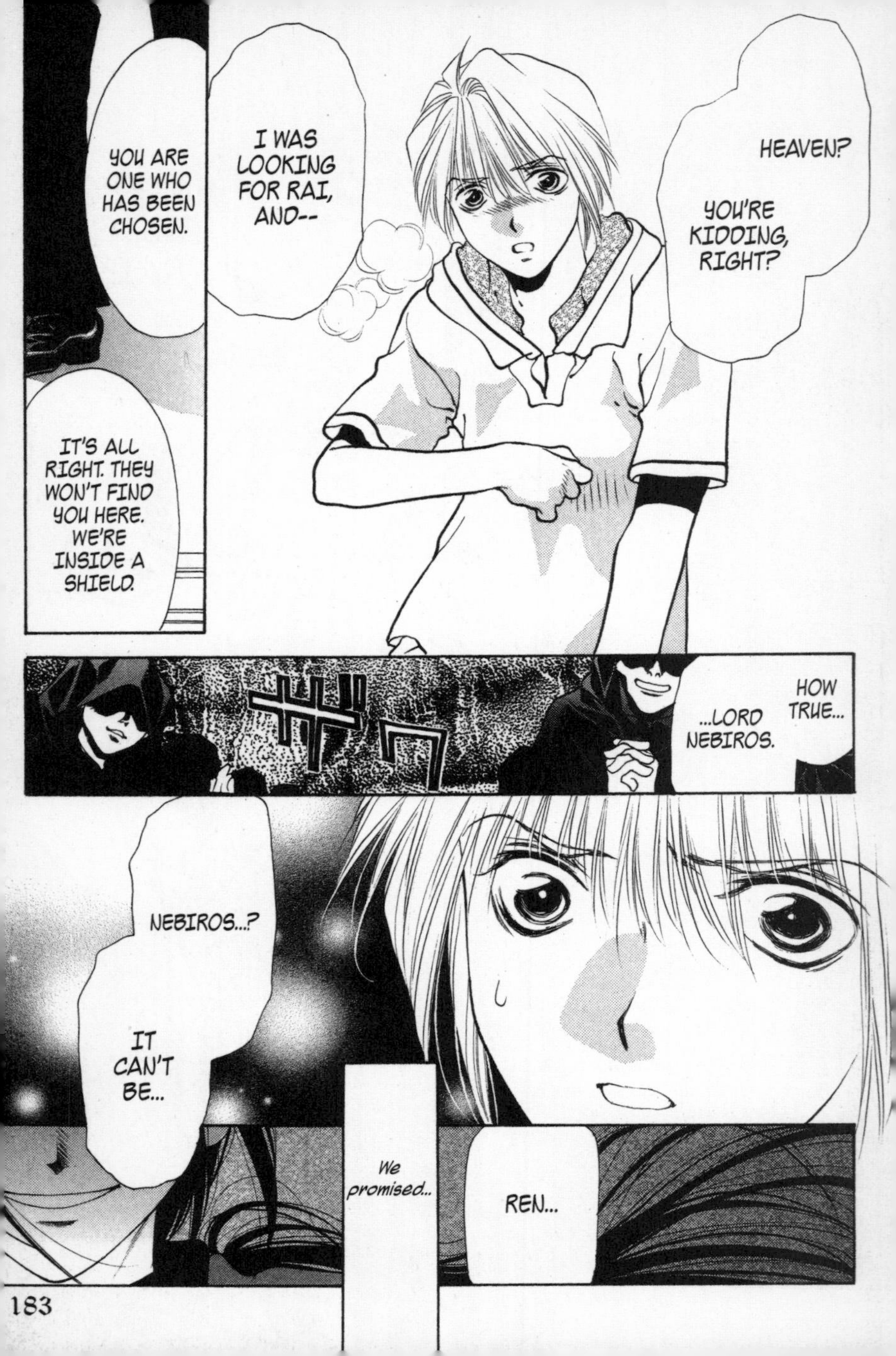
HEAVEN?
YOU'RE KIDDING, RIGHT?
I WAS LOOKING FOR RAI, AND--
YOU ARE ONE WHO HAS BEEN CHOSEN.
IT'S ALL RIGHT. THEY WON'T FIND YOU HERE. WE'RE INSIDE A SHIELD.
HOW TRUE...
...LORD NEBIROS.
NEBIROS...?
IT CAN'T BE...
REN...
We promised...

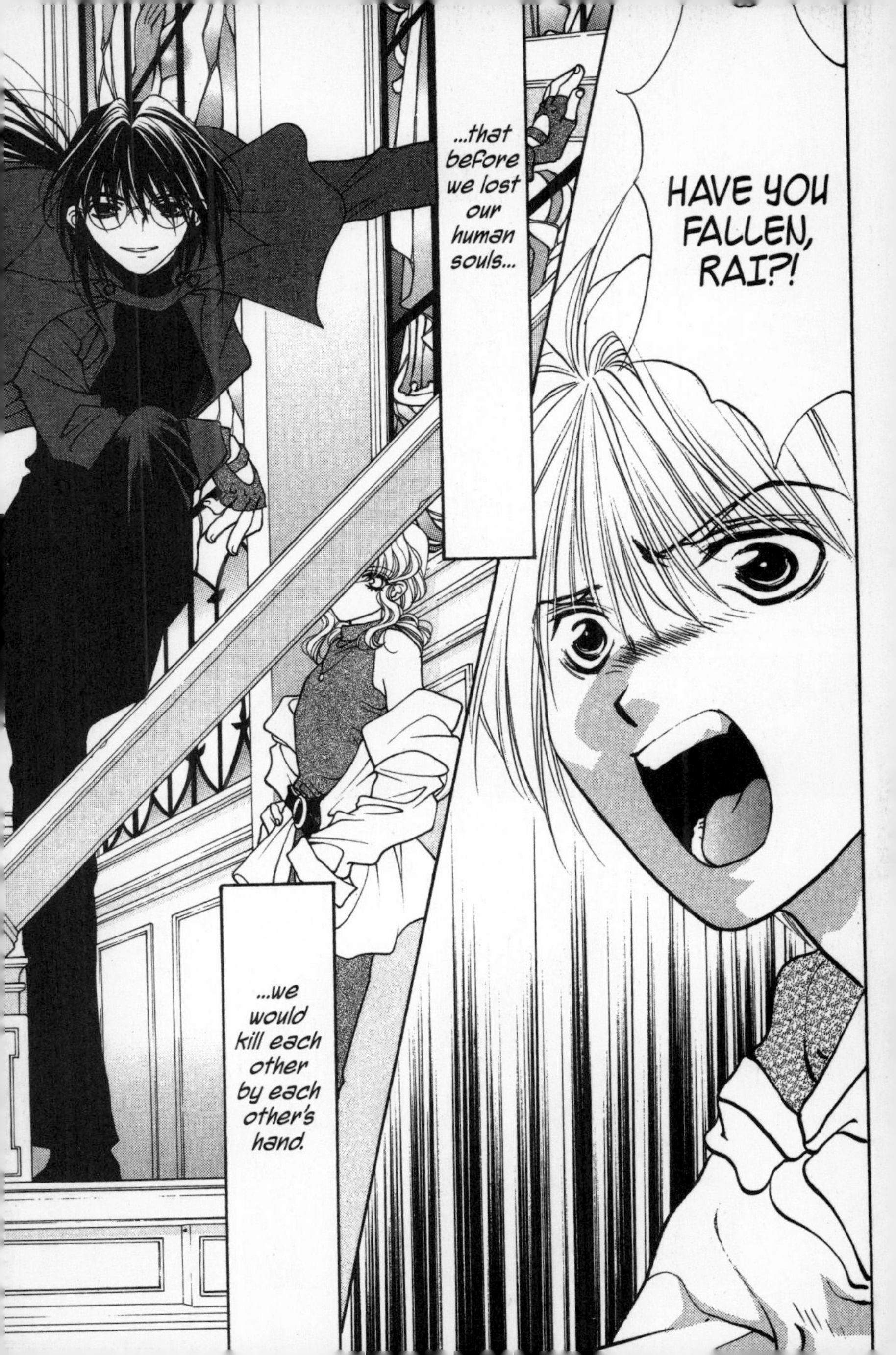
HAVE YOU FALLEN, RAI?!
...that before we lost our human souls...
...we would kill each other by each other's hand.

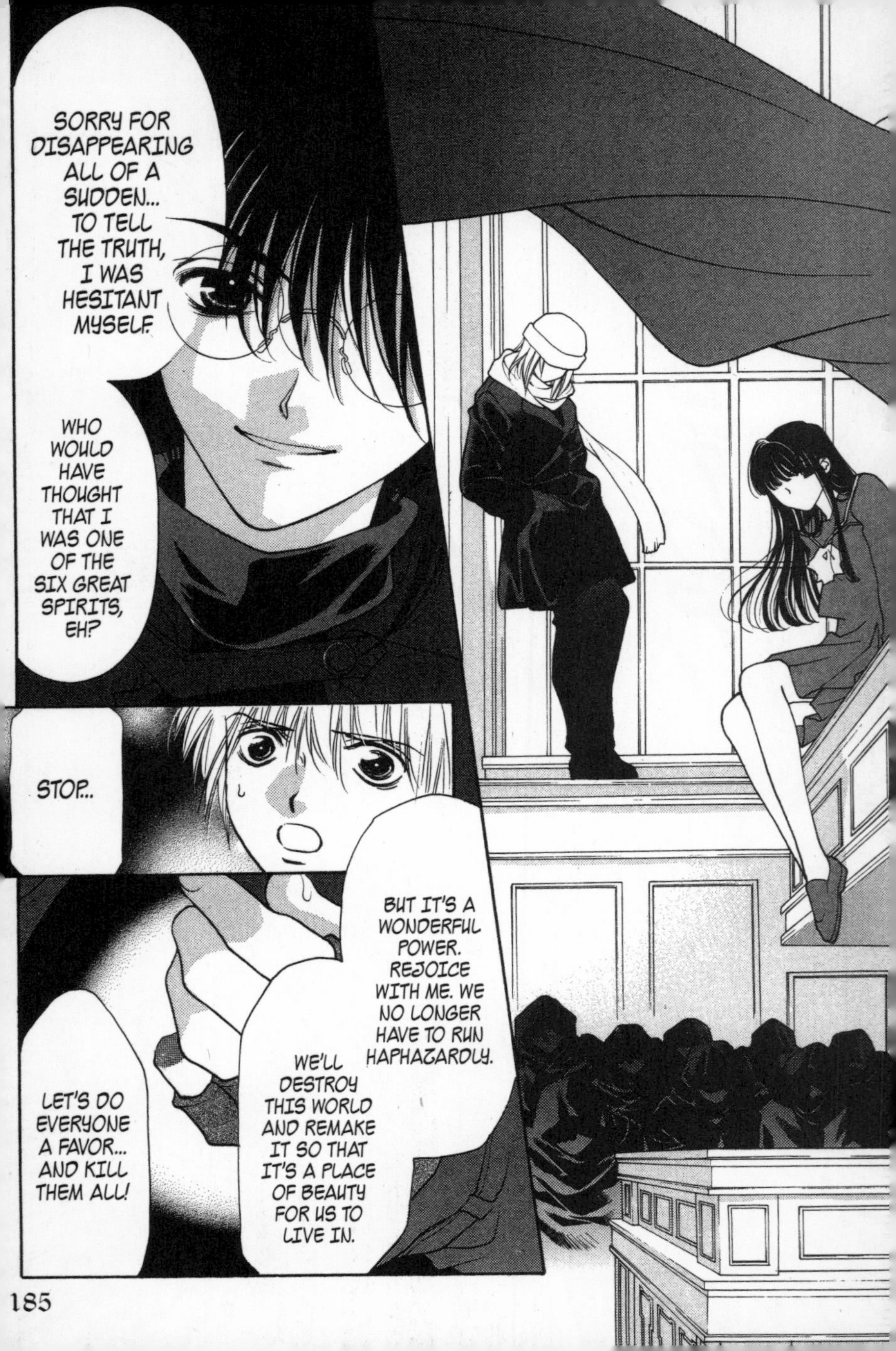
SORRY FOR DISAPPEARING ALL OF A SUDDEN... TO TELL THE TRUTH, I WAS HESITANT MYSELF.
WHO WOULD HAVE THOUGHT THAT I WAS ONE OF THE SIX GREAT SPIRITS, EH?
STOP...
BUT IT'S A WONDERFUL POWER. REJOICE WITH ME. WE NO LONGER HAVE TO RUN HAPHAZARDLY.
WE'LL DESTROY THIS WORLD AND REMAKE IT SO THAT IT'S A PLACE OF BEAUTY FOR US TO LIVE IN.
LET'S DO EVERYONE A FAVOR... AND KILL THEM ALL!

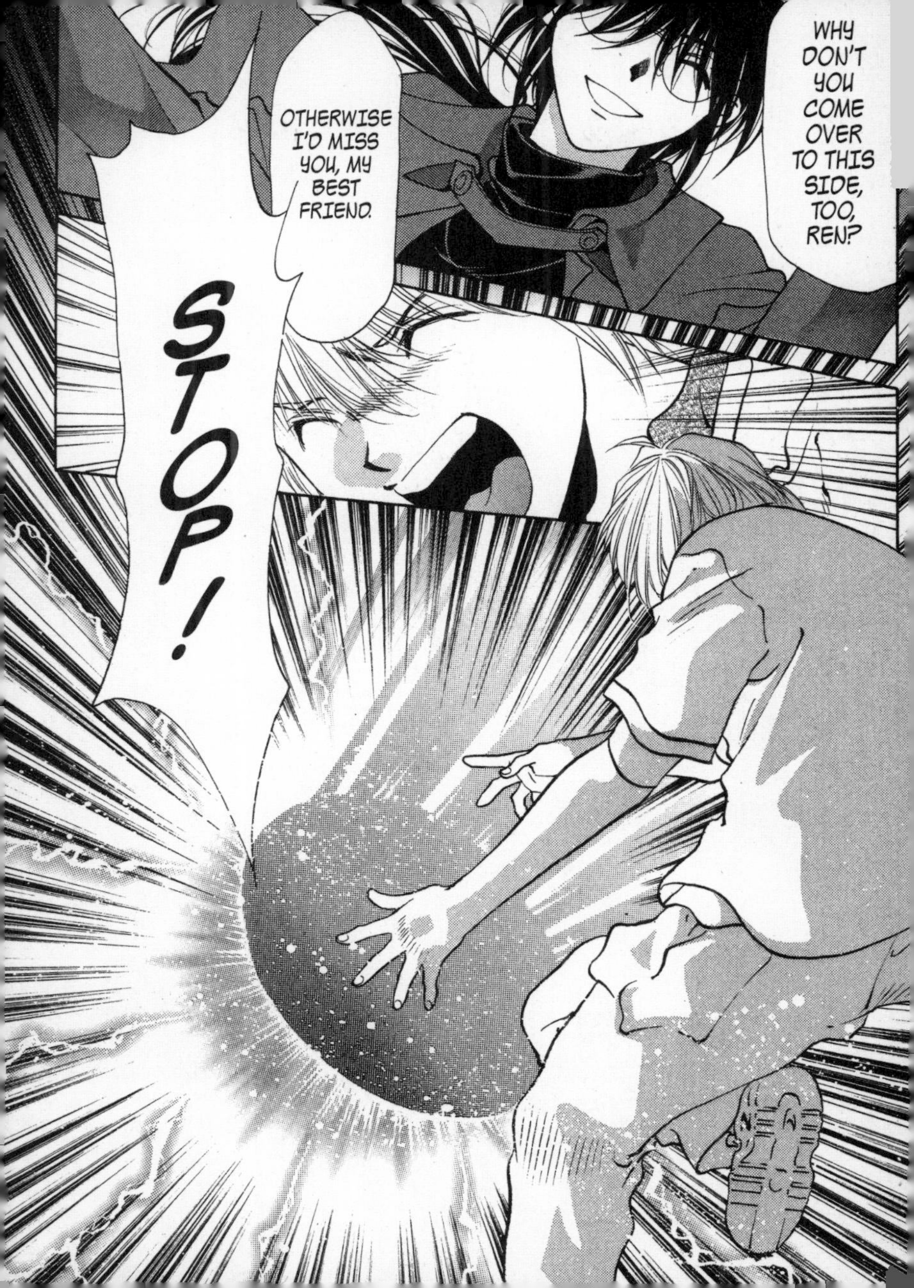
WHY DON'T YOU COME OVER TO THIS SIDE, TOO, REN?
OTHERWISE I'D MISS YOU, MY BEST FRIEND.
STOP!

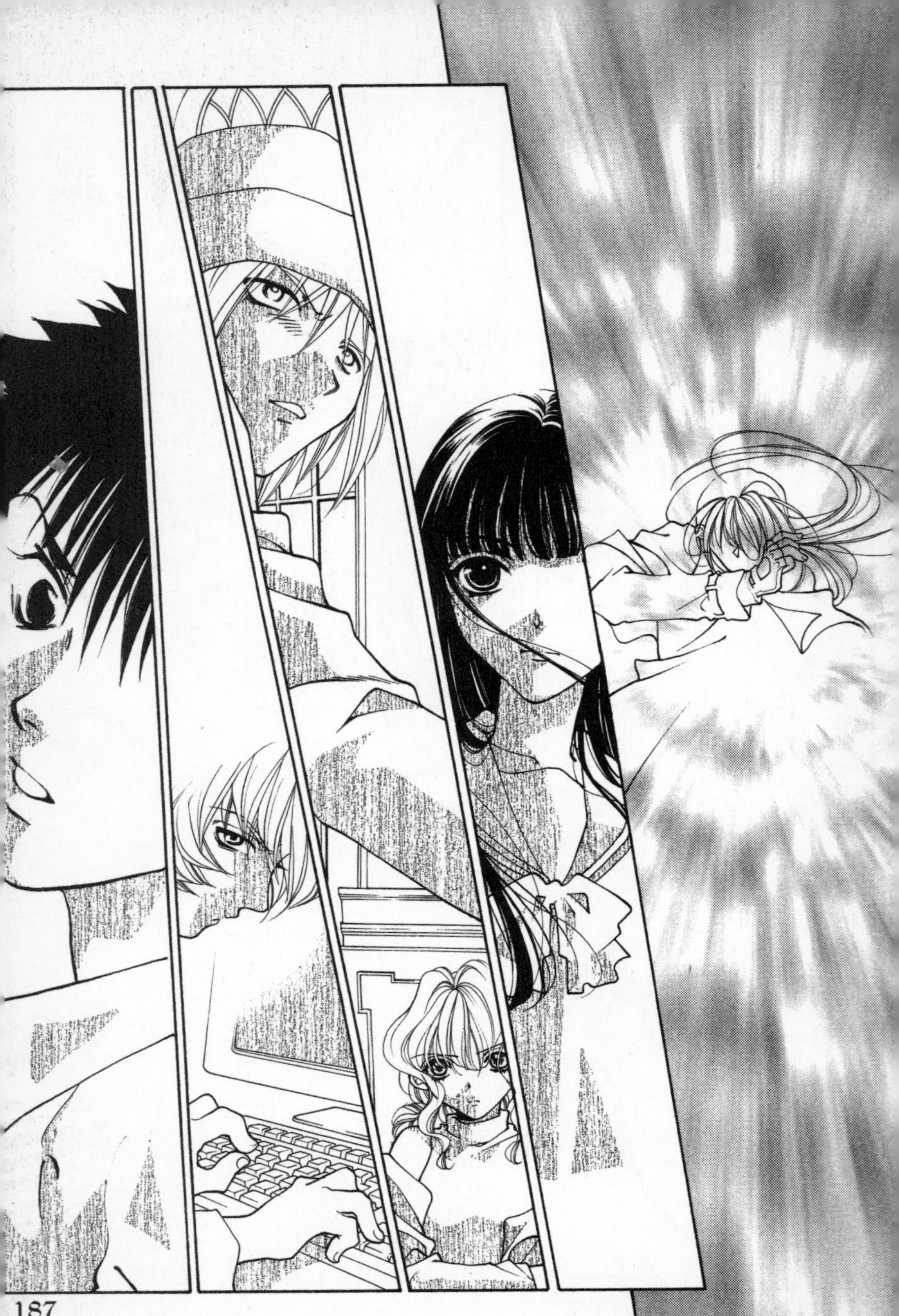

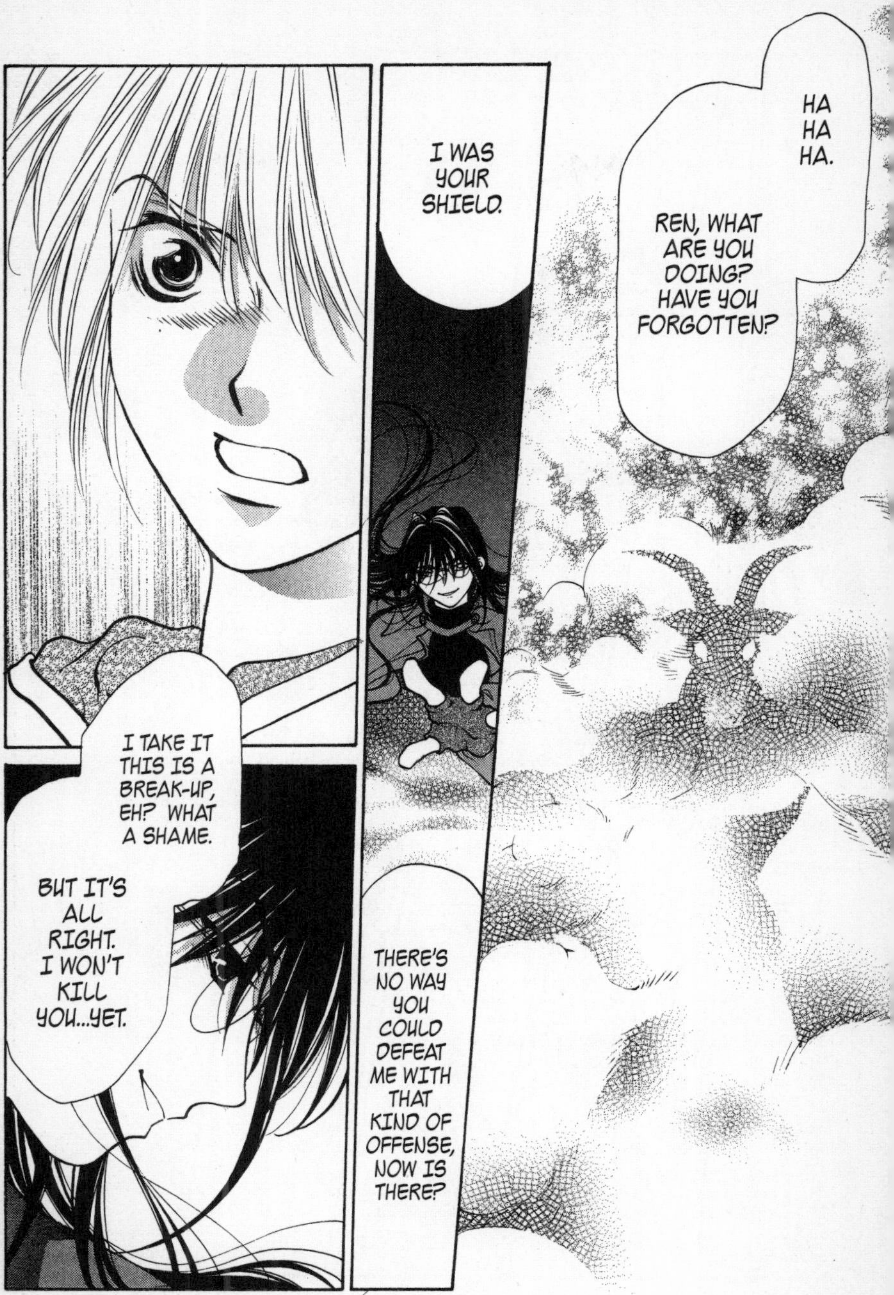
HA HA HA.
REN, WHAT ARE YOU DOING? HAVE YOU FORGOTTEN?
I WAS YOUR SHIELD.
THERE'S NO WAY YOU COULD DEFEAT ME WITH THAT KIND OF OFFENSE, NOW IS THERE?
I TAKE IT THIS IS A BREAK-UP, EH? WHAT A SHAME.
BUT IT'S ALL RIGHT. I WON'T KILL YOU...YET.

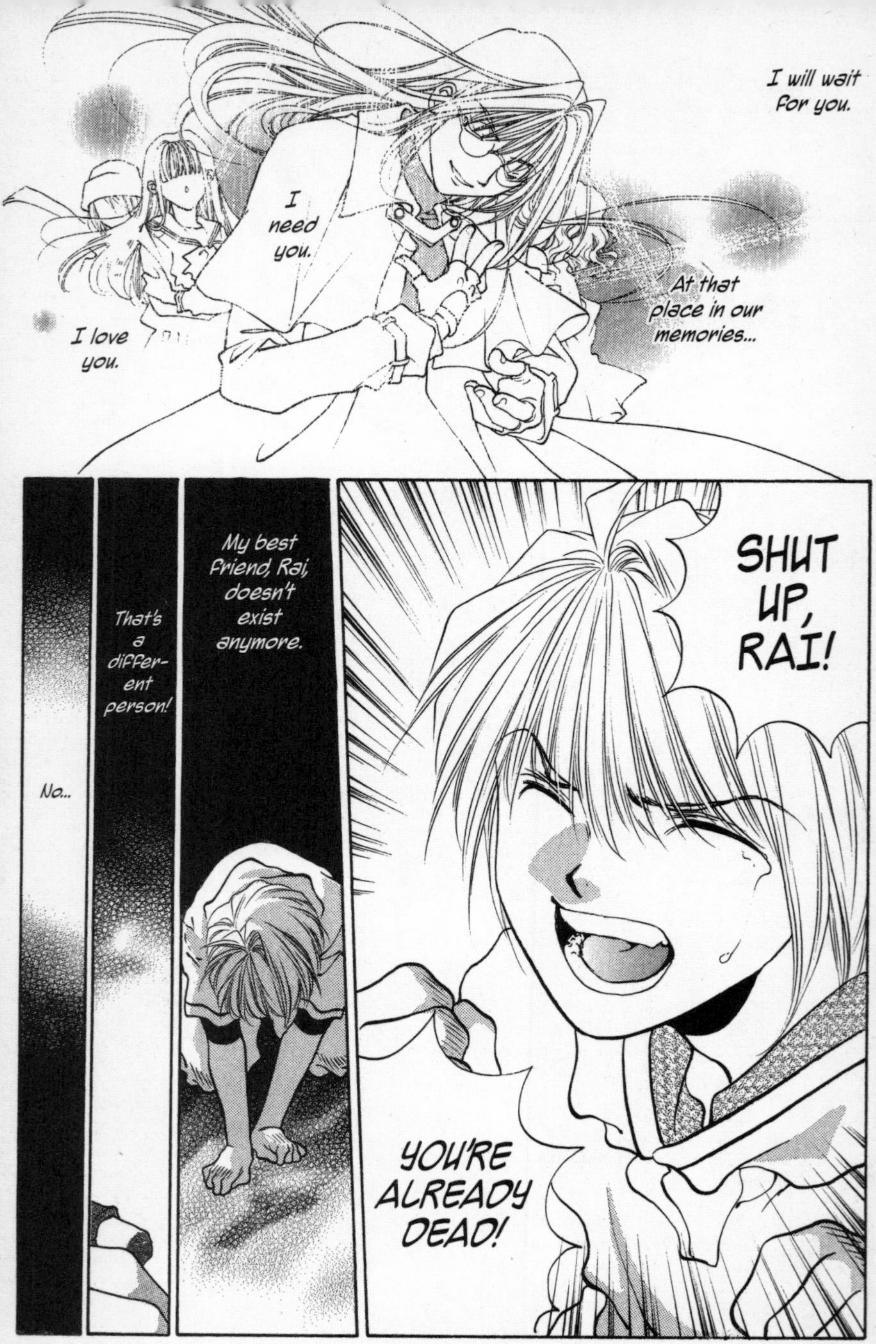

I will wait for you.
At that place in our memories...
I need you.
I love you.
SHUT UP, RAÍ!
YOU'RE ALREADY DEAD!
My best friend, Rai, doesn't exist anymore.
That's a different person!
No...

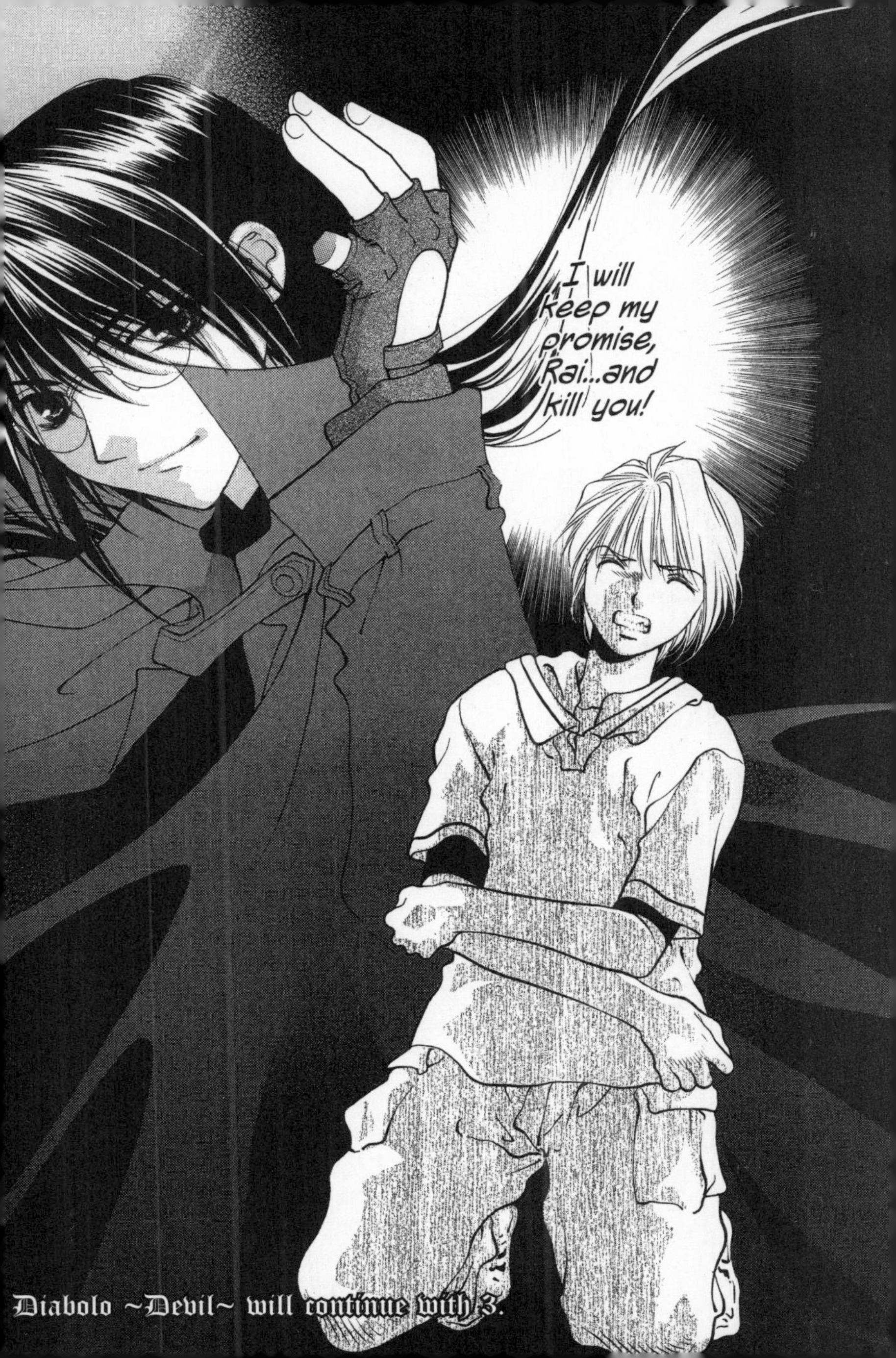
I will keep my promise, Rai...and kill you!

Diabolo ~Devil~ will continue with 3.

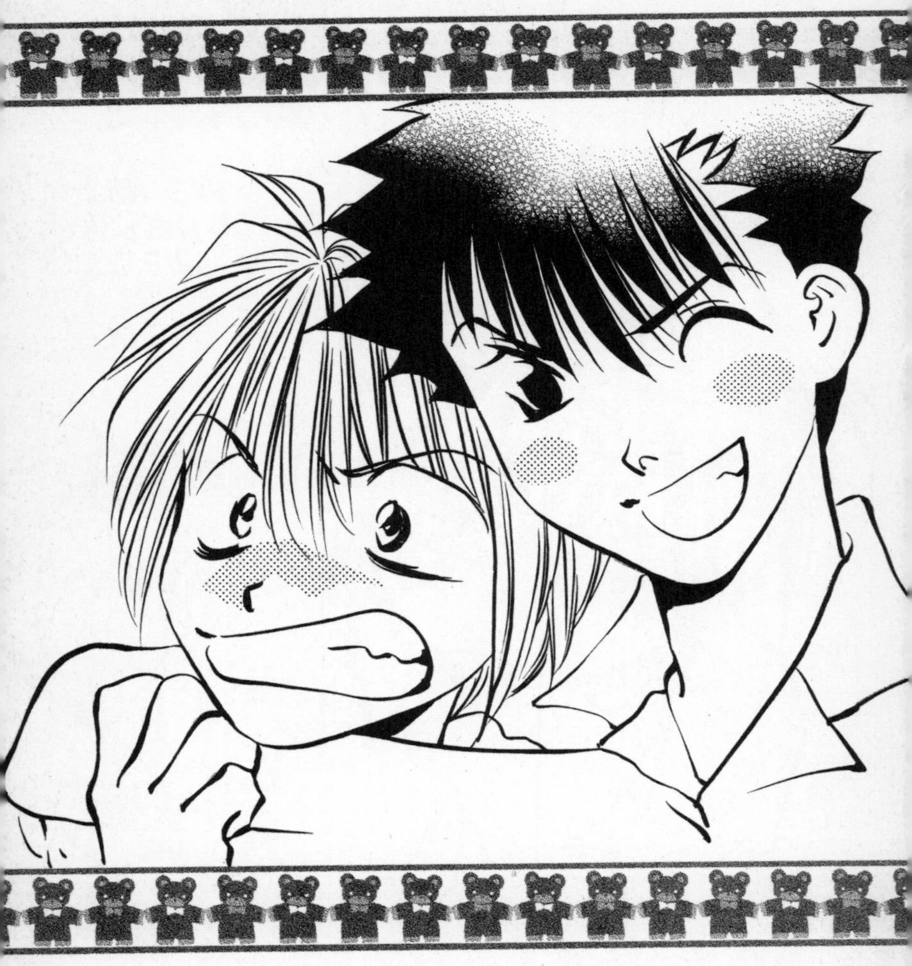

CO-AUTHORING IS HARD! EVEN FOR TWINS.

HOWEVER, SORRY THAT MOST OF THE BURDEN WAS ON YOU, KAORU-CHAN. THANK YOU!

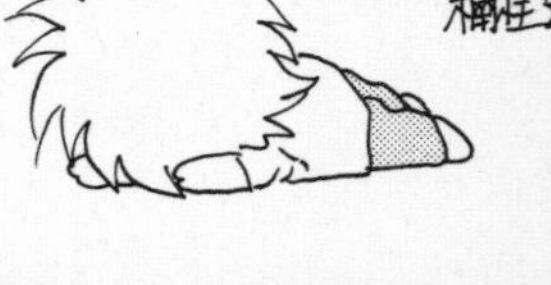

Kei Kusunoki

楠桂

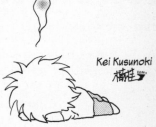

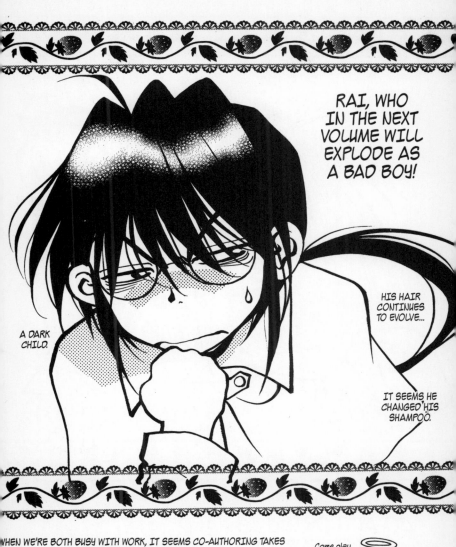

RAI, WHO IN THE NEXT VOLUME WILL EXPLODE AS A BAD BOY!

HIS HAIR CONTINUES TO EVOLVE...

A DARK CHILD.

IT SEEMS HE CHANGED HIS SHAMPOO.

WHEN WE'RE BOTH BUSY WITH WORK, IT SEEMS CO-AUTHORING TAKES AN INORDINATE AMOUNT OF TIME...

BUT, IT'S AMAZING WHEN WE'RE FAST!

BECAUSE KUSUNOKI COVERS FOR ME IN MANY WAYS...

I'M SORRY THAT I ALWAYS LEAVE THE BUSY SCENES TO YOU. THANK YOU.

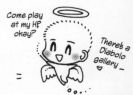

Come play at my HP okay?

There's a Diabolo gallery─

Kaoru Ohashi 大橋薫

In the next installment of

Diabolo

Ren is on a desperate mission to find Rai and save him while he still retains a remnant of his human soul. But this will be no easy task, as Rai decides to engage in a deadly game of cat-and-mouse with his frantic comrade. Adding to the danger are the other Six Great Spirits who will do anything to stand between Ren and his spiritually-lost friend. Meanwhile, Hiromi has vital information that will aide Ren in his search, but when her mother becomes convinced that she is a member of the terrifying Heaven Cult, Hiromi just may find herself in a fight for her own life.

The battle between Good and Evil escalates in DIABOLO volume 3!

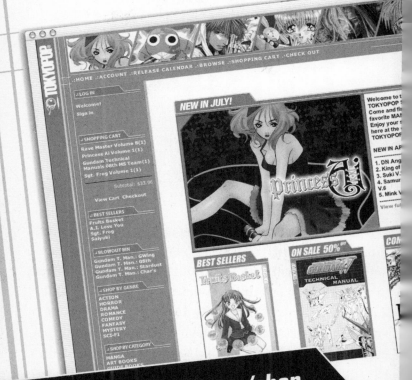
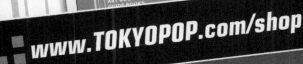

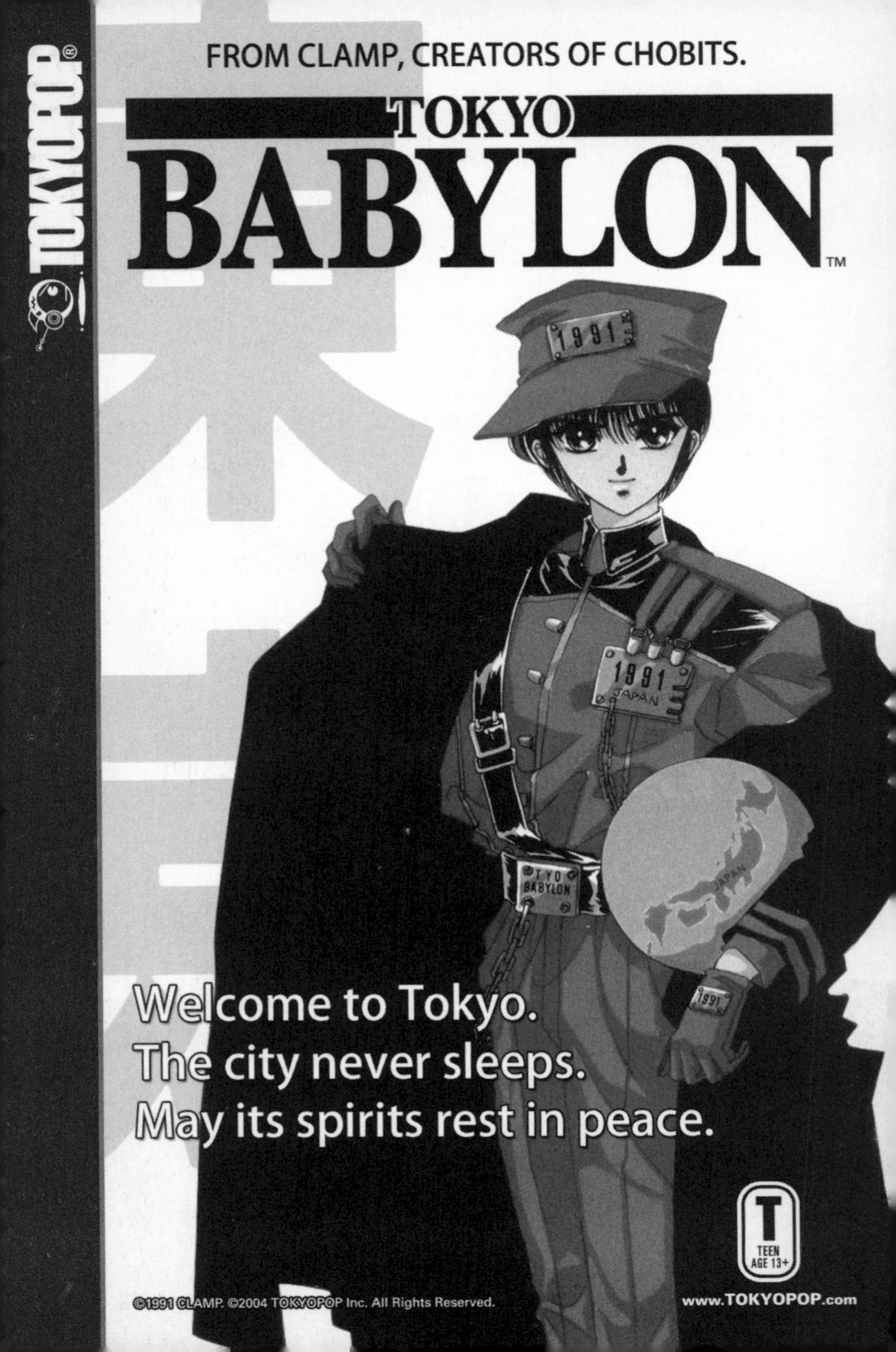
TOKYOPOP®
FROM CLAMP, CREATORS OF CHOBITS.
TOKYO BABYLON™
1991
1991 JAPAN
TYO BABYLON
JAPAN
1991
Welcome to Tokyo.
The city never sleeps.
May its spirits rest in peace.
T TEEN AGE 13+
©1991 CLAMP. ©2004 TOKYOPOP Inc. All Rights Reserved.
www.TOKYOPOP.com

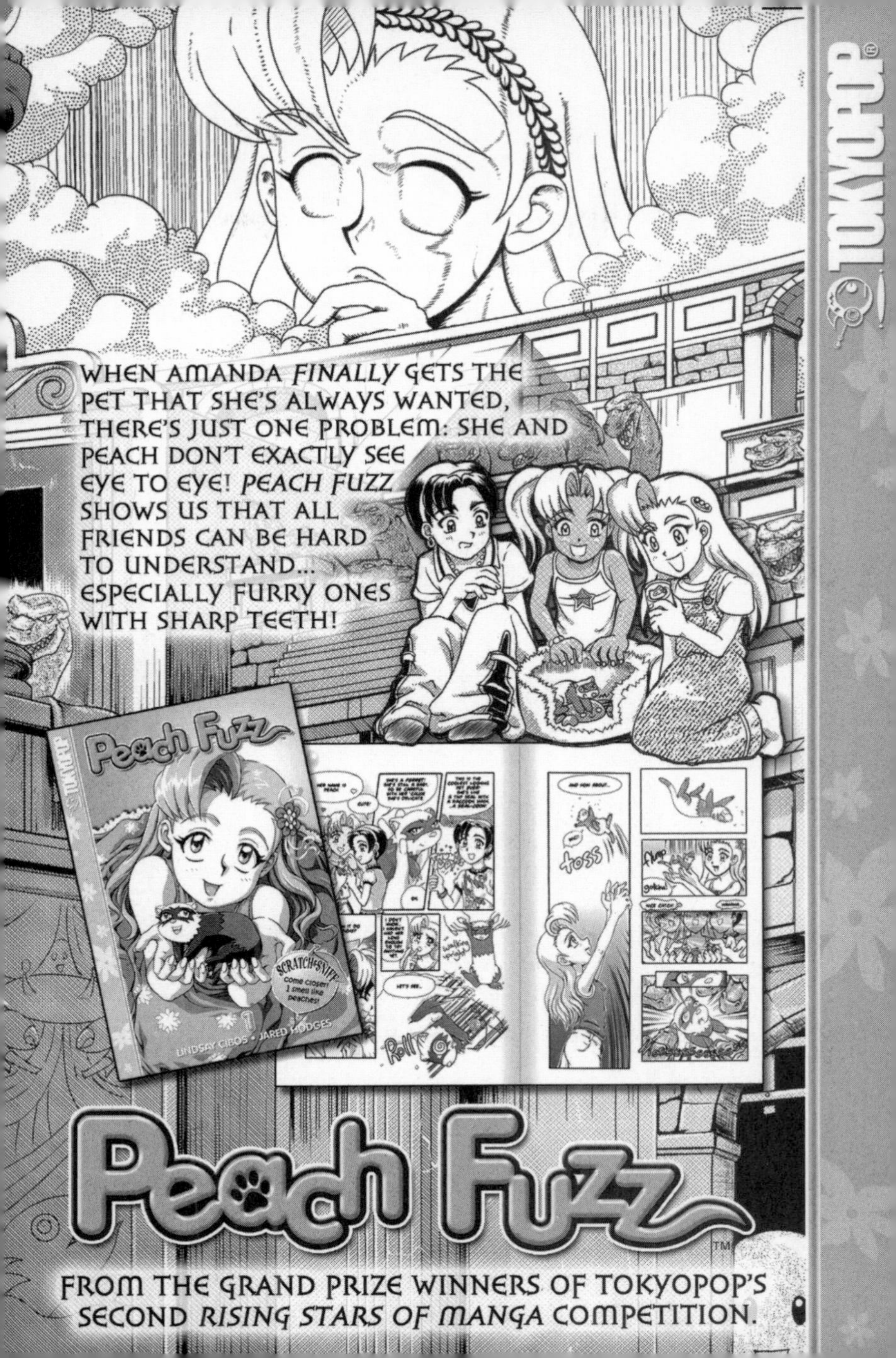
TOKYOPOP®
WHEN AMANDA *FINALLY* GETS THE PET THAT SHE'S ALWAYS WANTED, THERE'S JUST ONE PROBLEM: SHE AND PEACH DON'T EXACTLY SEE EYE TO EYE! *PEACH FUZZ* SHOWS US THAT ALL FRIENDS CAN BE HARD TO UNDERSTAND... ESPECIALLY FURRY ONES WITH SHARP TEETH!
Peach Fuzz
SCRATCH & SNIFF come closer! I smell like peaches!
LINDSAY CIBOS • JARED HODGES
Peach Fuzz™
FROM THE GRAND PRIZE WINNERS OF TOKYOPOP'S SECOND *RISING STARS OF MANGA* COMPETITION.

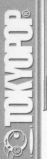

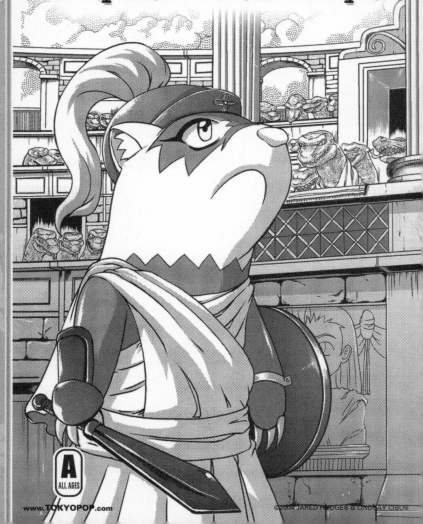

THE EPIC STORY OF A FERRET WHO DEFIED HER CAGE.

ALSO AVAILABLE FROM TOKYOPOP®

PLANETES
PRESIDENT DAD
PRIEST
PRINCESS AI
PSYCHIC ACADEMY
QUEEN'S KNIGHT, THE
RAGNAROK
RAVE MASTER
REALITY CHECK
REBIRTH
REBOUND
REMOTE
RISING STARS OF MANGA
SABER MARIONETTE J
SAILOR MOON
SAINT TAIL
SAIYUKI
SAMURAI DEEPER KYO
SAMURAI GIRL REAL BOUT HIGH SCHOOL
SCRYED
SEIKAI TRILOGY, THE
SGT. FROG
SHAOLIN SISTERS
SHIRAHIME-SYO: SNOW GODDESS TALES
SHUTTERBOX
SKULL MAN, THE
SNOW DROP
SORCERER HUNTERS
STONE
SUIKODEN III
SUKI
TAROT CAFÉ, THE
THREADS OF TIME
TOKYO BABYLON
TOKYO MEW MEW
TOKYO TRIBES
TRAMPS LIKE US
UNDER THE GLASS MOON
VAMPIRE GAME
VISION OF ESCAFLOWNE, THE
WARCRAFT
WARRIORS OF TAO
WILD ACT
WISH
WORLD OF HARTZ
X-DAY
ZODIAC P.I.

NOVELS

CLAMP SCHOOL PARANORMAL INVESTIGATORS
SAILOR MOON
SLAYERS

ART BOOKS

ART OF CARDCAPTOR SAKURA
ART OF MAGIC KNIGHT RAYEARTH, THE
PEACH: MIWA UEDA ILLUSTRATIONS
CLAMP NORTHSIDE
CLAMP SOUTHSIDE

ANIME GUIDES

COWBOY BEBOP
GUNDAM TECHNICAL MANUALS
SAILOR MOON SCOUT GUIDES

TOKYOPOP KIDS

STRAY SHEEP

CINE-MANGA®

ALADDIN
CARDCAPTORS
DUEL MASTERS
FAIRLY ODDPARENTS, THE
FAMILY GUY
FINDING NEMO
G.I. JOE SPY TROOPS
GREATEST STARS OF THE NBA
JACKIE CHAN ADVENTURES
JIMMY NEUTRON: BOY GENIUS, THE ADVENTURES OF
KIM POSSIBLE
LILO & STITCH: THE SERIES
LIZZIE MCGUIRE
LIZZIE MCGUIRE MOVIE, THE
MALCOLM IN THE MIDDLE
POWER RANGERS: DINO THUNDER
POWER RANGERS: NINJA STORM
PRINCESS DIARIES 2, THE
RAVE MASTER
SHREK 2
SIMPLE LIFE, THE
SPONGEBOB SQUAREPANTS
SPY KIDS 2
SPY KIDS 3-D: GAME OVER
TEENAGE MUTANT NINJA TURTLES
THAT'S SO RAVEN
TOTALLY SPIES
TRANSFORMERS: ARMADA
TRANSFORMERS: ENERGON

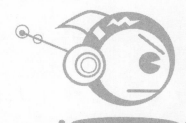

You want it? We got it!
A full range of TOKYOPOP
products are available now at:
www.TOKYOPOP.com/shop

09.21.04T

ALSO AVAILABLE FROM 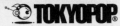TOKYOPOP®

MANGA

.HACK//LEGEND OF THE TWILIGHT
@LARGE
ABENOBASHI: MAGICAL SHOPPING ARCADE
A.I. LOVE YOU
AI YORI AOSHI
ALICHINO
ANGELIC LAYER
ARM OF KANNON
BABY BIRTH
BATTLE ROYALE
BATTLE VIXENS
BOYS BE...
BRAIN POWERED
BRIGADOON
B'TX
CANDIDATE FOR GODDESS, THE
CARDCAPTOR SAKURA
CARDCAPTOR SAKURA - MASTER OF THE CLOW
CHOBITS
CHRONICLES OF THE CURSED SWORD
CLAMP SCHOOL DETECTIVES
CLOVER
COMIC PARTY
CONFIDENTIAL CONFESSIONS
CORRECTOR YUI
COWBOY BEBOP
COWBOY BEBOP: SHOOTING STAR
CRAZY LOVE STORY
CRESCENT MOON
CROSS
CULDCEPT
CYBORG 009
D•N•ANGEL
DEARS
DEMON DIARY
DEMON ORORON, THE
DEUS VITAE
DIABOLO
DIGIMON
DIGIMON TAMERS
DIGIMON ZERO TWO
DOLL
DRAGON HUNTER
DRAGON KNIGHTS
DRAGON VOICE
DREAM SAGA
DUKLYON: CLAMP SCHOOL DEFENDERS
EERIE QUEERIE!
ERICA SAKURAZAWA: COLLECTED WORKS
ET CETERA
ETERNITY
EVIL'S RETURN
FAERIES' LANDING
FAKE
FLCL
FLOWER OF THE DEEP SLEEP
FORBIDDEN DANCE
FRUITS BASKET

G GUNDAM
GATEKEEPERS
GETBACKERS
GIRL GOT GAME
GRAVITATION
GTO
GUNDAM SEED ASTRAY
GUNDAM WING
GUNDAM WING: BATTLEFIELD OF PACIFISTS
GUNDAM WING: ENDLESS WALTZ
GUNDAM WING: THE LAST OUTPOST (G-UNIT)
HANDS OFF!
HAPPY MANIA
HARLEM BEAT
HYPER RUNE
I.N.V.U.
IMMORTAL RAIN
INITIAL D
INSTANT TEEN: JUST ADD NUTS
ISLAND
JING: KING OF BANDITS
JING: KING OF BANDITS - TWILIGHT TALES
JULINE
KARE KANO
KILL ME, KISS ME
KINDAICHI CASE FILES, THE
KING OF HELL
KODOCHA: SANA'S STAGE
LAMENT OF THE LAMB
LEGAL DRUG
LEGEND OF CHUN HYANG, THE
LES BIJOUX
LOVE HINA
LOVE OR MONEY
LUPIN III
LUPIN III: WORLD'S MOST WANTED
MAGIC KNIGHT RAYEARTH I
MAGIC KNIGHT RAYEARTH II
MAHOROMATIC: AUTOMATIC MAIDEN
MAN OF MANY FACES
MARMALADE BOY
MARS
MARS: HORSE WITH NO NAME
MINK
MIRACLE GIRLS
MIYUKI-CHAN IN WONDERLAND
MODEL
MOURYOU KIDEN: LEGEND OF THE NYMPH
NECK AND NECK
ONE
ONE I LOVE, THE
PARADISE KISS
PARASYTE
PASSION FRUIT
PEACH FUZZ
PEACH GIRL
PEACH GIRL: CHANGE OF HEART
PET SHOP OF HORRORS
PITA-TEN
PLANET LADDER

09.21.04T

STOP!

This is the back of the book.
You wouldn't want to spoil a great ending!

This book is printed "manga-style," in the authentic Japanese right-to-left format. Since none of the artwork has been flipped or altered, readers get to experience the story just as the creator intended. You've been asking for it, so TOKYOPOP® delivered: authentic, hot-off-the-press, and far more fun!

DIRECTIONS

If this is your first time reading manga-style, here's a quick guide to help you understand how it works.

It's easy… just start in the top right panel and follow the numbers. Have fun, and look for more 100% authentic manga from TOKYOPOP®!

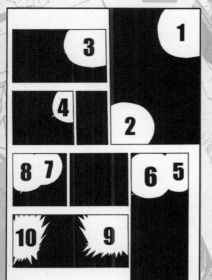

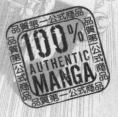